Journey to Indo-América

The American Popular Revolutionary Alliance (APRA) was a Peruvian political party that played an important role in the development of the Latin American left during the first half of the 1900s. In *Journey to Indo-América*, Geneviève Dorais examines how and why the anti-imperialist project of APRA took root outside of Peru as well as how APRA's struggle for political survival in Peru shaped its transnational consciousness. Dorais convincingly argues that APRA's history can only be understood properly within this transnational framework, and through the collective efforts of transnational organization rather than through an exclusive emphasis on political figures like APRA leader, Víctor Raúl Haya de la Torre. Tracing circuits of exile and solidarity through Latin America, the United States, and Europe, Dorais seeks to deepen our appreciation of APRA's ideological production through an exploration of the political context in which its project of hemispheric unity emerged.

Geneviève Dorais is Professor of Latin American history at the Université du Québec à Montréal (UQÀM). She is engaged in research projects exploring the involvement of non-state actors in solidarity networks in the Americas.

CAMBRIDGE LATIN AMERICAN STUDIES

General Editors

KRIS LANE, Tulane University
MATTHEW RESTALL, Pennsylvania State University

Editor Emeritus

HERBERT S. KLEIN
Gouverneur Morris Emeritus Professor of History, Columbia University and Hoover Research Fellow, Stanford University

Other Books in the Series

122. *Nationalizing Nature: Iguaza Falls and National Parks at the Brazil-Argentina Border*, Frederico Freitas
121. *Islanders and Empire: Smuggling and Political Defiance in Hispaniola, 1580–1690*, Juan José Ponce-Vázquez
120. *Our Time is Now: Race and Modernity in Postcolonial Guatemala*, Julie Gibbings
119. *The Sexual Question: A History of Prostitution in Peru, 1850s-1950s*, Paulo Drinot
118. *A Silver River in a Silver World: Dutch Trade in the Rio de la Plata, 1648–1678*, David Freeman
117. *Laboring for the State: Women, Family, and Work in Revolutionary Cuba, 1959–1971*, Rachel Hynson
116. *Violence and The Caste War of Yucatán*, Wolfgang Gabbert
115. *For Christ and Country: Militant Catholic Youth in Post-Revolutionary Mexico*, Robert Weis
114. *The Mexican Mission: Indigenous Reconstruction and Mendicant Enterprise in New Spain, 1521–1600*, Ryan Dominic Crewe
113. *Corruption and Justice in Colonial Mexico, 1650–1755*, Christoph Rosenmüller
112. *Blacks of the Land: Indian Slavery, Settler Society, and the Portuguese Colonial Enterprise in South America, Weinstein/Woodard/Montiero*
111. *The Street Is Ours: Community, the Car, and the Nature of Public Space in Rio de Janeiro*, Shawn William Miller
110. *Laywomen and the Making of Colonial Catholicism in New Spain, 1630–1790*, Jessica L. Delgado
109. *Urban Slavery in Colonial Mexico: Puebla de los Ángeles, 1531–1706*, Pablo Miguel Sierra Silva

(*Continued after the Index*)

Journey to Indo-América

APRA and the Transnational Politics of Exile, Persecution, and Solidarity, 1918–1945

GENEVIÈVE DORAIS
Université du Québec à Montréal

CAMBRIDGE
UNIVERSITY PRESS

CAMBRIDGE
UNIVERSITY PRESS

University Printing House, Cambridge CB2 8BS, United Kingdom

One Liberty Plaza, 20th Floor, New York, NY 10006, USA

477 Williamstown Road, Port Melbourne, VIC 3207, Australia

314–321, 3rd Floor, Plot 3, Splendor Forum, Jasola District Centre, New Delhi – 110025, India

103 Penang Road, #05–06/07, Visioncrest Commercial, Singapore 238467

Cambridge University Press is part of the University of Cambridge.

It furthers the University's mission by disseminating knowledge in the pursuit of education, learning, and research at the highest international levels of excellence.

www.cambridge.org
Information on this title: www.cambridge.org/9781108838047
DOI: 10.1017/9781108937030

First published 2021

A catalogue record for this publication is available from the British Library.

Library of Congress Cataloging-in-Publication Data
NAMES: Dorais, Geneviève, 1982– author.
TITLE: Journey to Indo-América : APRA and the transnational politics of exile, persecution, and solidarity, 1918–1945 / Geneviève Dorais.
DESCRIPTION: Cambridge, United Kingdom ; New York, NY : Cambridge University Press, 2021. | Series: Cambridge Latin American studies ; 123 | Includes bibliographical references and index.
IDENTIFIERS: LCCN 2021019476 (print) | LCCN 2021019477 (ebook) | ISBN 9781108838047 (hardback) | ISBN 9781108947695 (paperback) | ISBN 9781108937030 (epub)
SUBJECTS: LCSH: Partido Aprista Peruano–History–20th century. | Right and left (Political science)–Peru–History–20th century. | Right and left (Political science)–Latin America–History–20th century. | Anti-imperialist movements–Peru–History–20th century. | Anti-imperialist movements–Latin America–History–20th century. | Peru–Politics and government–1919–1968. | Latin America–Politics and government–20th century. | BISAC: HISTORY / Latin America / General | HISTORY / Latin America / General
CLASSIFICATION: LCC JL3498.A6 D67 2021 (print) | LCC JL3498.A6 (ebook) | DDC 324.285/07–dc23
LC record available at https://lccn.loc.gov/2021019476
LC ebook record available at https://lccn.loc.gov/2021019477

ISBN 978-1-108-83804-7 Hardback

Contents

Acknowledgments

This book required the efforts of many friends and peers I wish to celebrate. Eleni Schirmer has coached me during every mile of this several-year marathon with love, patience and precious intellectual insight, making sure that I reached the finish line. Robert Whitney began his advising enterprise over coffee in Montréal many years ago; he initiated me to transnational American Popular Revolutionary Alliance (APRA) and has continued to offer guidance, encouragements, and sound feedback ever since. The publication of this book would never have happened without their respective intellectual support and encouragement in the past few years. Thank you both for your outstanding cheering.

Several sources of financial support made the publication of this book possible. I am grateful for the early and generous sponsorship of the Conseil de recherches en sciences humaines du Canada (CRSH) during my doctoral studies. I thank the University of Wisconsin – Madison History Department and Graduate School for their support in the form of research and writing fellowships. The Beca Teixidor, from the Instituto de Investigaciones Históricas, Universidad Nacional Autónoma de México, and the Tinker Nave Short-Term Field Research Grant helped fund important preliminary research travels to Mexico and to US archives in 2009. The Vilas and Mellon Foundations also provided crucial financial assistance. More recently, the Programme d'appui aux Nouvelles professeures-chercheures (PANP) de la Faculté des sciences humaines, Université du Québec à Montréal (UQÀM) offered critical funding.

Research money would do little, however, without the expertise and assistance of well-trained and devoted archivists and librarians. In France, staff members at the Archives Nationales de Paris, Archives de la Préfecture de Police de Paris, and the Bibliothèque nationale de France all cheerfully assisted their “cousine du Canada.” In Mexico and Peru, I am fortunate to have benefited from the help and guidance of knowledgeable archivists. I especially thank the Pontificia Universidad Católica del Perú, Centro de documentación de ciencias sociales (CEDOC) for courteously bringing in collections I needed for review. On the North American side, the staff at the University of Texas Libraries received me with dedication and facilitated my forays into the Benson Latin American Collection beyond expectations. I owe special thanks to the Institute of Historical Studies at the University of Texas at Austin, and Julie Hardwick in particular, for helping me gain access to the University of Texas's extensive resources. William LeFevre, at the Archives of Labor and Urban Affairs at Wayne State University, was both patient and kind enough to accommodate my fast-paced research schedule. In Pennsylvania, Wendy E. Chmielewski provided invaluable guidance through the rich material of the Swarthmore College Peace Collection. Rarely have I seen a curator so knowledgeable about the historical protagonists who live in the archives she supervises. Leah Gass graciously received me at the Presbyterian Historical society in Philadelphia on a last-minute notice. The staff and librarians at Memorial Library in Madison, and especially Paloma Celis Carbajal, have helped my project in more ways than they can imagine.

In the course of two years, I visited over twenty-five archives spread between four countries (Mexico, the United States, France, and Peru) and approximately thirteen cities. My multi-site research agenda was ambitious, and I owe special thanks to certain guardian angels who helped along the way. I would have never emerged alive from these incessant travels without the warm generosity of friends who offered me shelter, emotional comfort, and intellectual camaraderie along the way. Among them are Tony Chapa, Ponciano del Pino, Katherine Eade, Clare and Daniel Friedrich, Kelly Jakes, Jessie Manfrin, Alice McGrath, Molly Noble, Carmen Yasmina López Morales, Christopher Walker, Helen Webb, James Wallace, and every single member of my marvelous Schirmer family in Madison, WI.

Loyal mentors have accompanied this research journey from day one. Cynthia Milton and Catherine LeGrand introduced me to the field of Latin American history in Montréal, Québec. It is under their influence that I first fell in love with history as a discipline of creation. I thank my doctoral advisors at the UW-Madison – Florencia E. Mallon, Steve

J. Stern, and Francisco Scarano – for their generous and remarkable advising. These historians set the bar high for themselves and request the same of their students, encouraging us to take intellectual risks and to stand by them. I feel proud to have been influenced by scholars who believed in their students and their craft with passion.

This project began during graduate school in the US. I'm grateful for the intellectual companionship of friends and colleagues in the Ph.D. program in history who have contributed in more ways that I can account for to the ideas and reflections that gave rise to this book. They are: Jake Blanc, Ingrid Johanna Bolívar Ramírez, Charlie Cahill, Marcelo Casals, Adela Cedillo, Ponciano del Pino, Jessica Kirstein, Annie Massa-MacLeod, Andrés Matías-Ortiz, Gladys McCormick, Valeria Navarro-Rosenblatt, Alberto Ortiz, Debbie Sharnak, Dustin Welch, Bridgette Werner, and especially (perhaps because our magic often happened later at night, prompted by that last round of bourbon old-fashioned) Sean Bloch, Chris Dols, Katherine Eade, Tamara Feinstein, Julie Gibbings, Robbie Gross, Simon Fisher, Katie Jarvis, Yeri Lopez, Jessie Manfrin, Elena McGrath, Carrie Ryan, Vikram Tamboli, Kate Waterman, and Naomi R Williams.

My research on trans-American solidarity profited from my participation in the Tepoztlán Institute in Morelos, México, in July 2018. It also gained a lot from the expertise of the colleagues and graduate students who attended the solidarity workshops in New York (February 2019) and Toronto (May 2019) hosted by the International Solidarity Action Research Network (ISARN). I'm particularly grateful to Tony Alessandrini, Anna Bernard, and Jessica Stites-Mor for organizing these events. I was also fortunate to give a public lecture at the University of Toronto in March 2018, thanks to the gracious invitation of Luis van Isschot, where I received sound feedback on the book.

Several colleagues have read early versions of this work and contributed to making the book stronger. I thank the anonymous readers chosen by Cambridge University Press for their attentive reading of the manuscript and for offering shrewd comments and recommendations. David Sheinin believed in this book and offered incisive feedback at an early stage. Daniel Ross graciously helped with the Introduction. Robert Whitney attentively read and commented on every single chapter. Eleni Schirmer attentively read and commented on every single word of this book. I also thank Paul Adler, Marie-Christine Dugal, Maurice Demers, Julie Gibbings, Danijel Matijevic, Hannah Oberman-Breindel, Nicolás Rodríguez, Maria del Carmen Suescun Pozas, Vikram Tamboli,

Guillaume Tremblay, and Naomi R Williams for providing invaluable comments and advice along the way.

In the Department of history at UQÀM, the best academic home I could hope for, I thank my colleagues Andrew Barros, Magda Fahrni, Martin Petitclerc, and Daniel Ross for providing guidance and support during the publication process. I thank my graduate students for bringing so much meaning and insight to my scholarly work. I'm especially grateful to Louis-Charles Cloutier Blain for his resourceful work as a research assistant, and to Charles Bénard, Dominik Charron, Olivier Dufresne, Marc-Edmond Lamarre, Frédérique Montreuil, and Alexandre Raymond-Desjardins for delighting with me in the pursuit of ideas on the Americas. The Latin Americanists with whom I collaborate in the Réseau d'études latino-américaines à Montréal (RÉLAM) and the Laboratoire interdisciplinaire d'études latino-américaines (LIELA) in Montréal have gifted me with an inter-disciplinary community of peers and friends with whom it's a pleasure to learn and exchange ideas.

In the research field, I thank many scholars and colleagues who have shared with me their knowledge and enthusiasm as I explored transnational APRA and its Indo-American project. From the early stages of the project, Ricardo Melgar Bao provided attentive guidance and assistance every time I needed it. With Martín Bergel, I shared the intellectual excitement of asking new questions to the field. Exchanges that contributed to shaping my thoughts at different stages of this project also include those I had with Iñigo García-Bryce, Fernando Camacho Padilla, Daniel Iglesias, Horacio Crespo, Mina Navarro, Enrique Plasencia, Juan Pablo Scarfi, Livia Schubiger, Leandro Sessa, and Daniela Spenser. In Peru, I thank Javier Barreda Jara, Víctor Caballero, Ponciano del Pino, Stefanie Graeter, Iván Hinojosa, Hugo Vallenas, and Armando Villanueva for sharing with me their love and knowledge of the Peruvian political landscape.

This is for my parents, Louise et Jacques Dorais, and also for Eleni, my *compañera*.

Introduction

"La nueva revolución de nuestra América será revolución de base y de sentido indio. De conciencia o de subconsciencia indígena expresada en una renovación económica y social."[1] Thus advocated the Peruvian politician Víctor Raúl Haya de la Torre in 1930, while living in Berlin, Germany. Indo-América, he argued, is "la expresión de la nueva concepción renovadora de América" and stems from the continental revolution under way.[2] Indo-América emerged at the beginning of the last century as a hemispheric and anti-imperialist revolutionary ideal, one that claimed to emphasize the Indigenous roots of Latin American culture and society. The American Popular Revolutionary Alliance (APRA), a highly influential populist and anti-imperialist movement in twentieth century Peru and Latin America more broadly, first envisioned and theorized Indo-América as a project of anti-imperialist and anti-colonial resistance, making it a key element of its political program during the interwar period.

This book has two intertwined objectives. First, it examines how and why the anti-imperialist project of the APRA took root outside of Peru. Second, it investigates the ways in which struggles for political survival in Peru shaped APRA's consciousness of the global. Unlike most studies that

1 All translations are mine unless otherwise stated. "The new revolution of our America will have Indian foundations and meaning. It will be based on an Indigenous consciousness or sub-consciousness, which will be expressed through economic and social renewal." Víctor Raúl Haya de la Torre, "La cuestión del nombre," In *¿A dónde va Indoamérica?*, Santiago de Chile: Editoriales Ercilla, 1935, p. 29.

2 Haya de la Torre,"The expression of the new renovating conception of America,"*¿A dónde va Indoamérica?*, p. 23.

interpret APRA's formation as entirely within the framework of Peruvian national history, the conclusions of this book show how the experience of exile and transnational solidarity decisively shaped the formation and the ideology of this major populist movement. Furthermore, by evincing the role that local politics in Peru and international politics abroad played in shaping APRA's call for hemispheric unity and Latin American solidarity, *Journey to Indo-América* explores more broadly how local dynamics shape global connections and collaborations.

SOLIDARITY AND ANTI-COLONIAL VISIONS OF LATIN AMERICAN UNITY

The American Popular Revolutionary Alliance (APRA) emerged in the mid-1920s as a hemispheric anti-imperialist movement. Established by a handful of leftist Peruvian exiles, this international organization demanded political, economic, cultural, and spiritual sovereignty for the people of Latin America. Its adherents, Apristas, rejected political institutions and revolutionary ideologies that came from Europe or the United States. They proposed instead to build a revolutionary doctrine Indigenous to the Americas, one that reflected Latin American realities rather than emulating ideologies that grew out of very different European conditions. As a result, Apristas positioned continental unity at the forefront of their fight against economic imperialism and mental colonialism. This vision, which they described by coining the term Indo-América, was intended to bring both freedom and moral revival to Latin Americans. The founders of APRA were university students and labour activists who had engaged in anti-governmental activities and attacked the political and social conditions that reigned in early twentieth-century Peru. The price they paid for their political activism was persecution, with arrests and waves of deportations starting in the spring of 1923.

The Peruvian students and labour activists who founded APRA initially conceived of their movement as an international organization, reflecting the context of its genesis in exile. The first Aprista committees were concurrently established in Paris, Buenos Aires, and Mexico City between 1926 and 1928. From exile, Aprista members came face to face with Latin American realities. Many echoed Haya de la Torre's reflection on the impact that exile had left on his political beliefs: "mi reciente viaje por Centroamérica, tan fecundo en trascendentes experiencias, me ha permitido ver de cerca la lucha de uno de los más importantes sectores de la América Latina contra el imperialismo invasor de los Estados

Unidos del Norte."[3] From exile, Aprista members also pursued militant activities, and organized and expanded their political movement into Europe and most of the Americas. They started to return to Peru in the summer of 1930 in order to found a national party, the Peruvian APRA party (PAP), in the hope of participating in the 1931 Peruvian elections.[4]

Today, Latin Americans continue to associate Indo-América with a form of resistance against Pan-American visions that are either entrenched in European outlooks or dependent on US dominance in the region. The discursive use of Indo-América, the name Apristas gave to the vast region south of the Río Grande, conveyed a forceful anti-colonial argument. By the end of the interwar period, Apristas came to prefer this name over Hispanic America, which they thought was too close to the legacy of Spain's colonialism. They similarly rejected Latin America as a nineteenth-century French invention meant to feed anti-Spanish sentiments. Pan-Americanism was also problematic, they claimed, because of its links with economic imperialism and because it included the continent as a whole without distinction between North America and South America. This early political statement partly explains Indo-América's enduring legacy as a symbol of Latin American resistance against foreign powers.[5] The resilience of APRA's Indo-América as a continental utopia and as a political weapon for anti-imperialist resistance also relied, as we shall see, on a surprising ideological malleability put at the service of a political cause in Peru.

APRA's vision of Latin American unity was hardly new. Aspirations for hemispheric integration have shaped the continent's political, social, and economic history for over two hundred years. From Simón Bolívar's dream of a united Spanish America in the early nineteenth century to Hugo Chávez's "Bolivarian revolution" in the early twenty-first century, Latin America has seen many attempts to forge collective projects that went beyond the confines of the nation-state. To be sure, individual

[3] "My recent trip to Central America, which fuelled transcendental experiences, enabled me to closely observe the struggle that one of the most important sectors of Latin America was leading against the invading imperialism of the United States." Haya de la Torre, *¿A dónde va Indoamérica?*, p. 41.

[4] On August 25, 1930, Lieutenant Colonel Luis M. Sánchez Cerro fomented a military coup and successfully seized power. The end of Leguía's *oncenio* (eleven-year term) marked a short-lived political opening in Peruvian politics.

[5] Harry Kantor, *The Ideology and Program of the Peruvian Aprista Movement*, New York: Octagon Books, 1966, pp. 28–29. Luis Alberto Sánchez, "A New Interpretation of the History of America," *The Hispanic American Historical Review*, 23: 3 (1943), 442.

countries in Latin America have asserted nationalist claims to exclusive sovereignty over territories and populations. At the same time, broad-based movements have championed unity and solidarity among Latin American peoples as the best vehicle to oppose foreign territorial expansion and cultural and economic influence. Continental nationalism first emerged in modern Latin America as an expression of hemispheric rather than national consciousness – a sense of belonging to the same continent-wide imagined community. Though different linguistic, cultural, and racial ideals formed the basis for an imagined Latin American community, the project of continental nationalism always carried an anti-colonial meaning against foreign intruders.[6]

In the wake of the Mexican Revolution and in the aftermath of the First World War, the first half of the twentieth century saw across Central America, the Caribbean, and South America a diverse, unorthodox constellation of radicals, revolutionaries, reformists, and populists take up the banner of Latin American unity and anti-imperialist struggle.[7] Their reasons for doing so varied, and as a result so did their perspectives on regional identities. Some of these anti-imperialist thinkers advocated *Hispanicidad*, specifically a return to the spiritual and moral values of Spain, as the best way to contest US imperialism and excessive materialism in the Southern Hemisphere.[8] Others preferred the larger European and cosmopolitan outlook Latin America provided to resist US

[6] Aimer Granados and Carlos Marichal (eds), *Construcción de las identidades latinoamericanas. Ensayos de historial intelectual siglos XIX y XX*, México: DF, El Colegio de México, 2004; Luis Tejada Ripalda, "El americanismo. Consideraciones sobre el nacionalismo continental latinoamericano," *Investigaciones sociales* 8: 12 (2004): 167–200; Jussi Pakkasvirta, *¿Un continente, una nación? Intelectuales latinoamericanos, comunidad política y las revistas culturales en Costa Rica y el Perú*, San José: Editorial de la Universidad de Costa Rica, 1997.

[7] Barry Carr, "Pioneering Transnational Solidarity in the Americas: The Movement in Support of Augusto C. Sandino, 1927–1934," *Journal of Iberian and Latin American Research* 20: 2 (2009): 141–152; Alexandra Pita González (ed.), *Redes intelectuales transnacionales en América Latina durante la entreguerra*, México: Universidad de Colima, Miguel Ángel Porrúa, 2016; Alexandra Pita González, *La Unión Latino Americana y el Boletín Renovación: Redes intelectuales y revistas culturales en la década de 1920*, México, DF: Colegio de México, Colima: Universidad de Colima, 2009; Ricardo Melgar Bao, "The Anti-Imperialist League of the Americas between the East and Latin America," *Latin American Perspectives* 35: 2 (2008): 9–24.

[8] Fabio Moraga Valle, "¿Una nación íbero o indoamericana? Joaquín Edwards Bello y el *Nacionalismo continental*," in Alexandra Pita González and Carlos Marichal Salinas (eds), *Pensar el antiimperialismo: Ensayos de historia intelectual latinoamericana, 1900–1930*, México, DF: El Colegio de México, Colima, Universidad de Colima, 2012, p. 247–282.

intervention, or else celebrated the democratic character of the "Latin race" in contradistinction with foreign expansionism.[9] By the late 1920s and 1930s, Indo-América surged as yet another model of anti-imperialist and hemispheric unity for the region. Whatever the successes, failures, or limitations of these movements, there is no doubt that such aspirations became, and are still, deeply embedded in Latin American political cultures.[10]

One such transnational project was that of Peru's APRA. Between the 1920s and the 1940s, APRA became a powerful national party and saw its calls for Indo-American solidarity, Latin American unity, and anti-imperialist struggle resonate well beyond Peru's borders throughout the Americas. While *aprismo* was never an ideologically or organizationally united movement, it generated social imaginaries and political symbols that became an enduring part of Latin American politics and culture for generations to come. APRA's anti-imperialist ideology of the 1920s and 1930s inspired a generation of Latin American intellectuals, artists, and political activists in their quest for social justice.[11] It likewise influenced a diverse network of internationalists and self-proclaimed anti-imperialists in the United States who strived to improve inter-American relations during a period characterized by extremely tense US–Latin American relations.[12] Many of these people, Latin Americans and non-Latin Americans alike, would play important roles in the growth and survival of APRA throughout the interwar period, with lasting consequences for APRA's critiques of Latin America's structural inequalities. This book

[9] Michel Gobat, "The Invention of Latin America: A Transnational History of Anti-Imperialism, Democracy, and Race," *American Historical Review*, 118: 5 (2013). 1345–1375; Alexandra Pita González and Carlos Marichal Salinas (eds), *Pensar el antiimperialismo: Ensayos de historia intelectual latinoamericana, 1900–1930*, México, DF: El Colegio de México, Colima, Universidad de Colima, 2012.

[10] Aldo Marchesi, *Latin America's Radical Left: Rebellion and Cold War in the Global 1960s*, New York: Cambridge University Press, 2018.

[11] Daniel Iglesias, *Du pain et de la Liberté. Socio-histoire des partis populaires apristes (Pérou, Venezuela, 1920–1962)*, Villeneuve d'Ascq: Presses Universitaires du Septentrion, 2015; Leandro Sessa, "'Semillas en tierras estériles': La recepción del APRA en la Argentina de mediados de la década de los treinta," *Revista Sociohistórica*, 28 (2011): 131–161; Robert Whitney, *State and Revolution in Cuba: Mass Mobilization and Political Change, 1920–1940*, Chapel Hill and London: The University of North Carolina Press, 2001, p. 36–53.

[12] Geneviève Dorais, "Missionary Critiques of Empire, 1920–1932: Between Interventionism and Anti-Imperialism," *The International History Review* 39: 3 (2017): 377–433; Anita Brenner, "Student Rebels in Latin America," *The Nation*, December 12, 1928, pp. 668–669.

traces the ways in which engaging in interwar trans-American and transnational solidarity networks, while assisting in crucial ways the organizing efforts of young Peruvian and Latin American radicals and political exiles, also limited the radical possibilities for social and political change that first drove APRA's anti-imperialist project of hemispheric unity.

Doing so places me in dialogue with a divided field of study regarding the revolutionary and transformative potential of *Indoamericanismo* for the Americas. A branch of the literature situates in Indo-América the first true alternative to Eurocentric modernity the region has known in the modern period.[13] Scholars likewise celebrate the early Marxist interpretations of APRA leaders for vindicating the rights and demands of "Indigenous America" and for including the emancipation of the Indigenous peoples in their strategic vision for Latin America's social revolution.[14] Indo-América, especially its early (though brief) socialist inflections, appears in these analyses as the point of junction between the Andean tradition and the new modernity, a mediating force around which the collective and millenarian forces of the Indigenous masses found common grounds with Marxism.[15] Indo-América has also been enthusiastically portrayed as a fusion of welded temporalities, an imagined uchrony (*ucronia*) where past legacies transcendentally bequeath to Latin Americans the possibility of emancipated futures.[16]

But Indo-América can also be reproved for its conservatism. APRA's Indo-American project lends itself to the same criticisms launched against *Indigenismo*. *Indigenismo* was a political and aesthetic movement that

[13] See for example Luis Arturo Torres Rojo, "La semántica política de Indoamericana, 1918–1941," in Aimer Granados and Carlos Marichal (eds), *Construcción de las identidades latinoamericanas. Ensayos de historial intelectual siglos XIX y XX*, México, DF: El Colegio de México, 2004, p. 207–240; César Germaná, *El 'Socialismo Indoamericano' de José Carlos Mariátegui: Proyecto de reconstitución del sentido histórico de la sociedad peruana*, Lima: Amauta, 1995; Aníbal Quijano, "Modernity, Identity, and Utopia in Latin America," *Boundary* 2, 20: 3 (1993): 140–155; Quijano, *Introducción a Mariátegui*, Mexico: Ediciones Era, S.A, 1981.

[14] Harry E. Vanden and Marc Becker (eds), *José Carlos Mariátegui: An Anthology*, New York: Monthly Review Press, 2011, p. 128. One of these celebrated leaders is the Peruvian socialist José Carlos Mariátegui, whose initial affiliation with APRA is often obliterated from historical narratives. I will return to this subject in Chapter 3.

[15] Ricardo Melgar Bao, *Mariátegui, Indoamerica y las crisis civilizatorias de Occidente*, Lima: Editora Amauta S.A, 1995, pp. 32–33.

[16] Torres Rojo, "La semántica política de Indoamericana, 1918–1941"; Luis Arturo Torres Rojo, *Ucronia y alteridad: notas para la historia de los conceptos políticos de Indoamérica, indigenismo e indianismo en México y Perú 1918–1994*, La Paz: Universidad Autónoma de Baja California Sur, 2016.

sought to save and redeem the marginalized Indigenous peoples of Latin America from the perspectives of white and mestizo intellectuals.[17] Not incidentally, the Indigenist movement proliferated during the period under study in this book, particularly in countries like Peru and Mexico with large Indigenous populations, and had a marked influence on APRA's anti-imperialist project of hemispheric unity. Nonetheless, whereas the *idea* of Indo-América initially foregrounded the racialized inequities of Latin America's economic and political development, its consolidation in later years as a *political concept* of anti-imperialist resistance and Latin American solidarity winded up having very little to do with the Indigenous peoples of the Americas.[18] That is not to say that APRA's vision of global resistance to imperialism should be dismissed as a fraud. But we must bear in mind this pointed limitation in our attempts to decipher and reckon with Indo-América's lasting ethos of Latin American unity and trans-American solidarity in the face of foreign power and global capitalism.

This is particularly the case since the interwar years saw the United States aggressively promoting its own hemispheric vision of Pan-Americanism, a vision that reflected its growing political, economic, and cultural power in the Americas. It was within this context of expanding US hegemony that APRA's message of anti-imperialist Latin American

[17] Kim Díaz, "Indigenismo in Peru and Bolivia," in Robert Eli Sánchez, Jr. (ed.), *Latin American and Latinx Philosophy: A Collaborative Introduction*, New York: Routledge, 2020, pp. 180–197; Marisol de la Cadena, *Indigenous Mestizos*, The Politics of Race and Culture in Cuzco, Peru, 1919–1991, Durham, NC and London: Duke University Press, 2000. In the past decade, scholars have returned to *Indigenismo* with a critical gaze on the movement's shortcomings while also reckoning with its historical and transformative significance for the meaning of modernity and of inclusive citizenship in early-twentieth-century Latin America. See Laura Giraudo and Stephen E. Lewis, "Introduction: Pan-American Indigenismo (1940–1970): New Approaches to an Ongoing Debate," *Latin American Perspectives* 39: 5 (2012): 3–11; Laura Giraudo and Juan Martín-Sánchez (eds), *La ambivalente historia del indigenismo. Campo interamericano y trayectorias nacionales, 1940–1970*, Lima: Instituto de Estudios Peruanos, 2011; Priscilla Archibald, *Imagining Modernity in the Andes*, Lewisburgh, PA: Bucknell University Press, 2011; Jorge Coronado, *The Andes Imagined: Indigenismo, Society, and Modernity*, Pittsburgh: University of Pittsburgh Press, 2009.

[18] What distinguishes a concept from an idea, according to the Latin American conceptual historians' readings of Reinhart Koselleck, is the concept's capacity to transcend its initial context of enunciation and to project itself in time. Elías J. Palti, "La nueva historia intelectual y sus repercusiones en América Latina," *Histórica Unisinos*, 11: 3 (2007): 297–305; Elías J. Palti, "The 'Theoretical Revolution' in Intellectual History: From the History of Political Ideas to the History of Political Languages," *History and Theory* , 53: 3 (2014): 387–405.

solidarity first emerged. From the mid-1920s through the mid-1930s, this message provided a powerful and compelling counter-narrative to US imperialism. Yet by the following decade, APRA's attacks against the United States had receded. More striking still is how APRA leaders ultimately accepted and fully engaged in the 1940s with the US-led vision of hemispheric integration as a viable political option. The new Pan-Americanism featuring non-intervention as a function of the Good Neighbor Policy (1933), as well as the rise of European Fascism, can only account in small measure for this political turnabout.

Journey to Indo-América argues that Indo-América, APRA's project of hemispheric unity, came to be understood in the 1940s as a democratic bulwark against the rise of Fascism in Europe, rather than the anti-US movement originally intended not only as a result of world events, but more importantly out of the necessity of political survival at the national level. The ideological and political evolution of the anti-imperialist APRA cannot be fully understood without attention to the state persecution and exile of APRA members. Because of its anti-government activities, before 1945 APRA was never able to participate fully and openly in Peruvian politics. Its survival therefore hinged on the capacity to remain connected to foreign allies. *Journey to Indo-América* explores how the necessity of engaging with international networks of solidarity – on the one hand, in order to withstand repression in Peru, while on the other simultaneously organizing labour and the middle sectors and vying for control of their fast-growing party at the national level – shaped APRA's anti-imperialist theses over time, as well as the project of hemispheric unity it promoted both inside and outside Peru. *Journey to Indo-América* simultaneously underscores the internal conflicts that rocked the Aprista movement from its inception onward. It advances that recurrent experiences of exile and ties to international solidarity contributed to firmly establishing the dominion of a moderate and anti-communist faction in the movement by the mid-to-late 1930s.

APRA'S ANTI-IMPERIALIST THESES

The first political platform of APRA reflected its international roots. In 1926, it released a five-plank program, which it called the "maximum program," or program for Latin America, as a means to orient and coordinate the struggles of national liberation it hoped to help bring about at the continental level. Its fundamental proposals were: (1) action against Yankee imperialism; (2) the political unity of Latin America; (3)

the nationalization of land and industry; (4) the internationalization of the Panama Canal; and (5) solidarity with all peoples and all oppressed classes.[19] The APRA rejected political institutions and revolutionary ideologies that came from Europe or the United States. They proposed instead to build a revolutionary doctrine Indigenous to the Americas, one that reflected Latin American realities rather than emulating European conditions.[20] The influence of APRA's anti-imperialist theses expanded well beyond Peru. Nationalist parties similar to the Peruvian APRA party surged in other Latin American countries, including: The *Acción Democrática* (Venezuela), the *Liberación Nacional* (Costa Rica), the *Movimiento Nacionalista Revolucionario* (Bolivia), the *Partido Febrerista* (Paraguay), the *Partido Revolucionario Dominicano* (Dominican Republic), the *Mouvement Ouvrier* (Haiti), the *Partido Popular Democrático* (Puerto Rico), and the *Autentico* and *Ortodoxo* parties (Cuba).[21]

In the 1920s and parts of the 1930s, Apristas defined imperialism primarily in economic terms. They had read John A. Hobson's thesis on imperialism attentively and understood that territorial expansion was but one expression of imperialist phenomena.[22] Travels to Europe in the 1920s introduced José Carlos Mariátegui and Víctor Raúl Haya de la Torre, two prominent founders and ideologues of APRA, to dialectical materialism, which contributed to shaping their reading of the Peruvian and Latin American realities.[23] Although they initially flirted with communism, Apristas ultimately rejected the rule of the Third International and proposed to create instead an original movement Indigenous to the Americas. Aprista ideologues conformed to what Sheldon B. Liss has called "plain" Marxists, that is, Marxists "who work openly and flexibly, as did Karl Marx, and believe that his ideas are

[19] Víctor Raúl Haya de la Torre, "What is the A.P.R.A.?" *The Labour Monthly*, December 1926, pp. 756–759.

[20] Sánchez, "A New Interpretation of the history of America," p. 444.

[21] Robert J. Alexander, *Aprismo: The Ideas and Doctrines of Víctor Raúl Haya de la Torre*, Kent, WA: Kent State University Press, 1973, pp. 27–28; Víctor Alba, *Historia del movimiento obrero en América Latina*, México: Libreros Mexicanos Unidos, 1964, pp. 284–314.

[22] John A. Hobson is one of the first to have explained and theorized the origins of modern economic imperialism. See Hobson, *Imperialism: A Study*, New York: J. Pott and Company, 1902.

[23] Mariátegui later helped form the Peruvian Socialist party and Peru's General Confederation of Workers.

applicable to present situations."[24] Apristas were, in sum, Marxists who refused ideological dogmatism. They dreaded one size-fits-all interpretations and would rather have abandoned Marxist claims than try to force social realities onto a given doctrine.

APRA's most compelling work on anti-imperialism appeared during the 1930s. According to Apristas, capitalism in Latin America should not be destroyed, but rather controlled.[25] This conclusion stemmed from their peculiar reading of Leninism. Apristas argued that Lenin's theses on imperialism did not reflect the historical and economic development particular to Latin American countries. They came to view communism as essentially a European phenomenon. Because the socio-economic problems of Europe and Latin America were different, the solutions that their respective problems called for were necessarily different as well, they argued, especially in regard to the relation between capitalism and imperialism. Here probably lies the single most important and original contribution of Apristas to Marxist thought in Latin America: Apristas, as Jeffrey L. Klaiber once wrote, turned Lenin on his head.[26] In contrast to what Lenin posited in his seminal work *Imperialism: The Highest Stage of Capitalism*, APRA argued that in non-industrialized nations imperialism represented the first rather than the final stage of capitalism.[27] Haya de la Torre first exposed and developed this thesis in El *Antimperialismo y el Apra* (1936) and refined it in later years in *Espacio-Tiempo-Histórico* (1948).[28] "El imperialismo es la ultima etapa del capitalismo en los pueblos industriales," he maintained, writing on behalf of all Latin Americans, "pero representa en los nuestros la primera etapa. Nuestros capitalismos nacen con el advenimiento del imperialismo moderno. Nace pues, dependiente, y como resultado de la culminación del

[24] Sheldon B. Liss, *Marxist Thought in Latin America*, Berkeley and Los Angeles: University of California Press, 1983, p. 2.

[25] Víctor Raúl Haya de la Torre, "El Antiimperialismo y el APRA," in *Obras Completas*, Vol. 4, Lima: Editorial Juan Mejía Baca, 1976–1977, n.p.

[26] Jeffrey L. Klaiber, "The Non-Communist Left in Latin America," *Journal of the History of Ideas*, 32: 4 (October–December, 1971): 613–615.

[27] Haya de la Torre, "El Antiimperialismo y el APRA...," pp. 18–21.

[28] Ibid., pp. 9–24. This work came as a response to the critique that the Cuban communist and revolutionary Julio Antonio Mella directed against APRA. Haya de la Torre argues that this work was meant to counterbalance the advance of both leftist and rightist extremism in Latin American revolutionary proposals. Although Haya de la Torre claims to have written this book in 1928 while in Mexico, this work was first published in 1936.

imperialismo."[29] Other Aprista ideologues produced important works on Latin American anti-imperialism as well, including Carlos Manuel Cox, Fernando León de Vivero, Pedro Muñiz, Magda Portal, and Manuel Seoane.[30]

APRA's ideological take on imperialism had one major consequence in terms of political organization. In countries understood as still grappling with feudal and semi-feudal economies, as was the case in Peru and most Latin American republics, the proletarian class was weak or non-existent and could therefore not successfully lead the socialist revolution. The APRA proposed instead a multi-class alliance between the workers, peasants, and the middle classes, one that would constitute the anti-imperialist state. The idea of an "anti-imperialist state" is central to APRA's thesis on imperialism. At the national level, the anti-imperialist state would exert control over foreign capital and orient it toward national development; it would not eliminate it. It would likewise work against the feudal oligarchies that had taken over the region as a result of the export-led economy of the late nineteenth century.[31]

TRANSNATIONAL PERSPECTIVE ON APRISMO: POPULISM, EXILE, AND SOLIDARITY ACTIVISTS FROM THE NORTH

Traditional scholarship on APRA has generally looked exclusively to the Peruvian national scene to grasp the complex evolution of this political group. In these studies, the movement's foundational years passed in exile throughout the 1920s are merely mentioned, not studied.[32] In contrast,

[29] Víctor Raúl Haya de la Torre, cited in Alba, *Historia del movimiento obrero*, p. 278 ("Imperialism is the highest stage of capitalism in industrialized countries, but it represents the first stage in ours. Our capitalisms first emerged with the advent of modern imperialism. Thus, they came to life dependent, and as a result of the culmination of imperialism.")

[30] See for example Magda Portal, *América latina frente al imperialismo*, Lima: Editorial Cahuide, 1931; Carlos Manuel Cox, *En torno al imperialismo*, Lima: Editorial cooperativa aprista "Atahualpa," 1933; Víctor Raúl Haya de la Torre, *¿A dónde va Indoamérica?*; Fernando León de Vivero, *Avance del imperialismo fascista en el Perú*, México, DF: Editorial Manuel Arévalo, 1938.

[31] Klaiber, "The Non-Communist Left," p. 615. Mariano Valderrama, "La evolución ideológica del APRA, 1924–1962," in Mariano Valderrama, Jorge Chullen, Nicolás Lynch and Carlos Malpica (eds), *El APRA: Un camino de esperanzas y frustraciones*, Lima: Ediciones El Gallo Rojo, 1980, p. 14.

[32] Works that provide critical and original perspectives on the Peruvian APRA party began to appear in the 1970s. Important contributions include: Peter F. Klarén, *Modernization, Dislocation, and Aprismo: Origins of the Peruvian Aprista Party, 1870–1932*, Austin and

I argue that we cannot adequately understand APRA's history without considering the international dimensions of *aprista* activity. APRA's vision of Latin American unity and of an Indo-American imagined political community was produced by a few prominent leaders of the party in dialogue with *aprista* supporters both outside and inside Peru. As such, the study shifts the focus away from exclusively APRA's charismatic leader, Víctor Raúl Haya de la Torre, taking pains to highlight the ideas and activities of lesser-known activists.[33]

By attempting to trace the worlds of transnational activism that carried the growth of APRA and of its anti-imperialist Indo-American project, *Journey to Indo-América* argues that the yearnings for inclusion that propelled the populist moment to the forefront of Latin American politics between the 1930s and 1960s are best understood as the result of collective and radical labours of transnational organization rather than the leadership of unique, purportedly larger-than-life political figures. This argument deviates from the more classical top-down approach to Latin American populism in which the study of the "charismatic bond between

London: The University of Texas Press, 1973. Jeffrey L. Klaiber, *Religion and Revolution in Peru, 1824–1976*, Notre Dame and London: University of Notre Dame Press, 1977. Steve Stein, *Populism in Peru: The Emergence of the Masses and the Politics of Social Control*, Madison: The University of Wisconsin Press, 1980. Imelda Vega-Centeno, *Aprismo popular: Cultura, Religión y Política*, Lima: Tarea, 1991. A trend of literature on APRA is currently seeking to move away from Haya de la Torre-centric studies, including Jaymie Patricia Heilman, "We Will No Longer Be Servile: Aprismo in 1930s Ayacucho," *Journal of Latin American Studies* 38 (2006): 491–518; Nelson Manrique, *"¡Usted fue Aprista!":Bases para una historia crítica del APRA* (Lima : Fondo Editorial Pontifica Universidad Católica del Perú, 2009); Iñigo García-Bryce, "A Revolution Remembered, a Revolution Forgotten: The 1932 Aprista Insurrection in Trujillo, Peru," *A Contra Corriente*, 7: 3 (Spring 2010): 277–322; Paulo Drinot, "Creole Anti-Communism: Labor, The Peruvian Communist Party, and APRA, 1930–1934," *Hispanic American Historical Review*, 92: 4 (2012): 703–736.

33 For a recent and non-partisan biography of Haya de la Torre, see Iñigo García-Bryce, *Haya de la Torre and the Pursuit of Power in Twentieth-Century Peru and Latin America*, Chapel Hill: The University of North Carolina Press, 2018. Scholars have also increasingly turned to marginalized Aprista leaders and vindicated the weight of their contributions to the movement. Peruvian poet Magda Portal has been, to date, the hub of these renewed efforts. See Myrna Yvonne Wallace Fuentes, *Most Scandalous Woman: Magda Portal and the Dream of Revolution in Peru*, Norman: University of Oklahoma Press, 2017; Iñigo García-Bryce, "Transnational Activist: Magda Portal and the American Popular Revolutionary Alliance (APRA), 1926–1950," *The Americas*, 70: 4 (April 2014): 667–706; Kathleen Weaver, *Peruvian Rebel: The World of Magda Portal. With a Selection of Her Poems*, Philadelphia: Pennsylvania State University Press, 2009.

political leaders and mass followers" prevails.[34] This scholarship's emphasis on the patron–client style of leadership and charisma insufficiently addresses how populist regimes fostered popular support among the marginalized sectors of Peruvian and Latin American societies. In an attempt to expand this view, revisionist scholars in the 1990s and early 2000s shifted their focus toward the militancy of the rank and file of the labour movements affiliated with populist regimes. These scholars argued that Latin American populist leaders did not rely on mere feelings and emotional appeals to gather support for their cause. Rather, they had political program and developed political ideologies that supported their populist platforms, as was the case with APRA. This literature also demonstrated that grassroots mobilization and rank and file negotiations contributed to shaping populist programs and ideologies in the region.[35]

These different approaches to Latin American populism, nevertheless, share the same national-centric framework of analysis.[36] With some recent and welcome exceptions, scholars have generally failed to explore in greater depth the extent to which interwar internationalism, as well as trans-American connections, informed the social and nationalist demands that infused the early populist platforms in Latin America.[37] This transnational study of APRA as an anti-imperialist movement, but also as a persecuted populist party composed of a multi-class alliance in Peru, contributes toward disclosing the transnational and trans-American

[34] Kenneth Robert, "Preface," in Michael L. Conniff (ed.), *Populism in Latin America: Second Edition*, Tuscaloosa: The University of Alabama Press, 2012, p. [illegible].

[35] See for example Daniel James, *Resistance and Integration: Peronism and the Argentine Working Class, 1946–1976*, New York and Cambridge: Cambridge University Press, 1988; John D. French, *The Brazilian Workers' ABC: Class Conflict and Alliances in Modern São Paulo*, Chapel Hill and London: The University of North Carolina Press, 1992; W. John Green, *Left Liberalism and Popular Mobilization in Colombia*, Gainesville: University Press of Florida, 2003. In the case of Peru, see the avant-garde work of Peter F. Klarén, *Modernization, Dislocation, and Aprismo*.

[36] Studies on Peruvian populism from a national perspective include Robert S. Jansen, *Revolutionizing Repertoires: The Rise of Populist Mobilization in Peru*, The University of Chicago Press: Chicago, 2017; Steve Stein, "The Paths to Populism in Peru," in Michael L. Conniff (ed.) *Populism in Latin America: Second Edition*, Tuscaloosa: The university of Alabama Press, 2012, pp. 110–131; Stein, *Populism in Peru*, 1980.

[37] Three exceptions in the case of Peru stand out. They are Daniel Iglesias, *Du pain et de la liberté*; Martín Bergel, *El oriente desplazado. Los intelectuales y los orígenes del tercermundismo en la Argentina*, Bernal: Universidad Nacional de Quilmes Editorial, 2015; Nelson Manrique, "*¡Usted fue aprista!*".

networks that bred the rise of the Latin American populist moment of 1930–1960.[38]

Another major theme of this book highlights the fact that exile, state persecution, and international solidarity were decisive for APRA's anti-imperialism and for the creation of its Indo-American political project. Specifically, I show that Indo-América as a political project was not consolidated in the heyday of transnational exile in the 1920s, as is often suggested in the scholarship. Rather, Indo-América is best understood as a form of universal appeal developed in the 1930s by one democratic and non-communist faction of the APRA movement, called the Hayista faction, precisely to advance a political struggle inside Peru. The book comes to this conclusion by tracing the political struggles that foregrounded the idea and political vision of Indo-América, from the moment it first emerged as a new hemispheric consciousness during the 1920s to its transformation into the Peruvian APRA party's main defensive strategy in the face of state persecution during the 1930s and 1940s.

The arguments I bring forth in this book about the weight that exile and state persecution exerted on the political activism of major APRA leaders place it in dialogue with the work of a small group of contemporary historians who have paid increasing attention to the APRA during its successive periods of political exile. Starting in the 1990s with the work of Ricardo Melgar Bao, a pioneering historian of the APRA exile in Mexico, recent scholarship has reconstructed Aprista networks of exile. This scholarship traces intellectual exchanges among Latin American political communities and studies APRA's mythic and symbolic construction of exile.[39] Together, these scholars have added to our knowledge of exile

[38] For theoretical frameworks that insist on Latin American populism's characteristics as a multi-class coalition and an antagonist force against political power and authority, see Torcuato S. Di Tella, "Populism and Reform in Latin America," in Claudio Veliz (ed.) *Obstacles to Change in Latin America*, London: Oxford University Press, 1965, pp. 47–74; Ernesto Laclau, "Towards a Theory of Populism," in *Political and Ideology in Marxist Theory*, Thetford, Norfolk: Lowe and Brydone Printers Limited, 1997, pp. 143–198.

[39] Important contributions in this field include: Martín Bergel, *La desmesura revolucionaria. Cultura y política en los orígenes del APRA*, Lima: La Siniestra, 2019; Bergel, "Un partido hecho de cartas. Exilio, redes diasporicas, y el rol de la correspondencia en la formación del aprismo peruano (1921–1930)," *Políticas de la Memoria*, 15 (2014–2015): 71–85; Bergel, "Con el ojo izquierdo. Mirando a Bolivia, de Manuel Seoane. Viaje y deriva latinoamericana en la génesis del antiimperialismo aprista," in Alexandra Pita and Carlos Marichal (eds), *Pensar el antiimperialismo*, pp. 283–311; Bergel, "Nomadismo proselitista y revolución. Notas para una caracterización del primer exilio aprista (1923–1931)." *E.I.A.L.*, 20: 1 (2009): 41–66; Bergel, "Manuel Seoane y Luis Heysen:

and transnational solidarity networks as major catalysts of the leftist political projects that emerged in, and influenced, twentieth-century Latin America.[40] My book builds on these studies.

Beyond its original historiographic contributions to the study of APRA, this book more importantly centres APRA's networks of solidarity and experience of exile as a detailed case study to understand better how political exile, including the experience of territorial displacement and "post-exilic relocation" in the homeland, shaped the growth of interwar Latin America's left.[41] As such, *Journey to Indo-América* adds to the studies that analyze the growth and political implications of transnational solidarity networks in the Southern Hemisphere from within the framework of studies of exile.[42] In past decades, this scholarship has granted much attention to Latin American exiles and refugees who fled state authoritarianism during the last phases of the Cold War. It resulted in a rich and interdisciplinary field of study that has explored from different analytical perspectives how individual and collective experiences fostered

el entrelugar de los exiliados apristas en la Argentina de los veinte," *Políticas de la memoria* 6/7 (2007): 124–142; Iñigo García-Bryce, "Transnational Activist: Magda Portal and the American Popular Revolutionary Alliance (APRA), 1926-1950," The Americas 70: 4 (April 2014): 667–706. Leandro Sessa, "Los exiliados como 'traductores.' Las redes del exilio aprista en la Argentina en la década de los treinta," *Trabajos y Comunicaciones*, 2nd season, 40 (2014); Sessa, "Aprismo y apristas en Argentina: Derivas de una experiencia antiimperialista en la 'encrucijada' ideológica y política de los años treinta," Ph.D. diss., Universidad Nacional de La Plata, 2013; Daniel Iglesias, "Articulaciones relacionales y redes transnacionales: Acercamiento critico para una nueva historiografía del Aprismo continental," *Nuevo Mundo Mundos Nuevos*, 2007, DOI: https://doi.org/10.4000/nuevomundo.8602; Iglesias, *Du pain et de la liberté*; Ricardo Melgar Bao, *Redes e imaginario del exilio en México y América Latina: 1934–1940*, Argentina: LibrosenRed, 2003; Bao, "Redes del exilio aprista en México (1923–1924), una aproximación," in *México, país refugio*, ed. Pablo Yankelevich. México, DF: Plaza y Valdés, 2002, p. 245–263.

40 Particularly influential to my work is the scholarship of Latin American intellectual historian Martín Bergel, who studied APRA's transnationalism in sophisticated and instructive ways.

41 Post-exilic relocation generally refers to the return to the homeland, though it can also mean to establish home elsewhere. Luis Roniger, "Paisajes culturales en cambio bajo el impacto del exilio, las diásporas y el retorno de le emigración," *Araucaria. Revista Iberoamericana de Filosofía, Política, Humanidades y Relaciones Internacionales*, 20: 40 (2018): 185–208; Roniger, Leonardo Senkman, Saúl Sosnowksi and Mario Sznajder, *Exile, Diaspora and Return: Changing Cultural Landscapes in Argentina, Chile, Paraguay, and Uruguay*, New York: Oxford University Press, 2018; Mario Benedetti, *El desexilio y otras conjeturas*, Buenos Aires: Nueva Imagen, 1985.

42 Luis Roniger, "Displacement and Testimony: Recent History and the Study of Exile in Post-Exile," *International Journal of Politics, Culture, and Society*, 9: 2 (2016): 111–133.

political and cultural changes in mid-to-late-twentieth century Latin America.[43]

My book adds to these scholarly efforts by studying the particular dynamics of Latin American exile during the interwar years, a period that has received less attention despite being marked by recurrent territorial displacements of radicals and student and union activists.[44] It also joins my peers' ambitions to move away from mere heroic or victimized assessments of exile, a common binary narrative found in the testimonial literature of exile.[45] To do so, I analyze the gains and losses associated with the exilic experiences of APRA activists at both the personal and political level. This includes tracing how these gains and losses experienced in exile shaped the re-encounter of continental problems and fed the rise of Pan-Latin American consciousnesses. It also demands that I heed the conditions under which the return of Apristas to the homeland took place, at both the local and national levels. As this book shows, the story of rising global consciousnesses in exile doesn't begin and end with territorial displacement abroad. Rather, for Peruvian leftist activists who politically came of age in exile, the experience of "post-exilic relocations" are what prompted the consolidation of their newly-gained cultural and political consciousnesses into the concept of Indo-América as a vision of continental solidarity and of modernity for Latin America's future.

A third and complementary theme of the book underlines interactions between *apristas* and APRA allies in Latin America and pacifist and Christian social justice activists from the United States and Europe. These solidarity activists cultivated an extensive correspondence with

[43] María Eugenia Horvitz, *Exiliados y desterrados del cono sur de América, 1970–1990*, Chile: Erdosain Ediciones Ltda, 2017; María Soledad Lastra, *Volver del exilio: Historia comparada de las políticas de recepción en las posdictaduras de la Argentina y Uruguay (1983–1989)*, La Plata: Universidad Nacional de La Plata, Universidad Nacional de Misiones and Universidad Nacional de General Sarmiento, 2016; Tanya Harmer, "The View from Havana: Chilean Exiles in Cuba and Early Resistance to Chile's Dictatorship, 1973–1977," *Hispanic American Historical Review*, 96: 1 (2016): 109–146; Silvina Jensen and Soledad Lastra (eds), *Exilios: Militancia y represión. Nuevas fuentes y nuevos abordajes de los destierros de la Argentina de los años setenta*, La Plata: EDULP, 2014; Marina Franco, *Exilio. Argentinos en Francia durante la dictadura*, Buenos Aires: Siglo XXI, 2008; Silvina Jensen, *La provincia flotante. El exilio argentino en Cataluña, 1976–2006*, Barcelona: Casa de América Cataluña, 2007; Silvia Dutrénit Bielous (ed.), *El Uruguay del exilio: Gente, circunstancias, escenarios*, Montivedo, Uruguay: Ediciones trilce, 2006.

[44] Ricardo Melgar Bao, "Los ciclos del exilio y del retorno en América Latina: una aproximación," *Estudios Latinoamericanos*, 23 (2009): 50.

[45] Roniger, "Displacement and Testimony."

apristas both in Peru and elsewhere, and they used the information they gathered to attract international attention to the Hayista faction within APRA. As such, my work contributes to the renewed scholarly interest in hemispheric history, specifically by paying attention to the fluid and heterogenous nature of the interwar international movements and the political consciousnesses that informed the growth of APRA's anti-imperialist theses for Indo-América.[46] Of particular interest to my work is the attention that historians Ian Tyrrell and Jay Sexton ask that we grant to "the missionaries' role as critics of empire and as brokers between imperial power and those subject to that power."[47] Doing so helps nuance the typical portrayals of missionaries and US civil society actors as agents of imperialism abroad. Examining the anti-imperialist currents of Protestant missions as well as US civil society actors involved in Latin America, and specifically those connected with APRA, reveals their contribution to US hegemony and informal empire to be far more complex and multifaceted, even contradictory, than suggested by earlier

[46] In a recent appraisal of the Western Hemisphere idea, historians Juan Pablo Scarfi and Andrew R. Tillman invite us to upend the traditional approach to US–Latin American relations. They invite scholars to search for instances of "cooperation and commonalities" in the history of inter-American relations rather than focus exclusively on stories of division and conflict: Juan Pablo Scarfi and Andrew R. Tillman (eds), *Cooperation and Hegemony in US–Latin American Relations: Revisiting the Western Hemisphere Idea*, New York: Palgrave Macmillan, 2016. The renewed scholarly interest in hemispheric history builds on the rich scholarship that has sought in the past two decades to move away from exclusive diplomatic-centric approaches to Pan-Americanism. A first, groundbreaking endeavour in that direction was David Sheinin (ed.), *Beyond the Ideal: Pan Americanism in Inter-American Affairs*, Westport: Greenwood Press, 2000. Also see, on social and cultural dimensions of Pan-Americanism, Mark Petersen, "Argentine and Chilean Approaches to Modern Pan-Americanism, 1888–1930," Ph.D. diss., Corpus Christi College, 2014; Ricardo D. Salvatore, "Imperial Mechanics: South America's Hemispheric Integration in the Machine Age," *American Quarterly*, 58: 3 (September 2006): 662–691. On different legal initiatives and interpretations, see Juan Pablo Scarfi, *The Hidden History of International Law in the Americas: Empire and Legal Networks*, New York, Oxford University Press, 2017; Scarfi, "In the Name of the Americas: The Pan-American Redefinition of the Monroe Doctrine and the Emerging Language of American International Law in the Western Hemisphere, 1898–1933," *Diplomatic History* 40: 2 (2016): 47–68; Scarfi, *El imperio de la ley: James Brown Scott y la construcción de un orden jurídico interamericano*, Buenos Aires: Fondo de Cultura Económica, 2014. Liliana Obregón, "Regionalism Constructed: A Short History of 'Latin American International Law," *ESIL Conference Paper Series*, 2: 1 (2012).

[47] Ian Tyrrell and Jay Sexton (eds), *Empire's Twin: U.S. Anti-Imperialism from the Founding Era to the Age of Terrorism*, Ithaca and London: Cornell University Press, 2015, p. 14.

scholarship.[48] These ties of international solidarity between sectors of the Latin American left and critiques of empire from the North created a unique body of political and cultural work that widens our understanding of the complexities and contradictions associated with hemispheric relations, imperial power, and anti-imperialist struggle.

"As historians, we have been trained to identify our historical figures through the lens of geography or political groups rather than recognizing the intersections between socialism, communism, nationalism, pacifism, and civil liberties worldwide," Michele L. Louro recently wrote in her outstanding monograph on Nerhu's interwar internationalism. This is indeed how most scholars of Latin American anti-imperialism have so far approached the conflicts and tensions, but also the friendships and solidarities between different sectors of the Latin American left. These studies give the impression that the interwar left in Latin America was divided between clearly defined political groups and parties for whom collaboration was out of the question. But, as Louro argues, "What was so unique about the 1920s and 1930s was the ability to move across and within such categories and to rethink solidarities beyond the rigid frameworks afforded by strict orthodoxies or institutionalization."[49] This fluidity also characterized the growth and formation of the APRA movement

[48] One branch of this literature considers specifically the role played by US Protestant missions in facilitating US hegemony in Latin America. See for example Daniel R. Rodríguez, *La primera evangelización norteamericana en Puerto Rico, 1898–1930*, México, DF: Ediciones Borinquen, 1986. Mariano C. Apilado, *Revolutionary Spirituality: A Study of the Protestant Role in the American Colonial Rule of the Philippines, 1898–1928*, Quezon City: New Day Publishers, 1999. Jason Yaremko, *U.S. Protestant Missions in Cuba: From Independence to Castro*, Gainsville: University Press of Florida, 2000. Other studies similarly approach Protestantism as cultural force though they more carefully delineate the contradictions that underlay the Protestant missionary project. See Samuel Silva-Gotay, *Protestantismo y política en Puerto Rico 1930. Hacia una historia del protestantismo evangélico en Puerto Rico*, San Juan: Editorial de la Universidad de Puerto Rico, 1997; Luis Martinez Fernandez, *Protestantism and Political Conflict in the Nineteenth Century Hispanic Caribbean*, New Brunswick: Rutgers University Press, 2002; David Stoll, *Is Latin America Turning Protestant?: The Politics of Evangelical Growth*, Berkeley: University of California Press, 1990. Starting in the mid-1990s, attempts to view Latin American Protestantism through cycles of negotiations and local re-appropriations rather than as mere North American mimicry emerged. See Virginia Garrard-Burnett and David Stoll (eds), *Rethinking Protestantism in Latin America*, Philadelphia: Temple University Press, 1993. Ellen Walsh, "'Advancing the Kingdom': Missionaries and Americanization in Puerto Rico, 1898–1930s," Ph.D. Diss., University of Pittsburgh, 2008.

[49] Michele L. Louro, *Comrades against Imperialism: Nehru, India, and Interwar Internationalism*, New York: Cambridge University Press, 2018, p. 7.

during the interwar period. The alliances between Apristas and US anti-imperialists and Christian social activists were helpful, but also fraught and difficult to maintain. They eventually gave way to contentious and fragile relationships. Nevertheless, they did contribute to providing the context in which APRA's ideological production happened, and particularly the Indo-American project. This context, framed by trans-American solidarity, I show in this book, comprised a central tension that drove historical change in two opposite directions all at once; trans-American solidarity enabled the survival and support of Latin American anti-imperialist thinkers, but while doing so it eventually curbed the critiques of US empire that Apristas were willing and able to formulate.

THEORY, METHODS, AND HOW TO EVADE THE CHARISMATIC STRONGMAN

Methodologically, it is crucial that my study reflects the plasticity and resilience of collaborations between historical actors who did not see eye to eye on every subject, but who put the same premium on global and international unity as remedies for the crises they sensed creeping worldwide. To do so, I seek to challenge the widespread belief that conflict never lasted, or even truly existed for that matter, in the APRA movement. The story goes two ways. Either Víctor Raúl Haya de la Torre, by far the most celebrated (and detested) historical leader of APRA, exercised such iron discipline over party members that only harmony prevailed between them. Or conspicuous ruptures regularly cleansed APRA of dissident elements, each time adding to the sway of the moderate party leadership as well as the internal cohesion of its membership. In the first version, the possibility of conflict is dismissed by negation: the myth of a united APRA refuses any likelihood of disagreement or quarrel in the history of the party. The second version, in contrast, eschews the possibility of conflict by inflation: occasional political ruptures realigned APRA in clearly defined and easily recognizable factions that henceforth jousted with one another – the legitimate APRA on one side, the dissidents on the other. Lingering conflict, in other words, did not exist within the organization. Only its final expression did.[50]

[50] APRA enemies and defectors alike published copious critiques, from both left and right ends of the political spectrum, to render public what they deemed deceitful manoeuvres amid APRA. These often included open and abrupt rupture from the APRA. See Mariano Valderrama, "La evolución ideológica del APRA, 1924–1962," in Mariano Valderrama

In contrast, my objective is to centre conflictive relationships, political negotiation and organizing, and the complexities of transnational solidarity work at the core of my story about APRA. This goal is informed by the work pioneered in the past fifteen years by scholars who revolve around two prominent research groups in the field of Latin American intellectual history – the Seminario de Historia Intelectual de América Latina, Centro de Estudios Históricos – Colmex, México, and the Centro de Historial Intelectual (CHI), Universidad Nacional de Quilmes, Argentina. Together, these research groups encouraged the growth of a renewed scholarship on the intellectual history of continental nationalism. This cohort of innovative intellectual historians has been committed to approaching their primary source material dynamically, not hesitating to borrow from other social science disciplines in their attempts to unveil and historicize the creative processes at play behind published texts[51]. As

Jorge Chullen, Nicolás Lynch and Carlos Malpica (eds), *El APRA: Un camino de esperanzas y frustraciones*, Lima: Ediciones El Gallo Rojo, 1980; Hernando Aguirre Gamio, *Liquidación histórica del APRA y del Colonialismo Neoliberal*, Lima: Ediciones Debate, 1962; Alberto Hernández Urbina, *Los partidos y la crisis del Apra*, Lima: Ediciones Raíz, 1956; Magda Portal, *La Trampa*, Lima: Ediciones Raíz, 1956; Portal, *¿Quienes traicionaron al pueblo?*, Lima, 1950; Alberto Hidalgo, *Por qué renuncié al Apra*, Buenos Aires: Imprenta Leomir, 1954; Luis Eduardo Enríquez Cabrera, *Haya de la Torre, la estafa política más grande de América*, Lima: Ediciones del Pacifico, 1951.

51 For examples of this rich scholarship, see Marco Frank and Alexandra Pita González, "Irradiador y Horizonte: Revistas de un movimiento de vanguardia y una red estridentista," *Catedral Tomada. Revista de Critica Literaria latinoamericana*, 6: 11 (2018): 13–47; Tomás Pérez Vejo and Pablo Yankelevich (eds), *Raza y política en hispanoamérica*, Madrid: Iberoamericana, Ciudad de México: Bonilla Artigas Editores, Colegio de México, 2018; Alexandra Pita González, "Panamericanismo y nación," *Anuario IEHS* 32: 1 (2017): 135–154; Pita González (ed.), *Redes intelectuales transnacionales en América Latina durante la entreguerra*, México: Universidad de Colima, Miguel Ángel Porrúa, 2016; Alexandra Pita González and Carlos Marichal Salinas (eds), *Pensar el antiimperialismo*, 2012; Pita Gonzalez (ed.), *Intelectuales y antiimperialismo: entre la teoría y la practica*, Colima: Universidad de Colima, 2010; Mariano Di Pasquale and Marcelo Summo (eds), *Trayectorias singulares, voces plurales: Intelectuales en la Argentina, siglos XIX–XX*, Buenos Aires: Editorial de la Universidad Nacional de Tres de Febrero, 2015; Rogelio De la Mora and Hugo Cancino (eds), *La Historia Intelectual y el movimiento de las ideas en América Latina, siglos XIX–XX*, México: Universidad Veracruzana, 2015; Martín Bergel, "El anti-antinortemaricanismo en América Latina (1898–1930): Apuntes para una historia intelectual," *Nueva Sociedad*, 236 (2011); Marta Elena Casaus Arzu (ed.), *El Lenguaje de los ismos: Algunos conceptos de la modernidad en América Latina*, Guatemala: F & G Editores, 2010; Elías J. Palti, "La nueva historia intelectual y sus repercusiones en América Latina," Histórica Unisinos, 11: 3 (2007): 297–305; Patricia Funes, *Salvar la nación: intelectuales, cultura y política en los años veinte latinoamericanos*, Buenos Aires: Prometeo libros, 2006; Marta Elena Casaús Arzú and Teresa García Giráldez, *Las redes intelectuales centroamericanas: un siglo de imaginarios nacionales (1820–1920)*, Guatemala: Editores F&G,

a result, one of the major and ongoing contributions of this field in recent years has been to draw attention to the transnational intellectual networks that underpinned the formation of projects of hemispheric unity in Latin America from the mid-nineteenth to early-twentieth centuries. My work on the history of transnational APRA, including their collaboration with non-Latin American allies, builds from this insight.

Additionally, my theoretical framework is inspired by the German sociologist Karl Mannheim's warning regarding the pitfalls that await those who study ideology through exclusive individual perspectives.[52] "The aim [...] is to investigate not how thinking appears in textbooks on logic, but how it really functions in public life and in politics as an instrument of collective actions."[53] Writing in the 1930s, Mannheim took issue with the individual-centric approach that recent advances in psychology had brought forth in works that studied the action of thinking. Mannheim stressed that the ways in which individuals think are constrained and delineated by the group from which they think. According to Mannheim, understanding how individuals think *with and against each other* in a given historical and sociological context can bring us, if not to the truth, at least close to it – to what he calls the "optimum of truth."[54] This warning assists my analysis of the relationship between political activism and intellectual production. By paying too much attention to published material or to official Aprista propaganda, we lose sight of the collective struggles that underpinned the unsteady creative process of the historical actors I study. Behind the lure of polished pages lie murkier realities associated with the lived experience of exile and the struggle to survive politically.

The Aprista web was dispersed throughout the Americas and Europe, and so are its remaining traces. Though an impressive number of primary sources exist on APRA, its lack of geographical concentration is a challenge for the researcher. When Aprista actors moved between Peru and exiled communities, they often brought personal letters and political documents along with them. In the space of exile, they were also persecuted and sometimes arrested. Police forces from different countries worked in collaboration and exchanged seized APRA material.

2005; Aimer Granados García and Carlos Marichal (eds), *Construcción de las identidades latinoamericanas*, 2004.

[52] Karl Mannheim, *An Ideology and Utopia: An Introduction to the Sociology of Knowledge*, New York: Harcourt, Brace and Company, 1949 (1st ed. 1936).

[53] Ibid., p. 1. [54] Ibid., p. 71.

Likewise, Peruvian diplomats located in foreign countries with communities of Aprista exiles shipped back to Peru important information on the Aprista committee's activities. Finally, over the course of the century, various United States institutions have acquired, unsystematically, APRA pamphlets and publications. The search for APRA material, in other words, is not territorially bounded to the places in which Aprista exiles resided. Researching Indo-América through the lens of APRA exile, therefore, required that I myself embark on a transnational journey. The book is based on original research in a total of eighteen Peruvian, Mexican, French, and US archives. It is based on a wide variety of sources, including personal correspondence, diplomatic reports, criminal files, religious publications, political flyers, propaganda material, cultural magazines, newspapers, as well as official studies and scholarship produced by APRA.

One caveat is in order regarding the challenges that reckoning with the one historical figure I wanted to ignore forced on my historical practice. When I began to delve into APRA's past a decade ago now, the last thing I wanted to do, as this Introduction I trust makes clear, was yet another study that associated this political movement with Haya de la Torre's leadership. My objective at that point was not only to decentre the history of the APRA by adopting a transnational lens of analysis, but to *remove* Haya de la Torre altogether from my historical narrative. Too much had been said and written about this leader. Too much passion for or against him made it impossible to see clearly in the collective dynamics of this anti-imperialist movement. I wanted him out.[55]

As a result, during my time in graduate school, I found myself drifting in endless archival detours, desperately seeking ways to forego the work and life of Haya de la Torre in my attempts to understand better the collective dynamics of APRA's exile, only to be thrust, without fail, right back to him and to the significance he had for the movement. Of course, one reason for Haya de la Torre's omnipresence in the history of the party is that most of the archives that exist on APRA, whether located in Peru or abroad, are organized in accordance with the leaders of APRA that official histories of the party have recorded. Yet the same thing happened

[55] For a critique of the charismatic strongman, see Kevin E. Young, "Revolutionary Actors, Encounters, and Transformations," in Young (ed.) *Making the Revolution: Histories of the Latin American Left*, New York: Cambridge University Press, 2019, pp. 1–18. Contributors to this edited volume all played a part in building and expanding this scholarship.

again and again when I spoke with contemporary Aprista sympathizers in Peru. They would share with me personal memories of their time in the party without even realizing, it seemed, that the recollection of events that they were describing to me wasn't actually theirs, but rather that it came from passages they had probably read over and over again, and which I recognized from official histories of the party in which Haya de la Torre took up the whole place. It proved impossible in Peru to talk about my project without reverting to the figure of Haya de la Torre. Everybody made sense of the research questions I was asking – whether it be about APRA's anti-imperialism, its foundational years in exile as a political diaspora, or the originality of its continental program for all of Latin America – through this single historical figure.

Every time the archives or a sympathizer of APRA forced upon my reflections a return to Haya de la Torre, it made clearer the inescapability of this historical figure to fully understand the development of APRA, both inside and outside Peru. This character invaded as much the lore and the collective memory of the Peruvian Apristas as he did the US state department archives or the official propaganda of the party. Was I wrong to try to walk away from him, I began to wonder? Did he, after all, control the movement from its foundation onward, as the literature suggested? I was not wrong, and Haya de la Torre, as we shall see in this book, did not control the movement alone or at all times. And yet, to say that things did not go as planned is a euphemism: Haya de la Torre, it turns out, lurks around every single chapter of this book.

Though my repeated attempts to dodge this historical character did not pan out the way I had foreseen when I first embarked on this research project, I was at least able to question and recast his so-called unique leadership. In that sense, Haya de la Torre still appears in the book, but less as the focal point of the study than as the narrative thread around which the story unfolds. If his archival presence was inescapable, I indeed began to realize, then I needed to adapt my research questions in a way that gestured to this historical figure but did not make the story about him. Doing so opened a whole new set of historical questions about the ways that exile, solidarity work, and calls for Latin American unity-shaped part of Latin America's left during the interwar period. Specifically, granting attention to moments of conflict in my sources forced me to trace the options made available to APRA leaders to exert dominion over their widespread and ideologically diverse movement. This, in turn, forced me to make sense of the connections I had observed, but failed to analyze, between the prevalence of a Latin American ethos of solidarity and resistance in APRA on one side, and the centrality of transnational solidarity work to APRA's political survival during the interwar period on the other. *Journey to Indo-América* tells the story I uncovered as I threaded my way through these connections.

ORGANIZATION OF THE BOOK

Six chapters structure the central arguments of the book. Documenting the transnational history of APRA, specifically how exile and state persecution shaped the growth and evolution of this major populist movement in Peru, demands that I foreground the collaborations that APRA leaders developed with non-Latin American allies. The first chapter begins this task by tracing the common ideological grounds that made possible the formation of an alliance in the early 1920s between Reform-minded students in Peru and a number of Christian missionaries and religious pacifists from Europe and the United States. These students, many of whom formed the APRA movement shortly after, viewed in continental solidarity a remedy to the moral crises they sensed around them. For many Christian pacifists, who like the Scottish Reverend John A. Mackay and the US internationalist Anna Melissa Graves dismissed the right of nations to claim territorial possessions, the references they saw in the Peruvian student reform movement to the Bolivarian ideal of a united America was inspiring. They viewed in these young Latin American radicals an opportunity for spiritual renewal in the Western World.

The next two chapters tackle the weight that exile had in the formation of this political movement between the mid-1920s and early 1930s. Chapter 2 traces how the lived experience of exile contributed to fostering new political consciousnesses in Apristas who were deported abroad in the 1920s. It traces as a case study the rocky relationship that the young student activist and future APRA leader Víctor Raúl Haya de la Torre maintained during his first years in exile with the foreign allies, specifically Mackay and Graves, who assisted him, and who tried to politically influence him. Chapter 3 turns to the discursive use of exile following the return to the homeland and the foundation of the Peruvian APRA Party (PAP) in 1930. It argues that APRA leaders who experienced exile in the 1920s used references to their past travels as regimes of authority in Peru. Discourses of deep connection to and knowledge of the Americas assisted in consolidating the political authority of exiled leaders as they began to convert the continental APRA into a national mass-based party.

Chapters 4 and 5 together explore deeper the transnational solidarity networks that worked in favour of the Hayista faction in the APRA movement in the 1930s. Following the arrest by Peruvian authorities of Víctor Raúl Haya de la Torre in May of 1932, a number of foreign allies organized a movement of solidarity with PAP. Their cross-border calls for a new democratic order in the Americas, as I show in Chapter 4, took Haya de la Torre as a symbol of their fight against dictatorships and communism. By delving deeper into this specific transnational advocacy campaign, the chapter argues that, in addition to providing access to external resources, international connections gave the Hayista faction the opportunity to acquire symbolic capital in Peru and helped to assert its authority in the APRA movement. Chapter 5 turns to the roles of APRA exiles and the workings of APRA's transnational solidarity networks during the 1930s, a period during which Apristas suffered unremitting state persecution in Peru. It argues that the deportations of party leaders paradoxically gave to the APRA movement political opportunities impossible to leverage otherwise, re-asserting the tight entanglement between exile and the development of the APRA movement in Peru. APRA leaders in exile connected with foreign allies in the Americas to create and sustain solidarity networks that assisted the persecuted PAP in Peru.

The final chapter reveals the impacts that APRA's engagement with transnational solidarity networks had on the evolution of its ideology, particularly of its Indo-American project. I suggest that it is precisely during the 1930s and early 1940s, after the foundation of the Peruvian APRA party and a national political platform, that APRA propelled Indo-América to the centre-stage of its political doctrine. Indo-América had emerged in APRA as a new cultural and anti-imperialist consciousness in the late 1920s thanks to the experience of exile, but, as this last chapter concludes, it became politically consolidated as a result of the experience of recurrent persecution in Peru after the first homecoming of Apristas in 1930. Recurrent state persecution against PAP, I argue, combined with APRA's innovative political strategies in exile, contributed to imagining an Indo-American project that moved beyond the rejection of US imperialism originally at its core to focus on the defence of electoral political rights and liberal democracy in Peru and the Americas. By that time, Apristas had all but stripped from their continental program pledges of social and moral revival for Indigenous people it had once, if briefly, included.

1

Crisis and Regeneration: Peruvian Students and Christian Pacifists, 1918–1925

"Europe is sinking! America is the hope of the world!" John A. Mackay, a Protestant missionary envoy to Peru, declared to an assembly of fellow missionaries in 1925. As the ashes of the First World War slowly settled, a constellation of missionaries, Christian pacifists, and internationalists reflected with dread upon the state of human civilization. Enlightened modernity had betrayed Western hopes. Instead of promises of universal brotherhood, it had wrought massive destruction and the experience of collective trauma. The lead up to war, the war itself, and the postwar crisis throughout the world generated a profound questioning of the very meanings of "civilization" and "progress." The Enlightenment narratives that dominated much of global politics since the late eighteenth century led to barbarism and war on an unprecedented scale. As a consequence, by 1918, the aspiration to find a path to a more civilized future provided the impetus for people throughout the world to create new political and social projects.

The notion of Latin American unity, and that of a political project rooted in a continental imagined community rather than in nationalist sentiments, gained new energy in North and South America alike. For a number of liberal- minded Christians from the US and Europe, who like Mackay were deeply affected in their worldviews by the global existential crisis, the Americas rose as a visionary geography where peace and

Extracts from Chapter 1 first appeared in Geneviève Dorais, "Missionary Critiques of Empire, 1920–1932: Between Interventionism and Anti-Imperialism," *The International History Review*, 39:3 (23017): 377–403, DOI: 10. 1080/07075332.2016. 1230767. Visit the Journal's website: www.tandfonline.com/.

universal brotherhood might bloom.[1] This conviction was in itself nothing new. It fed into a long tradition dating back to colonial times in both South and North America in which the land west of the Atlantic was perceived as a geography where utopian dreams came true. But, as of 1918, the moral crisis that had rocked Latin America in the early decades of the twentieth century also resulted, on the other hand, in drastic revisions of its governing liberal-conservative order.[2] From the cycle of independences in early nineteenth century to the end of the First World war, clashes between liberal and conservative political factions had dictated the pace of nation-state formation in Latin American republics, leading to profoundly unequal societies. Oligarchic minorities, in alliance with foreign capital, had ruled their respective countries to serve their unique interests. As a result, by the beginning of the interwar period, a new generation of middle-class intellectuals and university students came of age in Latin America, joining forces to oppose national oligarchic power and imperialism and to find solutions to the evils that plagued their region.

Chapter 1 traces the common ideological grounds that made possible the formation of an alliance in the 1920s between this Peruvian vanguard and Christian missionaries and religious pacifists. This chapter begins by locating the origins of the anti-imperialist American Popular Revolutionary Alliance (APRA) in the Latin American student movement and its opposition to oligarchic rule in Peru. It likewise details how Reform-minded students in Peru engaged with the tradition of continental nationalism particular to nineteenth- and early twentieth-century Latin America as a way to oppose the prevailing liberal-conservative order of the Republican era. These students, many of whom formed the APRA movement shortly afterward, saw continental solidarity as a remedy to the crises erupting around them. Yet, as this chapter demonstrates, the Peruvian Reform-minded students and the radical poets who founded the APRA movement did not ponder the future of their nation and of their collective identity as *americanos* exclusively amongst Peruvians or Latin

[1] For an introductory survey on the concept of the Americas as utopian geography since the "discovery" of the New World by Europeans, consult Alberto Flores Galindo, *In Search of An Inca: Identity and Utopia in the Andes*, Cambridge, UK: Cambridge University Press, 2010, pp. 10–17.

[2] Patricia Funes, "El pensamiento latinoamericano sobre la nación en la década de 1920," *Boletín Americanista*, 49 (April 1999): 108–109.

Americans.[3] On the contrary, they read and enthusiastically debated with US and European actors who were also concerned with projects, if inchoate and fledgling, of hemispheric unity and with questions of continental realities and utopian identities in the Americas. Whereas they often disagreed on the means to the end, still these actors agreed on which end to pursue. For all of them, in effect, the Americas provided a foil for the wrongs of Western civilization. In projects of hemispheric unity seemed to lay the promise of better days ahead. Once reinvented, the Reform-minded students and radical poets in Peru thought, alongside a number of Christian pacifists, that this utopian geography would be able to shepherd the world toward better days.

Concurrently, Chapter 1 shows that many Christian pacifists – like the Scottish Reverend John A. Mackay and the US internationalist Anna Melissa Graves – saw in nationalism a malign force that led only to war and catastrophe. The references to the Bolivarian ideal of a united America they saw in the Peruvian student reform movement were inspiring. Mackay and Graves' interest in this young generation of idealist Latin Americans stemmed from the widespread belief in postwar religious and pacifist circles that Western civilization was on the brink of implosion.[4] In the early 1920s, I argue, Mackay and Graves came to view the young Víctor Raúl Haya de la Torre as a spiritual prophet who would fulfill the spiritual revolution they deemed underway in Latin America. This conviction that the young Haya de la Torre was a harbinger of moral regeneration in the Western Hemisphere, due as much to his intellectual affinities with anti-materialism and Christian pacifism as to his political capacities, explains why Graves and Mackay established a mentoring relationship with him: they wanted this prodigy to serve their respective agendas in the region.

Doing so, these Christian allies tapped into a fundamental tension that lies at the heart of national continentalism between nationalist sentiments and internationalist beliefs. While Latin American student activists searched continental identities and *lo americano* for a way to oppose Eurocentric modernity, their main reason for this was to find a model of national development for their countries that affirmed the rights and

[3] Waldo Ansaldi, "Como carrera de antorchas. La Reforma Universitaria, de Cordoba a Nuestra América," *Revista de la Red de Intercátedras de Historia de América Latina Contemporánea*, 5: 9 (December 2018–May 2019): 7.

[4] Patricia Appelbaum, *Kingdom to Commune: Protestant Pacifist Culture between World War I and the Vietnam Era*, Chapel Hill, NC: The University of North Carolina Press, 2009.

demands of the oppressed. Thinking about what it meant to be Latin American and what it meant to be Peruvian, in other words, were two sides of the same coin. Graves and Mackay sensed this tension early on. They entered the fray head-on, determined to persuade future Apristas to relinquish nationalism, too prone in their view to chauvinist and bellicose positions, in favour of ideals of peace and internationalist cooperation as the basis for opposing creole oligarchies and foreign imperialism.

Whereas other historians have acknowledged APRA's alliances with foreign allies, the development of these relationships has yet to be drawn out as a constitutive element of APRA's budding anti-imperialist and populist project. Thus, this first chapter foregrounds in global perspectives the origins of the lasting and complicated friendships between APRA and these Christian allies who played a crucial part in shaping APRA's political agenda in the 1920s–1930s and, as we shall see in following chapters, in assessing the leadership of Víctor Raúl Haya de la Torre in this movement.

LATIN AMERICAN STUDENT REFORM MOVEMENT

Many scholars locate the origins of the Peruvian APRA party in the Latin American student movement. Often referred to as *La Reforma*, this movement started in July 1918 with a student strike at the University of Córdoba, Argentina. Demands to modernize higher education motivated the strike. The Argentine movement snowballed across the continent and led to the creation of organized student movements in many other Latin American countries. Reform-minded students knitted their academic demands with outward political and social vindications, pursuing their goals through struggles both inside the classroom and outside. According to them, the democracy they strove for in their classrooms also had to expand to society as a whole.[5] What started as a protest against a system that kept universities disconnected from students' concerns, then, soon turned into an overt battle against the prevailing social order.[6] Reform-minded students deemed the Republican order of the past hundred years

[5] Carlos Tünnermann, *Sesenta años de la reforma universitaria de Córdoba, 1918–1978*, Costa Rica: Editorial Universitaria Centroamericana (EDUCA), 1978.

[6] Gabriel del Mazo, "Hace Cuarenta Anos," in *La Reforma Universitaria, Tomo 1: El Movimiento Argentino*, Lima: Universidad Nacional Mayor de San Marcos, [1967?], p. xiii. Scholars have questioned the capacity of the Latin American student reform movement to bring forth true revolutionary change. See Dardo Cúneo, *La Reforma Universitaria*, Caracas: Biblioteca Ayacucho, 1988 (1st ed. 1978). Enrique Bernales,

decrepit and immoral. In addition to demanding democracy, and in countries like Peru attacking the political might of the Catholic Church, Reform-minded students forcefully opposed national oligarchic power as well as dominant positivist philosophies. They proposed in their stead models of continental community, in which beauty, morals, and anti-materialism constituted the mainstay of modernity and future hemispheric unity.[7]

This theme of hemispheric unity was particularly important to Reform-minded students. They saw in continental solidarity a remedy to the moral crises they sensed around them. By uniting the young generations of the Americas, student leaders believed they would be better equipped to free Latin America both spiritually, from mental colonialism, and politically, from the neocolonial order they blamed for the social and racial inequities pervading the region. The university youth of Córdoba tellingly titled its reform manifesto "La juventud argentina de Córdoba a los hombres libres de sud América." The authors claimed to set forth "una hora americana" and invited the "compañeros de la América toda" to become involved in the work of freedom (*obra de libertad*) they were initiating.[8] Latin American student federations responded enthusiastically to this plea of continental solidarity. Indeed, Reform-minded students sensed that returning to the Bolivarian ideal of a united Latin America might help them imagine solutions to the problems that afflicted not only Latin American nations, they thought, but also Western civilization more broadly. This coming-of-age generation hoped to find in these American utopias political alternatives that could transform the social fabric of their societies.[9]

Movimientos sociales y movimientos universitarios en el Perú, Lima: Pontificia Universidad Católica del Perú, 1974.

[7] Jeffrey L. Klaiber, "The Popular Universities and the Origins of Aprismo, 1921–1924," *The Hispanic American Historical Review*, 55: 4 (November 1975): 693–715; Tünnermann, *Sesenta años de la reforma universitaria.*

[8] "La juventud Argentina de Córdoba a los hombres libres de Sud América," Argentina, 1918, in Cúneo, *La Reforma universitaria*, pp. 3, 7. ("From the Argentine Youth of Córdoba to the free men of South America." "An American moment." "Fellows and comrades from all over the Americas.")

[9] Hugo Biagini, *La Reforma Universitaria y Nuestra América. A cien anos de la revuelta estudiantil que sacudió al continente*, Buenos Aires : Editorial Octubre, 2018; Pablo Buchbinder, "La Reforma y su impacto en América Latina: aportes para la actualización y revisión del problema," *Revista de la Red de Intercatedras de Historia de América Latina Contemporánea*, 5: 9 (December 2018–May 2019); Martín Bergel and Ricardo Martínez Mazzola, "América Latina como practica. Modos de sociabilidades intelectual de los reformistas universitarios (1918–1930)," in Carlos Altamirano (ed.), *Historia de los intelectuales en América Latina*, Buenos Aires: Tomo II, Katz editores, 2010, pp. 119–145.

In Peru, the student reform movement that began in 1919 reflected the same ideals. Like their peers, Peruvian Reform-minded students were imbued with a sense of social responsibility. Historian Jeffrey L. Klaiber remarks that they were wary of only improving "certain aspects of the lives of lower classes," demanding instead transformation for society as a whole. Student leaders in Peru, who like Víctor Raúl Haya de la Torre participated in the foundation of the APRA shortly thereafter, "came to realize that the social regeneration of Peru could only be effected through a total transformation of all of society itself."[10] One way to advance social change in their country was to help raise the social awareness of the workers of Peru. To that effect, university students created in 1921 the González Prada Popular Universities in Lima and Vitarte. Other Popular Universities opened in Peru and elsewhere in Latin America shortly thereafter. These cultural centres, run by students, offered night classes to the poor and uneducated. They federated other community spaces as well – such as libraries and medical centres – in which further associations between students and workers took place.[11]

In harmony with Reform-minded students elsewhere in the region, another important issue for the Peruvian student federation was that of continental solidarity. To be sure, Indo-América as APRA's political project had yet to be formulated, let alone conceived. But the content of this generation's socio-political and cultural publications already reflected in the early 1920s its firm commitment to rethinking the nation in light of shared continental realities. For example, the official organ of the Reform-minded students in Peru, *Claridad*, took pains to reproduce in its pages internationalist discourses by famous intellectuals who declared obsolete the concept of nationality or who claimed, like José Vasconcelos did, to be dreaming of a "bandera iberoamericana flotando una misma en el Brasil y en Méjico, en el Perú y la Argentina, en Chile y el Ecuador."[12] Likewise, the editorial committee celebrated the work that Latin American and US intellectuals were doing at the time for what they called "la nueva América."

[10] Klaiber, "The Popular Universities and the Origins of Aprismo," p. 715.

[11] Ibid., pp. 698, 715. Ernesto Cornejo-Coster, "Creación y funcionamiento," (n.d.) in Dardo Cúneo, *La Reforma universitaria*, Caracas: Biblioteca Ayacucho, 1978, pp. 71–72.

[12] José Vasconcelos, "Un sensacional discurso de Don José de Vasconcellos [*sic*]," *Claridad: Órgano de la juventud libre del Perú*, 1: 1 (1923): 3. ("Single Ibero-American flag displayed in the same way in Brazil and Mexico, Peru and Argentina, Chile and Ecuador.)

Concern about political projects in Peru wasn't simply the focus of students or the press; Peru's poets also mused over the matter. Future APRA leaders and Peruvian poets Magda Portal and Serafin Delmar took part in debates in important and innovative ways. Not only did this generation of artists move closer to the workers and the masses of Peru, they also engaged in political struggle and were willing and ready to place their art at the service of collective endeavours. Portal remembered in hindsight the effervescent thirst for creation and active participation particular to the early 1920s in Peru and elsewhere in the continent: "America, its youth, searched for action, not contemplation. It desired to demonstrate its active presence, its desire to intervene in the happenings of History not just as simple spectators, but instead as participants in the great tasks of the intelligentsia."[13] The literary magazine *Flechas*, which Portal and Delmar helped found in 1924, demonstrates their resolve to originally reflect upon new continental identities. *Flechas* was committed to assisting the instigation of spiritual renovation in Peru. It publicized in its pages "los nuevos valores que surgen en América," using art produced in Peru and in Latin America as a means to unlock avenues of creation and avant-garde imaginations.[14] In aesthetics lay regenerative power, thought Portal and Delmar. In them, they stressed, also lay the potential for unity and closer cooperation between the youth of Peru and the rest of Hispano-America.[15]

Reform-minded students in Peru repeatedly called for social change, political dissent, and moral purification.[16] However, before the late

[13] Magda Portal, cited in Myrna Yvonne Wallace Fuentes, "Becoming Magda Portal: Poetry, Gender, and Revolutionary Politics in Lima, Peru, 1920–1930," Ph.D. Diss., Duke University, 2006, p. 29.

[14] "Prólogo-Manifiesto," *Flechas: Revista Quincenal de Letras*, Lima, October 1923, Year 1, no. 1, p. 2.

[15] *Flechas: Revista Quincenal de Letras*, Lima, Octubre 1923, Year 1, no. 1. Vicky Unruh, *Latin American Vanguards: The Art of Contentious Encounters*, Berkeley: University of California Press, 1994.

[16] The *Clarté* movement initially developed in France between 1919 and 1921. A handful of pacifist intellectuals came together to honour their hatred of war and promote social regeneration worldwide. They labored to expand their movement worldwide, thereby regrouping an international elite of intellectuals able to guide the masses toward a better social order. Following in the footsteps of the *Clarté* movement in France, Peruvian reform students aspired to partake in a movement international in nature, based on the hatred of war and a revolt against the old order. They claimed to be seeking social transformations by dint of a revolution of the spirits worldwide. For an introduction on the Clarté Movement, see Nicole Racine, "The Clarte Movement in France, 1919–1921," *Journal of Contemporary History*, 2: 2 (April, 1967): 195–208.

1920s, when their initial intuitions began crystallizing into political proposals, notably with the consolidation of the APRA movement in exile, student leaders found it hard to express clearly what they wanted beyond a vague, if romantic "revolution of the spirits." This explains why the nature of the "new America" they kept referring to remained largely unspecified. To be sure, they knew very well what they did not want. Anything that had to do with the old order and forms of authority must be destroyed, they stressed over and over again. Still, what these actors opposed was much more clearly stated than the solutions they aspired to bring forth to replace this old order. In the early to mid-1920s, more work of creation was necessary to better define the global utopias they sought through the replacement of Western modernity.

Between 1918 and the mid-1920s, the declarations made by Reform-minded students in Peru and elsewhere in the Southern Hemisphere made clear that the revolutionary proposal they championed would bear continental dimensions or would not exist at all. They also agreed that the social change they wanted for their respective societies would first occur through a spiritual regeneration of the Latin American people. The consensus surrounding their revival of American utopias, however, stopped here. Student leaders and artists agreed their revolution must be rooted in American ideals, but the specific content of their continental revolution was left up for grabs. What constituted the essence of what they called, after the famous Cuban poet José Marti, "*Nuestra América*"? Was it a set of cultural and moral values specific to the region, as Uruguayan José Enrique Rodó described in his appraisal of *Hispanic América*?[17] Or was this continental body a political imperative in the making – an instrument of defence against US expansionism, as Argentine José Ingenieros' *latino-americanismo* suggested?[18] How to imagine projects of hemispheric unity truly original in form and content? Which type of continental design would concurrently challenge oligarchic powers from within and imperialist threats from without? To find answers to these questions, Reform-minded students in Peru collaborated with Latin American peers. They were also ready to engage and debate with a group of Christian US actors who were taking great interest in the Latin American student reform movement, particularly in its vow of moral and spiritual regeneration for the hemisphere.

[17] José Enrique Rodo, *Ariel*, México, DF: Editorial Calypso, 1948 (1900).

[18] Alexandra Pita González, *La Unión Latino Americana y el Boletín Renovación. Redes intelectuales y revistas culturales en la década de 1920*, México, DF: El Colegio de México, Universidad de Colima, 2009, pp. 39–68.

SAVING CIVILIZATION WITH JESUS AND LATIN AMERICAN STUDENTS

"Aunque escocés por nacimiento y educación, merece muy bien, como él modestamente se llama, ser apellido ciudadano espiritualmente naturalizado del continente americano."[19] This statement, made in 1927 by one of Mackay's peers, encapsulates the legacy of this influential missionary leader to Latin America and staunch advocate of inter-cultural dialogue between North and South America. Reverend John A. Mackay (1889–1983) was a Scot by birth, but his early commitment to a life of Christian religious vocation led him to travel and take residency in a variety of countries in the Americas for most of his lifetime. Mackay's lifelong journey to the other side of the Atlantic began in 1913. Then, aged twenty-four, Mackay left his homeland to study at the Princeton Seminary, in the state of New Jersey, US. He attended and read lectures by Robert E. Speer, an influential Presbyterian missionary leader who appeared in the 1910s as a lone wolf advocating the organization of missionary work in Latin America – a region profoundly Christian, in his view, but problematically still very much under the sway of the Catholic Church. The young Mackay was deeply struck by Speer's lessons and resolved to walk in his footsteps. He embarked on a six-month missionary tour to South America in May–September 1915 to report on the spiritual needs of the region to the Free Church of Scotland, a Presbyterian and reformed denomination formed in the mid-nineteenth century to which Mackay belonged.

These first experiences in the Americas were conclusive for Mackay: he would devote the rest of his life to advancing the spiritual betterment of the Western Hemisphere. He did this through the missionary work he accomplished in Peru between 1916 and 1925, and during his tours to South America on behalf of the YMCA in 1922 and again from 1925 through 1932. He also occupied prestigious executive positions in a number of religious institutions in the United States, including the Presbyterian Board of Foreign Missions and the Princeton Theological Seminary, where he served as president from 1937 through 1959, and collaborated with the Committee on Cooperation in Latin America and wrote in its mouthpiece publication, *La Nueva Democracia*, for

[19] Introduction of article by John A. Mackay, "La Desaparición del Panamericanismo y Qué Viene Después," *La Nueva Democracia*, New York, August 21, 1927, p. 5.

more than thirty years.[20] To this day, Mackay is renowned in the Presbyterian community for his contributions to the development of a world Christian movement.[21]

Many Latin American Protestants, in turn, highlight the important theological legacy that Mackay left to the region, insisting on the respect and the interest he showed for Latin American culture and traditions.[22] Mackay believed that "The first step toward exercising a spiritual influence upon a people is to understand its life," which explains why he took pains to learn as much as he could about the countries he visited in Latin America and to befriend the local populations. This evangelizing style, based on dialogue, reflected the turnabout that a handful of missionary leaders, regrouped in the Committee on Cooperation in Latin America (CCLA) – a forum established in 1913 in New York City by representatives of the National Evangelical Churches and the Mission Boards working in Latin America – were trying to push in the Christian missionary movement worldwide. From the early 1920s, Mackay and his peers from the CCLA advocated the importance "for the fulfillment of the spiritual task in which missionaries are engaged that they should have an adequate and sympathetic comprehension of the people who are the object of their solicitude."[23] This, they thought, might help increase cooperation and mutual understanding between North and South Americans, and as a result, improve inter-American relations during a time period characterized by heavy tensions in US–Latin American relations.[24] More importantly, taking interest in the very people they wanted

[20] John Alexander Mackay, Interview 4 conducted by Gerald W. Gillette, Hightstown, NJ, 21 October 1975, pp. 1–3, Record Group (hereafter cited as RG) 563, Cassette Tapes 4–5, Mackay, John Alexander, 1889–1983, Transcripts of Interview, Presbyterian Historical Society, Philadelphia, PA. The Department of Publicity, Presbyterian Church in the United States of America, "Authentic Biographical Sketch of Dr. John Alexander Mackay," p. 1, June 1953, RG 360, Historical Society, Philadelphia, PA.

[21] John Mackay Metzger, *The Hand and the Road: The Life and Times of John A. Mackay*, Louisville, Westminster: John Know Press, 2010.

[22] José Míguez Bonino, "Presentación," in John H. Sinclair (ed.), *Juan A. Mackay: Un Escocés con Alma Latina*, México, DF: Ediciones Centro de Comunicación Cultural CUPSA, 1990, p. 15.

[23] John A. Mackay, "Special Religious Problems in South America," in Robert E. Speer, Samuel G. Inman, and Frank K. Sanders (eds), *Christian Work in South America*, London and Edinburgh: Fleming H. Revell Company, 1925, p. 300.

[24] Juan Pablo Scarfi and Andrew R. Tillman, *Cooperation and Hegemony in US–Latin American Relations*, New York: Oxford University Press, 2016. Samuel G. Inman, *Problems in Panamericanism*, New York: George H. Doran Company, 1925 (1921 1st ed.); Inman, *Ventures in Inter-American Friendship*, New York: Missionary Education Movement of the United States and Canada, 1925.

to sway helped them to bolster the legitimacy and influence of their missionary work abroad.

In Peru, historians recall Mackay more specifically for the friendships that he established in the 1920s with a number of Reform-minded students, and particularly with future APRA leaders, including Haya de la Torre, José Carlos Mariátegui, Raúl Porras Barrenechea, and Oscar Herrera.[25] The story of their friendship began in August 1916, when the Free Church of Scotland selected Mackay, then a young graduate from the Princeton Theological Seminary (1915), to set up a mission in Peru. The Free Church's decision to open this institution in Peru was in line with recent developments in the Christian missionary movement that advocated that Protestants challenge the clout of the Catholic Church in Latin America.[26] In Peru, "Christ is absent, but the cross is present everywhere," concluded a 1924 report of the Free Church Foreign Mission Committee.[27] Mackay's peers advanced that Peruvians needed to be saved because their country was immersed in "spiritual ignorance" – not so much despite the presence of the Catholic Church in the region, but precisely because of it.[28]

The ascendancy of the Roman Catholic Church was still very strong in Peru in the early 1920s. Though the Catholic Church had begun to lose influence with the liberal elites following the end of the colonial era, its authority remained largely unchallenged by the popular classes for most of the nineteenth century.[29] When Mackay set foot in the Peruvian capital, this state of affairs was beginning to change and Protestant missionaries played an important role in accelerating this change. During Leguia's *Oncenio*, they actively participated in the process of modernization from below that was gripping Peru at that time, taking

[25] Tomás J. Gutiérrez, *Haya de la Torre y los Protestantes Liberales (Perú, 1917–1923)*, Lima: Editorial "Nuevo Rumbo," 1995; Raúl Chanamé, *La Amistad de dos Amautas: Mariátegui y John A. Mackay*, Lima: Editora Magisterial, 1995.

[26] Geneviève Dorais, "Missionary Critiques of Empire, 1920–1932: Between Interventionism and Anti-Imperialism," *International History Review*, 39: 3 (2017): 377–403; John H. Sinclair, *Juan A. Mackay*: Un Escocés con Alma Latina, México, DF: Ediciones Centro de Comunicación Cultural CUPSA, 1990, pp. 63–68.

[27] The Mission in Peru of the Free Church of Scotland, *Light in the Dark Continent*, Edinburgh, 1924, pp. 8–9, The Anna Melissa Graves Collection (hereafter cited as AMGC), 1921–1948, Series 7, Box 12, Folder "Spanish Articles 1920s," Archives of Labor and Urban Affairs, Wayne State University.

[28] Ibid., p. 9.

[29] Jeffrey Klaiber, *The Church, Dictatorships, and Democracy in Latin America*, New York: Orbis Books, 1998, p. 5–6.

pains, for instance, to develop relationships with liberal and progressive elites as well as with several social movements. Protestantism, in fact, recruited most of its membership between 1915 and 1930 from emerging popular sectors, such as artisans, miners, rural workers, and university students. The impetus for individual regeneration drove the social work of their missions. So did the wish to foster state secularization and religious pluralism in Peru.[30]

Within a few months of arriving in Lima, Mackay and his wife, Jane Logan Well, took over the primary school established a few years earlier by Scottish missionary John Ritchie and founded in its stead, on June 3, 1917, the Colegio Anglo-Peruano.[31] The school grew rapidly. By 1922, the number of students had increased tenfold since its foundation, increasing from thirty to 387 enrollments in only five years.[32] The Colegio Anglo-Peruano offered primary and secondary school instruction for the educated classes of Peru, aiming to form those they viewed as the leaders of tomorrow. The number of staff members increased, too, as enrollments rose. By 1923, the Free Church of Scotland had recruited additional teachers to partake in its mission to Peru, including V. R. Browne, Reverend J. Calvin Mackay, Miss Netta Kemp, Miss Mary Hutchison, Miss Christina Mackay, and L. J. Cutbill. Mackay, for his part, had hired Peruvian student leaders to work in his missionary school. Raúl Porras Barrenechea, Oscar Herrera, Jorge Guillermo Leguía, and Víctor Raúl Haya de la Torre, to name but a few, were among those he recruited to teach Spanish and history classes at the Colegio Anglo-Peruano.[33]

The missionaries who worked at the Anglo-Peruvian College went to great lengths to distance themselves from the English and Scottish community in Lima. They claimed they wanted to stay as close as possible to the national culture of Peru and to learn as much as they could about Peru and its people. Mackay took special pride, for example, in establishing Spanish rather than English as the chief language of the Anglo-Peruvian College, an initiative no other Protestant institution in Peru had ever

[30] Juan Fonseca Ariza, *Misioneros y civilizadores: Protestantismo y modernización en el Perú (1915–1930)*, Lima: Fondo Editorial de la Pontifica Universidad Católica del Perú, 2002, pp. 117–184, 221–274.

[31] Sinclair, *Juan A. Mackay*, p. 87.

[32] Gutiérrez, *Haya de la Torre y los Protestantes Liberales*, p. 17.

[33] John M. MacPherson, *At the Roots of a Nation: The Story of San Andrés School in Lima, Peru*, Edinburgh: The Knox Press, 1993, pp. 1–12.; Chanamé, *La amistad de dos Amautas*, pp. 30–32.

taken before.[34] He also made it a point to mix with, and learn about, the Peruvian youth. To do so, Mackay studied and taught philosophy classes at the San Marcos University, Peru's leading university. There, he debated and exchanged with leaders of the Peruvian student reform movement; he also attended the weekly reunions of the Limean bohemia, where students, artists, and intellectuals convened to discuss literature and politics.[35] Mackay collaborated with the student's mouthpiece publication *Claridad* and invited student leaders to write about the current social problems of Peru in *La Nueva Democracia*[36].

Why did Mackay, a Scottish Presbyterian, concern himself with the urges and dreams of Peruvian student leaders? Historians stress the Latin American student reform movement's anti-clericalism – specifically the fight that the Federation of Peruvian Students (FEP) led for the secularization of university education from 1919 onward – to explain why Mackay so closely supported and mixed with student leaders. To be sure, like many Protestant missionaries at the time, Mackay identified in the liberal and progressive elites of Peru valuable allies in the pursuit of state secularization and religious pluralism.[37] Yet Mackay's support of student leaders went far beyond anti-clerical considerations. During his stay at San Marcos University, Mackay had become closely acquainted with the anti-materialist currents that were rocking Peruvian youth. He praised the student movement for rejecting positivist philosophies and for seeing in José Enrique Rodó, an influential Uruguayan writer who commended the spiritual aesthetics of the Hispanic American culture, an alternative to excessive materialism. Mackay's rejection of materialism was in accordance with a growing cohort of Christian missionaries who felt the onus was on them to oppose not only the papal system in Latin America, but also the rise of materialist philosophies, mainly in the form of capitalism and communism, across the continent.[38]

[34] John Alexander Mackay, Interview 4 conducted by Gerald W. Gillette, Hightstown, NJ., 21 October 1975, pp. 3–4, RG 563, Cassette Tapes 4–5, Mackay, John Alexander, 1889–1983, Transcripts of Interview, Presbyterian Historical Society, Philadelphia, PA.

[35] M. MacPherson, *At the Roots of a Nation*, pp. 1–12; Chanamé, *La amistad de dos Amautas*, pp. 30–32.

[36] Víctor Raúl Haya de la Torre, "Aspectos del Problema Social en el Perú," *La Nueva Democracia*, New York, 1924, p. 11.

[37] Juan Fonseca Ariza, "Dialogo intercultural y pensamiento religioso: John A. Mackay y la Generación del Centenario," in Carlos Aguirre and Carmen McEvoy (eds), *Intelectuales y poder. Ensayos en torno a la republica de las letras en el Perú e Hispanoamerica (ss. XVI–XX)*, Lima: Instituto Francés de Estudios Andinos, 2008, pp. 281–302.

[38] Dorais, "Missionary Critiques of Empire."

Mackay voiced his admiration for the work of Peruvian students whenever he could. "These young men and the great masses of workmen with whom they are in contact and whose spiritual leaders they are," he remarked to his peers in the 1925 Montevideo missionary conference, "are strong internationalists, are opposed to militarism and refuse to have anything to do with professional politicians."[39] For Christian pacifists who, like Mackay, opposed nationalist warmongering, the references they saw in the student's paper *Claridad* and in other avant-garde publications to the Bolivarian ideal of a united America were enticing. This was especially the case for his peers from the CCLA, who championed a Pan Americanism based on democratic principles and cooperation. There was in Peru "a new sense of the glorious destiny that awaits America," rejoiced Mackay. "Narrow nationalism" was propitiously "giving place to internationalism"[40]

In addition to praising their political, if inchoate, designs for hemispheric unity, Mackay celebrated the students he met in Peru for a number of deserving personal features he believed they had and which Anglo-Saxons lacked. The Peruvians' eagerness to learn was impressive and commendable, noted Mackay.[41] So was their opening to the world: "Their conversation on modern literature is a veritable education," he claimed, "and the breadth of their acquaintanceship with foreign authors often makes one feel ashamed of his ignorance."[42] Mackay's comments echoed the critique widely adopted by the Latin American modernists, that of scorning Anglo-Saxon America for being superficial and overly materialist and praising in contradistinction the high cultural and moral values of Hispanic or Latin America.[43]

There was no doubt in Mackay's mind that the key to ending nationalist wars and racial discrimination in the Americas – and to working toward the spiritual revival of the Western world – rested in

[39] Mackay, "The Report of Commission Eleven on Special Religious Problems in South America," p. 308.

[40] Ibid., p. 305.

[41] John A. Mackay, "Student Life in a South American University," *The Student World*, July 1920, p. 93.

[42] John A. Mackay, "Religious Currents in the Intellectual Life of Peru," *Biblical Review Quarterly*, 6: 2 (April 1921): 196.

[43] This critique was prevalent in the Americanist thinkers from the previous generation, or the *generación del 900*. Luis Tejada Ripalda, "El americanismo. Consideraciones sobre el nacionalismo continental latinoamericano," *Investigaciones sociales*, 8: 12 (2004): 167–200; Jean Franco, *The Modern Culture of Latin America: Society and the Artist*, New York, Washington, London: Frederick A. Praeger Publishers, 1967.

building alliances with these Latin American student leaders. In his reflections upon the role that intellectuals had to play in the face of decaying and non-Christian civilization, Mackay positioned both evangelical Christians and university students from the growing middle class in Latin America as agents of social change.[44] It was their common responsibility, he believed, to eradicate the "destructive forces" of nationalism and racism from the face of the earth.[45]

Mackay came to view in the student reform movement not only a potent source of anti-Catholic opposition in Latin America, but also a harbinger of moral and spiritual regeneration in the Western Hemisphere. Postwar Latin America looked ripe for receiving spiritual and social change. Moreover, a growing number of Christian missionaries in fact believed that it would lead the way for all the Americas. According to reports and speeches that Mackay authored between 1918 and the mid-to-late 1920s, this southern geography offered a world of opportunities to help salvage spiritual truth and work against rising materialist forces worldwide.[46] The lingering disaster in European affairs, he pointed out, let alone the absence of satisfying proposals coming from Europe to deal with the postwar reconstruction, had produced in his view a new sense of destiny and of responsibility in the republics of South America.[47] "South American thinkers and scientists have discovered a new confidence in their own powers," stressed Mackay, correctly so. "Europe has lost a great deal of its traditional prestige and South American intellectuals have taken themselves out of their classic sense of inferiority, and have the feeling that in some spheres of life and thought, they are even called upon to give the world a lead."[48]

Many missionary leaders in Latin America, particularly religious leaders active in the CCLA, concurred with Mackay. "Above all, the spiritual awakening among all classes [in Latin America], especially among university students, offers great opportunities for helpful

[44] John A. Mackay, *Los Intelectuales y los Nuevos Tiempos*, Lima: Librería e Imprenta "El Inca," 1923, pp. 22–24.

[45] Ibid., p. 7.

[46] Mackay, "Student Life in a South American University"; Mackay, *Los intelectuales y los Nuevos Tiempos*; Mackay, "The Report of Commission Eleven on Special Religious Problems in South America"; Mackay, "La Desaparición del Panamericanismo y Qué Viene Después," *La Nueva Democracia*, New York, August 21, 1927, p. 5.

[47] Mackay, "The Report of Commission Eleven on Special Religious Problems in South America," p. 308.

[48] Ibid., p. 305.

guidance," confirmed a 1925 report authored by the Committee on Cooperation in Latin America.[49] Samuel G. Inman, the director of *La Nueva Democracia*, likewise saw the Western Hemisphere as the bell-wether of world peace.[50] While detailing the historical mission that befell the Americas to save the world from a degenerate Europe, Inman liked to remind his audience of the pacifist lessons brought forth by Latin Americans – "by nature a peaceful people," whose "statesmen have advocated the peaceful solution of all international problems" ever "since the days of Bolivar."[51] For Reverend W. Stanley Rycroft, Mackay's peer from the Anglo-Peruvian College, the Peruvian student movement merited attention for its capacity to hinder the progress of communism in the region. "May God's blessing rest on the work among the youth of Peru," Rycroft reported in 1923 in the Free Church's periodical, "may the day not be distant when the leaders of the movement towards liberty and freedom and a better order of things come to acknowledge the true Christ as their Saviour and save Peru from the fate of Russia."[52]

By the early 1920s, following the rise to power of the Bolshevik Party in Russia (1917) and the foundation of the Third International in 1919, the Christian missionaries who established relationships with the Peruvian vanguard and future Apristas were especially worried about the surge of world communism. The first Peruvian socialist party would not be created until 1928, under the guise of the Peruvian Marxist intellectual José Carlos Mariátegui. And when it was created, it remained fairly independent from Moscow's leadership.[53] But, even though communism remained absent from Peru for most of the 1920s, the Free Church feared the attraction it might exert on the students and workers of Peru. They hated class wars as much as they hated nationalism and racism. One flyer prepared by the Free Church Foreign Mission Committee in 1924 explained the matter in blunt terms to their Scottish

[49] The Committee on Cooperation in Latin America, *Christian Work in South America*, p. 4.

[50] Samuel G. Inman, "Nuestra Campana: Llamamiento a América Latina," *La Nueva Democracia*, New York, November 1, 1922, p. 1.

[51] Samuel G. Inman, "Message of the Magazine," *Nueva Democracia*, New York, October 1, 1921, p. 12.

[52] William Stanley Rycroft, "An Upheaval in Peru," *The Monthly Record of the Free Church of Scotland*, August 1923, p. 135, AMGC, Series 3, Box 3, Folder 3.2.

[53] Alberto Flores Galindo, *La agonía de Mariátegui. La polémica con la Komintern*, Lima: Centro de Estudios y Promoción del Desarrollo, 1980.

parishioners.[54] While Peru's educated classes' rejection of traditional authorities boded well for the advance of Protestantism in the region, the Mission Committee stressed that this rejection of traditional authorities also risked devolving into an open war against all religions. The surge of anti-religious sentiment in Peru, reasoned the flyer, therefore could potentially result in a breeding ground for the worst materialist doctrine of all – Russian communism.[55] These missionaries' worst-case scenario was in short that a revolt against the Catholic Church would devolve into an all-out opposition to all religions, including Protestantism. State secularism and anti-religious feelings, they insisted, were quite different things.

Nevertheless, their rejection of communism did not mean that the Christian missionaries who worked at the Colegio Anglo-Peruano were opposed to social change or reluctant to change the social order. To the contrary, these historical actors favourably viewed the advent of a social revolution in Peru, and in Latin America more broadly. By the turn of the century, the influence of the Social Gospel movement in US Protestantism had extended to both sides of the Atlantic, convincing leaders of the Free Church of Scotland to address the social consequences of brutal capitalism. These religious leaders championed solidarity with the British labour movement and summoned their followers to oppose social inequities. "[The Christian] may, or may not, be a Socialist," thundered one Church leader in 1910, "but a defender of this social order he cannot be."[56] This Christian doctrine of social transformation likewise encouraged the Free Church's missionaries to actively address the social ills that plagued the Americas rather than focusing their attention exclusively on individual redemption.[57] But there was one condition to their support. They believed it was of paramount importance to first achieve a spiritual revolution in the Americas before the social revolution could begin. Otherwise, they advanced, the new social order was doomed to failure;

[54] The Mission in Peru of the Free Church of Scotland, *Light in the Dark Continent*, AMGC, Series 7, Box 12, Folder "Spanish Articles 1920s," p. 9.

[55] Ibid., p. 9.

[56] As cited in Wilfred Barnard Faraday, *Socialism and the United Free Church of Scotland. A Reply to the four pamphlets of the Committee on Social Questions*, Westminster: Anti-Socialist Union of Great Britain, 1911, pp. 3–4.

[57] Ronald C. White, Jr. and C. Howard Hopkins, *The Social Gospel: Religion and Reform in Changing America*, Philadelphia: Temple University Press, 1976. Paul A. Carter, *The Decline and Revival of the Social Gospel: Social and Political Liberalism in American Protestant Churches, 1920–1940*, Ithaca, NY: Cornell University Press, 1954.

only the right set of Christian ethics and morals would prevent the world from relapsing into the dreadful dead-end then facing Western civilization.

This is why Mackay warned Peruvian students against the threats that "un proletario inculto e inescrupuloso" were then posing to Western civilization. Proletarian rule led nowhere constructive, he explained to them: "El poder a todo costo, a sangre, a fuego y a engaño, he allí el lema del nuevo imperialismo proletario, según su vocero más autorizado, el propio Lenin."[58] This is also why Mackay enthused about the prospect of an alliance between his Christian missionary peers and Reform-minded students in Peru. One way to prevent the surge of communism in Peru while fomenting social change, he trusted, was to build alliances with young student leaders, who like Haya de la Torre and future Apristas, were ready to reject the Catholic Church without, however, altogether denying God.

These views, disseminated by Mackay and leaders of the CCLA in their respective homelands, contributed toward building up a certain level of attention from Europe and the United States directed at student leaders in Peru. The favourable reviews of the Peruvian student reform movement that members of the Colegio Anglo-Peruano published in foreign publications and their church's periodicals confirms this acclaim for students' anti-clericalism. Perhaps never was this embrace clearer than in May 1923, when the crisis between Peruvian state authorities and Reform-minded students reached a climax.[59] In response to Leguía's attempt to consecrate Peru to the Sacred Heart of Jesus, which would augment the symbolic power of the Catholic Church, student activists, in collaboration with union leaders, spearheaded a mass protest in the streets of Lima to oppose this measure.[60] Violence against protestors ensued, resulting in two deaths and many more injured. The clash ended in a bitter victory for the protestors: Leguía ultimately balked and halted the project, but the

[58] "An ignorant and unscrupulous proletariat." "Power at all costs, by blood, by fire and by deception. That is the motto of the new proletarian imperialism, according to its most famous spokesman, Lenin himself." Mackay, *Los Intelectuales y los Nuevos Tiempos*, p. 8.

[59] Jorge Basadre, *Vida y la historia. Ensayos sobre personas, lugares y problemas*, 2nd ed., Lima: Lluvia Editores, 1981, pp. 239–336.

[60] Steven J. Hirsch, "Peruvian Anarcho-Syndicalism: Adapting Transnational Influences and Forging Counterhegemonic Practices, 1905–1930," in Steven Hirsch and Lucien van der Walt (eds), *Anarchism and Syndicalism in the Colonial and Postcolonial World, 1870–1940: The Praxis of National Liberation, Internationalism, and Social Revolution*, Leiden and Boston: Brill, Hotei Publishing, 2012, p. 242.

price to pay came in the form of arbitrary arrests and deportations of students and workers.

The Christian community revolving around the Anglo-Peruvian College mobilized quickly to assist the movement. Members of the Colegio Anglo-Peruano offered enthusiastic first-hand reports of the student revolt they had witnessed in Peru. In the August 1923 issue, *The Monthly Record of the Free Church* published a report by William Stanley Rycroft which extolled the student upheaval that had just rocked the Peruvian capital: "Last week was one of the most remarkable in the history of the Peruvian people," stated Rycroft in reference to the student protest on May 1923. Rycroft's story enthusiastically chronicled how the Peruvian student movement led "a violent attack on the whole religious system" of Peru, where a greedy government and a despotic Catholic Church were to blame, the article highlighted, for the social and political ills that afflicted the country.[61]

The editorial board of *The Nation*, a US leftist magazine, ran a story on April 9, 1924, on the student upheaval in Peru which quoted extensively from Rycroft's piece. *The Nation* in fact replicated most of Rycroft's argument. As a result, it disseminated among its progressive US readership a story that equated persecuted Peruvian students and intellectuals with pacifism and Christian values. Similar to Rycroft's piece, this article focused on the Peruvian student leader Víctor Raúl Haya de la Torre. It introduced him to *The Nation*'s subscribers as an impassioned Christian pacifist, "absolutely opposed to violence of any kind."[62] This journal was not the only press media in the United States to give favourable attention to the Peruvian student movement. Likewise, in March 1924, the *New Student* enthusiastically portrayed the student protests that had been rocking Peru the year before. Under the auspices of the New Student Forum, a moderate antiwar student body in the United States, this US bi-monthly publication congratulated the students of the "University of Lima" who had risked their "necks" and "fortunes" to oppose the consecration of Peru to the "Sacred Heart of Jesus" – an act, it was esteemed, that would have culminated in the subjugation of the Peruvian state to the Catholic juggernaut.[63] Student leader Víctor Raúl

[61] Rycroft, "An Upheaval in Peru," pp. 133–135.

[62] *The Nation*, April 9, 1924, pp. 406–407; Memorial Library Microforms/Media Center, Micro Film 2920.

[63] "Peruvian Students in Revolt," *The New Student*, New York, Vol. 3, No. 12, March 15, 1924, p. 1, Wisconsin Historical Society Library Microforms Room, Microfilm Collection, Micro film pp. 71–1579 2p [1922–1929]; Patti McGill Peterson, "Student

Haya de la Torre received particular attention.[64] This "pleasant fellow," the editorial read, had sailed above the fray with courage and dignity, inspiring his fellow students to withstand governmental repression without violence or demeaning actions. "The attack of the government had stirred the people, and the report is that only the pacifism of de la Torre prevented retaliation by them," the *New Student* claimed in its March issue.[65] *The New Leader*, a weekly publication dedicated to questions of interest for socialist groups and labour movements, ran an article on April 26, 1924, that similarly sang the praises of Peruvian student leader Haya de la Torre. "When [Haya de la Torre] became president of the Student Federation of Peru," wrote the author, "... immediately a new spirit—a searching for light—became manifest among the students and his approach to social questions has always been that of one who desired to make the people see that more light and more sweetness should be their aim rather than more rights only."[66]

The plotlines of these articles, if slightly different in form, share a common denominator. They all presented the Peruvian student reform movement as an inspiring model of moderate radicalism and Christian integrity – a roadmap for bringing students and workers together in the fight for social justice and political rights while eschewing violence.[67] Significantly, in these narratives, the Peruvian student leader Víctor Raúl Haya de la Torre stood as a symbol of advisable leadership in the face of unfair persecution. The articles all stressed how much approval Haya de la Torre was attracting in Peru because of his alleged religious values and absolute pacifism. They disseminated abroad the promise of a rising Latin American youth ready to take the commands of a moral regenerative movement in the Americas.

Organizations and the Antiwar Movement in America, 1900–1960," *American Studies*, (AMSJ) 13: 1 (Spring 1972): 131–147.

64 "Peruvian Students in Revolt," "Peruvian Revolt Continues," *The New Student*, New York, Vol. 3, No. 3, March 29, 1924, p. 8, Wisconsin Historical Society Library Microforms Room, Micro film, pp. 71–1579 2p [1922–1929].

65 "Peruvian Students in Revolt."

66 Anna Melissa Graves, "Haya de la Torre," *The New Leader*, Saturday, April 26, 1924, AMGC, Series 3, Box 3, Folder 3.2.

67 The expression "moderate radicalism" comes from Robert N. Gross in *Keeping the Faith Outside School: Liberal Protestant Reform and the Struggle for Secular Public Education in the Upper Midwest, 1890–1926*, M.A. Thesis, University of Wisconsin-Madison, Department of History, 2009. Also see Gross, *Public vs. Private: The Early History of School Choice in America*, New York: Oxford University Press, 2018.

HEADING SOUTH WITH GRAVES: PACIFISM AND WORLD CITIZENSHIP

In addition to the Christian missionaries who revolved around the Anglo-Peruvian College, Anna Melissa Graves, a Christian pacifist and self-proclaimed internationalist, is another influential figure in the early history of the APRA movement. Graves is a rather strange character. She belongs to the past of the APRA the way a prized actress plays a secondary role: the story is not meant to be about the character she personifies, but her presence on the screen is so remarkable that she steals the show regardless. It is indeed surprising that historians of APRA have granted so little attention to this historical figure; Graves is literally everywhere in the early history of this movement. The archives disclose how, through a combination of grassroots organizing and sustained correspondence between religious leaders and peace activists in Europe and the Americas, Graves, assisted by Mackay and other pacifist peers, helped weave a large web of solidarity networks that would assist the work of Reform-minded student leaders and the APRA movement shortly thereafter. Certainly, the history of this anti-imperialist movement would not have been the same had Graves not showed interest in the endeavours of the Peruvian Reform-minded students and avant-garde artists she met in Peru in 1922. Whereas Mackay connected future APRA leaders in Peru with Christian missionaries who aspired to advance cooperation and mutual understanding between the people of the Americas, Graves offered them international connections to religious pacifist organizations, such as the Fellowship of Reconciliation (FOR), in both Europe and the Americas.

Graves' motivations for contacting Reform-minded students and avant-garde artists in Peru in the early 1920s (such as the student leader Victor Raúl Haya de la Torre, with whom she became especially close) originated in a short but traumatic stay in Europe at the end the First World War. In the essay "I Have Tried to Think," Graves recounts the path that led her to choose absolute pacifism as a form of political activism. She arrived on the Old Continent in 1917, at the age of thirty-two, to serve as a social worker with the war-disabled.[68] What she witnessed in wartime Europe, she explains, induced life-altering changes in her worldview. Confronted first-hand with the horrors of the war,

[68] Anna Melissa Graves, "I Have Tried to Think, 1916–1919," in *"I Have Tried to Think" and Other Papers* (Baltimore, MD, s.n., n.d.), pp. 7–9.

Graves came to view differences based on racial or national character as deceptive illusions that needed to be fought and brought down. Hence began for her a lifelong quest against national divides and racial discrimination and in defence of world peace.[69] She left Europe in the summer of 1919 with the resolve, she wrote, to "devote the rest of my life to doing all that I could to prevent war."[70]

Between 1922 and 1934, Graves travelled the world hoping to collect evidence through direct observation of the universality of the human condition. "If the knowledge that [racial and national differences] did not exist," she reasoned, "if this knowledge could become universal, could the people be so easily stampeded into phobias? Would not the propagandists have much greater difficulty in producing these phobias? And hence greater difficulty in making men kill their brothers?"[71] Like Mackay, Graves opposed nationalist sentiments for being inherently belligerent, and thereby unfit for the cause of absolute pacifism she defended so adamantly. The countries that Graves visited in the Americas after leaving Europe were, in chronological order, Peru, Bolivia, Chile, Argentina, Uruguay, Brazil, and Mexico.[72] During these early travels to Latin America, Graves pursued militant activities and worked to recruit allies committed to absolute pacifism.[73] By 1923, Graves had become an active member of a number of pacifist organizations, including the Women's International League for Peace and Freedom (WILPF), the Peace Society, the Union of Democratic Control, and the US branch of the Fellowship of Reconciliation (FOR). The extensive correspondence that she maintained with Latin American pacifists and leftwing activists throughout the interwar period reveals how much she contributed in the early 1920s to establishing local branches of these pacifist organizations in the region south of the Río Grande.[74]

Graves passed most of 1922 in Peru. In Lima, she taught English classes at the North American Institute, a Methodist college originally founded in 1906 by the Methodist Women's Foreign Missionary

[69] Ibid., pp. 1–21. [70] Ibid., p. 17. [71] Ibid., p. 18.

[72] Graves to Romain Rolland, Septembre 17, 1923, Mexico DF, Mexico, Fonds Romain Rolland, NAF 28400, Bibliothèque nationale de France (hereafter cited as BNF), département des manuscrits.

[73] Graves, "I Have Tried to Think," p. 19.

[74] Graves to Miss Black, June 20, 1923, Mexico City, Mexico, Swarthmore College Peace Collection (hereafter cited as SCPC), Records of the Women's Peace Union, 1921–1940, Box 13, Correspondence G and Correspondence H, 1921–1931, Graves, A., 1923–1931 (Reel 88.12).

Society.[75] Teaching was for Graves a source of income as she travelled the world, but most importantly, in Peru, it also provided the ground for mixing with the small but active community of Christian missionaries present in the capital city. Through her connection with Reverend John A. Mackay, W. Stanley Rycroft, and Margaret Robb, all staff members at the Colegio Anglo-Peruano, a protestant missionary school in Lima, Graves developed friendships with Peruvian students and artists who, like her, insisted on the need to include moral and spiritual incentives in revolutionary endeavours.

Graves took pain to maintain her correspondence with the Peruvian youth she met in Peru because doing so presented the opportunity to influence them. The epistolary exchanges that she developed with several of them after she left Peru indeed points to her lasting influence in these circles. For example, the Peruvian artist Julia Codesido enjoyed reading the books on pacifism and the Christian US magazines that Graves forwarded to her even after she left Peru. Codesido was then studying at the School of Fine Arts under José Sabogal, a prominent Indigenist muralist who had recently returned from Revolutionary Mexico. Codesido tellingly disagreed with José Sabogal's embrace of Mexican nationalism, for according to a letter she wrote to Graves, she believed that "perfect beauty can't exist in nationalism."[76] Edwin Elmore, on the other hand, shared Graves' commitment to organizing the spiritual forces of the American continent as a necessary springboard toward the union of all spiritual forces of the world.[77] He furthermore confessed to her respecting very much the work that foreign pacifist institutions, such as the FOR or the Young Men's Christian Association (YMCA), were then conducting to help redress what Elmore found to be "false" and "vapid" in "Western culture and civilization."[78]

Of all Peruvians she met during her short stay, none impacted her as much as Haya de la Torre did. "The Señor Haya de la Torre of Lima, Peru is, I believe, the most selfless man I have ever met anywhere in the world,"

[75] Biographical data in letter of Graves to Elinor Byrns, Moscow, January 9, 1927, SCPC, Records of the Women's Peace Union, 1921–1940, Box 13, Correspondence G and Correspondence H, 1921–1931, Graves, A., 1923–1931 (Reel 88.12); Juan Fonseca, "Educación para un país moderno: El 'Lima High School' y la red educativa protestante en el Perú (1906–1945)," *Pontificia Universidad Católica del Perú*, n.d., 7.

[76] Julia Codesido to Graves, Lima, September 19, 1923, AMGC, Series 4, Box 4, Folder 4.6.

[77] Edwin Elmore to José Carlos Mariátegui, Alta Mar, January 9, 1925, José Carlos Mariátegui, *Correspondencia (1915–1930)*, Lima: Biblioteca Amauta, 1984, pp. 71–72.

[78] Edwin Elmore to Graves, February 27, 1924, AMGC, Series 4, Box 5, folder 5.9.

wrote Graves to a peer pacifist in September 1923.[79] Upon meeting him through Mackay in late 1922, Graves rapidly understood Haya de la Torre's potential as a powerful political leader. She was particularly impressed with his stamina and resolve in helping the workers of Peru achieve a better education, something she had witnessed in his work with the Popular Universities.[80] Articles and letters she authored celebrated his charisma and intelligence. Above all, Graves liked to compare this young student leader to the figure of Tolstoy as a paragon of Christian faith and pacifism.[81] "He has the spirit of Tolstoy," she wrote in 1924 in the US socialist journal *The New Leader*, "in that he looks straight into the soul of every man and finds God."[82] Similarly to Mackay, who saw in Haya de la Torre a powerful spiritual leader for the Americas, Graves pledged to assist Haya de la Torre in his political training. Latin America, she thought, needed leaders like him who were committed to pacifism and internationalism. And she wanted to make sure that in his budding political coming of age, she would stay close to him intellectually to assert her authority on his ideas.

From her travels to Latin America, Graves observed that Latin Americans could be divided into three main categories. The first category comprised those who were neither "nationalists nor internationalists," but whom according to Graves were ready to "play either game, if they think [...] that one or the other will further their interests." She abhorred this category of Latin Americans for worshipping "material progress" and for being "willing to borrow any amount of money from the capitalists of the United States, or any other country, in order that their field and forest and mines may be exploited."[83] The "Nationalists" constituted the second category. Graves understood the Nationalists in Latin America as "earnest" and "sincere" political actors. She respected these actors, but she did not support their cause. Graves had indeed observed how many Latin American nationalists believed, in her view candidly so, that their

[79] Graves to Romain Rolland, September 17, 1923, Mexico DF, Mexico, Fonds Romain Rolland, NAF 28400.

[80] Graves to Rolland, September 17, 1923, Mexico DF, Mexico, Fonds Romain Rolland, NAF 28400.

[81] Anna Melissa Graves, "Haya de la Torre," *The New Leader*, Saturday, April 26, 1924, AMGC, Series 3, Box 3, Folder 3.2. See also letters of Graves to Rolland in Fonds Romain Rolland, NAF 28400.

[82] Graves, "Haya de la Torre."

[83] Graves to Rolland, September 17, 1923, Mexico DF, Mexico, Fonds Romain Rolland, NAF 28400.

nationalism was "creative" and "for the good of the world." She explained in 1923 to her pacifist peer Romain Rolland that nationalists trusted "that the trouble with Latin America countries is that they have never realized that they were nations, that a burning consciousness of a national soul is necessary step in development."[84] Graves was correct in her assessment. For many nationalists in the 1920s, the spiritual freedom of their people went hand in hand with rejection of the cultural, economic, and political sway of external powers, notably those of the United States. For many of them, nationalist pride became a weapon against mental colonialism and economic domination.[85]

Nevertheless, like Mackay, Graves ultimately opposed nationalist sentiments for being inherently belligerent. She considered them unfit for the cause of absolute pacifism, which she defended so adamantly. This explains why Graves did not enthuse about the revolutionary process underway in Mexico as so many foreign actors did.[86] She had witnessed with anguish a wave of nationalism sweep revolutionary Mexico in the early 1920s.[87] This phenomenon was "partly due to the feeling against the United States, which Mexico thinks forced it to give up its revolution," Graves explained; but in her view, it was also "partly due to contagion from the wave of nationalism which is taking possession of the world."[88]

Graves disapproved all types of nationalism, whether it supported imperialist projects or fed anti-colonial struggles. She situated instead in a third category of Latin American actors the harbingers of moral and spiritual regeneration in the Western Hemisphere. Graves called this third

84 Graves to Rolland, September 17, 1923, Mexico DF, Mexico, Fonds Romain Rolland, NAF 28400.

85 Casaús Arzú, Marta Elena and Teresa García Giráldez, Teresa *Las redes intelectuales centroamericanas: un siglo de imaginarios nacionales (1820–1920)*, Guatemala: F&G Editores, 2005; Michel Gobat, *Confronting the American Dream: Nicaragua under U.S. Imperial Rule*, Duke University Press, 2005; Richard Grossman, "The Nation Is Our Mother: Augusto Sandino and the Construction of a Peasant Nationalism in Nicaragua, 1927–1934," *The Journal of Peasant Studies*, 35: 1(2008), pp. 80–99.

86 Helen Delpar, *The Enormous Vogue of Things Mexican: Cultural Relations between the United States and Mexico, 1920–1935*, Tuscaloosa: University of Alabama Press, 1992.

87 Graves to Miss Byrns, Mexico, DF, September 4, 1923, SCPC, Records of the Women's Peace Union, 1921–1940, Box 13, Correspondence G and Correspondence H, 1921–1931, Graves, A., 1923–1931 (Reel 88.12).

88 Anna Melissa Graves, excerpt from a letter written in October 1923, reproduced in "Nationalisme: L'Infâme," in *"I Have Tried to Think,"* p. 32.

group "the forerunners." In them, she thought, lay the possible salvation of Western civilization. These forerunners were, according to Graves, men and women "who realize that any idea, any sentiment which develops separateness is not creative." She billed these Latin Americans, like Peruvian Julia Codesido, Edwin Elmore or Víctor Raúl Haya de la Torre, "world citizens" and urged pacifist activists in Europe and the Americas to encourage them and support their growing, if inchoate, internationalism. It's important to understand that, in the early to mid-1920s, Graves did not embrace projects of hemispheric unity per se. Yet her internationalism dovetailed with the Latin American reform students' dismissal of the nation-state as a proper form of political organization. "Latin America has before her the possibility of continental development without the causes of separateness embedded in every other continent," she stressed in 1923. "She can be saved [from] the evils inherent in nationalism if she is made to see that they are inherent."[89] Like Mackay, Graves found inspiration in their discourses of continental unity. She admired their determination to engage seriously in political philosophies that sought to highlight what Latin American countries had in common rather than emphasize their differences. This, thought Graves, was a first and exemplary step toward world peace.

Latin America was at a historical crossroad, thought Graves. She trusted the onus was on pacifist activists to make sure that Latin American internationalists did not fall prey to nationalist sentiments. "Latin America is worthy of Faith," she told one peer pacifist in 1923, "but an encouraged nationalism in each one of these countries will make of this Continent the waste of carnage and agony which it has made of Europe."[90] There was still hope, thought Graves. She was convinced that, with the right allies and a careful process of persuasion, the progression of pacifism in the region would follow its right course. She held that belief because, according to her, nationalism was not yet rooted deeply enough in Latin America to cause the ravages it had wrought in Europe. More encouraging still were the budding pacifist and internationalist forces indigenous to the Americas which promised to counter Mexican nationalism. According to Graves, the Latin American student reform movement, and particularly the forces that she had witnessed coalesce

[89] Graves to Rolland, September 17, 1923, Mexico DF, Mexico, Fonds Romain Rolland, NAF 28400.

[90] Ibid.

in Peru around the Anglo-Peruvian College and the Limean bohemia that Mackay had befriended, was one of them.

In sum, Graves shared with Mackay the same animosity toward nationalist and materialist philosophies. According to them, none of these philosophies could help achieve world peace. Graves argued that internationalism provided an attractive alternative model of socio-political organization precisely because it forewent the nation-state. Internationalism, she stressed, promised to eliminate frontiers from world maps, the corollary of which was a world without divisions or discord – a world, in short, made for peace. To be sure, the subject of internationalism in Latin America was not black and white. The budding critiques of empire in Latin America often conceived the road to liberation in steps, including a nationalist period before the march toward universal peace and freedom could resume. As a result,many in Latin America approached nationalism and internationalism as two sides of the same coin. In contrast, these two concepts were for Graves two distinct and absolutely irreconcilable philosophies. Nationalism, she thought, belligerent by nature, inevitably subsumed the pacifism of internationalism.[91] According to her, true pacifists were de facto internationalists. To achieve this feat, however, Graves knew she needed help in orienting the Peruvian youth.

CONCLUSION

Understanding the transnational history of APRA exposes the fundamental forces of exile and state persecution in shaping the growth and evolution of this major populist movement in Peru. Exile and persecution forced APRA leaders to build vital political and emotional ties with non-Latin American allies in order to ensure the survival of their political movement in the first half of the twentieth century. Chapter 1 reveals how APRA leaders' connections with foreign allies began even prior to the foundation of the APRA movement in the mid-to-late 1920s. The social and political ideals of the Peruvian student movement, which advocated hemispheric unity, and aesthetic and spiritual revolution in addition to social change in Latin America, cracked open space for the possibility of exchange and dialogue with a number of Christian missionaries and

[91] Graves to Miss Byrns, Mexico, DF, September 4, 1923, SCPC, Records of the Women's Peace Union, 1921–1940, Box 13, Correspondence G and Correspondence H, 1921–1931, Graves, A., 1923–1931 (Reel 88.12).

pacifists who took interest in their work. John A. Mackay and his peers from the Free Church of Scotland were primarily drawn to this Peruvian vanguard for their bulwark against communism and materialism in the Western Hemisphere. Anna Melissa Graves, a staunch advocate of internationalism and absolute pacifism, praised above all their pancontinental visions. Both saw in these Peruvian actors the allies they needed to advance their respective and converging agendas in Latin America.

That the period in which these alliances took place was one of rapid changes in Peru and deep trauma worldwide facilitated these exchanges. The global existential crisis that prevailed during the interwar period, in effect, convinced many European and US actors to look to the region south of the Río Grande to find solutions to the evils of their times. The postwar crisis and the rise of radical political projects, such as different kinds of socialism and anarchism, compelled these actors from the North to rethink in dialogue with Latin Americans their ideas about what social justice meant and what proselytizing and missionary activity should entail. Meanwhile, as the Peruvian vanguard had more questions than answers about how to salvage their country and challenge Eurocentric modernity, they remained open to collaboration with liberal minded Christians who not only opposed oligarchic power in the region, but who similarly placed their hopes of regeneration for mankind in projects of hemispheric unity in the Americas. The global existential crisis that prevailed during the interwar period, then, threw people together who might otherwise have never communicated with each other. Their common search for a new path toward new dreams of civilization and progress brought them into dialogue.

Underscoring the prevalence of these global connections in defining APRA's future challenges a predominant and incorrect narrative in the history of the anti-imperialist APRA. Alliances between Apristas and North Americans were not the result of later betrayals, as often suggested by those who left the party. Rather, they were an inherent part of the inception of this Latin American anti-imperialist movement. Global connections between the Peruvian vanguard and Europeans and North Americans contributed to defining the worldviews and aspirations of future Apristas even prior to their coming of age as anti-imperialist and Indo-Américan advocates. What began as a peculiar friendship between foreign Christian actors and young university students would have important consequences for the leadership of APRA down the road. These non-Latin American allies repeatedly tapped into their own networks of peer activists to assist student leaders and future APRA leaders during their early years in exile in the 1920s and beyond, with important consequences for the growth of their movement. The next chapter turns to this lived experience of exile and to the ways in which Mackay and Graves, by supporting and trying to influence the young Haya de la Torre, contributed to the genesis of the APRA movement and to the rise of a new hemispheric consciousness. Apristas hoped such consciousness would be strong enough to limit European dominance over the region's identity.

2

Coming of Age in Exile: Víctor Raúl Haya de la Torre and the Genesis of APRA, 1923–1931

Shortly before returning to Peru to participate in the 1931 presidential elections, Víctor Raúl Haya de la Torre brooded over the misery that the past few years of exile had forced upon him. "He sufrido y sufro demasiado," he wrote to French intellectual and pacifist activist Romain Rolland. Reflecting on the recent past, the presidential candidate of the Partido Aprista Peruano (PAP) confessed he endured the worst times of his youth in the years following his deportation from Peru: "Y tengo sobre mi espíritu el peso de cuatro años, de 1924 a 1928, que considero los años malditos de mi juventud."[1] This statement sheds light on a human reality often dismissed by official historians of APRA: suffering and yearning for better days compounded with the early political formation of many of its main leaders and ideologues. "The experience of living in a different culture and communicating in a foreign language irrevocably alters an individual's world view and self-identity," write historians Ingrid E. Fey and Karen Racine. "For some, it is traumatic; for others, liberating. For all of them, however, the experience is intensely

"Coming of Age in Exile: Víctor Raúl Haya de la Torre and the Genesis of the American Popular Revolutionary Alliance, 1923–1931," was originally published in *Hispanic American Historical Review*, Vol. 97: 4, pp. 651–679. (c) 2017, Duke University Press. Republished by permission. www.dukeupress.edu.

[1] "I have suffered and I suffer too much." "And I have on my soul the weight of four years, from 1924 to 1928, which I consider the cursed years of my youth." Víctor Raúl Haya de la Torre (hereafter referred to as VRHT in footnotes) to Romain Rolland, Berlin, February 5, [1930?], Fonds Romain Rolland, NAF 28400, BNF, département des manuscrits.

personal."[2] Chapter 2 underlines this reality by tracing the ways in which the lived experience of exile of Peruvian intellectual Víctor Raúl Haya de la Torre, one of the historical leaders of APRA, shaped his coming of age as a political activist and anti-imperialist thinker. Doing so also contributes to exploring how personal self-transformations in exile triggered the rise of new social and hemispheric consciousnesses among Apristas, particularly regarding the rampant injustices experienced by Indigenous populations as well as the imminent danger of US expansionism. These realizations sustained the rocky formation of their anti-imperialist movement throughout the 1920s.[3]

The mythology particular to the APRA party, and especially the one of its years in exile, has silenced private stories that risked harming the party's reputation in the public eye. As a result, celebratory narratives remain prevalent in tales of exile, omitting the emotionally challenging and unsettling experiences that came with deportation. This is particularly true of the literature that focuses on the historical leader of APRA, Víctor Raúl Haya de la Torre. Even after his death in 1979, hagiographic narratives of his early years in exile continued to invade the field.[4] This is partially explained by logistics: Aprista militants and scholars have few sources to offer alternative perspectives. More problematically, this is explained by an urge to preserve the myth of Haya de la Torre. Seeing this leader as a god rather than a man with flaws and weaknesses provided important symbolic fodder for the cohesion of the Peruvian APRA party. Nonetheless, the stories behind the myths, especially the stories of exile, yield important understandings of APRA leaders. Sometimes ecstatic, sometimes dreadful, exile was always intimately personal.[5]

[2] Ingrid E. Fey and Karen Racine (eds), *Strange Pilgrimages: Exile, Travel, and National Identity in Latin America, 1800–1990s*, Wilmington: Scholarly Resources, 2000, p. xvii.

[3] For a reflection on how territorial displacement can help to materialize the idea of Latin America see Martín Bergel, "Con el ojo izquierdo. Mirando a Bolivia, de Manuel Seoane. Viaje y deriva latinoamericana en la génesis del antiimperialismo aprista," in Carlo Marichal Salinas and Alexandra Pita González (eds), *Pensar el antiimperialismo. Ensayos de historia intelectual latinoamericana, 1900–1930*, México, DF: Colima, El Colegio de México, Universidad de Colima, 2012, pp. 283–315.

[4] For examples of celebratory narratives, see Luis Alberto Sánchez, *Víctor Raúl Haya de la Torre o el político. Crónica de una vida sin tregua*, Lima: Imprenta Editora Atlántida S. A., 1979; Roy Soto Rivera, *Víctor Raúl. El hombre del siglo XX*, Lima: Instituto Víctor Raúl Haya de la Torre, 2002.

[5] Edward Said, "Réflexions sur l'exil" dans *Réflexions sur l'exil: et autres essais*, Arles: Actes Sud, 2008 [1st ed. 2000], pp. 241–257; Abril Trigo, *Memorias migrantes: Testimonios y ensayos sobre la diáspora uruguaya*, Buenos Aires and Montevideo: Beatriz Viterbo

By focusing on the lived experience of this Peruvian student activist during his first exile between October 1923 and July 1931, Chapter 2 accomplishes two goals. First, it provides a window into the types of negotiations, often emotionally painful, that many APRA exiles had to address on a daily basis while living abroad. By tracing the ways in which Haya de la Torre's political philosophy emerged progressively and unsteadily during his first period of exile, this analysis destabilizes the common belief that Haya de la Torre had a precise political vision for APRA from the moment of its alleged foundation in 1924. In fact, as historians have begun to suggest, APRA was neither fully formed as a political organization nor keenly defined as anti-imperialist movement as of 1924.[6] The experience of exile was necessary in the 1920s for the young Haya de la Torre, as it was for many other APRA leaders, to break away from his past and fully engage with the formation of the anti-imperialist APRA.[7]

Second, because the question of survival in exile was intimately connected with the necessity of finding communities of support abroad, Chapter 2 concurrently traces the rocky relationship that Haya de la Torre maintained with foreign allies following his arrest and deportation from Peru in October 1923. Herein began for him nearly eight years of exile, during which he would transit through countries as diverse and far apart as Mexico, Cuba, Costa Rica, El Salvador, the United States, Russia, England, France, and Germany, to name but a few.[8] As we shall

Editora and Ediciones Trilce, 2003; Eugenia Meyer, *Un refugio en la memoria: la experiencia de los exilios latino-americanos en México*, México, DF: Facultad de Filosofía y Letras, Universidad Nacional Autónoma de México, 2002; Carlos Ulanovsky, *Seamos felices mientras estamos aquí*, Buenos Aires: Editorial, Sudamericana, 2001; Pablo Yankelevich, "¿Usted no es de aquí, verdad? Huellas de identidad entre los exiliados sudamericanos en México," *Taller: Revista de sociedad, cultura y política*, 4: 9 (1999): 107–123; Ana Vásquez-Bronfman and Ana María Araujo, *Exils latino-américains. La malédiction d'Ulysse*, Paris: L'Harmattan, 1988.

6 Martín Bergel, "La desmesura revolucionaria: Prácticas intelectuales y cultura del heroísmo en los orígenes del aprismo peruano (1921–1930)," *Nuevo Mundo/Mundos Nuevos* (2007), doi: 10.4000/nuevomundo.5448; Ricardo Melgar Bao, "Redes del exilio aprista en México (1923–1924), una aproximación," in Pablo Yankelevich (ed.), *México, país refugio*, México F: Plaza y Valdés, 2002, pp. 245–263.

7 See Myrna Yvonne Wallace Fuentes, *Most Scandalous Woman: Magda Portal and the Dream of Revolution in Peru*, Norman: University of Oklahoma Press, 2017. This study splendidly details the personal struggles that underpinned Magda Portal's political activism from her coming of age as a young and radical poet in the early 1920s through her rise to leadership in the Peruvian APRA party in the 1930s.

8 Eugenio Chang-Rodríguez, *La Literatura Política de González Prada, Mariátegui y Haya de la Torre*, México: Ediciones de Andrea, 1957.

see, Haya de la Torre's feeling of alienation during his first months in exile markedly affected his approach to intellectual production. In the mid-1920s, Haya de la Torre seemed more occupied with everyday survival than with the production of meaningful political knowledge. Courting foreign allies was a crucial strategy, if not the only one, for meeting his basic needs. A combination of grassroots organizing and sustained correspondence between religious leaders and peace activists in Europe and the Americas, particularly Graves and Mackay, supported this young student leader during his first years in exile. These transnational solidarity networks would assist in crucial ways APRA's early formation as a persecuted political group. But this reliance on foreign assistance came with a price for the movement's autonomy: it cracked open a space for progressive US allies and Christian missionaries to peddle their own agenda to Latin American critiques of empire.

SURVIVAL IN EXILE

"Yo recibo con amor sus consejos. Los necesito. Usted debe decirme todo lo que piensa y todo lo que quiere porque yo soy buen hijo sumiso."[9] The Haya de la Torre who addressed these words to Anna Melissa Graves on December 26, 1923, had yet to grow into the charismatic APRA leader so many have praised for the legendary control he allegedly exerted over party members. Graves and Haya de la Torre first met in Peru in 1922, but archival evidence suggests that their relationship remained for the most part superficial until the latter was forced into exile in October 1923. Their paths overlapped again in Mexico City for a period of approximately two weeks, this time with lasting consequences. Cut from his homeland and from his community of student activists, Haya de la Torre was desperate for emotional comfort and material support.

The feelings of alienation that Haya de la Torre first experienced in exile provide an important frame for his correspondence with Graves. Literary scholars and postcolonial theorists have amply studied the way that feelings of alienation intimately mesh with experiences of exile.[10]

[9] "I welcome your advices with love. I need them. You must tell me everything you think and everything you want because I'm a good, submissive son." VRHT to Anna Melissa Graves (hereafter AMG), San Angel, México, 29 Nov. 1923, The Anna Melissa Graves Collection (AMGC), 1921–1948, Series 1, Box 1, Archives of Labor and Urban Affairs, Wayne State University.

[10] See for example Edward W. Said, *Reflections on Exile and Other Essays*, Cambridge, MA: Harvard University Press, 2000; Homi Bhabba, *Location of Culture*, New York:

Haya de la Torre did not escape this reality. Archival material suggests that the first months of impromptu travels left him feeling disconnected. Letters from Peru, when they reached him, took a long time to do so. Writing from San Angel, a neighbourhood on the outskirts of Mexico City, where he had arrived on November 16, 1923, this student leader at the helm and heart of thrilling battles earlier that year now demanded updates on recent developments of the Peruvian student reform movement.[11] Yet nearly two months passed before any news of family and friends back home made it to Mexico. The news that eventually arrived unfortunately offered no solace: more abuses, more arrests, more affliction for students and workers back home.[12] The situation was not to be ameliorated. On January 19, 1924, Haya de la Torre expressed having one wish: "solo espero que pase el invierno y que vengan noticias del Perú."[13] Likewise, friends and acquaintances in Peru confirmed they had a hard time getting in touch with him, scrambling to gather news of his whereabouts either through newspapers or chasing rumors.[14]

The initial months of exile replicated the experience of despair that Haya de la Torre felt, in retrospect, after three unsuccessful years of student struggle in Peru. "Yo pretendí morir en las últimas y dramáticas jornadas que culminaron con mi prescripción pero ni siquiera esa esperanza alcancé," he confessed to Romain Rolland on February 16, 1924, referring to the time he spent in prison before his deportation from Peru.[15] In light of this confession, the hunger strike that this student leader had launched in the face of unfair persecution – what the official history of APRA traditionally portrays as a proud fight against the arbitrary rule of Leguía – seemed little more than a suicide attempt.[16]

Routledge, 1994. Rajagopalan Radhakrishnan, *Diasporic Mediations: Between Home and Location*, Minneapolis: University of Minnesota Press, 1996.

[11] Haya de la Torre, "El primer mensaje del destierro a la juventud del Perú," (1923) in *Por la Emancipación de América Latina, Artículos, Mensajes, Discursos (1923–1927)*, Buenos Aires: Editor Triunvirato, 1927, p. 35.

[12] VRHT to AMG, Mexico, December 8, 1923, AMGC, Series 1, Box 1.

[13] "I just hope that the winter ends and that news come from Peru." VRHT to AMG, Mexico, January 19, 1924, AMGC, Series 1, Box 1.

[14] Julia Codesido to AMG, Lima, January 11, 1924, Swarthmore College, Peace Collection, AMGC (1919–1953), Reel 74.7.

[15] "I hoped to die in the last and dramatic days that culminated with my prescription, but even that wish I couldn't achieve." VRHT to Romain Rolland, Mexico City, February 16, 1924, Fonds Romain Rolland, NAF 28400, BNF.

[16] See for example Felipe Cossío del Pomar, *Víctor Raúl. Biografía de Haya de la Torre*, México DF, Editorial Cultura T.G., S.A., 1961, pp. 210–213.

From late November 1923 through February 1924 – less than three months – the contents of the letters that Haya de la Torre sent to Graves from Mexico suggest that a bond of friendship grew ever more intensely between them, charged by their shared political struggles and mutual admiration. So much so, in fact, that the tone of their initial epistolary exchanges, replete with praise and cajolery, came to resemble something close to courtship. "Continuamente pienso en V. y más que nunca admiro su gran corazón," Haya de la Torre told Graves on December 8, 1923, shortly after her return to the United States.[17] Two days later he wrote again, this time to respond to the missive that Graves had left him before leaving Mexico. "Mi corazón se ha estremecido ante su bondad, ante su cariño, ante su ternura maternal," he stated. "Yo la admiro y la quiero a V. cada vez más, porque su espíritu es muy grande, quizá el más grande espíritu de mujer que yo he conocido."[18]

Haya de la Torre's admission to feelings of love before Graves' maternal tenderness was not spontaneous. Indeed, Graves insisted that the international youth with whom she maintained epistolary exchanges referred to her and imagined her as a spiritual mother.[19] Like many of her other correspondents, Haya de la Torre complied with Graves' request without hesitation or, not initially at least, any sign of discomfort. The day after Christmas, after thanking Graves for the gift she had recently sent him, Haya de la Torre assured her that he thought of her as a mother.[20] By January 1924, he started addressing his letters to her with "mi querida segunda mama."[21] In September 1924, Graves claimed that she still maintained a feeling of maternal love for him.[22]

Haya de la Torre's thirst for connection and intimacy in the face of a lonely exile could partly explain the dramatic tone of his letters to Graves. The illusion of genuine intimacy provided by letter-writing lent itself particularly well to a style of political courtship that made room for passionate bonds to develop. Incidentally, the fact that he was not

[17] "I think of you constantly and I admire more than ever your big heart," VRHT to AMG, México, December 8, 1923, AMGC, Series 1, Box 1.

[18] "My heart melted before your kindness, before your tenderness and your maternal affection." "I admire you and I love you more and more. Because your soul is very great, perhaps the greatest soul of a woman that I have ever known," VRHT to AMG, San Angel, México, December 10, 1923, AMGC, Series 1, Box 1.

[19] Anna Melissa Graves, *"I Have Tried to Think" and Other Papers*. Baltimore, MD: s.n., n.d.

[20] VRHT to AMG, San Angel, México, December 26, 1923, AMGC, Series 1, Box 1.

[21] "My dear second mom," VRHT to AMG, January 2, 1924, AMGC, Series 1, Box 1.

[22] AMG to Romain Rolland, London, September 12, 1924, NAF 28400, BNF.

particularly close or intimate with his biological parents probably facilitated the emergence of a maternal metaphor in his correspondence with Graves.[23] His complaints about the inconsistency of his parents' communication in exile, and especially his intention in February 1926 to definitely break with his family relatives in Peru because they had forgotten about him, seem to confirm this emotional distance.[24]

But the experience of loneliness in and of itself cannot satisfactorily explain the flattering letters that he forwarded to Graves following her return to the United States in December 1923. Nor can the possibility of a love affair between them, whether it be because of Haya de la Torre's alleged homosexuality or Graves' repeated attempts to have him marry Margaret Robb, a young Protestant missionary to Peru.[25] This is because emotional hardships belied more pressing matters. Losing access to his community of support and affiliation in Peru not only had emotional consequences for Haya de la Torre; his need to cope with disconnection came hand in hand with the need to cope with scant resources. Courting allies and scouting around for new communities of support were therefore essential to compensate not only for his affective loss but also for his sparse access to material support. In exile, one had to engage in this activity as a means to ensure, at best, the pursuit of political activities and, at worst, the guarantee of everyday survival.

In this context, the words of encouragement that foreign allies extended to Haya de la Torre must have come as a soothing balm in his otherwise lonely life. On April 28, 1924, Mackay wrote a moving and

[23] Frederick B. Pike, *The Politics of the Miraculous in Peru: Haya de la Torre and the Spiritualist Tradition*, Lincoln and London: University of Nebraska Press, 1986, p. 24, pp. 116–117.

[24] VRHT to AMG, London, February 5, 1926, AMGC, Series 1, Box 1.

[25] VRHT to AMG, Moscow, August 9, 1924, AMGC, Series 1, Box 1. William Stanley Rycroft, Oral history, p. 4, RG MSC, Box 272, Folders 912–914, Presbyterian Historical Society, PA. Rumors about Haya de la Torre's homosexuality have so far been largely confined to political attacks by dissenting party members or political enemies of APRA; see for instance Alberto Hidalgo, *Por qué renuncié al Apra*, Buenos Aires, 1954. Official biographies of Haya de la Torre and party propaganda, on the other hand, aim to control the public image of the *líder máximo* by either denying or silencing any piece of evidence that could hint at the possibility of his homosexuality; see Roy Soto Rivera, *Víctor Raúl*. For a scholarly work that seeks to address the subject responsibly, see Iñigo García-Bryce, *Pragmatic Revolutionary: Haya de la Torre and the Pursuit of Power in Peru and Latin America, 1926–1979*, Chapel Hill: University of North Carolina Press, 2018. Another interesting attempt is a chapter devoted to Víctor Raúl Haya de la Torre in Toño Angulo Daneri, *Llámalo amor, si quieres. Nueve historias de pasión*, Lima: Santillana, 2004, pp. 15–43.

very kind letter to Haya de la Torre, who still lived in Mexico City at the time. Mackay compassionately inquired about his condition. "He tratado de ponerme en tu situación," he wrote, in reference to Haya de Torre's exile, "sentir el dolor y hasta cierto punto la desilusión que tu debes haber sentido en los últimos meses, mirar el presente y el futuro con tus ojos, y me he preguntado: 'Que haría yo en tales circunstancias?'."[26] He assured Haya de la Torre that he had been on his (Mackay's) mind more than usual as of late: What did he think? How did he feel? For how much longer was he planning to stay in Mexico? Mackay wanted to know. To better define the particular goal and pursuit of his mission on earth, Mackay encouraged Haya de la Torre to follow "every prophet" before him and leave, like Moses or Lenin, for the desert, for a place of seclusion ancillary to finding the peace and the inspiration necessary to reflect upon the moral and social problems that afflicted Latin America. There were indeed not many options available in the face of hardship and exile, thought Mackay: "Si vas a realizar la obra que te propones," he pointed out to Haya de la Torre, "si vas a servir los verdaderos intereses humanos en este continente, necesitas la soledad."[27]

In addition to emotional comfort, Graves and Mackay offered financial assistance to their protégé. At their behest, a number of Christian intermediaries dispensed precious financial resources to see that the exiled Haya de la Torre would not lack the basics essential to everyday survival. On February 19, 1924, Haya de la Torre confirmed the receipt of Graves' money from an acquaintance of hers who worked at the YMCA.[28] The following year a certain P. Hopkins, who lived in London, England, penned a note to Graves promising that he would soon make time to see her protégé. "I've been so busy during the past month that I haven't had a chance to see Haya," he apologized, "but I'm now in touch with him and expect to have a chat with him on Monday or so. I received your check for 45 dollars, and I'll give this to him at that time or before Christmas.[29] These efforts did not fully eradicate the financial hardship that necessarily came with exile, but the Christian missionaries' culture of

[26] "I have tried to put myself in your situation, feel the pain and to some extent the disappointment that you must have felt in recent months, look at the present and the future with your eyes, and I have asked myself: 'What would I do in such circumstances?" [John A. Mackay] to VRHT, April 28, 1924, AMGC, Series 3, Box 3, Folder 3.2.

[27] "If you are going to carry out the work that you have set out to do, if you are going to serve true human interests on this continent, what you need is solitude," ibid.

[28] VRHT to AMG, Mexico, DF, February 19, 1924, AMGC, Series 1, Box 1.

[29] P. Hopkins to AMG, London, December 1925, AMGC, Series 3, Box 3.

mutual assistance regularly channelled Mexican pesos or British pounds into Haya de la Torre's pockets when most needed.[30]

Support from the Christian intermediaries took different forms besides cash. YMCAs in Mexico City and later in London provided community and cheap lodging.[31] Letters of introduction penned by either Graves or Mackay helped connect Haya de la Torre to renowned intellectuals such as Romain Rolland.[32] Graves also connected him to US journals, where he published articles in exchange for small but welcome monetary compensations. Protestant circles in Peru also helped Haya de la Torre get access to communist credentials in order to go to Russia in the summer of 1924. They likewise paid part of his tuition fees at the Ruskin College, England, in 1925.[33]

Furthermore, in the face of intense government surveillance, external agents helped him to coordinate with allies and friends back home. To escape censorship, Haya de la Torre would send to Graves letters and political writings bound for Peru; the latter, usually travelling between the United States and European destinations, mailed Haya de la Torre's packages under her name so that they safely reached her Protestant friends in Lima without being searched or raising suspicion; these friends, in turn, arranged the distribution of material within Peru. Christian intermediaries in Lima also collected and shipped materials destined for Haya de la Torre.[34] This network enabled Peruvian student leaders and family members to remain in touch.

From the fall of 1923 through the first half of 1924, Haya de la Torre reiterated his loyalty to those who had helped him smoothly transition into life abroad. Christian intermediaries had displayed a growing commitment to helping him both fight persecution and combat the burden of solitude that came with exile. Graves and Mackay constituted the central hub of a complex network of communication and assistance, which made

[30] For more examples, consult the series of letters that Graves exchanged between 1924 and 1925 with the director of the Ruskin College, the director of the sanatorium in Leysin, Switzerland, and other actors such as Mackay, Hopkins, and Vargas. AMGC, Series 3, Box 3.

[31] VRHT to AMG, Mexico, DF, February 8, 1924, AMGC, Series 1, Box 1; VRHT to AMG, London, December 17, 1925, AMGC, Series 1, Box 1.

[32] AMG to Rolland, Mexico City, September 17, 1923, Fonds Romain Rolland, NAF 28400, BNF.

[33] AMGC, Series 3, Box 3.

[34] Abundant yet scattered evidence allowed me to re-construct this two-way system of communication. Consult the collection of correspondence between AMG and VRHT that is comprised in AMGC, Series 1, Box 1.

it very difficult, if not impossible, for the recently deported Haya de la Torre to eschew their authority and power.[35] Soon, discrepancies in opinions and respective longings for self-assertion hindered this initial, synergistic epistolary relationship. The honeymoon period between Graves and Haya de la Torre would not last more than two seasons.

EXPERIENCING REVOLUTIONS

In Mexico City in 1924 things were about to change for the lonely Víctor Raúl Haya de la Torre. The correspondence that he and Anna Melissa Graves had exchanged between winter and summer that year reveals that a spiritual rupture had been under way between the future APRA leader and his Christian mentors. While the latter group laboured to refine the symbolic politics necessary for the pacifist agenda they were forwarding in the Americas, Haya de la Torre, in exile in Mexico, slowly began to seek greater independence of thought and action. In this section of the chapter, I suggest that this leader was shaken by what he saw and whom he met abroad between 1923 and 1928. Exile changed his intellectual beliefs as well as his approach to politics.

Soon after departing from Peru, a series of unforeseen experiences changed Haya de la Torre's worldview. "La conciencia del peligro imperialista norteamericano es en mi nueva," he stated shortly after his arrival in Mexico in November 1923.[36] His brief travels to Panama, Cuba, and Mexico initially honed his appraisal of US imperialism. They sparked awareness of the threat that the northern giant posed to the region.[37] In addition to first-hand experiences, reading expanded Haya de la Torre's worldview beyond Peru and the student reform movement, especially the anti-imperialist theses of the Argentinean intellectual Manuel Ugarte.

[35] Haya de la Torre's talent for political courtship, especially via correspondence, is well known. He knew how to cater to human sensitivities when asking for favours. Nelson Manrique, *"¡Usted fue aprista!" Bases para una historia critica del APRA*, Lima: Fondo editorial PUCP, 2009, p. 14.

[36] "The awareness of the US imperialist danger is new to me," Haya de la Torre, "La unidad de América Latina es un imperativo revolucionario del más puro carácter económico," in *Por la emancipación de América Latina.* Artículos, Mensajes, Discursos (1923–1927), Buenos Aires: Editor Triunvirato, 1927, p. 23; Manuel Ugarte, *El destino de un continente*, Buenos Aires: Ediciones de la Patria Grande, 1962 [1st ed. 1923].

[37] Haya de la Torre, "La unidad de América Latina es un imperativo revolucionario," pp. 23–24.

Ugarte offered him the language and the analytical tools he needed, he felt, to start making sense of the social realities that he had witnessed.[38]

From then on, things accelerated at a staggering rate. Mexico bombarded Haya de la Torre with discoveries and fresh influences that escaped the sole purview of his Christian mentors. The country was going through a very particular moment of its history. For one, the rise to power of President Álvaro Obregón in November 1920 ushered in a period of remarkable transformations in Mexican politics. Under Obregón, the Mexican State rose from the rubble of its violent revolutionary period (1910–1920) and launched a unique program of nation-state formation based on cultural regeneration and national consolidation. The Obregón administration devised and began implementing reforms that aimed to propel the Mexican nation into modernity. Furthermore, the example of the Mexican Revolution sparked imaginations worldwide. "Until now the Revolution was promises," wrote US communist organizer Bertram D. Wolfe about 1920s Mexico. "Now the bright promises were to become reality in a new, marvelous, unpredictable world."[39] Wolfe was part of the large contingent of US expatriates who had heard of Mexico and rushed there in search of utopia.[40] On the Latin American side, anti-imperialist advocates and intellectuals of all leftist hues began to praise the Mexican Revolution. It provided an example for the rest of the continent, many argued, which should be emulated.[41]

Haya de la Torre was not indifferent to this scene. As he travelled in the Mexican countryside, he appears to have first grasped the importance as well as the social implications of paying heed to the Indigenous masses in a process of national redefinition.[42] To the best of my knowledge, it was upon returning from this expedition that the term "Indian," as a social category of people, first appeared in his discourse. Travels to Mexico,

[38] Ibid., pp. 23–29.

[39] Bertram D. Wolfe, *The Fabulous Life of Diego Rivera*, New York: Stein and Day, 1963, p. 131.

[40] Helen Delpar, *The Enormous Vogue of Things Mexican: Cultural Relations between the United States and Mexico, 1920–1935*, Tuscaloosa: University of Alabama Press, 1992.

[41] José Ingenieros, *Por la Unión Latino Americana. Discurso pronunciado el 11 de octubre de 1922 ofreciendo el banquete de los Escritores Argentinos en honor de José Vasconcelos*, Buenos Aires: L. J. Rosso y Cia., Impresores, 1922, pp. 4–5; Pablo Yankelevich, "La revolución Mexicana en el debate político latinoamericano: Ingenieros, Palacios, Haya de la Torre y Mariátegui," *Cuadernos Americanos*, 3: 111 (2005): 161–186.

[42] Haya de la Torre, "Emiliano Zapata, apóstol y mártir del agrarismo mexicano," in *Por la emancipación de América Latina*, pp. 55–59.

then, and not the Pre-Inca ruins of Chan-Chan in Peru, as asserted by Haya de la Torre after the official foundation of APRA, enabled him to gain awareness of the Indigenous question in Peru.[43] Only two weeks after attending a commemorative event in honour of revolutionary Emiliano Zapata, Haya de la Torre wrote to Graves to inform her that he felt a growing loyalty toward the workers but also the Indigenous of Peru.[44]

The classic body of scholarship on APRA locates in these initial months of exile in Mexico the foundational stepping stone for the future ideological development of APRA. There, it is claimed, the "jefe máximo" travelled extensively and met with prominent Mexican personalities. This series of adventures ostensibly enabled Haya de la Torre to get fully acquainted with both the "mentalidad agrarista" and the Mexican agrarian reform process. Haya de la Torre's process of literally absorbing the spirit of the Mexican Revolution was perhaps most important for the foundational myth of APRA, and for the defence of its staunch nationalist positions in later years.[45] These narratives insist on the success that Haya de la Torre had with groups of students and workers in Mexico. They also take pains to portray him as a leader in control of his destiny, politically mature and already knowledgeable about Indo-American ideology. Although scholars have more recently countered the argument that Haya de la Torre founded APRA in Mexico City on May 7, 1924, this foundational myth continues to persist in the popular imagination.[46] Yet his Torre's first exile in Mexico did have lasting consequences for his

[43] Haya de la Torre, *Espacio-Tiempo-Histórico: Cinco Ensayos y Tres Diálogos*, Lima: s.n., 1948, pp. vii–xi.

[44] VRHT to AMG, Mexico, April 22, 1924, AMGC, Series 1, Box 1.

[45] Luis Alberto Sánchez, *Víctor Raúl Haya de la Torre o el político*, pp. 107–111; Eugenio Chang-Rodríguez, *La literatura Política*, pp. 227–228; Jorge Luis Cáceres Arce, "Haya de la Torre estudiante peregrino," in Jorge Luis Cáceres, Enrique de la Osa, Tatiana Goncharova and Carlos Lúcar (eds), *III Concurso Latinoamericano de Ensayo Vida y Obra de Víctor Raúl Haya de la Torre*, Lima: Instituto Cambio y Desarrollo, 2006, pp. 15–150; Víctor Manuel Ibáñez Avados, "La influencia de la Revolución Mexicana en la formación ideológica y doctrinaria del aprismo," in Carlos Espá, et al. *VI Concurso Latinoamericano de Ensayo Vida y Obra de Víctor Raúl Haya de la Torre*, Lima: Instituto Cambio y Desarrollo, 2010, pp. 75–126.

[46] In his re-evaluation of the first Aprista exile in Mexico (1923–1924), Melgar Bao perceptively argues that the foundation of the APRA in Mexico on May 7, 1924, came to life as part of a mythology, which had become necessary by 1927, to help dissociate the APRA from other anti-imperialist Latin American forces. Melgar Bao, "Redes del exilio aprista en México."

political formation and for the future of the PAP, even if the specific effects differ from those suggested by celebratory narratives.

When in the spring of 1924 Graves commanded that Haya de la Torre "esperamos de ti una realización de tu responsabilidad," she knew only too well that his new Mexican acquaintances were impinging on her and Mackay's plans for Haya de la Torre to study abroad (which they viewed as the prelude to having him return to South America prepared to spearhead the spiritual revolution they longed for).[47] In the course of his first months of exile in post-revolutionary Mexico, Haya de la Torre had befriended the Mexican bohemia. The artists and intellectuals who formed the "grupo de México" were indeed renowned not only for their involvement in the communist movement but also for their romantic liaisons ruled by free love, two things Graves and Mackay found intolerable.[48]

These new friendships began to nudge Haya de la Torre away from his pacifist position. By February 1924, he was meeting on a regular basis with Ella and Bertram Wolfe, two US communist organizers and members of the Mexican Communist Party.[49] In the middle of that month, Haya de la Torre relocated from San Angel to Mexico City to get closer to the action. He began to rent a small place a couple of floors above the Wolfes' apartment. His new friends took him under their wing: they introduced him to their social circles, taught him English, occasionally loaned him small amounts of money, and even forwarded to him an invitation to travel to Russia.[50]

Haya de la Torre's new communist friends and networks of support were a thorn in the side of Christian mentors for two reasons. First, thanks to the networks of solidarity they offered, these new contacts contributed toward weaning him off the exclusivity of their financial backing. This could not be well received for protagonists who aspired

[47] "We expect from you that you honor your responsibility," as cited by VRHT in a letter to AMG, Mexico, April 29, 1924, AMGC, Series 1, Box 1.

[48] "Mexican group"; Daniel Kersffeld, "La recepción del marxismo en América Latina y su influencia en las ideas de integración continental: el caso de la Liga Antiimperialista de las Américas." Ph.D. diss., Universidad Nacional Autónoma de México, 2008, pp. 51–64.

[49] Haya de la Torre began to be in touch with Bertram Wolfe by the end of 1923. VRHT to AMG, Mexico, December 26, 1923, AMGC, Series 1, Box 1; Barry Carr, *Marxism and Communism in Twentieth Century Mexico*, Lincoln and London: University of Nebraska Press, 1992, p. 37.

[50] VRHT to AMG, Mexico, February 16, 1924, and VRHT to AMG, Mexico, February 29, 1924, AMGC, Series 1, Box 1.

to shape his destiny. Second, and more importantly, these friendships brought about drastic changes in Haya de la Torre's worldview. The conversations that Haya de la Torre routinely had with the Wolfes, as well as the handful of encounters he had with Jay Lovestone, another US communist organizer in exile in Mexico, contributed toward shaping his approach to the role and purpose of revolution in new ways.[51]

New acquaintances and ambitions started tilting his interest away from the religious faith that had allegedly shaped his activist agenda in Peru and toward Marxist theories and atheism.[52] The militant language that he used in his letters and publications to discuss politics became increasingly, and ever more precisely, coated with socialist idiom, especially when dissecting the repercussions of "capitalist oppression."[53] Similarly, the Indo-American flag, which has to this day symbolized both the foundation of APRA and the originality of its project of continental integration, was in fact initially conceived in Mexico as a symbol for Latin American communism rather than for Indo-American resistance. On May 9, 1924, while recounting the series of student events he had recently helped organize, Haya de la Torre boasted to Lovestone: "Yo he obsequiado la bandera de Nuestra [Generación]. Es toda roja con la figura del continente latino en oro. [Es] una bandera comunista!"[54]

Grimly witnessing the radicalization of their disciple, Christian intermediaries reiterated their desire to see Haya de la Torre flee to England and, from there, resume his university studies.[55] They feared communist indoctrination and dreaded that he would fall prey to foreign influences that embraced violence as a valid instrument of social change.[56] But Wolfe and Lovestone's plans for Haya de la Torre to travel to Russia and see with his own eyes the worker's paradise that radicals in Mexico

[51] VRHT to Jay Lovestone, Mexico, May 9, 1924, Box 372, Folder 26, Correspondence, Haya de la Torre, 1924, 1958, Jay Lovestone Papers, Hoover Institution Archives.

[52] AMG to Rolland, London, September 12, 1924, Fonds Romain Rolland, NAF 28400, BNF.

[53] Haya de la Torre, *Por la emancipación de América Latina*, 64. VRHT to AMG, AMGC, Series 1, Box 1. For a glimpse at Haya de la Torre's early political writings sent or published from exile, consult: Haya de la Torre, *Por la emancipación de América Latina*.

[54] "I presented the flag of Our [Generation]. It is all red with the shape of the Latin continent in gold. [It's] a communist flag!" VRHT to Jay Lovestone, Mexico, May 9, 1924, Box 372, Folder 26, Correspondence, Haya de la Torre, 1924, 1958, Jay Lovestone Papers, Hoover Institution Archives.

[55] VRHT to AMG, Mexico, April 29, 1924, AMGC, Series 1, Box 1.

[56] AMG to Rolland, London, September 12, 1924, Fonds Romain Rolland, NAF 28400, BNF.

kept talking about were too tempting.[57] In late June 1924, after agreeing to pass some time in England afterward, Haya de la Torre left for Russia.

Although the authority that Graves and Mackay exerted over the young Haya de la Torre began to crumble within weeks of his arrival in Mexico City, complete spiritual rupture materialized in Moscow. There, he squarely rebelled against the symbol of Christianity and pacifism that his early mentors were so fervently disseminating across their transnational networks.[58] "No tengo ni la divinidad de un Jesús ni el Talento de un Tolstoy," he told Graves on August 20, 1924.[59] Haya de la Torre appeared eager to correct the discrepancy between himself as symbol and himself as a young man and mature political activist – what he was and what he aspired to become. Gaining in confidence, Haya de la Torre bluntly signalled his concern to Graves: "Yo creo que es un deber de mi conciencia decirle a U. que no soy sino un hombre común, sin valor ninguno, que ha jurado entregar su vida por la causa de los oprimidos, de los que en mi país son víctimas," he stated on August 20, 1924.[60]

The timing of this revolt was not fortuitous. A few weeks earlier, Haya de la Torre was powerfully and profoundly moved by the dizzying first impressions from his initial travels to Russia. Between July and August 1924, journeying in the humid weather particular to the Volga region, an illness that he attributed to his imprisonment in Lima the year before came back to afflict his lungs. Never had he imagined possible such genuine kindness and true abnegation as he witnessed in Russia, he told Graves upon his return to Moscow.[61] He highlighted how "obreras y obreras [sic] que nunca me habían conocido me cuidaron como a un hermano o hijo." "El pueblo ruso que no piensa tanto en el 'time-

[57] On the influence that the Bolshevik revolution had outside communist circles see Daniela Spenser, *The Impossible Triangle: Mexico, Soviet Russia, and the United States in the 1920s*, Durham and London: Duke University Press, 1999, pp. 55–58, 62–64; Carr, *Marxism and Communism in Twentieth Century Mexico*, p. 4.

[58] See for example Anna Melissa Graves, "Haya de la Torre," *The New Leader*, Saturday, 26 April 1924 and W. Stanley Rycroft, "An Upheaval in Peru," *The Monthly Record of the Free Church of Scotland*, Edinburgh, August 1923, pp. 133–135.

[59] "I have neither the divinity of Jesus nor the talent of Tolstoy," VRHT to AMG, Moscow, August 20, 1924, AMGC, Series 1, Box 1.

[60] "I believe it is conscience's duty to tell you that I am nothing but an ordinary man, with no bravery whatsoever, who has sworn to give his life for the cause of the oppressed, for those who are victims in my country," ibid.

[61] VRHT to AMG, Moscow, August 9, 1924, AMGC, Series 1, Box 1.

money,'" "puede amar así tan grandemente al prójimo."[62] The attentiveness with which workers in the Volga had taken care of him shook Haya de la Torre's deepest convictions. The feelings evoked by his experience in Russia were so intense that his ideas about peace were transformed.[63] He still cared for peace, but now he understood better its costs and therefore deemed defensive wars to be legitimate and justifiable.[64] The workers' paradise that Haya de la Torre's friends had raved so much about was indeed a paradise; a violent revolution had been necessary to bring it to life.

Shortly after, in a letter on August 23, 1924, Haya de la Torre voiced his need for self-assertion. He clearly marked the breach that now distanced his aspirations from Graves and Mackay's. "Usted me dice que ha perdido gran parte del respeto que antes tenía por mi y yo le contesto que a mi me pase igualmente," Haya de la Torre replied to Graves' accusations of betrayal.[65] His discourse shone with pride and independence: "Yo he roto para siempre mi subordinación a la familia y a la clase a que pertenecía, y estoy dispuesto a romper muchos otros vínculos, todos, por ser leal a mi mismo." He continued, "Así he escrito al Dr. Mackay: No acepto ayuda de amigos cuando ellos quieren que a cambio de su ayuda o de su amistad cambie de modo de pensar."[66] He argued that he would never be cowed again before the lure of financial support. He promised himself that, from now on, he would be the one imposing the conditions of his friendships.[67]

NEW POLITICAL CONSCIOUSNESSES AND THE FORMATION OF APRA

Despite his strong resolutions, Haya de la Torre struggled to completely cut the ties that bound him to the ambitions of his Christian sponsors. For

[62] "Workers who had never met me before took care of me like a brother or a son." "The Russian people can love their neighbor so deeply because they do not think in terms of time-money," ibid.

[63] VRHT to AMG, Moscow, July 24, 1924, AMGC, Series 1, Box 1.

[64] Ibid.

[65] "You tell me that you have lost much of the respect that you previously had for me. My answer is that the same happened to me with you," VRHT to AMG, Moscow, August 23, 1924, AMGC, Series 1, Box 1.

[66] "I have forever broken my subordination to the family and the class to which I belonged, and I am willing to break many other ties, all of them, to stay true to myself." "Thus I have written to Dr. Mackay: I do not accept help from friends when they want me to change my mind in exchange for their help or friendship," ibid.

[67] Ibid.

one, they were not willing to let go of him. When he voiced his desire in Mexico City to have more room for thinking on his own and for meeting new people, Graves countered with backroom manipulation. She used her connections in hopes of retaining some degree of influence over the kind of political formation that he received in exile.[68] What's more, exile forced material hardship upon Haya de la Torre, making it difficult to let go of his Christian mentors. In APRA's early years, between 1925 and 1928, the organization grew, certainly, but not fast enough to provide financial assistance to its members. Thus at least until 1929, the need for material support, more than emotional comfort, thwarted Haya de la Torre's attempts at self-assertion.

In the fall of 1925, after a silence of seven months, Haya de la Torre renewed contact with Graves. He claimed that he wasn't doing well. "I have lived more than seven months in England and always without any tranquility," he wrote in English on November 12.[69] He hated the weather in London, where it was cold and rained all the time. Also, he didn't have the means to buy appropriate winter clothing. Money went missing. Work opportunities were rare and paid badly.[70] These material hardships only served to compound the psychological distress that appeared to beset him at the time, and which not incidentally, he meticulously and unabashedly detailed to Graves in his letters. He confessed to feeling terribly lonely and missing home. Above all, he missed his friends. He missed being part of something bigger than himself.[71] "Morally and materially this year has been very bad. Never, after two years of exile have I wanted to go home so much," he stated on December 29.[72] The letters that Haya de la Torre sent to Graves between November 1925 and March 1926 report a great deal of suffering.[73] Europe was, according to the latter, "a bitter exile" filled only with "sorrows and troubles."[74]

As 1925 came to an end, Haya de la Torre rejoiced in the prospect of new beginnings. He tried to remain positive, he told Graves, for he trusted he would soon return to his America. "I wish to do my best next year in

[68] AMG to Rolland, London, September 12, 1924, Fonds Romain Rolland, NAF 28400, BNF. Gabriela Mistral to AMG, México, n.d.; José Vasconcelos to AMG, April 21, and May 21, 1924, AMGC, Series 3, Box 3.

[69] VRHT to AMG, London, November 12, 1925, AMGC, Series 1, Box 1.

[70] VRHT to AMG, London, January 24, 1926, AMGC, Series 1, Box 1.

[71] Haya de la Torre began to write his letters to Graves in English when he was in England. VRHT to AMG, London, December 29, 1925, AMGC, Series 1, Box 1.

[72] Ibid. [73] Consult letters from VRHT to AMG, AMGC, Series 1, Box 1.

[74] VRHT to AMG, London, December 29, 1925, AMGC, Series 1, Box 1.

my America," he wrote. "I think I will go back at [*sic*] summer and I will be glad, strong and happy again."[75] With new beginnings also came the possibility of reconciliation. Three days before the New Year, he communicated his wish to restore relations with Graves: "I hope in our particular way that 1926 shall be a year when you will be not in the material sens [*sic*], but in the spirtual [*sic*] sens [*sic*] a friend of mine"[76] Graves agreed; they would be friends again.

Yet why would the proud Haya de la Torre so brazenly disclose the slew of miseries that afflicted his life? He was desperate for money – so much so, in fact, that he admitted that the lack thereof had become an obsession in his life in London.[77] The erratic tone of his correspondence at the time tends to corroborate this confession of financial anxiety. His letters to Graves were littered with financial concerns and details of his precarious situation. Haya de la Torre carefully explained to Graves, for example, how difficult it was for him as a foreign and poor student in England to be successful in school. He worked by day in a press agency, wrote by night, and in between still tried to make it to lectures. Here and there he also sold articles to South American journals and sometimes received financial help from the Comité Latino Americano in Buenos Aires through the intermediary of the Argentine anti-imperialist José Ingenieros, with whom Haya de la Torre had developed a friendship.[78] But all that wasn't enough to make ends meet. He maintained that he had accumulated too many debts in London since his arrival in August. Besides, he stressed, he wanted to become more serious in his studies.[79]

Detailing the emotional toll of poverty proved to be an astute rhetorical strategy for attracting money. When in December 1925 Haya de la Torre wrote to Graves about his misery and pleaded to be friends again, he also communicated his hope to receive a weekly allowance from her instead of sporadic sums of money. "If you are able to make any arrangements with a Bank or office and if I could to [*sic*] get some money every week I would be much better, indeed."[80] Graves acquiesced to his wish. In fact, she had already resumed her financial support along with her friendship some time back. On November 16, 1925, Haya de la Torre

[75] Ibid. [76] Ibid.

[77] VRHT to AMG, London, February 5, 1926, AMGC, Series 1, Box 1.

[78] VRHT to AMG, London, November 16, 1925; VRHT to AMG, London, 12 November 1925; VRHT to AMG, London, December 29, 1925; AMGC, Series 1, Box 1.

[79] VRHT to AMG, London, November 12, 1925 and VRHT to AMG, London, 16 November 1925, AMGC, Series 1, Box 1.

[80] VRHT to AMG, London, December 17, 1925, AMGC, Series 1, Box 1.

acknowledged receipt of a twenty-dollar check from her.[81] One month later, he was waiting for more: "I have just received your post card and I hope to have your cheque [*sic*] from Mr. Hopkins soon."[82] Graves continued to send money through the remainder of this stay in England.

Yet while material hardships more likely led Haya de la Torre to reconnect with Graves, he took pains this time around to place limits on the nature of their friendship. "You know," he warned her, "friendship can not be forced and you forced it when you insist in to [*sic*] remember me that you give me materials [*sic*] help." Haya de la Torre was, in a way, establishing rules to make sure that he would be able to benefit from Graves' financial support without the burden of moral obligations in return. How they addressed their letters to each other was one of these rules. In the postscript added to the just-quoted letter, dated November 12, 1925, Haya de la Torre signalled his intention to use hereafter only formal salutations with Graves. The goal was to curb the passionate tone of their previous exchanges.[83]

In his letters to Graves, Haya de la Torre now claimed to be a free and unbending man, exempt from all obligations besides those dictated by his own conscience. At the very least, this was how he liked to imagine himself. Starting early in 1926, he began to feel that an important phase in his life was coming to an end. After introspection, he came to realize that the hardships of exile had transformed him into a man of action, a pragmatic political activist.[84] He now longed for mentors who chose realism over idealism.[85] By January 1926, Haya de la Torre thought of himself as an "active revolutionary" rather than an "intellectual revolutionary."[86]

From 1926 through 1927, the tone and content of Haya de la Torre's correspondence reflected the series of self-transformations that he had so far experienced in exile. In a letter addressed to Graves and dated February 5, 1926, he interprets the personal transformations that he had gone through in exile. This letter determines that his coming of age came as a result of a sustained process of self-transformations that began in Peru, in 1921, and that continued all through his early years in exile,

[81] VRHT to AMG, London, November 16, 1925, AMGC, Series 1, Box 1.
[82] VRHT to AMG, London, December 17, 1925, AMGC, Series 1, Box 1.
[83] VRHT to AMG, London, November 12, 1925, AMGC, Series 1, Box 1.
[84] VRHT to AMG, London, January 24, 1926, AMGC, Series 1, Box 1.
[85] VRHT to AMG, London, November 16, 1925, AMGC, Series 1, Box 1.
[86] VRHT to AMG, London, January 24, 1926, AMGC, Series 1, Box 1.

until 1925. "I am changing now. I am a new people [*sic*]," he wrote.[87] According to him, the end of 1925 marked an important rupture in his life. Then ended his "boyhood," he stated. Then he became a "man," a complete, individual adult in control of his own destiny.[88]

Haya de la Torre had needed to emotionally break away from his past and shatter the ties that kept him fettered to his early mentors before he was able to fully embrace his role as a politician and begin devising his own political thoughts about the future of the Americas. He believed that the hardships of exile had enabled him to reject the sentimentalism of his youth and that it assisted his evolution into a realistic fighter. A gendered metaphor helped him express this self-transformation: as a man, he proclaimed, he was a leader in control of his own destiny, capable of a rational and mature form of political leadership.

Significantly, the period of Haya de la Torre's coming of age as a mature political activist in exile corresponded with APRA's own growth as a mature political movement. A string of political achievements from 1926 onward contributed toward positioning APRA at the forefront of the Latin American anti-imperialist struggle, on a par with the communist Liga Antimperialistas de las Américas (LADLA) and the Argentine-based Union Latino Americana (ULA).[89] The further expansion of Latin American anti-imperialist solidarity networks in the late 1920s and especially the 1930s, after the foundation of the Peruvian APRA Party (PAP), made Haya de la Torre less reliant on the financial support of Christian intermediaries and freed up new resources to help support Latin American exiles active in APRA's development.[90]

Shortly after penning the February 5 confession to Graves, Haya de la Torre travelled to Paris, where a group of Peruvian exiles had begun to

[87] VRHT to AMG, London, February 5, 1926, AMGC, Series 1, Box 1. [88] Ibid.

[89] Haya de la Torre, "What is the A.P.R.A.?"; Alexandra Pita González, *La Unión Latino Americana y el Boletín Revocación. Redes intelectuales y revistas culturales en la década de 1920*, México, DF: El Colegio de México; Colima: Universidad de Colima, 2009; Daniel Kersffeld, *Contra el imperio. Historia de la Liga Antimperialista de las Américas*, México: Siglo Veintinuno editores, 2012.

[90] On the solidarity networks between APRA exiles and the anti-imperialist circles that revolved around the figure of Alfredo Palacios in Argentina in the mid-to-late 1920s, see exchanges between Oscar Herrera and José Carlos Mariátegui in José Carlos Mariátegui, *Correspondencia (1915–1930)*, Lima: Biblioteca Amauta, 1984. In the 1930s, APRA exiles in Chile received support from the Chilean left, Juan Manuel Reveco del Villar, "Influencia del APRA en el partido socialista de Chile," in Juan Manuel Reveco, Hugo Vallenas, Rolando Pereda and Rafael Romero, *Vida y Obra de Víctor Raúl Haya de la Torre*, Segundo Concurso Latinoamericano, Lima: Instituto Cambio y Desarrollo, 2006, pp. 19–134.

organize APRA.[91] He passed most of September 1926 in the French capital, assisting his peers in forming APRA and concretely defining its revolutionary line.[92] Interwar Paris was then a breeding ground for radicalization among Latin American critiques of empire and anti-colonial activists from the Global South. It provided refuge to expatriates from Latin America, Asia, and Africa where intellectual and political interchange bloomed, as these expats reflected upon their respective struggles for national liberation.[93] It was after this short but intense stay in Paris that mentions of APRA first appeared in Haya de la Torre's correspondence with Graves. He seemed thrilled, ecstatic even.[94] He was at long last participating in a project larger than himself: "Our APRA is every day [growing] up. It is magnificent," he wrote to Graves toward the end of 1926.[95] The release in *Labour Monthly* of one of APRA's foundational texts, "What is the A.P.R.A.?," authored by Haya de la Torre, came around this time.[96]

Historians of APRA have so far argued that Haya de la Torre was the leader of this political organization from its very beginning. And indeed the sub-title of the *Labour Monthly* article, which bills its author in the byline as the "leader of the 'United Front' Latin America Anti-Imperialist Party," suggests that he was the leader of APRA as early as December 1926. Yet evidence culled from the understudied archives that I have been citing suggests that this designation more likely stemmed from the need to

[91] Evidence shows that the APRA cell in Paris began to be operative toward the end of the summer 1926. AMGC, Series 1, Box 1. Also see Arturo Taracena Arriola, "La Asociación General de Estudiantes Latinoamericanos de Paris (1925–1933)" *Anuario de Estudios Centroamericanos*, 15: 2 (1989): 61–80.

[92] Involved in the organization of the APRA cell in Paris starting in 1926 were: Eudocio Ravines, Felipe Cossío del Polmar, César Vallejo, José Félix Cárdenas Castro, and Luis Heysen (Heysen arrived in Paris in 1928 after spending time in exile in Argentina); Leandro Sessa, "Aprismo y apristas en Argentina. Derivas de una experiencia antiimperialista en la 'encrucijada' ideológica y política de los años treinta," Ph.D. diss., Universidad Nacional de La Plata, 2013. See also the correspondence that Manuel E. Seoane exchanged with José Carlos Mariátegui between 1927 and 1928 from Buenos Aires, Argentina in Mariátegui, *Correspondencia*.

[93] Michael Goebel, *Anti-Imperial Metropolis: Interwar Paris and the Seeds of Third World Nationalism*, New York: Cambridge University Press, 2015, pp. 176–215; Goebel, "'The Capital of the Men without a Country': Migrants and Anticolonialism in Interwar Paris," *American Historical Review*, 121: 5 (2016): 1444–1467.

[94] VRHT to AMG, Oxford, [September or October] 29, 1926, AMGC, Series 1, Box 1.

[95] The use of the possessive pronoun "our" instead of "my" contrasts with customary scholarly interpretations that portray APRA as Haya de la Torre's political organization from its inception onward, VRHT to AMG, [1926], AMGC, Series 1, Box 1.

[96] Víctor Raúl Haya de la Torre, "What is the A.P.R.A.?," pp. 756–759.

boost the legitimacy of Haya de la Torre before a British readership that did not know him well. In effect, he was far from exercising sole control of what looked more like a promising political movement than an established anti-imperialist stronghold. He himself readily acknowledged in a February 1927 letter his subordinate status. Anticipating news from other Aprista exiles, Haya de la Torre was lingering in Oxford as the weeks passed by. As he explained to Graves, he was unable to make any plans, much less travel anywhere, because "I am wainting [*sic*] for the orders of my comrades. They want to [meet] me at Buenos Aires for a month and to pay my travelling over there. I am wainting [*sic*] for the decision of the differentes [*sic*] celules [*sic*] of the APRA. [...] They are who can advise or order my movements."[97]

It is plausible that Haya de la Torre wrote these lines to Graves only to escape her daunting and repeated demands. Yet archival evidence from the mid-to-late 1920s likewise hints at such indecision or lack of command. He wrote to Ella Wolfe at the very end of 1924, eager to learn more about a radical party forming in Peru.[98] He admitted knowing very little about this project to create an "international" and "anti-imperialist" party, and thanked Wolfe for the news she supplied.[99] "No tengo aun noticias exactas," he wrote, "pero parece que antes de seis meses tendremos ya un estremecimiento formidable."[100] These exchanges show Haya de la Torre as an interested participant, rather than a commanding leader.

More evidence that Haya de la Torre was not the sole leader of the budding APRA comes in the inconsistency with which the movement's members discussed the question of leadership within their diasporic community, discussion that points to how APRA's command was not yet centralized within a defined body of political executives, as it would be in later years. For example, one year after Haya de la Torre's pledge to Graves regarding his subordinate status in the organization, the Uruguayan poet Blanca Luz Brum, by then greatly involved in the organization of the APRA cell in Chile, reported to José Carlos Mariátegui how much she admired a certain Humberto Mendoza, "fundador del

97 VRHT to AMG, Oxford, Febuary 23, [1927], AMGC, Series 1, Box 1.

98 VHRT to Ella Wolfe, Leysin, Switzerland, December 12, [1924], Box 7, Folder 52, Bertram David Wolfe Papers (hereafter cited as BDWP); VHRT to Ella Wolfe, Leysin, December 31, [1924], Box 7, Folder 52, BDWP.

99 VHRT to Ella Wolfe, Leysin, Switzerland, December 31, [1924], Box 7, Folder 52, BDWP, 1903–1999 (hereafter referred to as BDWP).

100 "I do not yet have exact news." "But it seems that within six months we will already have a formidable impact," ibid.

Apra, y de grandes actividades obreras."[101] Depending on their respective geographical locations and local experiences with a specific APRA community, APRA members had different understandings of who led the organization and how it worked.[102] Despite the fact that Brum had joined APRA in Peru in 1926–1927, by February 1928 she thought of the movement's leadership in light of the initiatives spearheaded by this Mendoza in Chile.[103]

The growth of the APRA movement as a diasporic community in the mid-to-late 1920s accelerated following the publication of its seminal text "What is the A.P.R.A.?" in December 1926.[104] Aprista cells began to appear in a number of Latin American and European cities shortly thereafter. The first Aprista committees were concurrently established in Paris, Buenos Aires, and Mexico City between 1926 and 1928.[105] Involved in the organization of the APRA cell in Paris, France, starting in 1926 were: Eudocio Ravines, Felipe Cossío del Polmar, César Vallejo, José Félix Cárdenas Castro, and Luis Heysen (Heysen arrived in Paris in 1928 after spending time in exile in Argentina). Those who participated in the growth of APRA in Buenos Aires, Argentina, in the late 1920s were: Manuel Seoane, Luis Heysen, Fernán Cisneros, Oscar Herrera, Blanca Luz Brum, César Alfredo Miró Quesada, Enrique Köster Cornejo, and Juan de Dios Merel.[106] Active in the Aprista committee of Mexico City, Mexico, in 1927–1928 were: Carlos Manuel Cox, Manuel Vásquez Díaz, Esteban Pavletich, Serafín Delmar, Nicolás Terreros, Jacobo Hurwitz, and Magda Portal.[107] By the end of the decade, Aprista committees had appeared in a number of other cities as well, including Santiago de Chile

101 "...founder of APRA and of great labour work,"letter from Blanca Luz Brum to José Carlos Mariátegui, February 1, 1928, Mariátegui, *Correspondencia*, pp. 346–347.

102 "Founder of APRA, and of great labor activities." I have probed elsewhere this question of parallel leaderships in the 1920s. See Geneviève Dorais, "Indo-America and the Politics of APRA Exile, 1918–1945," Ph.D. diss., University of Wisconsin – Madison, 2014, pp. 143–191.

103 Blanca Luz Brum, *Mi vida. Cartas de amor a Siqueiros*, Santiago de Chile: Editorial Mare Nostrum, 2004, p. 52.

104 Víctor Raúl Haya de la Torre, "What is the A.P.R.A.?," pp. 756–759.

105 Bergel, "La desmesura revolucionaria"; Arturo Taracena Arriola, "La Asociación General de Estudiantes Latinoamericanos de París, 1925–1933," 61–80.

106 Sessa, "Aprismo y apristas en Argentina"; also consult the correspondence that Manuel E. Seoane exchanged with José Carlos Mariátegui between 1927 and 1928 from Buenos Aires, Argentina in José Carlos Mariátegui, *Correspondencia (1915–1930)*.

107 Daniel R. Reedy, *Magda Portal: La Pasionaria Peruana. Biografía Intelectual*, Lima: Ediciones Flora Tristán, 2000, p. 138.

(Chile), La Paz (Bolivia), San José (Costa Rica), Santa Ana (El Salvador), and New York City (United States).[108]

On paper, these APRA cells gave the impression that they were professional and sizable political organizations. The articles that they authored in Aprista journals founded in exile, such as *Indoamérica* in Mexico and *Atuei* in Cuba, or in foreign publications amiable to APRA, such as the cultural magazine *Repertorio Americano* in Costa Rica, contributed to this impression.[109] In reality, though, these committees comprised a handful of actors only.[110] The historian García Iñigo-Bryce records this fact in a vivid and very telling image: "Anecdotally," he writes, "Luis Alberto Sánchez recalled that the members of the Paris cell could all fit on one sofa."[111] This was true of all Aprista committees at the time. Nevertheless, what these Aprista exiles lacked in number, they made up for in heartfelt conviction and dedication. In addition to publishing their political writings in the foreign press, they used a number of different strategies to educate Latin Americans on the dangers of US imperialism and on the need for Latin American solidarity. Archival records show that they organized public conferences and lectures, spearheaded solidarity protests with Latin American nationalists, such as the Nicaraguan revolutionary Augusto César Sandino, and founded anti-imperialist studies centres abroad. APRA's events reputedly brought together influential Latin American and Caribbean anti-imperialist thinkers from all over Latin America and the Caribbean.[112]

108 R. M. de Lambert to Secretary of State; Legation of the United States of America, San Salvador, February 2, 1929; 810.43 A.P.R.A./1; CF, 1930–1939; RG59; National Archives and Records Administration (hereafter cited as NACP); APRA, "Declaration of Principles of Costa Rican Section of 'APRA'," *La Tribuna*, San José, December 23, 1928, pp. 6–7; 810.43 A.P.R.A./1; CF, 1930–1939; RG59; NACP.

109 Iñigo Garcia-Bryce, "Transnational Activist: Magda Portal and the American Popular revolutionary Alliance (APRA), 1926–1950," *The Americas*, 1: 2 (2014): 686.

110 Julio Antonio Mella, *¿Qué es el ARPA?* Miraflores: Editorial Educación, 1975 (1st ed. 1928), p. 17.

111 Iñigo-Bryce, "Transnational Activist," p. 686.

112 "Programme," N.D. The Anna Melissa Graves Collection, 1921–1948 (AMGC), Series 1, Box 1, Folder 1.8, Archives of Labor and Urban Affairs, Wayne State University; Report, January 14, 1927, Archives Nationales de Paris, Ministère de l'Intérieur, F713435 Pays Étrangers, Surveillance de leurs ressortissants résidents en France, Amérique Latine (1914–1933), Nicaragua 1927. "The secretary of the APRA in Paris," January 14, 1927, Archives Nationales de Paris, Ministère de l'Intérieur, F713435 Pays Étrangers, Surveillance de leurs ressortissants résidents en France, Amérique Latine (1914–1933), Nicaragua 1927. Víctor Raúl Haya de la Torre, "Que persigue el centro de estudios antiimperialista del A.P.R.A. en Paris," (1927), in *Por la*

As APRA kept expanding in the mid-to-late 1920s, geographical distance started to make political coordination increasingly difficult within the transnational APRA community. This was reflected in the anti-imperialist theses they began to sketch from distinct national and political contexts, and more specifically in the ways in which they envisioned differently the necessity of hemispheric unity to oppose US expansionism. Some in the movement saw in "Latin America" a satisfactory expression of continental sovereignty and anti-imperialist resistance, whereas others rejected the "romantic bluff" of Latinism and began to champion the anti-colonial essence of "Indo-América" for being altogether "against North America and far from Europe."[113] Beyond this double opposition to global powers, however, the idea of Indo-América that materialized in Aprista circles in 1928–1929 came without clear interpretations of what it meant or proposed to achieve politically. That is because the idea of Indo-América, let alone as a political concept, was not fully formed as of the late 1920s.

To be sure, most Apristas began to reckon with Latin America's racialized economic and political development during their stay in exile. They came to view the injustices experienced by the Indigenous populations – not only in Peru but wherever they went in the Americas, Apristas came to realize – in light of the colonial and neocolonial oppressions particular to that region.[114] Yet at the time, Aprista exiles neither fully incorporated this racial awareness into their vision for Latin America's unity nor imagined their shared continental identity in the same way. Throughout the 1920s, references to "América Hispana," "Latin America," "Nuestra América," "América," or "Indo-Iberian America" unsystematically dotted APRA's publications.[115] As for Haya de la Torre,

emancipación de América latina. Artículos, Mensajes, Discursos (1923–1927), pp. 205–212.

[113] Hernandez Franco, "Magda Portal en el Imperativo de Indoamérica," [newspaper clipping], Santo Domingo, 1929, [newspaper clipping], Magda Portal Papers, Benson Latin American Collection, University of Texas Libraries, the University of Texas at Austin, Box 10, Folder 10.11. Goebel, *Anti-Imperial Metropolis*, p. 205; Anita Brenner, "Student Rebels in Latin America," *The Nation*, December 12, 1928, pp. 668–669. [n. a.], "El X Aniversario de la Reforma Universitaria," *Indoamérica*, 1: 2 (August 1928), p. 5.

[114] Bergel, "Con el ojo izquierdo," pp. 302–307; Kathleen Weaver, *Peruvian Rebel: The World of Magda Portal. With a Selection of Her Poems*, Philadelphia: Pennsylvania State University Press, 2009, p. 29.

[115] Victor Raul Haya de la Torre as cited in [n.a.], "La unidad política y económica de la América Hispana es la única solución," *La Prensa*, New York, Noviembre 12, 1927, p. 1; Brenner, "Student Rebels in Latin America," pp. 668–669; Magda Portal, "El Clero

it was only in 1930, while living in Berlin, that he welcomed and seriously pondered the use of Indo-América to name APRA's project of hemispheric unity.[116] I shall return to this point in the following chapters. For now, let us heed the malleability with which Aprista exiles envisioned continental consciousness during their first exile.

Part of APRA's strength as a growing and decentralized movement rested on this ideological flexibility. Theirs was a work in progress that welcomed inconsistencies. But distance also took a toll on the sense of shared community between activists spread out across the Americas and Europe. The years passed in exile ultimately destroyed the possibility of harmony in groups that were not well defined, let alone organized, to begin with.[117] If initially these actors had worked hard to remain politically attuned to one another, the years brought new aspirations and daily realities that undercut the need to remain closely in touch with the homeland. "Hace mucho tiempo que no leo periódicos del Perú," Haya de la Torre, still in Oxford, admitted to a friend in April 1927. "Casi estoy ignorante de todo lo que pasa allá."[118]

Two years later, due to internal disputes regarding APRA's political orientation as well as the exhaustion caused by constant travelling, Haya de la Torre confirmed to Luis Heysen, an active member of the APRA cell in Buenos Aires and Paris, that he was ready to end his political activism and definitively quit the movement that he had helped create.[119] According to letters that he sent from Berlin to Rolland in 1930, Haya de la Torre was eager to find the geographical stability and peace of mind

Católico de México Frente a la Revolución," *Indoamérica*, 1: 2 (August 1928): 6, 15; Serafín Delmar, "Interpretación del Arte en América," *Indoamérica*, 1: 2 (August, 1928): 8, Hoover Institution Library, Serial: México; José Carlos Mariategui, "Theory [1925]," *José Carlos Mariátegui: An Anthology*, Harry E. Vanden and Marc Becker ed., New York: Monthly Review Press, 2011, p. 126.

116 I shall return to this point in the next chapter. Haya de la Torre, "La cuestión del nombre," (1930) in *¿A dónde va Indoamérica?*, pp. 21–35.

117 On this subject, the scholarship has predominantly focused on the infamous break between José Carlos Mariátegui and Víctor Raúl Haya de la Torre, two major leaders of APRA, in 1927–1928. See Alberto Flores Galindo and Manuel Burga, *Apogeo y crisis de la republica aristocrática*, Lima: Ediciones "Rikchay Perú," 1979, pp. 185–196. Ricardo Martínez de la Torre, *Apuntes para una interpretación marxista de la historia social del Perú (I–II)*, Lima:, Empresa editora peruana, 1947–1949.

118 "I have not read Peruvian newspapers in a long time. I'm ignorant of almost everything that is happening there," VRHT to Luis Varela y Orbegoso, Oxford, April 15, 1927, Biblioteca Nacional del Perú, Fondo Raúl Porras Barrenechea.

119 Luis Heysen to AMG, Berlin, April 25, 1929, SCPC, Anna Melissa Graves Papers (hereafter cited as AMGP) (1919–1953), Reel 74.8.

that he felt necessary to think and finish a book project.[120] His letters to close friends corroborate the news that Heysen had forwarded to Graves the year before: Haya de la Torre wanted time to rest. Moreover, he craved a life away from politics for a while.[121]

Yet Haya de la Torre's disengagement from APRA, beginning in the spring of 1929, did not shake the movement's political organization, which suggests diffuse leadership as of the late 1920s. The APRA cells in France, Mexico, and Argentina remained active and efficient. The growing influence of Eudacio Ravines in the Parisian group of APRA exiles starting in 1927, as well as the importance of Buenos Aires as a centre of Aprista activities (as documented by Leandro Sessa and Martín Bergel), testifies to a logic of dispersed, non-vertical, and shared leadership during the first period of exile.[122]

Before the promise of a democratic Peru with the fall of Leguía in the Peruvian winter of 1930, APRA exiles returned home and began to organize their movement at the national level. By September of that year, a dozen or so of these Apristas had established themselves in Lima, whence they orchestrated the integration of APRA as a national political party. Haya de la Torre was nominated as the PAP's presidential candidate. He agreed to return to Peru in July 1931 to campaign for the upcoming elections and endeavoured to establish his leadership of APRA. Although ultimately defeated, he defiantly rebuffed his electoral opponent Luis Miguel Sánchez Cerro on the day of his inauguration as president, December 8, 1931, and declared himself the only true and moral leader of Peru.[123] The self-transformations that he had experienced in exile had prepared him, he felt, for the task at hand. Indo-América had

120 VRHT to Romain Rolland, February 5, [1930?], Berlin, Fonds Romain Rolland, NAF 28400, BNF.

121 VRHT to Romain Rolland, February 5, [1930?], Berlin, Fonds Romain Rolland, NAF 28400, BNF. VRHT to César Rospigliosi, Germany, October 1930, cited in María Luz Díaz, *Las mujeres de Haya: Ocho historias de pasión y rebeldía*, Lima: Editorial Planeta, 2007, p. 164.

122 Sessa, "Aprismo y apristas en Argentina," pp. 71–86. Bergel, "Un partido hecho de cartas" and "Manuel Seoane y Luis Heysen: el entrelugar de los exiliados apristas en la Argentina de los veinte," *Políticas de la memoria* 6/7 (2007): 124–142. On Ravines heading Aprista activities in the French capital, see Archives de la Préfecture de Police, Paris, France, BA 2143 (hereafter cited as AGELA): Association Générale d'Étudiants Latino-Américains, l'Association des Nouveaux Émigrés Révolutionnaires de Cuba, Amérique Centrale et Caraïbes (A.G.E.L.A.).

123 Haya de la Torre, 1931, "Discurso contra la fraude y la tiranía," in *Antología del pensamiento político de Haya de la Torre*, ed. Andrés Townsend Ezcurra, Lima: Biblioteca Nacional del Perú, 1995, pp. 30–32.

revealed itself to him as he travelled throughout the Americas.[124] Additionally, realism by then shaped his approach to power and political struggle. Exile, with the encounters it prompted and the emotional and practical challenges it thrust on Apristas, was the starting point, the incubator, for transformed political consciousnesses.

CONCLUSION

Chapter 2 revealed an untold story about how the young Víctor Raúl Haya de la Torre experienced exile following his deportation from Peru. It aimed to shift the analytical gaze away from tales of betrayal or celebration of this legendary and uncontested leader of APRA and focused instead on the social strains that he had to go through during his early years of political militancy in exile. The coming of age of Haya de la Torre in exile as an independent individual and pragmatic politician enabled him to fully engage with the formation of APRA and its anti-imperialist project in the late 1920s. To conceive differently of collective identities, Haya de la Torre first had to realign how he approached and conceived of his own individual identity. To be sure, we should be wary not to indiscriminately extrapolate his first experience of exile to all Apristas who were deported in the early to mid-1920s. Different socio-political contexts and personal development generated different responses and reactions in the face of hardship. Gender, in particular, can affect the experience and the meaning of exile in different ways.[125] Nonetheless, these conclusions point to how the lived experience of exile shaped the early militancy of other founding members of APRA. They also show that Haya de la Torre did not assume the leadership of APRA as early and as decisively as the scholarship suggests. Neither was he always a man as thoroughly in control of his destiny as portrayed in celebratory narratives. Like many of his peers in exile, Haya de la Torre often felt at a loss and isolated from the political struggles that were rocking Peru during the 1920s.

Additionally, this chapter attended to the movement and exchange within some of the transnational networks of solidarity that made viable

[124] It was in 1930, while living in Berlin, that Haya de la Torre fully embraced and seriously explained for the first time the use of Indo-América to refer to the project of hemispheric unity. Haya de la Torre, "La cuestión del nombre," (1930) in *¿A dónde va Indoamérica?*, pp. 21–35.

[125] Amy K. Kaminsky, *After Exile: Writing the Latin American Diaspora*, Minneapolis: University of Minnesota Press, 1999.

the formation, under persecution, of APRA. John A. Mackay and Anna Melissa Graves, two foreign allies who were close to Christian pacifist groups, constituted a beneficial hub of transnational networks in the 1920s for young Peruvian exiles, and for Haya de la Torre in particular, eager to foster the liberation of the Americas without as yet the means to do so. This situation changed starting in the late 1920s, when APRA gained momentum as a viable and functional political movement. The growth of Latin American anti-imperialist networks of solidarity in the late 1920s ultimately relieved part of the burden of financial support of Mackay and Graves as intermediaries and freed up new resources to help support Latin American exiles active in the development of APRA. The consolidation of the PAP at the national level in the early 1930s, as we shall see, also played an important part in explaining these changing relations. For now, however, let us continue our exploration of how exile affected the early formation of APRA as well as the role that a newly formed hemispheric consciousness came to play in this political movement. The next chapter traces how exile, from the lived experience that APRA leaders underwent in the 1920s, turned into a discursive referent that was used to boost the legitimacy of one specific faction within the APRA leadership following the return to Peru in 1930.

3

"Lo que escribo lo he visto con mis propios ojos": Travels and Foreign Contacts as Regime of Authority, 1928–1931

On October 27, 1930, the US consul of Lima-Callao in Peru, William C. Burdett, briefed the Secretary of State on key aspects of the anti-imperialist and Pan-American policies of APRA, a political organization increasingly active in Peru. "The argument of Apra," he noted, "places Peru in the same class with Nicaragua, Haiti, Santo Domingo and Cuba under American tutelage."[1] Burdett was correct to believe that APRA interpreted the reality of Peru through the gaze of Central American and Caribbean countries. This region indeed played a pivotal role in raising the awareness of influential APRA leaders like Víctor Raúl Haya de la Torre and Magda Portal to the imperialist dangers facing Peru. These leaders travelled to the region in the late 1920s to proselytize APRA. Both admitted shortly afterward being deeply shaken by what they witnessed there, as reported in their respective political writings. Haya de la Torre stated in 1928 that his recent travels to Central America "me ha permitido ver de cerca la lucha de uno de los más importantes sectores de la América Latina contra el imperialismo invasor de los Estados Unidos del Norte."[2] Following her return to Peru in October 1930, Portal similarly emphasized to journalists the lessons that she had learned during her travels in

[1] William C. Burdett, American Consulate general, Callao-Lima, Peru (Burdett); "Haya de la Torre, Peruvian Radical Leader," October 27, 1930, p. 5; 810.43 A.P.R.A./1; State Department Records; Central Files, 1930–1939 (CF, 1930–1939); RG59; US National Archives at College Park, College Park, MD (NACP).

[2] "Have allowed me to see closely the struggle of one of the most important sectors of Latin America against the invading imperialism of the Northern United States," Haya de la Torre, "La lucha de Centroamérica contra el imperialismo," (Costa Rica, 1928) in *¿A dónde va Indoamérica?* Santiago de Chile: Editorial Ercilla, 1935, p. 41.

the Caribbean. In contrast to South America, where according to Portal, imperialist penetration advanced more insidiously, namely in the form of foreign loans and investments rather than military interventions, "en estos pueblos, el Imperialismo no tiene ningún disfraz," she explained about the Caribbean countries.[3] Portal suggested she had come to see and understand this brutal reality because of her travels abroad.

APRA is largely renowned in the scholarship for the originality of its anti-imperialist theses, specifically its capacity to formulate critiques of empire in a way that reflected the historical and social conditions of Latin American countries rather than emulating European models of critical thinking. Exile, as we have seen in Chapter 2, played an important role in this. The experience of traveling abroad prompted the rise of new personal and political consciousnesses that in turn enabled the formation and growth of the continental APRA. The student activists and labour organizers who were deported from Peru in the 1920s, and who politically came of age in exile as APRA leaders, were strikingly self-reflective about the changes that they underwent as they organized their anti-imperialist movement abroad. Their political writings stressed the heuristic value of travel and exile. "Lo que escribo no es consecuencia de lo que he oído o leído," Haya de la Torre once wrote in exile. "Lo he visto con mis propios ojos."[4] Many APRA leaders likewise asserted that exile transformed them into men and women of action ready to engage in revolutionary politics.[5] Moreover, they squarely and very conspicuously inferred that their capacity for original reflections about the Americas, and Peru's social problems in particular, was due to the time they spent in exile.

Chapter 3 investigates these metaphors of exile and travel as regimes of authority and political formation in APRA. To do so, it builds on the work of the historian Martín Bergel, who has coined the term "cultura nomádica" (nomadic culture) to explain how Aprista exiles defined their form of political proselytism during the late 1920s.[6] As shown by Bergel,

[3] "In this region, imperialism has no disguise," Magda Portal, "Con Magda Portal," October 26, 1930, [newspaper clipping], Magda Portal Papers, Benson Latin American Collection, University of Texas Libraries, the University of Texas at Austin, Box 10, Folder 10.10. Magda Portal, *América Latina frente al imperialismo*, Lima: Editorial Cahuide, 1931, p. 15.

[4] "What I write is not the result of what I have heard or read. I have seen it with my own eyes." Haya de la Torre, "La suerte de Puerto Rico," Berlín, junio 1930, in *¿A dónde va Indoamérica?*, p. 54.

[5] Martín Bergel, "Nomadismo proselitista y revolución. Notas para una caracterización del primer exilio aprista (1923–1931)," *E.I.A.L.*, 20: 1 (2009): 41–66.

[6] Bergel, "Nomadismo proselitista y revolución," pp. 2–3.

the development of a nomad culture by the late 1920s, associated with world travel and militant action, helped Aprista exiles differentiate their movement from previous generations of Peruvian intellectuals as well as from other anti-imperialist leagues, such as the Communist Anti-Imperialist League of the Americas (LADLA) and the Argentine-based Latin American Union (ULA), which were also simultaneously growing in the Americas.[7] Chapter 3 likewise suggests that the experience of exile had consequences far beyond the ideological formation imparted by the emotional and practical challenges that exile thrust on Apristas. Yet it expands the scope of the research to include the ways in which exile shaped the political identity of these APRA leaders as they were enmeshed in political struggles to retain control of their fast-growing political movement.

In this chapter, I argue that the development of this "nomad culture" in the late 1920s, associated with world travel and militant action, helped define who were authentic revolutionaries in the APRA movement as conflict began to grow in their continent-wide movement. By highlighting the symbolic importance that travel came to occupy in APRA's political imaginary abroad, I aim to shed new light on the clash that, in 1928, opposed two major APRA leaders – Víctor Raúl Haya de la Torre and Carlos José Mariátegui – and which scholars have so far studied exclusively through the prism of ideological or tactical disagreements. Doing so reframes this episode as a prolonged conflict rather than a clear-cut rupture between *aprismo* and socialism, as portrayed by the historiography of the Peruvian left. Important ideological differences did emerge in the early APRA as a result of different sites of political action in the movement. But they lingered in the movement, more so and for a longer time than often assessed, with important consequences for the transformation of the anti-imperialist APRA into a Peruvian national-popular party in the early 1930s.

Chapter 3 shows that the regime of travel authority carried on the Peruvian scene in the early 1930s as APRA exiles began their homecoming following the downfall of Augusto B. Leguía in August 1930. Indeed, discourses of deep connection to and knowledge of the

[7] Alexandra Pita González, *La Unión Latino Americana y el Boletín Revocación: Redes intelectuales y revistas culturales en la década de 1920*, México, DF: Colegio de México; Colima: Universidad de Colima, 2009 ; Daniel Kersffeld, *Contra el imperio: historia de la Liga Antimperialista de las Américas*, México: Siglo Veintiuno Editores, 2012; Melgar Bao, "The Anti-Imperialist League of the Americas between the East and Latin America," *Latin American Perspectives*, 35: 2 (2008): 9–24.

Americas assisted in consolidating the political authority of exiled APRA leaders as they began to convert the continental APRA into a national mass-based party: the Peruvian APRA Party (PAP). Stories of past travels and international connections enabled them to dissociate their movement from that of their political opponents in Peru, specifically the newly founded Communist Party of Peru (PCP), but also from newcomers to the party who had not experienced exile. In the leadership struggle over APRA and over who organized the working and middle classes of Peru, exile, from the lived experience it once was, turned into a discursive referent used to boost celebratory narratives of the APRA leadership before a Peruvian audience. Here lies a fundamental contradiction in the rise of APRA as a populist force in 1930s Peru. On the one hand, Apristas who experienced exile insisted that their primary goal was to bring about a popular democracy that responded to Peruvians' concerns. On the other hand, they claimed that their travels across the Americas the previous decade, and thus their absence from Peru, best positioned them to achieve this nationalist goal. This paradox is reminiscent of the tension we observed in the previous chapters between nationalism and internationalism and which underpinned anti-imperialist iterations of Latin America's national continentalism. This tension, as we shall see, would continue to shape APRA's evolution throughout the 1930s as well.

DIVISIONS IN A DIASPORIC COMMUNITY

The previous chapter has primarily focused on the organizing activities of Víctor Raúl Haya de la Torre while gesturing to other Peruvian Apristas during their time in exile. Yet APRA exiles were not the only ones who contributed to the success of the anti-imperialist APRA in the 1920s. A small but influential group of Apristas had also simultaneously developed in Peru under the leadership of the Peruvian intellectual and famous Marxist thinker, José Carlos Mariátegui. The historian of APRA, Eugenio Chang-Rodriguez, once stated, correctly so, that "la historia peruana del lustro 1924–1928 corresponde en gran parte a Mariátegui."[8] During that time period, the great *Amauta*, as Mariátegui came to be billed, emerged in Lima as a key player in the labour of

[8] "... to a large extent, the Peruvian history of the 1924–1928 period corresponds to Mariátegui," Eugenio Chang-Rodríguez, *La literatura política de González Prada, Mariátegui y Haya de la Torre*, México: Ediciones de Andrea, 1957, p. 129.

organizing APRA in Peru.[9] Mariátegui returned to his home country in 1923 after having spent four years of exile in Europe (1919–1923). He devoted most of his time abroad to studying Marxist texts and to observing the nascent communist movement in the region and returned home, writes historian Thomas Angotti, with an important Marxist intellectual baggage and with the determination to help organize the anti-oligarchical forces of Peru.[10] Haya de la Torre passed over the direction of *Claridad* and the Popular Universities Gonzalez Prada to Mariátegui following his arrest and deportation from Peru in October 1923. Both grew into important APRA leaders shortly thereafter.

In Peru, Mariátegui excelled at coordinating the efforts of poets, intellectuals, and labour activists in a way that channelled them into a collective project of creation. To foster dialogue amongst the vanguard forces of Peru, he established in 1926 the journal *Amauta*, a monthly magazine where vanguard artists and leftist intellectuals from Latin America and other parts of the world wrote and debated about arts, politics, and culture. Apristas frequently collaborated in this magazine during the first years of its existence.[11] Those who lived in Lima also regularly gathered at the house of Mariátegui, where they discussed and argued over how best to foster change in Latin American societies.[12] Kathleen Weaver describes the effervescent and eclectic nature of these encounters as follows: "Frequenting Amauta's informal salon were writers, artists, students, labor leaders, archaeologists, historians, and sociologists. Foreign radicals were sometimes present, and delegations of factory workers or miners often stopped by to confer with Mariátegui on specific labor issues."[13] The Uruguayan poet and Aprista, Blanca Luz Brum, recalls in similar fashion in her memoirs the political and social

[9] In Quechuas *Amauta* means "sage" or "priest." Kathleen Weaver, *Peruvian Rebel*: The World of Magda Portal. With a Selection of Her Poems, Philadelphia: Pennsylvania State University Press, 2009, p. 34.

[10] Thomas Angotti, "The Contributions of Jose Carlos Mariátegui to Revolutionary Theory," *Latin American Perspectives*, 13: 2 (1986): 33–57; *José Carlos Mariategui: An Anthology*, ed. Harry E. Vanden and Marc Becker, New York: Monthly Review Press, 2011, p. 15.

[11] Oscar Terán, "Amauta: vanguardia y revolución," in Carlos Altamirano (ed.), *Historia de los intelectuales en América Latina, Tomo II*, Buenos Aires: Katz editores, 2010, pp. 169–191. Daniel Iglesias, "Nacionalismo y utlización política del pasado: la historia nacional desde la perspectiva de la revista Amauta (1926–1930)," *Histtórica*, 30: 2 (2006): 91–114. Alberto Tauro, *Amauta y su influencia*, Lima: Editora Amauta, 1960.

[12] Armando Bazán, *Mariátegui y su tiempo*, Lima: Empresa Editora Amauta, 1969.

[13] Weaver, *Peruvian Rebel*, p. 34.

excitement that she felt during her stay in Lima in 1926–1927. "Me llevaron a un mundo diferente al que yo hasta entonces conociera, a un mundo de conflictos y luchas sociales," she writes about the Apristas and socialist intellectuals she met in Mariátegui's house. "Estos tenían la piel oscura, estaban mal vestidos y algo desesperado y angustioso temblaba en el fondo de sus pupilas. ¡Eran apristas!"[14] Brum's recollection of her time in Peru reflects how the community of artists, workers, and reform students who were part of the nascent APRA circles in Peru first kindled her awareness of Latin America's plight. "Por el Perú entré a la cultura de América," she writes in her memoirs, "participando de los procesos políticos y sociales que por entonces agitaban las banderas americanistas de esos pueblos."[15]

During its first years of existence, the APRA operated on two fronts – one abroad, and one at home. This worked quite well for some time. To be sure, as shown in Chapter 2, the lived experience of exile empowered APRA leaders abroad to develop new forms of continental consciousness; it also shaped their anti-US and anti-imperialist sensibilities in ways that eventually differed from those who stayed in Peru and formed the "Lima Group" (grupo de Lima). But, as the burden of distance, miscommunication, and persecution created problems of political organization and ideological cohesion for the movement's leadership, these hurdles paradoxically contributed to boosting APRA's resilience. In effect, because the command of APRA was spread through space and not yet centralized into a single executive body, the meaning of APRA was still left open to interpretation. This flexibility had one important consequence for the group's unity: there was room for conflict to endure in the movement before definitive ruptures took place.

This relative peace began to crumble, starting in 1928. By that point in time, the leadership of APRA in exile agreed that the struggle for liberation had to move onto the Peruvian scene.[16] To carry through with this

[14] "They took me to a different world from the one I had known until then, to a world of conflicts and social struggles. They were dark-skinned, poorly dressed, and something desperate and anguished trembled deep inside their eyes. They were Apristas !," Blanca Luz Brum, *Mi vida. Cartas de amor a Siqueiros*, Santiago de Chile: Editorial Mare Nostrum, 2004, p. 51.

[15] "Through Peru I became part of the culture of America. There, I participated in the political and social processes that were rocking Americanist groups," ibid., p. 56.

[16] Juan de Dios Merel to José Carlos Mariátegui, Buenos Aires, September 7, 1928, José Carlos Mariátegui, *Correspondencia* (1915–1930), Lima: Biblioteca Amauta, 1984, p. 429.

task, the Comité Aprista de México founded in January 1928 a Peruvian political party, entitled the Partido Nacionalista Libertador, or Partido Nacionalista Peruano (PNL). In addition to seeking to translate APRA's revolutionary ideals to the Peruvian scene, the PNL worked to organize from abroad the onset of the revolution in Peru. It named Haya de la Torre as its de facto presidential candidate, and altogether announced the enactment of two central revolutionary measures upon taking power: (1) enact major land redistribution, and (2) overturn all national laws that favoured imperialist interests at the expense of the workers of Peru.[17] Although ideological discrepancies between Aprista circles in exile and those in Peru had surged beforehand, notably with the anti-Comintern positions that Haya de la Torre adopted during the Anti-Imperialist Congress in Brussels in February 1927, it is with the foundation of the PNL that minor hiccups in the growing APRA community turned into real problems.[18] A crisis burst into the open between the group of México and elements of the Peruvian vanguard back home.

The areas of disagreement were twofold. First, the foundation of the PNL rested on an ideological premise that directly contravened the political work that José Carlos Mariátegui was then spearheading in Peru. Its formation implied the projection of the united front strategy between all anti-imperialist forces of the continent into a national context, taking the form of a united front between the workers (which encompassed, for Apristas, the urban proletariat and the Indigenous peasant masses) and the middle class of Peru. Influenced by the experience of the nationalist Kuomintang in China, Haya de la Torre and others in the APRA began to question their communist allies, starting in 1927. They later disapproved of the class-against-class strategy adopted during the Comintern's Third Period (1928–1935), favouring anti-colonial nationalism over international communism to protect Peru and the Americas from US expansionism.[19] As a result, by 1928, Haya de la Torre and his peers in

[17] "Esquema del plan de México," in Ricardo Martínez de la Torre, *Apuntes para la interpretación marxista de la historia social del Perú (I–II)*, Lima: Impresa Editora Peruana, 1947–1949, pp. 290–293; Alberto Flores Galindo and Manuel Burga, *Apogeo y crisis de la republica aristocrática*, Lima: Ediciones "Rikchay Perú," 1979, p. 186.

[18] José A. Barba Caballero, *Haya de la Torre y Mariátegui frente a la historia*, Lima: Amauta, 1978, pp. 143–144; Galindo and Burga, *Apogeo y crisis de la republica*, p. 186; Julio Antonio Mella, *¿Qué es el ARPA?* , Miraflores: Editorial Educación, 1975 (1st ed. 1928), pp. 49–53.

[19] Though the possibility of an alliance with communists remained nevertheless open until the early 1930s. See Victor Jeifets and Lazar Jeifets, "Haya de la Torre… ¿Un comunista latinoamericano?," *Istoriia: la revista científica y educativa electrónica*, 12: 6 (2011),

Mexico claimed that it was possible for Peruvians to achieve national liberation within a worldwide capitalist order.

In contrast, Mariátegui and the Peruvian vanguard ruled out this option. According to them, it was simply impossible to realize any type of national sovereignty as long as capitalism reigned supreme. The notion, so central for the "grupo de México," that the creation of an anti-imperialist state in Peru would establish a bulwark against imperialist intrusions, facilitate national liberation, and therefore allow socialism to eventually come about afterward, was met with stern rejection by Mariátegui and the so-called "grupo de Lima."[20] To be sure, Mariátegui did not altogether deny the revolutionary potential that nationalism had for a semi-colonial nation like Peru. But he strongly disagreed with the Aprista exiles' proposal of a united front between the workers and the middle sectors of Peru. Mariátegui saw value in the class-versus-class strategy of the Comintern. He argued that because fighting imperialism necessarily involved waging a total war against capitalism, then it was of paramount importance that the working class, even if still a minority in Peru, remained the vanguard of the revolution.[21] In other words, there was no room in Mariátegui's reasoning for a revolutionary alliance with the growing middle sectors of Peru – an alliance from which soon emerged the national-popular political culture inherent in Latin American populism.[22] Mariátegui resented that some APRA ideologues contemplated the small bourgeoisie and the middle classes of Peru as viable conduits for the revolution. According to him, the Peruvian vanguard might as well abandon all hope of social transformation, for the promise of a socialist revolution tomorrow rather than today was tantamount to embracing the expansion of imperialist interests in Latin America.[23] Only a socialist revolution, he argued, independent of the

available at: https://arxiv.gaugn.ru/s207987840000141-4-2/?sl=en. Also see Martín Bergel's analysis on the influence of the Kuomintang for APRA's political formation, and for Latin American populism more broadly in Bergel, *El oriente desplazado.* Los intelectuales y los orígenes del tercermundismo en la Argentina, Bernal: Universidad Nacional de Quilmes Editorial, 2015, pp. 258–277.

20 Galindo and Burga, *Apogeo y crisis de la república*, p. 190.

21 José Carlos Mariátegui, "Replica a Luis Alberto Sánchez," in *Boletín de Defensa Indígena*, 1: 3, in *Amauta*, 2: 3, March 1927, pp. 38–39.

22 Bergel, *El oriente desplazado.*

23 Carlos Franco, "Acerca del surgimiento del marxismo latinoamericano y de las perspectivas de Víctor Raúl Haya de la Torre y José Carlos Mariátegui sobre el desarrollo, la nación y el socialismo en América Latina," in *Del marxismo eurocéntrico al marxismo latinoamericano*, Lima: Centro de Estudios para el Desarrollo y la participación, 1981,

course of the so-called universal Western history, had the power to free the oppressed masses of Peru.

The second disagreement was over the political role that the APRA movement was called to play in Peru. APRA exiles in Mexico supported the transformation of APRA into a national party (hence the creation of the PNL in January 1928), whereas those in charge of the movement in Peru rebuffed this position. They proposed instead that APRA had to remain a political alliance, not a party, so that it continued to marshal anti-imperialist forces across the continent while bequeathing to a national-level socialist party the responsibility for revolutionary work in Peru. On September 29, 1928, Mariátegui summarized the crux of the problem in the following terms: "Yo he tenido con Haya primero y con el grupo de México después un largo debate, en el cual he sostenido con abundantes y claras razones que el Apra, como su mismo título lo dice, no debía ser un partido sino una alianza y he desaprobado posteriormente la propaganda con la cual se pretendía presentar la candidatura de Haya."[24] In many ways, tactical deviations stemmed from different readings of the situation in Peru and of the logics of global capitalism, but they also had to do with how these historical actors perceived their place in the Peruvian vanguard and understood their role as agents of social transformation.

As a result of these ideological and tactical debates, two competing visions for Indo-América began to rise in the late 1920s between Apristas in Peru and those in exile: one Indo-América championed a socialist revolution while the other pressed for a social and anti-imperialist revolution. Mariátegui was by then a fierce advocate of the former. He came to view in "Indo-American socialism" a revolutionary project that spoke to the social and political realities of Peru.[25] Mariátegui is indeed known and celebrated for his promotion of the Indigenist movement in Peru and the Americas from a socialist perspective. His intellectual work vindicated the rights and demands of "Indian Peru" and made the

pp. 67–112; Flores Galindo and Manuel Burga, "La polémica Haya – Mariátegui," in *Apogeo y crisis de la republica*, pp. 185–196; Flores Galindo, "Haya, Mariátegui y el Europeismo," *Obras Completas V*, Lima: Casa de estudio del socialismo, 1993, pp. 127–129.

[24] "I have had a long debate, first with Haya, and later with the group of Mexico. I have argued with abundant and clear reasons that APRA, as its title says, should not be a party but an alliance and I have subsequently disapproved the propaganda with which they presented Haya's candidacy," Mariátegui to Carlos Arbulú Miranda, Lima, September 20, 1928, Mariátegui, *Correspondencia*, p. 444.

[25] "Aniversario y balance," *Amauta*, no. 17, September, 1928, p. 3.

emancipation of Indigenous populations the primary goal of the socialist revolution.[26] "The problem of the Indian, which is the problem of Peru, cannot find its solution in an abstract humanitarian formula," he wrote in 1924 shortly after returning to Peru. "The solution to the problem of the Indian must be a social solution. It must be worked out by the Indian themselves."[27] Mariátegui rebuked the discourse of cultural and moral salvation, so prevalent in positivist discourses, and advocated instead for the full agency of the Indigenous peasants as revolutionary actors. He nevertheless opposed the creation of an Indian Republic in South America, as proposed by the Comintern in the late 1920s, arguing that race oppression should always be primarily read as class oppression.[28]

Mariátegui's Indo-American socialism, then, was less a plan for integrating the Americas than a roadmap for Peruvians to bring socialism to life "con nuestra propia realidad, en nuestro propio lenguaje."[29] By 1928, it had become clear to Mariátegui and the Peruvian vanguard that the real problem surrounding them was not one that opposed Latin or Hispanic or Indo-América to North America, let alone Western civilization per se. Rather, the problem lay in the polarity between capitalism and socialism, and Indo-América's role as a concept was to help bring about the latter in Peru and the Americas.[30]

In contrast, for Haya de la Torre and for Apristas in Mexico, Indo-América was not a means to an end. It was the goal to achieve. This idea gained clarity in later years, but in 1930, it was already clear to Haya de la Torre that correctly naming the continent in a way that revealed to the Latin American peoples what united them rather than insisting on national distinctions in their respective *patria chica* (small nation), constituted a revolutionary priority. He reflected in 1930 upon distinct continental consciousnesses in tandem with their respective historical significance. His conclusions associated Hispano América with the colonial period, Latin America with the republican one, and Pan-América with the contemporary expression of US imperialism in the

[26] *José Carlos Mariátegui: An Anthology*, p. 128.

[27] José Carlos Mariategui, Mundial, Lima, December 9, 1924, in *José Carlos Mariátegui: An Anthology*, pp. 141–142.

[28] Marc Becker, "Mariátegui, the Comintern, and the Indigenous Question in Latin America," *Science and Society*, 70: 4 (October 2006): 450–479.

[29] "With our own reality, in our own language." "Aniversario y balance," *Amauta*, no. 17, September, 1928, p. 3.

[30] Ricardo Melgar Bao, *Mariátegui, Indoamérica y las crisis civilizatorias* de Occidente, Lima: Editora Amauta S. A, 1995.

region south of the Río Grande. Indo-América, following that logic, represented altogether the continental and the historical consciousness of a new, emancipated people south of the Río Grande, free at long last from colonial and neocolonial oppression. It was a form of revolutionary consciousness projected onto the future, one that did not exist yet, therefore nebulous, but which Aprista exiles were beginning to see more clearly and strived to bring about.[31]

Notwithstanding these differing Aprista positions regarding the essence or the indispensability of hemispheric unity, their visions for Indo-América shared one common denominator. In the late 1920s to early 1930s, Indo-América had overall much less to do with representing the Indigenous people of the Americas than with organizing one of two things – either a socialist revolution in Peru, or an original movement of Pan-Latin American resistance in the face of global capitalism and the US hegemon. Haya de la Torre brought home this point in 1930 when he favoured the use of "Latin America" over "Indo-América," since it was so widespread, he claimed, and accepted by many worldwide.[32] Besides, his early references to an "Indo-" América were mostly superficial; they more resembled José Vasconcelos' mixed-race utopia, or "cosmic race," than they did any attempt at paying serious attention to Indigenous agency.[33] The same was true of Mariátegui's approach to Indo-América. Mariátegui did celebrate the Inca past and the mythic cultural essence of the "Indio," and to be sure his Marxist interpretations have received much praise for that overture. But while rooted in an idealized past, observes the literary scholar Jorge Coronado, his social philosophy "slight[ed] present-day indigenous cultures".[34]

The current scholarship that is critical of the Indigenist movement helps to grasp how central was the concept of salvation and of a civilizing mission to Apristas' political endeavours, whether conducted in exile or in

[31] Víctor Raúl Haya de la Torre, "La cuestión del nombre," (1930), *¿A dónde va Indoamérica*, pp. 31–35.

[32] Haya de la Torre, "La cuestión del nombre," p. 33.

[33] José Vasconcelos argued that Latin Americans inherited a historical mission from their colonial past. Through mestizaje, he advanced, they must favour the advent of a new era, in which the instinct of beauty, emotions, and spiritual feelings, rather than reason or ethics, would rule human societies. José Vasconcelos, *La raza cósmica*, Baltimore and London: The Johns Hopkins University Press, 1997 (1st ed. In Spanish 1925).

[34] Jorge Coronado, *The Andes Imagined*: Indigenismo, Society, and Modernity, Pittsburgh: University of Pittsburgh Press, 2009, p. 28.

Peru.[35] This doesn't mean that the idea of Indo-América altogether forewent concerns for the impoverished Indigenous populations of the Americas, specifically that of Peru. From the late 1920s onward, APRA's fragmented program fiercely championed their cause and the improvement of their social conditions. Yet they did so in a way that ultimately erased those they claimed to represent.[36] In discourse, the figure of the "Indio" became associated with the new ideal of modernity that Aprista exiles and the Peruvian vanguard wanted to bring forth. In practice, however, these white and mestizo intellectuals never seriously included Indigenous agency and worldviews in their political philosophy.[37]

This shared oblivion in Aprista circles yields an important lesson: in the late 1920s, conflict had little to do with the nascent concepts of Indo-América, for Indo-América was neither hegemonic at the time, nor overly discordant regarding Apristas' approach to Indigenous agency. In contrast, distance, leadership struggles, and hurt feelings, as we shall see, were creating more important headaches for the movement.

UNITY IN CONFLICT

Now that we understand better the underlying tensions that ran through APRA's Marxist interpretations during its foundational phase, we must reckon with their persistence in the movement. These tensions fed conflicts and debates more than they precipitated ruptures. Besides, in contrast to what historians have so far suggested, the quarrel that arose between José Carlos Mariátegui and Víctor Raúl Haya de la Torre in 1928 was not only about ideological discrepancies and tactical incompatibilities. Mariátegui in fact resented that Peruvian exiles had taken the initiative to form a national party from afar. Most vexing was the fact that the Aprista cell in Mexico had moved along with the creation of the

[35] Kim Díaz, "Indigenism in Peru and Bolivia," in Robert Eli Sánchez, Jr. (ed.) Latin American and Latinx Philosophy: A Collaborative Introduction, New York: Routledge, 2020, pp. 180–197; Priscilla Archibald, *Imagining Modernity in the Andes*, Lewisburgh, PA: Bucknell University Press, 2011; Coronado, *The Andes Imagined*; Paulo Drinot, *The Allure of Labor. Workers, Race, and the Making of the Peruvian State*, Durham, NC and London: Duke University Press, 2011.

[36] Drinot, *The Allure of Labor*, pp. 17–50.

[37] Coronado, *The Andes Imagined*; Daniel Iglesias, "Redécouverte et idéologisation de l'Amérique latine par l'Alliance populaire révolutionnaire américaine," in Annie-Blonderl and Eliane Talbot (eds), *(Re)découvertes des Amériques. Entre conflits, rencontres et recherche d'identité*, Paris: L'Harmattan, 2013, pp. 155–166.

Partido Nacionalista Peruano without receiving prior consent from any of the vanguard elements present and active in Peru at the time. Apristas in Mexico had not even consulted them.[38] In a letter dated April 16, 1928, Mariátegui reminded his intractable peers of the organizing work that homebred activists were already doing in Peruvian provinces. Intellectuals, students, schoolteachers, union leaders, and professionals of all sorts appeared, in light of Mariátegui's assessment, to have joined forces on the national scene to mobilize the masses of Peru and stir up their revolutionary potential.[39] What could a group of Peruvian exiles possibly bring to the political organizing underway in Peru that vanguard elements, who lived and worked there, did not know already? "*Les absents ont toujours tort*," says the French adage.[40] So thought Mariátegui: "Si de lo que se trata, como sostiene Haya en una magnifica conferencia," he gibed, referring to ongoing Marxist debates about how to best interpret Latin American societies, "es de descubrir la realidad y no de inventarla, me parece que Uds. están siguiendo un método totalmente distinto y contrario."[41]

Beneath this statement lay the assumption that the state of being in Peru rather than abroad gave a comparative advantage to the Peruvian vanguard that revolved around the leadership of Mariátegui. Aprista exiles were too far away. According to Mariátegui, they were too removed and disconnected from Peruvian realities to fully grasp what types of radical politics their country needed. He mused later that year, still in reference to Aprista exiles in Mexico, "Yo no los apruebo. Y creo que estoy más cerca de la realidad y más cerca del Perú que ellos, a pesar de mi presunto europeismo y de mi supuesto excesivo doctrinarismo."[42] For Marxist theorists, immediate surroundings are crucial to analyzing the historical development of a given society. Only with an accurate

[38] Mariátegui to La Célula Aprista de México, Lima, April 16, 1928, Mariátegui, *Correspondencia*, pp. 371–373.

[39] Mariátegui to La Célula Aprista de México, Lima, April 16, 1928, Mariátegui, *Correspondencia*, p. 372.

[40] "Those who are absent are always wrong."

[41] "If what this is about, as Haya maintains in a magnificent conference, is to discover reality and not to invent it, it seems to me that you are following a totally different and contrary method," Mariátegui to La Célula Aprista de México, Lima, April 16, 1928, Mariátegui, *Correspondencia*, p. 372.

[42] "I do not approve of them. And I believe that I am closer to reality and closer to Peru than they are, despite my alleged Europeanism and my alleged excessive doctrinarism," Mariátegui to Eudocio Ravines, Lima, December 31, 1928, Mariátegui, *Correspondencia*, p. 492.

reading of a social context can they choose the appropriate theoretical lodestar for the war to be waged. Geographical distance, therefore, had the power to flaw an otherwise Marxist interpretation of a particular reality.

What ensued came in the form of personal squabbles. Haya de la Torre's response reached Lima the following month. His words dripped bitterness: "Está Ud. Haciendo mucho daño por su falta de calma, por su afán de aparecer siempre europeo dentro de la terminología europea." The rebuke went on, "Con eso rompe el Apra. Yo sé que está Ud. contra nosotros. No me sorprende. Pero la revolución la haremos nosotros sin mencionar el socialismo pero repartiendo las tierras y luchando contra el imperialismo."[43] To this pledge of rupture Mariátegui replied with silence. "¿Para que escribirnos?" he mused later that year, reflecting upon his estranged relationship with Haya de la Torre.[44] Mariátegui was aware that heeding each other's complaints would only compound their falling-out at this point. He also knew that petty squabbles could easily blow out of proportion. To avoid an "unpleasant rupture" with the grupo de México, Mariátegui resolved to stave off situations that risked adding fuel to the flames; he altogether stopped replying to Haya de la Torre. By the end of 1928, the two major Peruvian figures associated with APRA had ceased all communication with one another.[45]

Meanwhile, a restricted number of Apristas in exile appeared eager to bring this fight into the open. Significantly for my argument, they did so in a way that associated their geographical positions outside Peru with capacities for revolutionary thought. Take for example the case of Alejandro Rojas Zevallos, a Peruvian Aprista who lived and worked in New York City, and who openly sided with Haya de la Torre against the leadership of Mariátegui. In a letter he forwarded to the latter in September 1928, Rojas Zevallos used the geographical component to assess his superiority over Apristas in Peru. His text implied that peers back home could not understand the urgency to defend the national sovereignty of Peru. If they toyed with socialist ideas, even as their

[43] "You are doing a lot of damage by your lack of calm, by your desire to always appear European within the European terminology." "With that breaks the APRA. I know that you are against us. I'm not surprised. But we will make the revolution without mentioning socialism, by distributing the lands and fighting against imperialism," Haya de la Torre to Mariátegui, México, May 20, 1928, Mariátegui, *Correspondencia*, p. 379.

[44] "Why write to one another?" Mariátegui to Eudocio Ravines, Lima, December 31, 1928, Mariátegui, *Correspondencia*, p. 490.

[45] Ibid., pp. 489–490.

country was still only a "colonia," Rojas Zevallos suggested, it was because they remained oblivious to the realities of persecution and imperialism in the Americas.[46] According to Zevallos, those who lived abroad were confronted with different points of view and benefited from experiences conducive to original creation.[47] Rojas Zevallos was terse and unforgiving. The solution he envisioned to save APRA and protect Peruvians from misguided revolutionaries took the form of overt rupture: "En nombre de los amigos de Haya," he told Mariátegui, "le invito a declararse contra Haya, a proclamar su rebeldía en nombre de su 'acendradas convicciones' y anunciar que usted es ajeno a la campaña nacional contra el leguíismo."[48]

Other APRA leaders in exile thought along similar lines. This was the case of Alberto Hidalgo, an Aprista exiled in Buenos Aires, Argentina. Hidalgo reproached Mariátegui for his excessive focus on the Peruvian scene, which came to the detriment of the American continental scene, he argued. Hidalgo feared that socialist theories would hold Peru captive to narrow nationalist aspirations, pressing instead for a political agenda that apprehended the country in relation to its place within, as well as its connections to, the entire American continent.[49] "Yo no estoy de acuerdo con muchos de sus postulados. Es más. Estoy en contra de ellos," Hidalgo told Mariátegui in a letter dated 21 December 1928. He added examples to support his claim: "Así por ejemplo usted es nacionalista, así en política como en arte. Ha caído usted en la trampa del comunismo ruso, hecho con fronteras y divisiones raciales."[50]

Interestingly, Hidalgo criticized Mariátegui for being overly nationalist and not internationalist enough, whereas Rojas Zevallo rebuked Mariátegui's socialism for denying the importance of nationalism when

[46] Alejandro Rojas Zevallos to Mariátegui, Hamburgo, [New York], [septiembre] 1928, Mariátegui, *Correspondencia*, pp. 446–447. Zevallos, "De nuestros lectores," *La Prensa*, New York, April 30, 1929, p. 6.

[47] Rojas Zevallos, "El problema indígena de Hispano America," *La Prensa*, August 16, 1927, sec. *Tribuna Libre*, p. 5.

[48] "On behalf of Hayas' friends, I invite you to declare yourself against Haya, to proclaim your rebellion in the name of your 'solid convictions' and to announce that you are alien to the national campaign against Leguía," Zevallos to Mariátegui, Hamburgo, [New York], [September] 1928, Mariátegui, *Correspondencia*, p. 447.

[49] Alberto Hidalgo to Mariátegui, Buenos Aires, December 21, 1928, Mariátegui, *Correspondencia*, p. 486.

[50] "I do not agree with many of your reasonings. It's more. I am against them." "For example, you are a nationalist, in politics as well as in art. You have fallen into the trap of Russian communism, made of borders and racial divisions," Hidalgo to Mariátegui, Buenos Aires, December 21, 1928, Mariátegui, *Correspondencia*, p. 486.

fighting US imperialism. This discrepancy of opinion can be explained by the lack of cohesion at the time in a movement that grew fast and wide. Not all APRA exiles agreed over the importance of being nationalist or internationalist, and often a single individual looked confused about what exactly being a nationalist or an internationalist entailed, for at the time Apristas were still struggling to syncretize both concepts into a single plan of action. But one thing held true for most of them, and this was that they similarly understood their geographical location as a guarantee against inappropriate revolutionary paths for Peru.

The pugnacious tone of Rojas Zevallos, seen above, is consistent with common interpretations of the strife that opposed in 1928 the two major historical figures of APRA. This scholarship tends to bracket what happened between these two leaders with the outbreak of explicit and immediate divisions among Aprista circles. A consensual narrative proposes that, from then until the 1940s, when the Peruvian APRA party fully swerved to the right of the political spectrum, the intellectual history of Peru wavered between two leftist poles. A sharp divide between the Peruvian vanguard back home, which revolved around the figure of José Carlos Mariátegui, and Aprista exiles abroad, more loyal to Víctor Raúl Haya de la Torre, forcefully separated these circles starting in 1928. The former group was associated with socialism, whereas those who formed the latter came to be viewed as the only legitimate representatives of APRA.[51] José Carlos Mariátegui, Ricardo Martínez de la Torre, and Julio Portocarrero went on to organize the Socialist Party of Peru in October 1928. It became the Communist party of Peru shortly after the death of Mariátegui in April 1930.[52]

Problematically, this individual-focused perspective on political strife has led scholars to concentrate primarily on notions of rupture and division in their apprehension of the many conflicts that rocked the Aprista community from the late 1920s onward. They have found surprisingly little room in their reading of primary sources for notions of conciliation and cooperation. Yet a closer look at the correspondence that

[51] Alberto Flores Galindo and Manuel Burga, "La polémica Haya-Mariategui," in *Apogeo y crisis de la república* aristocrática, Lima: Ediciones "Rikchay Perú," 1979, pp. 185–196. José Barba Caballero and César Lévano, *La polémica: Haya de la Torre – Mariátegui*, s.l., n.d., 1979; Luis Alberto Sánchez, *Haya de la Torre y el APRA*, Santiago de Chile: Pacifico, 1955; Ricardo Martínez de la Torre, *Apuntes para una interpretación marxista*, 1947–1949.

[52] Alberto Flores Galindo, *El pensamiento comunista, 1917–1945*, Lima: Mosca Azul Editores, 1982, pp. 28, 84–85.

Apristas exchanged during these years reveals a different picture. Those who took clear and unwavering sides in the split between Haya de la Torre and Mariátegui, like Rojas Zevallos above, represented more an exception than the norm. The correspondence that Mariátegui continued to maintain with a panoply of Aprista exiles, even as his relationship with Haya de la Torre took a turn for the worse, brings home the resilience of cooperation in these political circles.

In effect, many Apristas maintained amiable relationships with one another despite the divergence of opinions. Most continued to collaborate in the pages of *Amauta* until the death of José Carlos Mariátegui. Others took pains to openly defend collaboration and solidarity of action in the face of mounting disagreements.[53] Discord was not born yesterday in these groups, nor was it about to die. In these radical and leftist circles, correspondence of action did not have to map onto precise political ambitions. It was possible to experience feelings of solidarity for a common cause of regeneration for Peru and the Americas despite deviating ideological or tactical alignments. Likewise, personal rivalries did not automatically require that allies join one particular faction. The practice of unity in conflict associated with the *Reforma* movement had led Peruvian radicals to place intellectual conflict at the core of their collective endeavours. This was still true in the late 1920s. Ten years after the Grito de Córdoba, the Peruvian vanguard continued to chisel social designs into the backbeat of debates and arguments.

The positions that Mariátegui proselytized in the summer of 1929 make clear that he continued to view the possibility of complementary goals between APRA and the newfound Socialist Party of Peru (PSP). On June 20, 1929, Mariátegui forwarded a series of instructions to Nicanor A. de la Fuente, a close collaborator in Chiclayo, Peru. His letter clearly states the necessity to carry on the fight against divisionism between elements of the Peruvian vanguard, therefore suggesting that as long as both groups clarified their respective functions and realms of actions, then cooperation could still prevail over internal warfare:

Como organización continental, el Apra depende de lo que resulta al congreso antiimperialista de Paris, a cuyas decisiones, inspiradas seguramente en la necesidad de unificar el movimiento anti-imperialista, ningún revolucionario puede oponer resistencia. [...] Nosotros trabajamos con el proletariado y por el

[53] Fernán Cisneros (H.) a José Carlos Mariátegui, Buenos Aires, October 4, 1928, Mariátegui, *Correspondencia*, p. 449; Hidalgo to Mariátegui, Buenos Aires, December 21, 1928, Mariátegui, *Correspondencia*, p. 486.

socialismo. Si hay grupos dispuestos a trabajar con la pequeña burguesía por un nacionalismo revolucionario, que ocupen su puesto. No nos negaremos a colaborar con ellos, si representan efectivamente una corriente, un movimiento de masas. Me parece que, planteada así, la cuestión es completamente clara y queda excluida toda posibilidad de divisionismo.[54]

To be sure, Mariátegui's text implies that it was incumbent upon the Lima Group to allocate resources and objectives, and to dictate who, in the end, organized an anti-imperialist alliance abroad and who stayed in Peru to prepare the socialist revolution. Nevertheless, Mariategui's call for cooperation with APRA is crucial, for it helps to demystify the rigidity with which most studies have approached group dynamics within the Aprista community. That Mariátegui was able to envision, still in 1929, an alliance between a continental APRA and a national-level socialist party, that he considered the possibility of a fruitful collaboration based on complementary objectives between them, runs counter to what most scholarship on APRA has inferred to this day about the divide that ostensibly kept aprismo and socialism hermetically apart from one another, starting somewhat in 1927, and then completely from 1928 onward.[55] The letter that Mariátegui wrote to Mario Nerval the following week concluded with similar call for cooperation between antagonist lines of action: "Los términos del debate quedan así bien esclarecidos," he stated, "y todo reproche por divisionismo completamente excluido. – No hay por nuestra parte divisionismo sino clarificación."[56] In the late 1920s, allegiances to both groups not only appeared plausible, but several members of APRA in fact trusted that this double affiliation had the power to facilitate revolutionary work and assist different realms of action between the national and the continental scene.

[54] "As a continental organization, APRA depends on the results of the anti-imperialist congress in Paris, to whose decisions, surely inspired by the need to unify the anti-imperialist movement, no revolutionary can contest. [...] We work with the proletariat and for socialism. If there are groups willing to work with the petty bourgeoisie for revolutionary nationalism, let them take their place. We will not refuse to collaborate with them, if they effectively represent a current, a mass movement. It seems to me that, put like this, the question is completely clear and any possibility of division is excluded," José Carlos Mariátegui to Nicanor A. de la Fuente, Lima, June 20, 1929, Mariátegui, *Correspondencia*, p. 584.

[55] An exception to this trend, however, is Harry E. Vanden and Marc Becker who also recognize this fact in *José Carlos Mariátegui: An Anthology*.

[56] "The terms of the debate are thus clarified, and any reproach for divisiveness completely excluded – There is no divisiveness on our part but clarification," José Carlos Mariátegui a Mario Nerval, Lima, June 28, 1929, Mariátegui, *Correspondencia*, p. 597.

This protracted struggle in the APRA movement meant that the need to confirm one's authority endured way beyond the formative years in exile, with consequences for the making of APRA's anti-imperialist project and its subsequent association with Indo-American solidarity a few years later. It is precisely because conflict repeatedly rattled the movement that a branch of the leadership clung so hard to Indo-América. There will be more to say about how this project of hemispheric unity, in addition to advocating Latin American sovereignty by way of continental unity, helped to establish political legitimacy within the movement during the 1930s and early 1940s. But first we must continue to explore the national context in which Aprista exiles returned to Peru in 1930–1931. Their homecoming took place in a context in which the Peruvian vanguard, united yesterday, began to divide. Organizing political parties demanded the dissociation of one party from the another. The experience of travel and exile would help a certain leadership in the movement achieve this task.

HOMECOMING

In Peru, Major Luis Miguel Sánchez Cerro's rise to power in August 1930 marked the onset of a democratic opening. A combination of frantic hopes and political shadows took hold of the country soon after this military revolt, launched in the southern province of Arequipa on August 22, 1930, toppled the unpopular government of Augusto B. Leguía within three days. Sánchez Cerro, a mestizo from modest origins, epitomized for the popular sectors the promise of a new Peru.[57] As highlighted by eminent historians of the country, this military coup presaged the beginning of mass politics in Peru.[58] To understand the rapid politicization of the Peruvian masses henceforth, one must consider the underlying tensions that were gripping the country in the preceding decade.[59] In effect, the deepening chasm between the expectations of change initially brought forth by the Leguía government (1919–1923) and the reality of his last term in office (1923–1930) had become untenable by the time Sánchez Cerro victoriously marched on the Peruvian

[57] Víctor Andrés Belaúnde, *La crisis presente, 1914–1939*, Lima: Ediciones "Mercurio Peruano" [1940]. Steve Stein, *Populism in Peru: The Emergence of the Masses and the Politics of Social Control*, Madison: The University of Wisconsin Press, 1980, p. 84.

[58] Belaúnde, *La crisis presente, 1914–1939*.

[59] Armando Villanueva and Pablo Macera, *Arrogante Montonero*, Lima: Fondo Editorial del Congreso del Perú, 2011, p. 48.

capital on August 29, 1930. Whereas the ascension of Leguía to the presidency of Peru in 1919 had put an end to the Aristocratic Republic, ultimately his attempts to liquidate the old political order and modernize Peru did not meet expectations. By the end of his *Oncenio* (eleven-year presidential period), Leguía had fallen in disgrace before the popular sectors of Peru. By 1930, they wondered whether this "Patria Nueva," so cheerfully announced at the beginning of his presidential mandate, had anything to do with them after all: Peru looked more like a playground for foreign investors and US administrative cadres than the modern Peruvian nation Leguía had promised to bring about.

APRA leaders in exile swiftly capitalized on these events. They sensed the imminence of political transformations in their country. The fall of Leguía in August 1930, then, brought not only promises of a democratic Peru, but also the return home of the APRA exiles shortly thereafter. By September of that year, a dozen or so APRA exiles had established themselves in Lima, whence they began orchestrating the integration of APRA into a national political party. They also worked hard to diminish the clout of socialist peers in Peru, since both factions competed with one another to organize the rising popular sectors of Peru.[60] The first party executive was founded soon after and placed under direction of Luis Eduardo Enríquez, a stalwart militant and leader of APRA who had campaigned for the movement in Paris starting in the mid-1920s (he would soon be exiled again, this time in Chile). Three departments oversaw the functioning of the executive committee of the Peruvian section of APRA: the Department of Propaganda (Departamento de Propaganda y Redacción), divided between the office of exterior propaganda and the office of national propaganda, the Department of Economics (Departamento de Economía), and the Department of Discipline (Departamento de Disciplina). Each department was made up of one or two sub-secretaries, in addition to incorporating a couple of

[60] On APRA's anti-communism, and more specifically on the strategies that the PAP deployed to garner support among organized labour in early 1930s Peru, see Paulo Drinot, "Creole Anti-Communism: Labor, The Peruvian Communist Party, and APRA, 1930–1934," *Hispanic American Historical Review*, 92: 4 (2012): 703–736. Steven Hirsch also studied the partnership established in the early 1930s between the non-communist labour movement and the Peruvian APRA party. Hirsch argues that anarcho-syndicalist unions allied with the PAP because they saw in this party a prudent left alternative to a more belligerent, and above all more controlling, Communist Party. Steven J. Hirsch, "The Anarcho-Syndicalist Roots of a Multi-Class Alliance: Organized Labor and the Peruvian Aprista Party, 1900-1930," Ph. D. Diss., George Washington University, 1997.

"miembros integrantes" as well.[61] Official party documents reported in mid-October 1930 that about twenty-six collaborators worked in or for the party executive, thereby confirming, or more accurately giving the impression that the Peruvian APRA Party (PAP) was already a well-run institution with viable and organized party structures at the national level. This was not the case, as we shall see, but setting out the design of party infrastructure, and doing so conspicuously, did point to a group of undaunted militants who were girding themselves for a solid comeback into Peruvian politics.

As APRA began to cohere into a national political party, between August 1930 and October 1931, the Apristas who had come of age politically in exile faced an important challenge in terms of the party's ideological adaptation. This cohort of APRA leaders needed to reconnect with the Peruvian population. They needed to convince their fellow citizens that their organization was not an international clique dissociated from Peruvian politics, as many of its enemies alleged from 1930 onward. Specifically, they needed to adapt the experiences and the political knowledge they had accumulated abroad, whether in Europe or in the Americas, in a way that would make sense to ordinary Peruvians. Very few people at the time had the opportunity to travel within their own country, let alone abroad. Most simply strove to eke out a living and to live decent and honourable lives. What good was studying imperialism for a peasant of Indigenous descent in the Andes, or a baker in Lima? Why were the United States so bad for them? How exactly did imperialist domination materialize in the lives of Peruvian people? To provide straightforward answers to these questions, the APRA leaders freshly returned from exile needed time to regroup. They needed time to reacquaint themselves with Peru and with the everyday realities of its people to be able to translate the lessons they had learned abroad about US imperialism and global capitalism and the way in which these powerful forces of oppression specifically worked in their country.

Stories of past travels assisted APRA leaders to introduce their movement to the Peruvian electorate prior to adapting its program to the national scene (which it did in August 1931, when Haya de la Torre unveiled the minimum program (*programa mínimo*) of PAP before a crowd of thousands in the Plaza de Acho, a colonial bullring in the city

[61] "Comité Directivo del A.P.R.A.," *APRA: Órgano del frente único de trabajadores manuales e intelectuales, Partido Aprista Peruano*, Lima, No. 2, October 20, 1930, p. 3.

of Lima).[62] In *Craft and the Kingly Ideal*, the anthropologist Mary W. Helms traces how concepts and interpretations conferred on geographical distance and remote areas affect the meaning that subjects grant to material artefacts acquired in these far-away and foreign places.[63] Helm tells us that geographical distance is not neutral. For members of traditional societies, she writes, "geographical distance is frequently thought to correspond with supernatural distance, such that as one moves away from the social center geographically one moves toward places and people that are increasingly 'different' and, therefore, regarded as increasingly supernatural, mythical, and powerful."[64] These conclusions help shed light on the role that travel narratives came to play for the APRA leaders who experienced exile in the 1920s and who returned home in 1930 to organize their movement at the national level from then onward. Upon returning to Peru, APRA exiles took on the habit of telling stories of their recent travels abroad. These travelling stories displayed a symbolic apparatus that implied that roaming foreign lands and exploring distant regions empowered them with rare and arcane knowledge about the world located outside Peru.

One such article cheerfully announced Magda Portal's imminent homecoming in October 1930, favourably insisting on the knowledge she was able to collect on the Americas: "Su ausencia ha sido fecunda y provechosa, pues ha ganado cultura y saber del conocimiento de la propia América."[65] Not only had exile permitted Portal to gain a deeper knowledge of the Americas; this article further argued that, in exile, Portal studied and assimilated European political theories, those very ones, the author stressed, which sheepishly applied to Latin American realities would give negative results. But Portal "ha comprendido a América,"

[62] Víctor Raúl Haya de la Torre, 1931, "Discurso Programa," in *Política Aprista*, Lima: Editorial Cooperativa Aprista Atahualpa, 1933. Two other documents, "Llamamiento a la Nación por el Partido Aprista" and "Manifiesto a la Nación," had appeared earlier that year, in January and February 1931 respectively. These documents began proposing a unified proposal analyses informed with questions of national and regional interests, "Documentos Políticos del Partido Aprista Peruano," *APRA: Órgano del Partido Aprista Peruano*, Lima, March 10, 1931, pp. 3–6.

[63] Mary W. Helms, *Craft and the Kingly Ideal: Art, Trade, and Power*, Austin: University of Texas Press, 1993, p. xi.

[64] Helms, *Craft and the Kingly Ideal*, p. 7. Also see Mary W. Helms, *Ulysses' Sail: An Ethnographic Odyssey of Power, Knowledge, and Geographical Distance*, Princeton, NJ: Princeton University Press, 1988.

[65] [n.d.], "Magda Portal" [newspaper clipping], [1930], Magda Portal Papers, Box 10, Folder 10.10.

insisted the article. "De allí que sea una de nuestras más fervorosas figuras del movimiento antiimperialista y de unionismo continental que el Apra propugna."[66]

Likewise, articles in the *APRA* journal, the mouthpiece of the Peruvian section of APRA, and in various other pro-APRA political flyers that I found in Peruvian archives took pains to publicize the cosmopolitan features of APRA's founding members, associating them with "la gran causa americana" rather than with exclusive Peruvian politics.[67] Appraisals of their capacity for leadership rested on their status as world travellers, able to feel and connect with the rest of the Americas.[68] In this political literature, it was crucial to specify where one had acquired his or her political knowledge since the experience of having lived abroad was allegedly what enabled Apristas to turn the dreams of Reform- students into serious and organized political projects. "Porque en el exterior," explained the APRA leader Manuel Seoane in a conference he gave upon returning to Peru, "viviendo en el estudio de las universidades o de las bibliotecas, y atendiendo a los experimentos sociales de otros pueblos, hemos aprendido el método científico que nos permitirá llegar a la realización de lo que antes era un sueño de románticos."[69]

Other stories sought to demonstrate the success that APRA as a continental movement had gained in the 1920s as a way to promote its cause in Peru. In November 1930, the Peruvian newspaper *Crítica* billed Magda Portal as "uno de los más altos exponentes del MOVIMIENTO APRISTA continental" to welcome her back in Peru.[70] The *APRA* journal similarly celebrated that month the return of the APRA leader Manuel Seoane in

66 "Has understood America." "Hence, she is one of our most fervent figures in the anti-imperialist movement and continental unionism advocated by APRA," ibid.

67 "The great American cause." "Serafín Delmar and Julián Petrovick," *APRA*, Lima, no. 1, October 12, 1930, p. 13.

68 Magda Portal, "Haya de la Torre y José Carlos Mariátegui," *APRA*, no. 2, Lima, October 20, 1930, p. 4; Luis Alberto Sánchez, *Haya de la Torre y el APRA*, Lima: Editorial Universo, 1980 (1954 ed.), p. 206.

69 "Because abroad, living in the study of universities or libraries, and attending to the social experiments of other peoples, we have learned the scientific method that will allow us to achieve the realization of what was previously a romantic dream," as cited in Martín Bergel, "La desmesura revolucionaria: Prácticas intelectuales y cultura del heroísmo en los orígenes del aprismo peruano (1921–1930)," p. 6.

70 "One of the greatest advocate of the continental Aprista movement." "Con Mui Explicable i Placentero Orgullo Saludamos el Retorno de nuestra Gran Poetisa Magda Portal; Uno De Los Mas Altos Exponentes Del MOVIMIENTO APRISTA continental," *Crítica*, November 1930, Lima, Newspaper clipping, Magda Portal Papers, Box 10, Folder 10.10.

light of the international prestige he had secured for himself in Argentina. Read one article: "Todo lo que de representativo tiene la gran nación del Plata en intelectualidad, en lucha, en acción, le ha dado su abrazo de despedida, enviando con él sus mensajes fraternales al pueblo peruano."[71] The display of travel narratives in this case was less about the creative and inner qualities of APRA leaders than about the networks they had built, or the people they had met, during their time in exile. Moreover, they supposed that because intellectuals and civil associations throughout the Americas recognized the merit of the continental APRA, then Peruvians were right to grant their trust to that party.[72]

APRA's strategy of flaunting travel stories in order to gain political prestige in Peru was nothing new in the region. Travel literature was in nineteenth-century Latin America one of the fundamental narratives that shaped reflections on the region's emerging nations.[73] Liberal elites and intellectuals travelled abroad, particularly to France and England, using foreign scenes as a foil to think and reflect upon their own identity.[74] Literary scholar Julio Ramos has specifically linked the United States and Europe to symbolic topographies where heuristic visions befell Latin American travellers. Those who travelled abroad were imbued, he notes, with a capacity to translate experiences accumulated from afar "with the objective of correcting the wrong track of his own tradition."[75] Similarly, Edward Said's work on the role of intellectuals in exile suggests that to think as outsiders from the margins of a given system enables intellectuals to move closer to universality. From spaces of exile, whether geographical or metaphorical, Said argues that intellectuals and artists are more likely to challenge the status quo.[76]

[71] "All that is representative of the great Argentine nation in intellectuality, in struggle, in action, have given him their farewell embrace, sending with him their fraternal messages to the Peruvian people." "El regreso de Manuel A. Seoane," *APRA : Órgano del Frente único de Trabajadores Manuales e Intelectuales, Partido Aprista Peruano*, Lima, no. 5, November 9, 1930, pp. 2, 11.

[72] Arturo Dubra y José Pedro Cordozo, "Los Universitarios del Perú y el Uruguay," *APRA*, Lima, no. 5, November 9, 1930, p. 12. "Pacto revolucionario," *APRA*, Lima, no. 1, October 12, 1930, p. 3.

[73] "Constructing Nations after Independence and Beyond," in Ingrid E. Fey and Karen Racine (eds), *Strange Pilgrimages: Exile, Travel, and National Identity in Latin America, 1800–1990s*, Wilmington: Scholarly Resources Inc., 2000, pp. 1–74.

[74] Julio Ramos, *Divergent Modernitie: Culture and Politics in Nineteenth-Century Latin America*, Durham, NC and London: Duke University Press, 2001, p. 151.

[75] Ibid., p. 153.

[76] Edward W. Said, "Intellectual Exile: Expatriates and Marginals," in *Representations of the Intellectual: The 1993 Reith Lectures*, New York: Pantheon Books, 1994, pp. 49–53;

This is certainly how APRA leaders liked to imagine themselves. Apristas presented their experience of exile and travel as the linchpin of revolutionary action and of nuanced ideological translations able to morph European theories into original Latin American Marxism. In 1930–1931, it wasn't clear exactly what these translations intellectually entailed, but one thing was certain. According to Aprista publications, Apristas were better equipped than sanchecerrista and communists to implement these translations and thus assess the place of Peru in the Americas. Though APRA leaders initially celebrated the military junta of Sanchez Cerro for successfully ousting the Leguía government, by late October of 1930 they contended that because military regimes lacked the capacity to think globally about national problems, the current administration could only offer short-sighted solutions to the complex predicaments that afflicted Peru as a result of the 1929 world economic crisis.[77]

APRA leaders ridiculed their political opponents who lacked their experience abroad. For example, that same month Portal diminished José Carlos Mariátegui for having experienced his intellectual coming of age in Europe rather than in the Americas.[78] Her attack stemmed from the rift that opposed APRA leaders in exile who were close to Haya de la Torre, and those in Peru who sided with Mariátegui and who manned the socialist party of Peru from 1928 onward. These appellations were tainted with pejorative or complimentary tropes depending on the side one favoured. Those who like Magda Portal sided with Haya de la Torre came to position in the urgency of action the condition for vanguard association.[79] This group faulted those who indulged in abstract thinking without daring to mingle with the surrounding world.[80]

In similar fashion, common Aprista attacks launched against the PCP in the early 1930s included reproaching Mariátegui for being overly theoretical and "Europeanist" in his approach to Latin American

Said, "Representations of the Intellectual," in *Representations of the Intellectual*, pp. 3–23.

77 A.G., "Comentario Sobre la Crisis Económica," *APRA*, Lima, no. 2, October 20, 1930, p. 13.

78 Magda Portal, "Haya de la Torre y José Carlos Mariategui," *APRA: Órgano del Frente Único de Trabajadores Manuales e Intelectuales*, Partido Aprista Peruano, Lima, no. 2, October 20, 1930, p. 4.

79 Bergel, "Nomadismo proselitista y revolución," p. 3.

80 Luis Alberto Sánchez, *Waldo Frank in America Hispana*, New York: Instituto de las Españas en los Estados Unidos, 1930, p. 122.

problems.[81] His sedentary lifestyle was partly to blame for this limitation, according to APRA leaders like Portal. Because of significant health problems, Mariátegui was confined to a wheelchair before his early death in 1930, and thus he never had a chance to explore his own country following his homecoming in the mid-1920s. Mariátegui prepared most of his political organizing through letter-writing, as evidenced by the hundreds of letters that he exchanged with allies and political activists in different parts of Peru.[82] Portal suggested that this sedentary lifestyle had hindered Mariátegui's capacity to develop political philosophies indigenous to the Americas. "Obligado por su invalidez a mirar la vida desde un sillón y a través de [sus] lecturas europeas, no podía despojarse del lente europeo para mirar América," noted Portal.[83] This rebuke reflected the views shared by many APRA leaders who had just returned to Peru to organize the Peruvian section of APRA. For APRA leaders who had come of age in exile, the context of creation underlying the production of a political philosophy was in the early 1930s as important, if not more so, than the accuracy of its ideology and social interpretations.

The recruitment of APRA members and sympathizers took on special importance starting in March 1931, after an internal military coup overthrew Sánchez Cerro and installed in his stead a new junta, headed by the Pierolista David Samanez Ocampo and backed by the pro-Aprista Colonel Gustavo Jiménez.[84] Soon after assuming power, the Samanez Ocampo Junta announced its intention to hold elections nationwide in October 1931 and to allow the participation of political parties, with the

[81] Galindo and Burga, *Apogeo y crisis de la republica*, p. 192. These attacks were unwarranted. For one, Mariátegui conducted an project of organization in Peru during the second half of the 1920s. And although the fame of Mariátegui as a prominent intellectual remained somewhat limited up until the 1960s, scholars of revolutionary thought usually concur nowadays in recognizing him as one of the most original Marxist thinkers Latin America has known. Harry E. Vanden, "Mariátegui: Marxismo, Comunismo, and Other Bibliographical Notes," *Latin American Research Review*, 14: 3 (1979): 74; Vanden, "The Peasants as a Revolutionary Class: An Early Latin American View," *Journal of Interamerican Studies and World Affairs*, 20: 2 (May, 1978): 198–199; Thomas Angotti, "The Contributions of José Carlos Mariátegui to Revolutionary Theory," pp. 42–43; Alberto Flores Galindo and Manuel Burga, "La Polémica Haya-Mariategui," *Apogeo y crisis de la republica*, pp. 185–196; Ricardo Melgar Bao, *Mariátegui, Indoamérica y las crisis civilizatorias de Occidente*.

[82] Mariátegui, *Correspondencia*.

[83] "Forced by his disability to look at life from an armchair and through [his] European readings, he could not shed the European lens to look at America," Portal, "Haya de la Torre y José Carlos Mariátegui," p. 4.

[84] Peter F. Klarén, *Peru: Society and Nationhood in the Andes*, New York: Oxford University Press, 2000, p. 269.

exception of the Communist Party. The PAP was allowed to openly take part in Peruvian politics and, for the first time, to pursue state power via democratic means. The Junta also passed a new electoral law, whose long-awaited provisions, including the introduction of the secret ballot and the removal of property qualifications for the right to vote, swelled the number of eligible voters in Peru.[85] Determined to take advantage of this opportunity, PAP organized rapidly. Party leaders in Peru officially named Víctor Raúl Haya de la Torre as the party's presidential candidate and ordered his return to Peru. They likewise put their propaganda activities into overdrive, as notified by the American Consul General in the region of Callao-Lima. "Aprista propaganda is being spread all over Peru," William C. Burdett reported to the State Secretary on March 23, 1931, "and there are several A.P.R.A. offices in Lima and in other cities. There is even a *célula* for women in Lima." Burdett also noted that, according to APRA's headquarters in Lima, "everyone who has joined the A.P.R.A. has become an enthusiastic propagandist."[86]

Crucial to APRA leaders was indeed the conquest of imaginations. They battled for the hearts and minds of the Peruvian people by way of seduction and dramatized portrayals of their movement.[87] Throughout the electoral campaign in view of the October 1931 elections, APRA leaders continued to insist on the value of travel as the premise for ideological accuracy regarding the fate of the Americas, even as the minimum political program focusing on national politics emerged in August 1931. Although the PCP remained outlawed, it continued in its attempts to organize the workers of Peru. The PCP operated from clandestine cells to "infiltrate trade unions and student groups" on one side, and it used the CGTP "to influence and to attempt to take control of the labor movement" on the other, as highlighted by historian Paulo Drinot.[88] The political material that Apristas produced, then, continued to flaunt the formative value of travel and exile as one way to validate their political credentials vis-à-vis their opponents in organizing Peruvian labour. In addition to augmenting and strengthening intellectual capacities, stressed APRA leaders and ideologues, the experience of travel and

[85] Ibid., p. 269; Klarén, *Modernization, Dislocation, and Aprismo: Origins of the Peruvian Aprista Party, 1870–1932*, Austin and London: University of Texas Press, 1973, p. 122.

[86] William C. Burdett to the Secretary of State; March 23, 1931, p. 4; 823.00/626 Aprista; CF, 1930–1939; RG59, NACP.

[87] Alfredo Saco Miro Quesada, *Tiempos de Violencia y Rebeldía*, Lima: OKURA Editores, 1985.

[88] Drinot, "Creole Anti-Communism," p. 712.

exile affected the inner qualities of those who travelled. Exile built character, they noted. It allegedly formed authentic and loyal APRA revolutionaries by testing them with hardships.[89] Another way that APRA leaders bolstered their political authority before the Peruvian workers, and the Peruvian electorate more broadly, still included flaunting their associations with foreign intellectuals and foreign political activists. APRA leaders emphasized, like they had the previous year, their authority as intermediaries between Peru and the rest of the continent by publicizing the web of acquaintances and friendships they had developed and collected during their travels in Latin America. This strategy focused on the creative potential and the political value of individuals rather than on the ideas that they proposed.[90]

WHO'S THE LEADER IN THIS TOWN?

Yet referring to stories of past travels served purposes other than boosting the legitimacy of unknown APRA leaders before the Peruvian people or competing with sanchecerrista and with communists for the trust of the labouring and middle sectors of Peru. This strategy also helped validate the authority of the APRA leaders who had experienced exile vis-à-vis peer colleagues and party followers in Peru. In the national context leading to the October 1931 elections, the travel trope came to the rescue of APRA leaders who had joined the APRA movement in exile and who had contributed to its development in the late 1920s. Once back in Peru, leaders like Magda Portal, Carlos Manuel Cox, Julián Petrovick, and Manuel Seoane integrated the National Executive Committee of the party (Comité Ejecutivo Nacional del PAP) from whence they spearheaded the transition from the continental APRA to the Peruvian APRA party (PAP) in Peru and prepared for the 1931 elections. They did so amidst a context in which they had to fight not only against political enemies to seduce the

[89] "Llego ayer Oscar Herrera después de seis años de destierro," Lima, *La Tribuna*, no. 105, August 26, 1931, p. 4. "Como se considera en el extranjero la personalidad e Haya de La Torre y su programa político, "(*The New York Herald Tribune*, August 2, 1931)," Lima, *La Tribuna*, no. 106, August 27, 1931, p. 6. William C. Burdett to Secretary of State; "Haya de la Torre, Peruvian Radical Leader," Callao-Lima, Peru, October 27, 1930, p. 4-5; 810.43 A.P.R.A./1; CF, 1930–1939; RG59; NACP.

[90] "Nos hace interesantes declaraciones el c. Manuel Vásquez Díaz sobre el Aprismo en México; su actuación en el Congreso Iberoamericano de Estudiantes y la repercusión de la dictadura sanchizta en la República Mexicana," *La Tribuna*, Lima, August 27, 1931, p. 3; Julio Cuadros Caldas, "Por la candidatura de Haya de la Torre a la presidencia del Perú," *APRA*, Segunda época, no. 3, Lima, March 18, 1931, p. 5.

Peruvian people, but also within their own party structures to make sure they were the ones in control of their fast-growing movement. In addition to introducing the APRA party to the Peruvian population, then, stories of past travels and exile served as an instrument of political control within the party itself.

Traditional scholarship on the APRA has contributed to the widespread but misguided belief that the Peruvian APRA party was an organized and disciplined entity from its inception onward. Many scholars have often incorrectly reproduced official histories regarding the control that Haya de la Torre allegedly exerted over the rank and file of the party from the foundation of the Peruvian section of the APRA from 1930 onward. The process of transition from APRA to PAP in 1930–1931 was in fact fraught with internal struggles, where competing factions jockeyed for leadership of the movement and wrestled to impose specific political orientations on the PAP. In the early 1930s, conflict between Apristas usually stemmed from tactical disagreements over how to take power. The executive committee of the party based in Lima advocated legal means of action to take power – the democracy they wanted for Peru, argued its members, necessarily had to rise from democratic means of action. In contrast, other factions of the Peruvian APRA, specifically on the northern coast of Peru, were inclined to choose violence over democracy to bring about the promised social revolution. This tension between using violence or legal means of action would continue to seep through APRA during most of the 1930s and 1940s, as shown by the literature on the subject.[91]

Yet the scholarship has failed to acknowledge beyond the rift opposing Haya de la Torre to Mariátegui just how much personal squabbles were also very often the cause of internal conflict in PAP. This was the case in the petty conflict that opposed (in the month prior to the October 1931 elections) two second-tier leaders of the PAP in Tumbes, a city located in northwestern Peru. This particular quarrel is instructive for my argument, for it touches on the intricate task of harmonizing the views and interests of a vast array of Apristas whose life experiences and political perspectives seldom squared with one another. As such, casting a spotlight on the feud between the Apristas Alfredo Perla Lapoint and Javier Valera aims to

[91] Nelson Manrique, *"¡Usted Fue Aprista!"* Bases para una historia critica del APRA. Lima: Fondo editorial PUCP, 2009; Víctor Villanueva, *El APRA en busca del poder, 1930–1940*, Lima: Editorial Horizonte, 1975.

showcase how references to persecution and exile helped reaffirm one's authority vis-à-vis party mavericks or pugnacious peers.

The respective life experiences of the Apristas involved in the conflict, Alfredo Perla Lapoint and Javier Valera, were drastically different, and so were their reasons for joining the PAP. Lapoint was young and had suffered repression under the Leguía government. His loyalty to PAP stemmed from his involvement with the continental APRA in the course of the 1920s. After six years of exile, Lapoint returned to Peru in 1930 and, like many of his peers at the time, established himself in the Peruvian capital. There, he worked as a journalist, writing articles in Peruvian newspapers to make a living. Lapoint revolved around the executive committee of the party based in Lima, but he wasn't officially part of it, which explains why the official history of APRA has not recorded his name. In contrast, Valera had never experienced persecution, let alone political exile. A middle-aged professional from the northern Department of Tumbes, his adhesion to APRA happened in Peru. Although less is known about Valera, archival evidence suggests he joined the party in 1931, soon after the foundation of the PAP.

Shortly before the conflict between them began, the Central Committee of Lima (Comité Central de Lima) had commissioned Lapoint to travel to the Department of Junín, in the central highlands of Peru, to begin propaganda work among the local population in view of the 1931 elections. Lapoint was then transferred to the neighbouring city of Huánuco, and then to the northern Departments of Ancash, Lambayeque, and Piura shortly thereafter, each time with the mandate to begin organizing local sections of the party or help new affiliates mount support for *Aprismo*.[92] Tumbes came last. There, Lapoint was so startled by the level of disorganization and by how steep intrigues ran in the local PAP that he felt compelled to report the case to the Central Committee back in Lima.[93] Lapoint blamed Valera for the mess that he witnessed in the region, "el que debía dar ejemplo de integridad, de abierto desinterés," he wrote in reference to the local leader Valera, but who had instead led the party in Tumbes astray. What remained of the PAP in Tumbes was, according to Lapoint, bogged down in divisions and "consumido por las ambiciones,

[92] Alfredo Perla Lapoint to Señor Doctor Don Javier Valera, Tumbes, September 18, 1931, Archivo General del la Nación, Perú (hereafter cited as AGN), Ministerio de Interior, Dirección de gobierno, Prefectura de Lima, Presos Políticos y Sociales, Legajo 3.9.5.1.15.1.14.3 (1932).

[93] Ibid.

por las bajas pasiones."[94] Valera quickly retaliated. He accused Lapoint of an offence whose nature remains unknown. But, as evidenced by the defence that Lapoint mounted for himself before the Central Committee of Lima as well as before Javier Valera, the attack coming from Tumbes inflicted a heavy blow to his reputation.

Evidently, Lapoint felt compelled to justify his credentials before provincial Apristas. The way he did it is instructive to understand how references to travel abroad and to political exile provided symbolic capital within the party itself. Lapoint started by inferring that part of his authority derived from the fact that the Comité Central de Lima had specifically commissioned him to do militant work in Tumbes. More importantly, Lapoint underscored his years passed in exile as a token of his selfless devotion to the party. "Nosotros los soldados fundadores del aprismo," he told Valera, in reference to those, who according to his letter, suffered persecution at the hands of tyrants, served prison sentences in foreign prisons, and would never dare use the cause of *Aprismo* to advance a political career. "Nuestras luchas eran y son abnegadas," he concluded, for "en el corazón del auténtico aprista [no] cabe la ambición personalista."[95]

That Lapoint took pains to highlight his status as a founding member of APRA was intended to dwarf the legitimacy of his rival in Tumbes, a newcomer to aprismo in Peru. His repeated reference to past travels and injustices suffered abroad sought to enhance the prestige that Lapoint allegedly drew from his position as a long-standing militant. Lapoint had seen worse, he claimed, much worse. Yet never had his faith in APRA wavered: "Es muy difícil Dr.," he warned Valera, "destruir un prestigio creado a la sombra del sacrificio, lealtad, integridad y desprendimiento puesto a toda prueba."[96] In addition to casting Lapoint, a Lima-based leader who meddled in local politics, as an outsider within his own political movement in Tumbes, the content of his defence speech evidences the inevitability in APRA of jostling for peer validation. Party leaders routinely had to negotiate the right to belong to the PAP, depending on where they stayed or with whom they did political work. Likewise, during most of the 1930s, and to be fair throughout its history

[94] "The one who should set an example of integrity, of open disinterest." "Consumed by ambitions, by low passions," ibid.

[95] "We, the founding soldiers of Aprismo." "Our struggles were and are self-sacrificing, in the heart of the authentic Apristas there is [no] room for personalistic ambition," ibid.

[96] "It is very difficult, Dr., to destroy a reputation created in the shadow of sacrifice, loyalty, integrity and disinterest put to the test," ibid.

from the mid-1920s onward, different APRA leaders had to validate their authority to define what exactly the PAP was about. In this particular case, alluding to a regime of past travels and suffering helped Lapoint distinguish "true" Apristas like himself, from opportunists like Valera who ostensibly saw in the PAP little more than a chance to boost their political career. In Lapoint's defence speech, it was precisely the experience of exile and persecution that gave meaning to his relationship to *Aprismo*. The lived experience of exile also defined the most intrinsic values of a good Aprista: those of abnegation and self-devotion.

ASSESSING CONTROL OF THE LIMA-BASED LEADERSHIP

As an instrument of political control within the party, stories of past travels and exile also helped APRA leaders based in Lima cope with Peru's manifold regional differences. In the political material that it disseminated around the country, the party leadership based in Lima voiced time and again the urgency to reject models that came from Europe – Spain and France in particular – and replace them with a democratic system in tune with Peruvian realities. Editorials in *APRA* and *La Tribuna* conjured up the betrayal that Peruvians had suffered twice: first with the conquest of the Americas by the Spaniards in the fifteenth and sixteenth centuries, then with the onset of the Republican era, from the early nineteenth century onward. These texts argued that Peru had inherited systems of law and governance and state institutions completely foreign to its reality. The importation of liberal democracy had failed the Peruvian people, explained APRA ideologues. It had served the interests of a restricted minority for too long. Now was the time to devise an original democracy: a democracy crafted by the Peruvian people, for the Peruvian people.[97]

This discourse of inclusion and democracy that APRA leaders put forth in their electoral campaign bore fruit in many different regions of the country. Peruvians were seduced by what they heard at public rallies or read in pro-APRA material. The intensity with which the second generation of APRA leaders, who like Victor Villanueva and Andrés Townsend Ezcurra joined the PAP in the early 1930s when they were teenagers, remembers these first, life-changing encounters with *Aprismo* via in the pages of the newfound *APRA* journal gestures to the success of the party's

[97] See, for example, "El Programa Analítico del Aprismo," *APRA*, Lima, no. 4, August 8, 1931, p. 1.

proselytizing discourse. Villanueva and Townsend Ezcurra similarly recall in their memoirs being in thrall to the articles they read in the *APRA*, and to APRA's political proposals more broadly, for these bore the promise of something new, something worth thinking about.[98]

Particularly heartening for the growing rank and files of PAP was the fact that they were asked to partake in the design of the party's program and structure. To that effect, calls for public participation in the design of *Aprismo* published in the *APRA* journal and in *La Tribuna* summoned up the image of an executive committee willing to hear out its members. APRA leaders based in Lima repeatedly asked in *La Tribuna* that their fellow citizens help them wrest politics from common political imaginaries.[99] Organizing Aprista forces nationwide by way of associations of different shapes and sizes, including committees, unions, cells, and professional associations, appeared to grant the promised flexibility so that Peruvians could carve out their own understanding of aprismo.[100] On the surface, then, party structures began to develop and expand in ways that reflected the discourse of democratic inclusion found in Aprista publications. This position on democratic party structures furthermore squared very well with another, where PAP emphasized the need to decentralize the Peruvian administration and devolve more executive power to municipalities.[101]

It looked only logical, then, that the leadership in Lima would want their actions to reflect their words. Except they did not. There was a fundamental contradiction in the party leadership based in Lima between a discourse of democracy and inclusion on one side, and a practice of provincial exclusion on the other. The band of APRA leaders who had experienced exile and established their headquarters in Lima reproduced the Lima-centric politics that determined the history of Republican Peru.

98 Andrés Townsend Ezcurra, *50 Años de aprismo: Memorias, Ensayos y Discursos de un Militante*, Lima: Editorial DESA, 1989, p. 34–35; Villanueva and Macera, *Arrogante Montonero*, pp. 46–55.

99 Small Aprista cells and Aprista sections blossomed all over the map of Peru. During the summer of 1931, a column in *La Tribuna* entitled "Actividades Apristas" reported on the rapid growth and the expanding activities of regional Aprista cells. Doing so gave the impression of a decentralized party administration. "Actividades Apristas," *La Tribuna*, Lima, July 31, 1931, p. 7.

100 "Citación," *La Tribuna*, no. 81, Lima, August 3, 1931, p. 2.

101 Manuel Seoane, "Nuestro Anticentralismo," *APRA*, Segunda Época, no. 1, Lima, March 10, 1931, p. 14; Luis Eduardo Enríquez, "Los Apristas somos regionalistas y anticentralistas," *APRA*, Segunda Época, no. 1, Lima, March 10, 1931, p. 13; "Democracia funcional," *La Tribuna*, no. 81, Lima, August 3, 1931, p. 1.

They walked a fine line between acknowledging the importance of members outside the capital while at the same time finding ways to retain control over the party.

The rising popularity of the PAP nationwide, and more especially in the northern coast of Peru though not exclusively, as the work of Jaymie Heilman has begun to disclose, had been creating unexpected headaches for those located in Lima, most of whom had either joined APRA or participated in its foundation in exile.[102] Because the Lima-based executive committee of PAP was the nerve centre that oversaw the institutionalization of *Aprismo* at the national level, provincial committees were expected to follow its instructions.[103] On March 14, 1931, a boxed text section in the *APRA* journal reminded party members that the only section of the APRA leadership that was entitled to authorize their initiatives was the one whose headquarters were located in Lima. Any other factions who claimed to exert leadership in the PAP, they stressed, were rebels that party members should dodge:

> Como una forma de ejercer un efectivo control sobre las fuerzas con que cuenta el aprismo, y para evitar que elementos revoltosos, aprovechen de la popularidad de nuestro partido y del nombre de nuestro Jefe, Haya Delatorre [sic], para cometer escándalos, rogamos a todos los compañeros apristas y a los simpatizantes que para efectuar manifestaciones públicas se pongan de acuerdo primero con la Directiva del Partido, que funciona en Belén 1065.[104]

In many ways, these APRA leaders became victims of their own success. The PAP grew too fast for the handful of leaders back from exile to maintain the control they wanted to exert. That the direction of the party, or more specifically those who manned the executive committee based in

102 Jaymie Patricia Heilman, "We Will No Longer Be Servile: Aprismo in 1930s Ayacucho," *Journal of Latin American Studies*, 38 (2006): 491–518.

103 Alfredo Perla Lapoint to Señor Doctor Don Javier Valera, Tumbes, September 18, 1931, AGN, Prefectura de Lima, 3.9.5.1.15.1.14.3; "Anoche en el salón Agurto, tuvo lugar un recital poético-literario por los apristas Dr. Francisco Mendoza Calle y por el líder Alfredo Perla Lapoint," *El corresponsal*, Chucalanas, [1931], AGN, Prefectura de Lima, 3.9.5.1.15.1.14.3. The relationship between the Central Committee of Lima and regional committees of PAP is understudied. More research is necessary to fully understand how the relations it established with provincial committees worked.

104 "To exercise effective control over the forces of the Aprismo, and to prevent unruly elements from taking advantage of the popularity of our party and of the name of our Chief, Haya Delatorre [*sic*], to commit scandals, we ask that all Aprista comrades and sympathizers who want to carry out public demonstrations that they first agree with the Party Directive, which operates in Belén 1065." "A todos los afiliados y simpatizantes del Partido Aprista peruano," *APRA*, Lima, Segunda Época, no. 2, March 14, 1931, p. 5.

Lima, felt compelled to reiterate who was in control of coordinating the different sections of its organization points to this section's lack of hegemony within the party. The northern section of PAP, headed by the Comité del Primer Sector del Norte del Partido Aprista Peruano, was particularly problematic for them, as it was wielding increasing influence in the Departments of Cajamarca, Lambayeque and La Libertad.[105] As provincial members began to push forward to adapt the party to their own demands, heeding the voice and demands of these provincial Apristas while at the same time retaining control over the party demanded careful planning. The way in which the First Aprista National Congress, an event organized by the executive committee of the party in August 1931, displayed a discourse of inclusion while making sure that only the APRA leadership associated with the experience of exile made executive decisions brings home this point.

Soon after returning to Peru in 1930, the handful of APRA leaders established in Lima had promised to bring together what they called the "vanguard elements" of Peru in order to develop in a collaborative effort "un programa nacionalista revolucionario de acción política," fit to solve problems particular to the Peruvian reality.[106] The provisional executive committee of PAP promised to hold a congress to that effect, but significantly, only when all APRA exiles had returned to the country.[107] If they were to gather together the "vanguard" forces of Peru, surely those who then manned the Peruvian section of APRA wanted to wait for their friends to return. This homecoming took quite a while to be completed – over a year, in fact, for it was expensive to sponsor the return of all APRA exiles and the new PAP lacked the funds to proceed rapidly.[108]

When the National Congress finally opened in Lima on August 10, 1931, the advertised goal was still to devise a pragmatic political program that best served the Peruvian people.[109] APRA leaders who manned the executive committee of the party held on to their discourse of national

105 This committee was based in Trujillo and comprised the following APRA members: Carlos C. Godoy, Federico Chávez, R. J. A. Haya de la Torre, Francisco Dañino Ribatto, Manuel J. Arévalo, Manuel V. Barreto, Alfredo Rebaza Acosta, Américo Pérez Treviño, Pedro G. Lizazaburu and Fernando Cárdenas. *APRA*, Lima, Segunda época, no. 3, March 18, 1931, p. 13.

106 "a revolutionary nationalist program of political action." [Boxed text], *APRA*, no. 1, Lima, October 12, 1930, p. 13.

107 Ibid., p. 13.

108 William C. Burdett to the Secretary of State; March 23, 1931, p. 4; 823.00/626 Aprista; CF, 1930–1939; RG59, NACP.

109 "El Programa Analítico del Aprismo," *APRA*, Lima, no. 4, August 8, 1931, p. 1.

inclusion, asking that local Aprista congresses participate in the elaboration of the Aprista political program. They claimed to want popular input into the design of their national program, for they recognized their lack of knowledge about many of the local scenes. "Tenemos demasiado respeto por el pueblo," read one passage of the *APRA* special issue of August 1931 on the political program of *Aprismo*, "para adjudicarnos, un grupito de lideres, el derecho de legislar sobre las necesidades de todas y cada una de las provincias, de las cuales desconocemos hasta la real ubicación geográfica."[110] These APRA leaders also felt, more pragmatically, that they needed the backing of the regional factions of the PAP if they were to ever claim legitimately that their party represented all of Peru.[111] According to the party leadership in Lima, this call to collaboration proved that they were not intent on devising impossible utopias while conversing in coffee shops. Rather, theirs would be a realistic and scientific political program that stemmed from the consideration of the Peruvian people, as their political discourse promised.[112] The plan was simple: regional congresses first brainstormed, and the National Congress held in Lima subsequently heeded regional proposals, sorted them out, and finally harmonized them into a single and realist program of political action.

But the promise of regional participation was harder to achieve in reality than in discourse. For one, provincial delegates were asked to either travel to the capital or entrust representatives who already lived in Lima with instructions as they partook in the National Congress.[113] This entailed provincial Apristas having access to resources, such as travelling money or time off from work, which they did not have. Then came the question of who in the party was entitled to speak during the panels. According to reports in *La Tribuna*, only members of the CEN, including Magda Portal, Carlos Manuel Cox, Julián Petrovick, Manuel Seoane, or Arturo Sabroso – in short, members of the Lima-based executive committee – appeared to have had the right to take the floor during the event.[114] All of them had experienced exile. All of them recognized

110 "We have too much respect for the people, to give ourselves, a small group of leaders, the right to legislate on the needs of each and every one of the provinces, of which we do not even know the real geographic location," ibid., p. 2.

111 Ibid., p. 1.

112 Ibid., pp. 1–2.

113 Ibid., p. 2.

114 "Más de 1500 personas asistieron a la sesión de inauguración del primer Congreso Nacional Aprista," *La Tribuna*, Lima, August 11, 1931, p. 1.

each other's value and legitimacy by way of the persecution and travel they had undergone in the past. To retain control over the organization of party infrastructure was challenging. The travel trope assisted members of the National Executive Committee of PAP in this task. In effect, except for the calls for collaboration uttered in view of the First Aprista National Congress, true and authentic leaders of APRA continued to be associated in these journals with the experience of travel and exile not only in 1930 but also all through 1931 as well.

The APRA leaders who manned or revolved around the CEN of PAP were the only ones entitled to define what, in the end, the Peruvian APRA party was truly about. If all were sometimes asked to give opinions, the travelled actors designed who was entitled to make decisions in the end. Besides, the party leadership in Lima had one major advantage over those who disagreed with its precepts. It benefited from access to resources that others in the party lacked. Because it controlled the board of direction of *La Tribuna* and the *APRA* journal, the Lima-based executive committee of PAP was the only one with the capacity to call official convocations of provincial offspring of the party and coordinate the activities of Aprista members nationwide. It also controlled the distribution of propaganda around Peru. Likewise, sending APRA organizers, such as Perla Lapoint, from Lima into the countryside equipped party leaders based in Lima with an informal surveillance system to rein in local initiatives and ensure that the development of Aprismo in Peru remained consistent with the vision they had for the PAP. This vision put forth travel and exile as the prime condition of original critical thinkers and authentic Apristas.

CONCLUSION

Chapter 3 deepened our understanding of the ways in which a regime of authority associated with travel abroad, particularly though not exclusively in the Americas, assisted in the late 1920s and early 1930s the APRA leadership who had come of age in exile. Here, the experience of exile was used rhetorically as an instrument of political power and persuasion. Stories of travels in Europe and the Americas helped these leaders to assert their political legitimacy and expertise vis-à-vis their peers who had stayed in Peru during the 1920s, especially from those who openly embraced socialism from 1928 onward. Once returned to Peru and trying to build up APRA from a political activism group to a political party, the Apristas who experienced exile sought to validate their authority before Peruvian audiences through associations with foreign contacts. They also played up their travels abroad to establish their distinction and legitimacy vis-à-vis new recruits to the party as well as socialist peers.

The APRA leaders who began organizing the Peruvian section of APRA suggested in their proselytizing material that because the Peruvian social and political realities were intimately connected with those of their sister republics in the Americas, the development of a continental consciousness was consequently the fulcrum around which Peruvians should envision their place in the world and design accurate political solutions to the problems that plagued their nation.[115] The creation of the Peruvian self, in other words, passed for Apristas through increased hemispheric consciousness. What mattered most, at the time, was less to define the Americas in a new way than to incite Peruvians to identify with this geographic body. This partly explains why the use of Indo-América to name Latin America remained mostly thin on the ground. There was furthermore very little time for creative intellectual work as Apristas campaigned across the country.

But boast about their grasp of the Americas they did. In the face of socialist peers who explained class struggles to the Peruvian population, the APRA positioned its expertise as one that relied on its complementary understanding of Latin American and imperialist realities, specifically its capacity to translate them for a Peruvian public. The political material they produced to proselytize their movement to the Peruvian people argued that, although most of APRA's leaders had not been living in Peru, the legitimacy of their political credentials, as well as their capacity to propose to Peruvians a revolutionary and authentic nationalism, rested precisely on the experiences gained while travelling around the Americas. These experiences had allegedly transformed Apristas into foreign experts bestowed with the intellectual capacity to translate to a Peruvian audience what they had learned and witnessed in Latin America during their travels abroad. These conclusions bring us back to the ongoing tension between nationalism and internationalism in the history of APRA; as the movement entered its populist phase, APRA's growing nationalism was cropping out from its early internationalism. In 1930–1931, more important

[115] APRA Sección Peruana, *APRA*, no. 1, Lima, October 12, 1930, 1.

than the content or accuracy of their ideological translation, however, was the validation of their authority as enlightened translators. The return in 1932 of unabashed persecution against Apristas only strengthened these positions, as APRA leaders continued to vie for survival and political control of their disbanded movement.

4

Life and Freedom for Víctor Raúl Haya de la Torre: Surviving Chaos in the Peruvian APRA Party, 1932–1933

On the night of August 22, 1932, a patrolman apprehended Manuel Villalobos Hihuayin as he meandered down "Veinte de Septiembre" street in Lima. Villalobos reeked of liquor. Thirty-two years old, Villalobos was originally from the northern province of Chiclayo. He was single and eked a living from construction jobs he contracted here and there. It was quite plausible that his habits included enjoying a few drinks at the local *pulpería* after a long day of work. This time, though, Villalobos was completely drunk. That he drank too much did not represent an offence to public order per se, but it did get him into trouble that night.[1] According to a police report filed three days later, Villalobos' crime consisted of having given "vivas al Apra," to which accusation he retorted having no recollection of what he did or said that night. But, even as the suspect denied any allegiance to the Peruvian APRA party (PAP) or to any other political group, and though Villalobos confessed to being so inebriated the night of his arrest that he neared unconsciousness, Peruvian authorities turned a deaf ear to his plea of innocence. Villalobos was charged with subversive activities and condemned to thirty days in prison.[2]

Earlier that year, police officers detained Jorge Alzamora for similar reasons. He spent two weeks in prison after the prefecture of Lima found him guilty of having publicly professed comments favourable to the cause

[1] Sub-prefectura to Prefectura de Lima, September 2, 1932 AGN, Ministerio de Interior, Dirección de gobierno, Prefectura de Lima, Presos Políticos y Sociales, Legajo 3.9.5.1.15.1.14.3 (1932).

[2] "Long live APRA," ibid.

of APRA.[3] Similarly, on July 12, 1932, Antero Muñoz was caught distributing political fliers, deemed subversive, to passers-by in Lima. The following month, Muñoz, who had confessed to his membership in PAP, was condemned to 180 days in jail.[4] On July 14, 1932, a certain Don José Loaiza denounced to his neighbourhood superintendent of Chorrillos the seditious activities conducted by Aprista Moises Morales. Although Loaiza's deposition brimmed with cracks and approximations, Morales was nonetheless taken into custody shortly thereafter.[5] The same happened to Aprista Carlos Alberto Izaguirre Alzamora and his brother Julio, both arrested in August 1932 at their home on charges of possession of subversive propaganda. Similar fates were suffered by the employees of the Hermanos Faura printing house: Eugenio Asencio Moscol, Orlando Vásquez Solano, Alberto Zuzunaga Effio, Victoriano Gonzáles Trochou, Emilio Espinoza Landaberi and Alfonso Abad Navas. The courts indicted the printers for clandestinely running off Aprista material.[6]

These actors were all abruptly detained and brought to stand before biased trials, where the whims of a few clerks were tantamount to the rule of law. The archives of the Peruvian Ministry of the Interior in 1932–1933 are full of similar cases. The Emergency Law, instigated in February 1932 by the government of Luis Miguel Sánchez Cerro, contained strict and dire provisions regarding the fate of political dissidents.[7] It thwarted freedom of expression. It allowed police forces to apprehend and incarcerate those who "disobeyed," namely Peruvian citizens suspected of Communist or Aprista affiliations. As such, the episodes of arbitrary arrests above reflect a much larger, and grimmer reality of prevailing state persecution in Peru. They signify the climate of fear and suspicion that the Sánchez Cerro government sought to instill among the

[3] "CF. No. 484 – Remite al detenido Aprista J. Alzamore," Prefectura de Lima, March 15, 1932–1939 April 1932, AGN, Ministerio de Interior, Legajo 3.9.5.1.15.1.14.7 (1932–1942).

[4] Cuerpo de investigación y vigilancia, Lima, July 13, 1932, AGN, Ministerio de Interior, Legajo 3.9.5.1.15.1.14.3 (1932). Sub-prefectura to Prefectura de Lima, August 9, 1932, AGN, Ministerio de Interior, Legajo 3.9.5.1.15.1.14.3 (1932).

[5] Cuerpo de investigación, Sección Chorrillos to Jefe General de Investigación, Chorrillos, July 15, 1932, AGN, Ministerio de Interior, Legajo 3.9.5.1.15.1.14.3 (1932).

[6] Cuerpo de investigación y vigilancia, Lima, August 29, 1932, AGN, Ministerio de Interior, Legajo 3.9.5.1.15.1.14.3 (1932). Prefectura de Lima, 19 October 1932, AGN, Ministerio de Interior, Legajo 3.9.5.1.15.1.14.3 (1932).

[7] Peter F. Klarén, *Modernization, Dislocation, and Aprismo: Origins of the Peruvian Aprista Party, 1870–1932*, Austin and London: University of Texas Press, 1973, p. 138.

Peruvian population. The preserve of national order had its price, according to military officers. In 1932, any excuse, any inkling of dissent became a reason to cart off potential agitators. These episodes of arbitrary arrests also point, more specifically, to an oppressive surveillance apparatus that rendered political organization for PAP particularly difficult following the presidential election of October 1931.

Chapter 4 studies the consequences that the return of full-fledged persecution in 1932–1933 had on the political capacities of PAP. When analysing the growth of the populist APRA in the early 1930s, scholars seldom consider the extent to which repression limited the party's political capacities in terms of internal cohesion and intellectual production. Yet the return of state repression in Peru following the 1931 election and the victory of Sánchez Cerro over PAP's presidential candidate threw the young party in disarray, leaving the door wide open for internal struggles to fester. The simultaneous experiences of persecution and exile in the early 1930s and of political contests to control the rank-and-file of the party, I suggest, pressed upon the Aprista community, and more specifically upon the Hayista faction within that community, the necessity to cling to a discourse of Latin American solidarity to ensure political survival in Peru. The underlying tensions between the local and the global analyzed in this chapter, then, shed light on the crucial interplay between APRA's experience of international solidarity work and the coordination of political struggles within the movement itself. Latin American solidarity for *Aprismo* was not just an idea to be debated. Before anything else, Latin American solidarity was a question of survival. It was a plan, a practice to be set in motion in order to defy the creole oligarchy within the nation.

Chapter 4 more specifically details how being connected to the outside world supplied to the Hayista faction two crucial political advantages as it vied for survival. For one, the APRA leaders who had experienced exile in the 1920s and who were deported in the early 1930s had access to transnational solidarity networks that others in the party lacked. Following the arrest of Víctor Raúl Haya de la Torre in May of 1932, as this chapter explains, a number of foreign allies organized a movement of solidarity with PAP. Their cross-border calls for a new democratic order in the Americas took Haya de la Torre as a symbol of their fight against both right-wing dictatorships and communism. The Hayista faction used this solidarity campaign to their advantage, wagering on the publicity that a pro-democratic international public opinion afforded to PAP. Hence, in addition to providing access to external resources, international connections gave the Hayista faction the opportunity to acquire symbolic capital. They disseminated in Peru stories of APRA's international connections and reputation, much like they had two years earlier as described in Chapter 3. However, by 1933 this discourse of international prestige and connections was conspicuously associated with the figure of a single leader: Víctor Raúl Haya de la Torre. By publicizing the international fame of Haya de la Torre, the Hayista faction bolstered the legitimacy of PAP before Peruvians and simultaneously asserted the faction's leadership within PAP's rank-and-file. Internationalism and trans-American solidarity, this chapter makes plain, prompted the Peruvian APRA's rise as a populist movement from the 1930s onward.

PERSECUTION AND THE DISMANTLING OF PAP

The new wave of political repression launched against PAP in 1932–1933 originated in Peru's presidential elections in October 1931. The official count declared majority for Sánchez Cerro, who had won with 50.7 percent of the votes. His main opponent, the presidential candidate for PAP, Víctor Raúl Haya de la Torre, came second with 34.5 percent of the votes.[8] PAP immediately decried the legitimacy of Sánchez Cerro as president of Peru. The party argued that fraud had tarnished the electoral process, a claim not entirely ludicrous given the country's past history of electoral frauds but persuasively debunked by the scholarship since.[9] On December 8, 1931, on the day of Sánchez Cerro's inauguration, Haya de la Torre rebuffed the latter as president and declared himself the only true and moral leader of Peru.[10]

As a result of PAP's refusal to comply with the electoral results, confrontations between governmental forces and APRA followers escalated rapidly. Apristas called for general strikes and organized large demonstrations in the streets of Lima to dispute Sánchez Cerro's victory.[11] Meanwhile, in the northern part of the country, where PAP had collected the majority of its votes, feelings of resentment translated into political

[8] Steve Stein, *Populism in Peru: The Emergence of the Masses and the Politics of Social Control*, Madison: The University of Wisconsin Press, 1980, p. 189.

[9] Ibid., pp. 189–196.

[10] Víctor Raúl Haya de la Torre, 1931, "Discurso contra la fraude y la tiranía," in *Antología del pensamiento político de Haya de la Torre*, ed. Andrés Townsend Ezcurra, Lima: Biblioteca Nacional del Perú, 1995, pp. 30–32.

[11] See diplomatic reports in Folder 2, Box 4696, Central Files, Record Group 59 (RG 59), 1930–1939, US National Archives at College Park, College Park, MD (NACP).

action. A series of face-offs broke out between small farmers and local authorities.[12] Rumours soon spread that PAP was organizing a revolutionary uprising and that party affiliates would not hesitate to resort to force and bloodshed, if need be, to take power and establish Haya de la Torre as president of Peru.[13] The Peruvian government retaliated with a series of counter-revolutionary actions that aimed to quell aprista opposition. Sánchez Cerro passed a decree in November 1931 that prohibited all public meetings and demonstrations by political parties. Three months later, the Congress approved the Emergency Law that the government had designed to restore order in the country. This law suspended personal liberties and brought the level of persecution against PAP to new heights with the arrest and exile of twenty-three Aprista congressmen. By May 13, 1932, eight party leaders had been executed, twenty-six sentenced to prison, and thirty-seven more deported to Chile.[14] It was this context that explained the many arrests described in the introduction of this chapter.

State persecution deeply affected PAP's ability to operate as a viable and effective political organization.[15] Failing to reckon with this grim reality risks replicating the widespread but misguided belief that PAP was an organized and highly disciplined entity from its inception in 1930 onward. As we shall see, this wasn't the case. The experience of ongoing repression created a number of hurdles that shaped APRA's complex and unsteady growth as an anti-imperialist and populist political movement.

For one, renewed repression in Peru made the task of educating inexperienced APRA militants more difficult. During an interview with the US ambassador Fred Morris Dearing in January 1932, Haya de la Torre acknowledged the hurdles that he faced when teaching ideological tenets of APRA to the party's rank-and-file in Peru. Haya de la Torre maintained that party members "felt the rightness of the Party's aim," but yet the

[12] Klarén, *Modernization, Dislocation, and Aprismo*, p. 137.

[13] See diplomatic reports in Folder 2, Box 4696, RG 59, 1930–1939, NACP.

[14] [Unknown author] to AMG, Lima, May 13th, 1932, Wayne State University, Detroit, Walter P. Reuther Library, Archives of Labor and Urban Affairs, AMGC, series 2, box 2, folder 2.15. Klarén, *Modernization, Dislocation, and Aprismo*, p. 138.

[15] Scholars are more interested in the emotional impacts of persecution than on its political implications. See for example Juan Aguilar Derpich, *Catacumbas del APRA: Vivencia y testimonios de su clandestinidad*, Lima: Ediciones del recuerdo, 1984, pp. 58–59 and Thomas M. Davies, *Indian Integration in Peru: A Half Century of Experience, 1900–1948*, Lincoln, NE: University of Nebraska Press, 1974, p. 113.

party faced "a long and tedious road to follow to bring the rank and file up to an understanding of the Party's aims."[16] This passage confirms, on the one hand, the difficulty of adapting an ideology first conceived from afar to the everyday concerns and aspirations of the Peruvian people. Yet it also suggests that attempting to do so in a context where APRA followers were busier staying out of jail than engaging in serious reflection was close to impossible.

Additionally, political repression exacerbated latent problems of party directions, noticeable even to outside observers. US diplomatic reports hint at the lack of clear leadership in PAP in 1932. According to one such report, penned by Fred Morris Dearing in February of that year, simmering tensions between factions of APRA appeared likely to explode. Ambassador Dearing stressed the lack of control that Aprista leaders had over some sections of the APRA party. He wrote in his report, "above all Haya de la Torre's central problem [is] that of controlling and reforming his lieutenants and party members can only be accomplished slowly."[17] The arrest and trial of Haya de la Torre on May 6, 1932, followed shortly after by the failed revolutionary uprising in Trujillo, only served to compound the situation.[18] On 7 July 1932, a group of APRA militants captured the northern city of Trujillo in an attempt to launch an insurrectionary war against the Sánchez Cerro dictatorship.[19] Those who participated in the uprising, a group opposed to the Hayista and pro-democratic faction, argued that violence had become necessary to oppose the persecution of APRA and to rise to power in Peru.[20] Instead of marking the beginning of a national revolution, as APRA rebels had envisioned, this

[16] Fred Morris Dearing, Embassy of the United States of America, to the Secretary of State, Lima, January 6, 1932, Folder 3, Box 4696, RG 59, 1930–1939, NACP.

[17] Dearing to the Secretary of State, Lima, February 21, 1932, Folder 3, Box 4696, RG 59, 1930–1939, NACP.

[18] "Víctor Raúl Haya de la Torre fue apresado esta mañana en Miraflores," *Última Hora*, Lima, May 6, 1932. Klarén, *Modernization, Dislocation, and Aprismo*, p. 141.

[19] Iñigo García-Bryce wrote one of the best accounts on the Trujillo Insurrection. Iñigo García-Bryce, "A Revolution Remembered, a Revolution Forgotten: The 1932 Aprista Insurrection in Trujillo, Peru," *A Contra Corriente*, 7: 3 (2010): 277–322. Other studies on the subject include: Hidalgo Gamarra and José Daniel, *1932: los excluidos combaten por la libertad: la Revolución de Trujillo*, Perú: [s.n.], 2011; Margarita Giesecke, *La insurrección de Trujillo: Jueves 7 de Julio de 1932*, Lima: Fondo Editorial del Congreso del Perú, 2010; Mariano Alcántara, *Arte y revolución, Trujillo 1932: de pie ante la historia*, Trujillo: Secongensa, 1994; Percy Murillo Garaycochea, *Revolución de Trujillo, 1932*, Lima: Editorial Nosotros, 1982.

[20] Nelson Manrique,"*¡Usted Fue Aprista!*" Bases para una historia critica del APRA. Lima: Fondo editorial PUCP, 2009, p. 98.

episode ended dramatically three days later with many dead and injured. Governmental military forces rapidly and easily quelled the staged revolution.[21]

By the Peruvian winter of 1932, state persecution had successfully crushed the cohesion of the party, leaving even its most fervent affiliates at a loss for clear direction. The circumstances in which the Aprista Perla Lapoint tried, to no avail, to resign from the party earlier that year casts a spotlight on the level of disorganization that was by then endemic to PAP. On August 13, 1932, Lapoint was arrested and taken into custody. The police officer who handled his case reported that he first apprehended Lapoint around four in the afternoon, "por haber estado dando vivas al Apra en estado de ebriedad," he wrote, and that after a summary search in his residence he found a number of incriminating documents. The documents effectively testified to Perla Lapoint's involvement with APRA. Yet these documents were all dated 1931 and, as Lapoint remarked, he now felt completely dissociated from PAP and wanted nothing more than to formally leave its ranks. Giving notice of departure to a fragmented PAP, however, was easier said than done. When his interrogators asked what he meant by a failed resignation, Lapoint retorted it was on account of "no existir la directiva del partido aprista."[22] The state of chaos in the party was such, Lapoint regretted, that he no longer knew where to present his resignation to make it official.[23]

APRA leaders readily acknowledged the state of chaos of their organization. Starting in March 1932, the National Executive Committee (CEN), under the direction of Haya de la Torre at the time, resolved to try to cope with the level of disorganization that beset not only the activities but also the resistance of the party in the face of state persecution.[24] It called an extraordinary plenary session in Lima to discuss the seriousness of the situation and reckon with the predicaments it faced. The party apparatus was dismantled. Its propaganda system was almost

[21] García-Bryce, "A Revolution Remembered," pp. 277–322.

[22] "For having been cheering APRA in a drunken state." "Of the nonexistence of the APRA party leadership," Jefe General de Investigación, [Interrogatorio de Alfredo Perla Lapoint,] Lima, August 16, 1932, AGN, Ministerio de Interior, Legajo 3.9.5.1.15.1.14.3 (1932).

[23] Ibid.

[24] Comité Ejecutivo Nacional del Partido Aprista Peruano (hereafter cited as CEN del PAP), *Boletín del Partido Aprista Peruano. Órgano del Comité Ejecutivo Nacional*, Lima, March 14, 1932, AGN, Ministerio de Interior, Legajo 3.9.5.1.15.1.14.3 (1932).

entirely shut down. Worse still, because of the impossibility of transmitting clear instructions to Apristas scattered across the country, the CEN had to reckon with the social disorder caused by individual party members who arbitrarily took their frustration to the streets and engaged in acts of violence.[25] The CEN attributed – in March of 1932 – the lack of discipline in Aprista ranks to the lack of central command in the party, as explained in the first issue of its underground mouthpiece, *the Newsletters of PAP*. Yet it concurrently condemned individual acts of violence for being impulsive, and, as a result, unworthy of the shrewd methods that ostensibly defined aprismo. Significantly, by portraying a wayward party in need of guidance, the Executive Committee indirectly championed its own cause. Implicit in this contention, in effect, was the role that the Lima-based leadership intended to recapture as the executive of PAP.

The CEN was on paper the top administrative unit of PAP. It was controlled by the APRA leaders who had experienced exile in the 1920s and who sided with the leadership of Haya de la Torre. Based in Lima, it sent out instructions to communities of APRA exiles abroad and coordinated the dissemination of pro-APRA propaganda throughout the country.[26] This access to underground networks abroad and in Peru, specifically the control it afforded over PAP's political propaganda, increased the leverage of the CEN in the party. The CEN was officially under the control of Haya de la Torre following the 1931 elections and until his arrest in May 1932. By and large, it is possible to equate the CEN during the 1930s with the positions held by the Hayista faction. For this reason, the CEN and the Hayista faction are terms I use alternately to designate the Lima-based, pro-democratic and anti-communist faction of the APRA movement from the early 1930s onward.[27]

By the first half of 1932, the CEN claimed that they had the capacity and the determination to "dignify" the political struggles that were then rocking Peru. Recalling the democratic tradition from which APRA came, the Hayista faction promised to instill order and method into a disorganized PAP.[28] To do so, one of the first noticeable initiatives launched by the

[25] CEN del PAP, *Boletín del Partido Aprista Peruano*, Lima, March 14, 1932.

[26] Fondo Luis Eduardo Enríquez Cabrera, ENAH, México, "APRA," 1930–1939, AGN, Ministerio de Interior, Legajo 3.9.5.1.15.1.14.3 (1932).

[27] For a sound description of APRA's party structure in 1931 and of the role played by the executive committee see Robert S. Jansen, *Revolutionizing Repertoires: The Rise of Populist Mobilization in Peru*, Chicago: The University of Chicago Press, 2017, pp. 157–158.

[28] CEN del PAP, *Boletín del Partido Aprista Peruano*, Lima, March 14, 1932.

CEN was to send to press a clandestine mouthpiece, entitled the *Newsletter of the Peruvian APRA Party* (*Boletín del Partido Aprista Peruano*). It usually came in the form of a rudimentary two-page leaflet that reported on the most recent undertakings of the CEN in Lima with the use of educational and upbeat articles.[29] Significantly, however, very few engaged in serious political reflection. From the uncertainty of clandestine retreats, there was indeed little time or energy left to engage in substantial analyses.[30] In 1932, in the midst of persecution, creating original political knowledge mattered less to APRA leaders than did the need to construct the image of a strong and active PAP. The arrest of Haya de la Torre on May 6, 1932, and the expressions of international solidarity it immediately triggered, gifted the CEN with a unique opportunity to accomplish that goal.

INTERNATIONAL SOLIDARITY CAMPAIGN WITH HAYA DE LA TORRE

Following the passage of the 1932 Emergency Law and the renewed spike of persecution it unleashed against PAP, Haya de la Torre became a prime target of the Sánchez Cerro government. The new president was determined to stop this radical from continuing to encourage political dissent. Haya de la Torre hid for several weeks before police located him on May 6, 1932.[31] News of his subsequent arrest spread rapidly. In Peru, a crowd of supporters spontaneously took to the streets of the capital upon hearing about the detention of this major APRA leader. Apristas marched on to the Plaza Mayor to oppose this new affront to Peruvian democracy and to what they correctly viewed as another assault on their political party. The exact number of participants is unknown, but according to the *New York Times*, the size or at least the energy of the demonstration was dramatic enough to cause commotion among Peruvian authorities.[32]

[29] A total of fourteen issues appeared between March 14 and June 14 of 1932.

[30] Police agents confiscated this material from APRA members placed under arrest. Several issues of the *Boletín del PAP* can be found in AGN, Ministerio de Interior, Legajo 3.9.5.1.15.1.14.3 (1932).

[31] Haya de la Torre had opportunities to leave the country but refused to do so. Testimony of Rufino Briceño y Ulloa, May 7, 1932, AGN, Ministerio de Interior, Legajo 3.9.5.1.15.1.14.7 (1932–1942).

[32] "Arrest Stirs Crowds to Protest in Peru: Radical Leader Is Seized as the Assassin's Accomplice – Presidential Palace Under Guard," *The New York Times*, New York, May 7, 1932, p. 4.

Yet the legal provisions that had led to the arbitrary arrest of Haya de la Torre applied to the protesters as well. The government refused to budge on Haya de la Torre's detention. Persecution against political agitators expanded.

International supporters quickly mobilized around Haya de la Torre. Between May 1932 and August 1933, when an Amnesty Law was promulgated to free all political prisoners, many Latin American actors drafted congressional motions and petitions, sent out cablegrams, and used newspapers and magazines to express solidarity with APRA and to decry the repressive regimes of Sánchez Cerro and his successor, Oscar Benavides (who assumed power in 1933 after the assassination of Sánchez Cerro by a presumed Aprista). Joaquín García Monge, a well-known Costa Rican democrat and anti-imperialist advocate, inveighed against "the Peruvian tyranny of Sánchez Cerro."[33] Sánchez Cerro's oppression of Peruvian Apristas, he scolded on July 26, 1932, in the pages of the *Diario de Costa Rica*, ran counter to the democratic and continental Hispano-American citizenship that intellectuals across the Americas aspired to build.[34] He demanded the immediate release of Haya de la Torre. "Esta es una forma de barbarie que urge combatir," stated García Monge. "Hay que organizar un movimiento de opinión para que el militarismo estúpido del Perú vea que la América tiene los ojos puestos sobre su sable levantado."[35] Many Latin American actors echoed García Monge's demand for democracy in Peru and for the release of the APRA leader Haya de la Torre. The San José Bar Association (Colegio de Abogados) and the Costa Rican University student association organized protests and issued pro-APRA communiqués addressed to Peruvian authorities.[36] Throughout Latin America, remarked the US ambassador to Peru, irate citizens came together in protest of the unfair treatment meted out to Haya de la Torre, "requesting that [the] Constituent Assembly of Peru" free him at once.[37] More significant still, an impressive

[33] Joaquín García Monge, "Haya de la Torre en Peligro de Ser Fusilado," *Diario de Costa Rica*, Tuesday, July 26, 1932, newspaper clipping in Folder 4, Box 4696, RG 59, 1930–1939, NACP.

[34] Ibid.

[35] "This is a form of barbarism that we must urgently combat. A movement of opinion must be organized so that the stupid militarism of Peru sees that America is ready to fight it," ibid.

[36] Charles C. Eberhardt to Secretary of State, Washington, DC, "Protests from Costa Rica. Re: Haya de la Torre," San José, Costa Rica, July 27, 1932, Folder 4, Box 4696, RG 59, 1930–1939, NACP.

[37] William C. Burdett to State Department, Desp. #1896, Peru, July 5, 1932, Folder 4, Box 4696, RG 59, 1930–1939, NACP.

number of legislative chambers in the region, including those of Colombia, Argentina, Mexico and Costa Rica, unanimously approved bills demanding amnesty for Haya de la Torre.[38]

The widespread coverage that Haya de la Torre's arrest received in Latin America showcases the symbolic capital that he had successfully accumulated in Latin America in the course of the previous decade. His travels across the Americas in addition to his extensive correspondence with anti-imperialist peers had indeed contributed toward making him a renowned leftist intellectual in the region by the time of his arrest in 1932. This coverage likewise hints at the struggles for democracy and social justice that were rocking the entire continent at the time. The 1930s were years shaped by political violence not only in Peru but also throughout Latin America. Soon after the stock market crash in late 1929, military takeovers swept the region as a result of growing economic and social unrest. Despite regional differences, these military governments shared the same aversion toward civilian rule. They were likewise committed to restoring peace and order in their respective countries, using violence against their own population if needed. Given that context, then, many Latin American intellectuals and politicians saw in the imprisoned Haya de la Torre a symbol that bore meaning not only for Peru but also for their respective national contexts and for the future of the Americas more broadly. The petitions signed by solidarity activists outside Peru effectively turned APRA, and specifically an APRA placed under the leadership of Haya de la Torre, into a symbol of Latin American solidarity and continental democracy.

Consider for example the petition that a series of distinguished Mexican intellectuals presented to the Peruvian Congress in July 1932.[39] According to an article that appeared on July 3, 1932, in *El Nacional*, an important Mexican newspaper, "the purpose of these Mexican intellectuals in making this petition [was] not to create a conflict

[38] "Gestiones de los congresos," *La Tribuna. En el destierro*, August 1932, p. 3, AGN, Ministerio de Interior, Ministerio de Interior, Legajo 3.9.5.1.15.1.14.3 (1932–1942).

[39] The petition included the following signatures: Alfonso Caso, E. González Martínez, Marino Silva and Aceres, L. Chico [Coarne], I. García Téllez, Pedro de Alba, D. Cosió Villegas, J. Silva Herzog, H. Villaseñor, A. Espinosa de los Monteros, F. Bach, Antonio Caso, Rafael López, J. De J. Núñez y Domínguez, Samuel Ramos, F. González Guerrero, Héctor Pérez Martínez, R. E. Valle, G. López y Fuentes, Julio Torri, Xavier Sorondo, F. Monterde, O. Icazbalosta, José Corostiza, E. Fernández Ledesma, Moisés Sáenz, Salvador Novo Carlos Pellicer, Humberto Rejera, Mariano Asuela, Alfonso Taracena, Salvador Azuela, Diego Córdova, Enrique Sarro, Roberto Montenegro and Fernando Leal, "Liberty of R. Haya de la Torre Requested," *El Nacional*, Mexico, July 3, 1932.

nor [*sic*] to criticize the action of the Peruvian Government, but, based on the merits of Haya de la Torre, to secure the liberation of the South American thinker."[40] Particularly important here is the reference to Haya de la Torre as a *South American thinker* rather than a *Peruvian politician*. Although the Mexican petitioners claimed they wanted to respect the sovereignty of Peru, they simultaneously claimed to be speaking on behalf of a higher continental ideal. In their petition, interestingly, the latter principle superseded the former: by protesting what they viewed as the unjustified repression of Haya de la Torre, Mexican intellectuals claimed to be defending the culture and progress of American republics at large. The petition offered three main justifications to explain why they requested the immediate liberation of Haya de la Torre and his fellow imprisoned Apristas.[41] Each provision made direct reference to a principle of continental solidarity, either in the form of a shared Indo-Latin identity or in the name of a democratic ideal that guaranteed freedom of thought and basic political rights:

1. "The personality of Haya de la Torre, as one of the greatest Indo-Latins and representative of the restlessness and aspirations of the present young generation for the advancement of social ideas [...], merits, in our opinion, protection and respect.
2. Whatever may be the details of the internal political struggle in Peru, upon which we do not feel ourselves qualified to express an opinion, there exists a well defined continental interest, in the name of which we are acting, for the defense of the exponents of culture and progress without whose constant and efficient action our republics would be unable to fulfill their historic destinies.
3. With the installation in Peru of a new government, the Indo-Latin mind trusts it will abolish the methods of coercion and terror which characterized dismal epochs, and, with ample generosity and feeling of the moment [...], will grant to Haya de la Torre and companions the liberty and guarantees to which they are entitled."[42]

[40] "Liberty of R. Haya de la Torre Requested," *El Nacional*, Mexico, 3 July 1932, as cited and translated in report from [J. R.] Clark, Jr., US embassy in Mexico City, to the Secretary of State, Washington DC, Mexico, July 8, 1932, Folder 4, Box 4696, RG 59, 1930–1939, NACP.

[41] Ibid.

[42] "Liberty of R. Haya de la Torre Requested," *El Nacional*, Mexico, 3 July 1932, as cited and translated in report from [J. R.] Clark, Jr., US embassy in Mexico City, to the Secretary of State, Washington DC, Mexico, July 8, 1932, Folder 4, Box 4696, RG 59, 1930–1939, NACP.

Later that year in Mexico, the states of Puebla, Michoacán, Nuevo León, and Coahuila urged the Congress of the Union, the legislative branch of the Mexican federal government, to use its influence before Peruvian authorities and other Latin American legislatures to demand at once the liberation of Haya de la Torre.[43] They requested that Peruvian and continental authorities protect the life and integrity of a Peruvian citizen who, they noted, was also a strong and valuable advocate of Latin American sovereignty. These actors justified their interference in Peruvian affairs by asserting that Haya de la Torre offered a model to emulate in the fight against foreign interests in Latin America.[44]

State representatives from other Latin American countries likewise alluded to a sense of continental solidarity that coalesced around the figure of Haya de la Torre. In the course of the Peruvian winter of 1932, the Congresses of Colombia and Costa Rica unanimously approved bills requesting amnesty for him. In Colombia, the Senate spearheaded the protest. The proposition formulated by Colombian Senators Serrano Blanco, Tirado Macias Holguín Julio, Cote Bautista and Umana Bernal reportedly rose from a democratic sentiment, deep-rooted in Colombia, which justified the need to defend an individual who had worked to advance the spiritual and administrative sovereignty of Latin America.[45] Costa Rican representatives similarly referred to a principle of Latin solidarity in order to justify their defense of Haya de la Torre, as highlighted in the telegram they sent to Peruvian authorities in July of 1932: "The Congress of Costa Rica, by unanimous decision, has agreed to address the Legislative Body of this sister Republic in order to request, in the name of Latin solidarity, the intercession of its high good offices to prevent the execution of the reported death sentence against Haya de la Torre."[46]

[43] Departamento de gobernación, "NOMBRE: Raúl Haya de la Torre. ASUNTO: La H. Legislatura del Estado de Puebla, gestiona la libertad del expresado ciudadano peruano," 1932, AGN, México, Secretaria de Gobernación, Dirección General de Gobierno, 2/000(29) 246, Caja 36, esp. 4.

[44] Filomeno González y Leopolido García, Diputados Secretarios del Congreso del Estado de Nuevo León, Acuerdo presentado al Ministro de Gobernación, México, D.F., November 21, 1932, Monterrey, Nuevo León, AGN, México, Secretaria de Gobernación, Dirección General de Gobierno, 2/000(29) 246, Caja 36, esp. 4, p. 7.

[45] "Gestiones de los congresos," *La Tribuna. En el destierro*, August 1932, p. 3, AGN, Ministerio de Interior, Ministerio de Interior, Legajo 3.9.5.1.15.1.14.3 (1932–1942).

[46] Eberhardt to Secretary of State, Washington, DC, "Protests from Costa Rica. Re: Haya de la Torre," San José, Costa Rica, July 27, 1932, Folder 4, Box 4696, RG 59, 1930–1939, NACP.

It is difficult to evaluate how many solidarity activists ultimately participated in the liberation campaign in favour of Haya de la Torre in 1932–1933. As we shall see in the next section, several non-Latin American allies also played an important role in orchestrating this international movement of support, making it difficult to precisely assess the number of initiatives that directly stemmed from Latin Americans. Its historical importance relies less on the specific number of those who signed the petition, than on the dissemination of these stories abroad and in Peru. These petitions point to one important reality for PAP in the early 1930s and beyond: moments of crises were oddly beneficial to PAP precisely because they acted as catalystic moments that attracted attention to its political cause.

Significantly, these petitions also reveal the flexibility with which an imagined community of democratic support coalesced around the international defence of APRA. The petitioners referred to Haya de la Torre sometimes as a *South American* thinker, sometimes as a *Latin-Indo* thinker. Some praised the work that APRA was achieving for *Hispano-America*, while others focused instead on its contributions to *Latin America*. The difference in labels used to name the continent mattered less to Apristas than having non-Peruvian allies praise their political work and imagine them as activists who served the Americas as a whole, not just Peru. Therefore, it was to Apristas' advantage to avoid dogmatism as they continued to hone their project of hemispheric unity and Latin American solidarity. Ideological flexibility was an asset a persecuted APRA could not afford to lose.

CHRISTIAN ALLIES AND TRANSNATIONAL ADVOCACY CAMPAIGN

Organizing a transnational advocacy campaign demanded a constant work of coordination and communication that weighed heavily on the shoulders of a few political refugees. Significantly, the international movement in support of Haya de la Torre could never have reached the magnitude it did without the assistance of key allies abroad, and especially that of Anna Melissa Graves and John A. Mackay, who used grassroots organizing and sustained correspondence to weave an intricate web of transnational support. Working together, these solidarity activists not only helped to expand this movement beyond the scope of Latin America; they were in fact responsible for setting much of this transnational advocacy campaign in motion. These international alliances were all the more important in the face of the changing global order of the interwar period.

"Hope proved elusive," Ira Katznelson, a leading US historian of the New Deal, eloquently wrote about the 1930s – a period marked by the rise of Communism and Fascism and by what looked like the disintegration of democracy worldwide. "The rumble of deep uncertainty, a sense of proceeding without a map, remained relentless and enveloping. A climate of universal fear deeply affected political understandings and concerns."[47] The Christian intermediaries who assisted Haya de la Torre in this solidarity campaign were not immune to this pervading feeling of alarm. In the 1920s, their fears originated in the recent experience of the First World War; by the early 1930s, the angst they felt was the result of forebodings about rising totalitarian regimes and impending global warfare. These actors sensed that Western civilization was at a historic crossroads. It would either face its internal contradictions or implode.

As to where to look for salvation, the Christian pacifists who were close to Haya de la Torre had a ready answer. "I have as I know you also have, unlimited faith in him," Mackay wrote to Graves about Haya de la Torre on January 10, 1933.[48] These mentors continued to see in him, and more specifically by the 1930s in a Peruvian APRA party placed under his leadership, a harbinger of moral, spiritual, and social regeneration not just in Latin America but across the Western Hemisphere as well. Positive appraisals of a PAP placed under his leadership ran through their writing. "[Haya de la Torre] is undoubtedly the most brilliant figure of the new generation," remarked Mackay in 1932, "and one who seems destined to play an important role in the future life of Peru and of the Continent as a whole."[49] Mackay was so confident he billed the APRA movement "la fuerza revolucionaria más constructiva de hoy día en la América Latina."[50] Graves shared his enthusiasm. In 1932, she was as enthralled by Haya de la Torre's "singularly magnetic and lovable personality" as when she had first met him in Lima ten years earlier. Importantly, she was

47 Ira Katznelson, *Fear Itself: The New Deal and the Origins of Our Time*, New York, London: Liveright, 2014 (1st ed. 2013), p. 12.

48 John A. Mackay to AMG, New York, January 10, 1933, AMGC, Series 2, Box 2, Folder 2.4.

49 John A. Mackay, *The Other Spanish Christ: A Study in the Spiritual History of Spain and South America*, New York: The Macmillian Company, 1932, p. 193.

50 "... the most constructive revolutionary force in Latin America Today," John A. Mackay, "Víctor Raúl Haya de la Torre. Semblanzas Americanas," *La Nueva Democracia*, New York City, May 25, 1933, p. 18.

also as fiercely committed to viewing in APRA's project of Latin American unity a first step toward world peace.[51] The imminent threat of warfare she sensed around her as she travelled to Europe in the early 1930s confirmed her in her views. She was ready to fight tooth and nail to make sure Peruvian authorities did not stand in the way of her dream of world peace.

As a result, on May 20, 1932, when Graves learned about the arrest of Haya de la Torre, she immediately took action. Graves did what she did best. She sat in front of her Remington and, one letter at a time, set about to weave together a substantial patchwork of international support in favour of her protégé. To say that Graves was a dedicated correspondent is a euphemism. She was fierce. She was relentless. She was unforgiving. Above all, she knew like no other how to bring people together around a common cause when she set her mind to persuading others she was right. The spectacular number of letters either published or preserved in her personal archives testify to Graves' staunch commitment to letter-writing as a form of political activism. For the remaining part of 1932, she worked doggedly to set an international protest in motion.

Graves' efforts bore fruit. Public outcry over the arbitrary arrest of Haya de la Torre soon spread from Latin America to the United States and Europe. Solidarity activists, upon Graves' request, wrote protest letters and drafted petitions addressed to Peruvian ambassadors in Washington, D.C., London, and Paris to request that the Peruvian government be held responsible in the face of a democratic international public opinion. These petitions denounced the harsh prison conditions under which Haya de la Torre was being held captive and protested "against the arrests of those apparently guilty of nothing but expressions of political opinion or membership in a political party."[52] International APRA supporters requested a fair trial or immediate deportation for Haya de la Torre. In the United States, the petition forwarded to the Peruvian embassy in Washington, D.C. was signed by renown US liberals, progressives and radical pacifists, including Carleton Beals, Jane Addams, John Dewey, Waldo Frank, Hubert Herring, Paul Kellogg, H. L. Mencken, Fred Rippy, Frederico de Onis, Jeannette Rankin, and

[51] AMG, [Enclosure #1, Dispatch No. 3980. Copy of manuscript by Graves on Haya de la Torre], September–October 1932, p. 2, Folder 4, Box 4696, RG 59, 1930–1939, NACP.

[52] Petition draft addressed to Manuel de Freyre y Santander, December 23, 1932, AMGC, Series 2, Box 2, Folders 2.1 to 2.17. To see efforts to publicize petitions in the US press consult AMGC, Series 3, Box 3, Folder 3.6.

Charles Thomson. In addition to rebuking the undemocratic action of the Peruvian government, this petition extolled the moral qualities and the "international significance" of the APRA leader. "We are sure that Your Excellency will respect this universal opinion concerning Haya," it stressed, "for we feel that you are truly anxious to uphold the good name of Peru before the world as a country where liberty and free government may prosper."[53]

In Europe, solidarity activists likewise pressured the Peruvian authorities into releasing the APRA leader. "The political imprisonment of a man such as Haya de la Torre," as stated by a dozen of British scholars and intellectuals in an open letter to the *Manchester Guardian*, "is a fact which in the eyes of international opinion, cannot but reflect discredit upon the Government which inflicts it."[54] Many more pacifist activists and renowned intellectuals from France, England, and Spain took part in the solidarity campaign for his release. They included the French pacifists Romain Rolland and Georges Duhamel, the Spanish intellectuals Miguel de Unamuno, Gregorio Marañon, and Ortega y Gassett, and British scholars and academics Harold Laski, Dr. Marett, Rector of Exeter College, and Barrett Brown, the principal of the Ruskin College where Haya de la Torre had briefly studied in the late 1920s.

Although Graves was the clear conductor of this campaign, as revealed by the hundreds of letters she received in response to her invitations to join the protest in favour of Haya de la Torre, she enlisted other recruits in her efforts.[55] For example, Mackay assisted Graves in writing the petition drafts and helped to forward the petitions to the relevant diplomatic authorities.[56] He used his contacts in Peru in an attempt to improve Haya de la Torre's prison conditions.[57] Mackay also kept his own missionary circles in Latin America abreast of the latest developments in Peru regarding the fate of persecuted Apristas. Significantly, nearly all the letters that Mackay received between the months of May and July of 1933, from US peers involved with the Presbyterian Board of Foreign

[53] Petition signed by Jane Addams, John Dewey, Waldo Frank, Hubert Herring, Paul Kellogg, H. L. Mencken, Frederico de Onis, George Mitchell, Jeannette Rankin and Charles Thompson, AMGC, Series 2, Box 2, Folder 2.3.

[54] Clipping of Manchester Guardian, n.d., AMGC, Series 5, Box 10, Folder 10.4.

[55] All of the solidarity activists who ultimately signed the US protest were initially contacted by Graves. See AMGC, Series 2, Box 2, Folders 2.1 to 2.17.

[56] Manual Freyre to Samuel G. Inman, February 14, 1933, and Mackay to AMG, November 10, 1933, in AMGC, Series 2, Box 2, Folder 2.17.

[57] Mackay to AMG, March 27, 1933, AMGC, Series 2, Box 2, Folder 2.17.

Missions, disclose acute interest and great concern for the life of Haya de la Torre.[58]

To reach intellectuals in Europe, in addition to writing to her peers in Great Britain, Graves benefited from the help of Rolland, who reached out to his networks to help mobilize a protest in Haya de la Torre's favour.[59] On the Latin American side, Graves corresponded with the Costa Rican democrat Garcia Monge, the Argentine intellectual Manuel Ugarte, the Mexican philosopher and politician José Vasconcelos, and the Chilean poet Gabriela Mistral, urging them to take action to save Haya de la Torre's life. These actors had been involved with Haya de la Torre and with the growth of the anti-imperialist APRA in the mid-1920s. All agreed to help Graves and to actively participate in the advocacy campaign underway.

Most petitioners outside Latin America, however, had never met or, for a few, even heard of the imprisoned political leader. Graves' intervention was in these cases all the more crucial. Among those who learned about APRA and its imprisoned leader through Graves' 1932–1933 efforts, several agreed to add their names to the petition not because they felt a sudden urge to defend a political party they barely knew, but because Graves, a peer pacifist activist whom they respected, asked them to. For example, although the Nobel Peace Prize recipients Jane Addams and Emily Greene Balch showed no indication of knowing anything about APRA, both signed the petition upon Graves' request.[60] They owed loyalty to Graves, their longtime activist friend and colleague from the Women's International League for Peace and Freedom, as well as to the ideals of peace, democracy, and civic rights that Graves' initiative purportedly defended. Archival evidence suggests that in addition to signing

[58] Webster E. Browning to Mackay, New York, May 2, 1933; Browning to Mackay, June 5, 1933 (Dictated June 2); unknown member of the Presbyterian Board of Foreign Missions to Mackay, July 6, 1933; unknown member of the Board of Foreign Missions to Mackay, June 10, 1933; unknown member of the Presbyterian Board of Foreign Missions to John A. Mackay, June 8, 1933; Folder 8.31, South America John Mackay, 1933, Record Group No. 81, Box No. 8, The United Presbyterian Church in the United States of America, C.O.E.M.A.R; Secretaries Files-Subject Material 1892–1965, Deputations: Corres., reports, travel letters 1916–1936, Presbyterian Historical Society, Philadelphia, PA.

[59] Romain Rolland to AMG, Villeneuve, May 27, 1932, BNF, Département des Manuscrits (hereafter cited as DM), NAF 28400: Fonds Romain Rolland NAF 28400.

[60] The Nobel Peace Prize was awarded to Jane Addams in 1931 and to Emily Greene Balch in 1946.

the petition, Addams and Greene actively promoted this case of injustice within their immediate social circles.[61] Similarly, when Graves first tested the waters with the pacifist Minister John Haynes Holmes, from the Community Church of New York, Holmes cheerfully thanked Graves, "for giving me this opportunity to help in a good cause."[62]

Significantly, others were seduced into the cause of supporting Haya de la Torre in the hopes of fighting communism. This is what appears to have secured the assistance of Christian actors such as Father MacGowan who, as the assistant director of the anti-communist National Catholic Welfare Conference, agreed to utilize his aura of authority to present the final version of the petition to the Peruvian ambassador in the United States.[63] By the early 1930s, as we have seen in Chapter 3, PAP and the Communist Party of Peru (PCP) had definitively and irreconcilably parted ways.[64] In the material that Graves and Mackay distributed in their solidarity networks and in their writings and correspondence, both insisted on this political break to depict Haya de la Torre's leadership as a model of proper and desirable resistance all at once to imperialism and communism. "Quite as revolutionary and socially-minded in his outlook as Mariátegui," concluded Mackay about Haya de la Torre in 1932, "he recognizes what the latter failed to recognize: that the human problem is spiritual before it is economic."[65]

When Graves first contacted potential supporters of APRA, she usually included a newspaper clipping of the open letter from the *Manchester Guardian*, which she had partially written, and which took pains to dissociate this political leader from any radical or violent wing of the

[61] Jane Addams was the Honorary President of the Women's International League for Peace and Freedom (WILPF) and founder of the Hull House in Chicago. Emily G. Balch was the National President of the US section of the WILPF. AMGC, Series 2, Box 2, Folder 2.3, 2.4, and 2.8. For archival material that traces the lasting relationships between Graves and Addams and Green see SCPC, AMGP, 1919–1953, Box 1 (Reel 74.1), Correspondence with "Jane Addams," Correspondence with "Emily Greene Balch, 1920–1942," "Emily Green Balch, 1943–1949," and "Emily Green Balch, 1950–1959."

[62] John Haynes Holmes to AMG, New York, January 30, 1933, AMGC, Series 2, Box 2, Folder 2.6.

[63] Catherine [Schaeger], Secretary to Father McGowan, to AMG, January 26, 1933, AMGC, Series 2, Box 2, Folder 2.6.

[64] The personal polemics of the late 1920s had crystallized into an open ideological opposition between proponents of the Comintern's class versus class strategy on one side and APRA's single front proposal on the other.

[65] Mackay, *The Other Spanish* Christ, p. 197.

APRA movement.[66] Despite initial communist inclinations, "towards the end of 1927," noted the letter, "those members of the Apra who stood for revolutionary action repudiated [Haya de la Torre's] leadership."[67] The petition that Roger Baldwin prepared, upon Graves' recommendation, for the International Committee for Political Prisoners similarly insisted on the non-communist nature of the APRA leader. "He is not a Communist," confirmed Baldwin; "in fact he is identified with the least radical wing of the Apra movement."[68] These documents suggested that between authoritarian regimes on one side and a Comintern class-based line on the other, an APRA placed under the leadership of Haya de la Torre posed an attractive lesser evil not only for Peru, but also for Latin America as a whole. In other words, this faction of APRA was attractive to international networks outside Latin America in part because of its anti-communist promise, a reality that only encouraged APRA's pivot to the right during the 1930s.

This is true not only because the concomitant experience of persecution and of international solidarity forced on APRA an increasing reliance on international support to survive politically. To be sure, the "good-moderate-left/bad-radical-left trope," which framed most of the campaign of support for Haya de la Torre, contributed to encouraging APRA, specifically the Hayista faction, to curb the revolutionary agenda it once held to comply with the image of a moderate Latin American left deserving of support.[69] But another element holds true to explain APRA's changing positions in later years vis-à-vis US expansionism: the benevolent interventionism of US liberals and progressives in the domestic affairs of Peru was suddenly *not* something to frown upon. In view of the 1932–1933 advocacy campaign, where national and Latin American sovereignty began and ended looked much blurrier to Apristas than it had in exile or in the books they read.

It is hard to assess precisely what international solidarity with APRA ultimately achieved when it came to the liberation of Haya de la Torre in

[66] See the numerous clippings of Manchester Guardian article collected by AMG in AMGC, Series 5, Box 10, Folder 10.4.

[67] Clipping of Manchester Guardian article, n.d., AMGC, Series 5, Box 10, Folder 10.4.

[68] Roger Baldwin, [Petition draft], December 6, 1932, AMGC, Series 2, Box 2, Folder 2.1.

[69] The good-left/bad-left trope is originally used by Kevin Young in his analysis of the liberal US press coverage of the Latin American leftists during the pink tide in the late 1990s and the 2000s. Kevin Young, "The Good, the Bad, and the Benevolent Interventionist: U.S. Press and Intellectual Distortions of the Latin American Left," *Latin American Perspectives*, 190: 40 (May 2013): 207–225.

August 1933. Did General Benavides, recently succeeding Sánchez Cerro to the presidency of Peru, cave in to public pressure, attempting to save face before the international community of nations? Or did individual networking play a more crucial role than political accountability? Solidarity activists disagreed over who or what ultimately wielded the most influence in forcing the promulgation of the Amnesty Law on August 10 of that year.[70] Nevertheless, crucial to my argument in this chapter is the opportunity that this international solidarity campaign gave to the Hayista faction, as it attempted to ensure the survival of PAP in Peru and simultaneously secure party leadership. Haya de la Torre and his persecution became an organizing tool for developing an international solidarity campaign in favour of PAP. APRA leaders rapidly understood the extent to which Hayade la Torre, as a political figure, carried meaning and symbolic capital for a large variety of Latin American actors who faced a similar national context to Peru or feared that they might very soon. Some saw in Haya de la Torre the bearer of a socio-democratic model for Peru, and possibly for all of Latin America, capable of both challenging the right-wing military dictatorships and eschewing violence and rejecting communism to achieve this end. Others placed in him their hopes of witnessing the rise of another Augusto César Sandino, a hero who doggedly opposed foreign interests in Latin American countries and abhorred national oligarchies, heirs of crooked republican orders. The APRA leaders who sided with the Hayista faction rapidly and ubiquitously tapped into those discourses as a line of defence back home.

PUBLICIZING IN PERU APRA'S INTERNATIONAL REPUTATION

The National Executive Committee (CEN) of the Peruvian APRA Party (PAP) rapidly learned to capitalize on international public opinion in favour of the APRA leader Víctor Raúl Haya de la Torre. To be sure, few other options were available. They could not lift a finger without having the state retaliate. A few attempts were made to have US diplomats intercede in favour of PAP, but they refused to get involved in an issue they deemed inflammatory.[71] One option that remained available to

[70] Luis E. Heysen to AMG, Mexico, D.F., March 6, 1933, SCPC, AMGP, Reel 74.8; Mackay to AMG, March 27, 1933, AMGC, Series 2, Box 2, Folder 2.17.

[71] Manuel Vásquez, for the CEN of PAP, to Fred M. Dearing, Ambassador of the United States, Lima, Perú, July 23, 1932, Box 4696, RG 59, 1930–1939, NACP. Dearing to the Secretary of State, "Subject: Alleged Proposal to Execute Haya de la Torre," Lima, July 27, 1932, p. 2, Box 4696, RG 59, 1930–1939, NACP.

persecuted Apristas, which required few resources and hardly any additional risk-taking, was to publicize in Peru the amount of support that Aprista exiles, and specifically Haya de la Torre, were securing at the international level. APRA leaders strategically used these foreign positions to build a storyline that aimed to convince Peruvians of one crucial point: Haya de la Torre was able to garner international support for his persona, the corollary of which was that he was also able to garner international support for his party and for Peruvians more broadly.

The CEN swiftly adapted its political propaganda to take benefit of the arrest of APRA's leader, specifically focusing on the international outcry it created. In a way that recalls the messages of continental solidarity that the *APRA* journal advertised during PAP's initial forays in Peru in 1930, references to the outside world began to proliferate in the underground publications controlled by the party direction after Haya de la Torre's arrest on May 6, 1932. Issues of the *Newsletter of PAP* appearing after that date repeatedly represented the new wave of APRA exiles as crucial intermediaries between Peru and the rest of the continent. One article in the June 6 issue, tellingly entitled "El sueño de Bolívar meta ideal del P.A.P.," reproduced the expressions of "solidaridad indoamericana" that a small contingent of Peruvian APRA exiles in Guayaquil, Ecuador, had recently forwarded to Alfredo Baquerizo Moreno, the president of their host country.[72] According to the *Newsletter*, the Ecuadorian president favourably replied to their good wishes. He likewise allegedly celebrated the work of APRA in trying to bring about the "verdadero sueño de Bolívar," that of bringing the Americas together.[73] The *Newsletter* argued in other issues that the political work of the recently deported Apristas was acclaimed outside Peru.[74] Reports publicized the proselytizing work of Aprista exiles like Manuel Seoane, Luis Alberto Sánchez, Pedro E. Muñiz, Carlos Cox, or Arturo Sabroso who allegedly organized networks and wrote political work abroad for the sake of the APRA movement, and as a corollary for the sake of Peru as well.[75]

Whenever they could, APRA leaders in exile attempted to blur the distinction between PAP and the Peruvian people. These storylines suggested that all suffered under the same repressive government; that all were denied democratic rights at the national level. For example, the

[72] "Bolívar's dream: PAP's ideal goal." "Indo-American solidarity." CEN del PAP, *Boletín del Partido Aprista Peruano*, Lima, June 6, 1932.

[73] "True dream of Bolívar," ibid.

[74] CEN del PAP, *Boletín del Partido Aprista Peruano*. Lima, May 23, 1932.

[75] Ibid.

August 1932 issue of *La Tribuna* in exile, another publication controlled by the Hayista faction, reported on the concern of Argentinean people for the political situation in Peru in a way that equated Peruvians with Apristas. Read one passage: "Hoy más que nunca podemos afirmar que en la República Argentina hay una gran inquietud, una verdadera preocupación por el destino político de nuestra patria. La Argentina contempla el dolor en que nos debatimos compartiéndolo y sintiéndolo como un dolor propio."[76] The use of the first-person plural pronoun gave the impression that all Peruvian citizens, and not only APRA members, were linked by a shared experience of sorrow and suffering in the face of state persecution. This strategy aimed to enable APRA leaders to speak in exile on behalf of all Peruvians.[77] Significantly, when the CEN reported in the pages of its *Newsletter* on growing continental solidarity protests against Sánchez Cerro, it similarly did so by highlighting that these protests demanded the end of indiscriminate violence against Peruvian citizens, not just against Apristas.[78]

As the Hayista faction forcefully condemned state censorship in Peru for concealing the growing expressions of solidarity with the persecuted PAP, the renewed wave of deportations paradoxically created political opportunities that APRA leaders were sure not to squander. For one, the deportation of Apristas to Chile gave the CEN access to sites of literary production abroad, which bolstered its capacity to broadcast to a Peruvian audience the level of international backing that a PAP under the leadership of Haya de la Torre was able to attract.[79] Santiago de Chile, especially, rapidly gained grounds as an important centre of APRA propaganda. Archival evidence points to this city as the new publishing platform for *La Tribuna*, which reappeared in August 1932 under the title of *La Tribuna. En el destierro*.[80] In stark contrast to a few rough pages

[76] "Today more than ever we can affirm that in the Argentine Republic there is great concern, a real concern for the political destiny of our country. Argentina contemplates the pain we're struggling with, sharing it and feeling it as their own." La protesta Argentina," *La Tribuna. En el destierro*, August 1932, p. 3.

[77] *La Tribuna. En el destierro*, August 1932.

[78] CEN del PAP, *Boletín del Partido Aprista Peruano*, Lima, May 23, 1932.

[79] CEN del PAP, *Boletín del Partido Aprista Peruano*, Lima, May 23, 1932.

[80] On April 18, 1932, the Peruvian ambassador in Chile wrote to the Ministry of Foreign Affairs in Peru to confirm receipt of three packages of anti-APRA propaganda. Each package contained fifty copies of a flyer entitled "Los documentos comprobatorios de la dirección comunista del Apra." In addition to this material, the ambassador had received earlier that month 350 more copies of the same flyer for anti-APRA propaganda purposes in Chile. This primary source suggests that the Peruvian government was concerned with

stapled together, which characterized issues of *La Tribuna* published in Peru prior to August 1932, the arrangement of the revamped edition of *La Tribuna* in exile hardly portrayed a party operating in hiding or suffering from repression and internal disorganization.[81] Quite the opposite, its presentation was slick. Its four-page format resembled that of any respectable, serious daily paper. The professional look of this mouthpiece increased the authority of its contents.

In addition to producing political propaganda, importantly, the community of APRA exiles in Chile clandestinely forwarded copies of *La Tribuna* to Peru via the intermediary of APRA exiles stationed in Arica, a city in the northern province of Chile.[82] The CEN had in turn devised a systematized and well-run propaganda apparatus that insured the diffusion in Peru of the political material they received from abroad. This work of mediation fell on the shoulders of subalterns and anonymous figures of the party. Indeed, the constant state surveillance to which APRA leaders were subjected in their home country precluded them from engaging in such activities. Apristas who were not known by the authorities shouldered the work of disseminating APRA's political propaganda in the different regions of Peru, keeping members of the party in contact with one another and transmitting directives to the rank-and-file of the party.[83]

the activities of Peruvian APRA exiles in Chile. Certainly their activism was significant enough to worry the Peruvian government and justify a smear campaign against Peruvian citizens outside Peru. Embazador de Perú en Chile al Señor Ministro de Estado en el Despacho de Relaciones Exteriores, Embajada del Perú. Santiago, abril 18 de 1932, Archivo Central del Ministerio de Relaciones Exteriores, Perú, Oficios de Chile, 5-4-A, 1932; Letter of José Chávez R. to Luis Eduardo Enríquez, Arica, Chile, May 30, 1933, *Fondo Luis Eduardo Enríquez Cabrera* (hereafter cited as FLEEC), Escuela Nacional de Antropología e Historia, México (hereafter cited as ENAH), "APRA," 1930–1939; Letter of Noé Ordoñez to Luis Eduardo Enríquez, Arica, Chile, June 3, 1933, FLEEC, ENAH, "APRA," 1930–1939.

81 *La Tribuna*, March 23, 1932, Año 1, No. [286 o 236], Lima, p. 1, AGN, Ministerio de Interior, Legajo 3.9.5.1.15.1.14.7 (1932).

82 José Chávez R. to Luis Eduardo Enríquez, Arica, Chile, May 30, 1933; Noé Ordoñez to Luis Eduardo Enríquez, Arica, Chile, June 3, 1933; FLEEC, ENAH, "APRA," 1930–1939.

83 Numerous cases of detention in the archives of the Ministry of the Interior in Peru helped piece together the strategies used by official party propagandists. See "El Vigilante de investigación al Señor Jefe de la Brigada de Asuntos Sociales, Prefectura del Departamento de Lima, Lima, June [*sic*] 5, 1932; Testimony of Edgardo Castro Agustí, Lima, July 5, 1932, AGN, Ministerio de Interior, Legajo 3.9.5.1.15.1.14.3 (1932). Comandancia General al Prefecto del Departamento, "No. 42 – Sobre propaganda activa," Lima, April 7, 1932, AGN, Ministerio de Interior, Legajo 3.9.5.1.15.1.14.7 (1932–1942).

By August 1932, Haya de la Torre's international reputation was vividly deployed as an instrument of political prestige for PAP. The Hayista faction doggedly and increasingly disseminated explicit associations between the good reputation of the APRA movement abroad and the leadership of Haya de la Torre in Peru throughout the first half of 1933. Having access to more resources and benefiting from freedom of speech, the editors of *La Tribuna* in exile took it upon themselves to publicize the content of the international press and the advocacy initiatives that supported him. They aggressively printed the expressions of solidarity with this APRA leader that swept through the continent, as evidenced in the first issue published abroad in 1932. One article showcased the list of every single expression of support of either APRA or Haya de la Torre and which APRA exiles had tracked down abroad as of August of that year.[84] Others copied excerpts from foreign newspapers that evinced the alleged continental outrage mounting against the regime of Sánchez Cerro.[85] Yet another reproduced in full the cablegram requesting the release and deportation of the imprisoned leader that eighty-five congressional deputies and four senators in Argentina forwarded to Sánchez Cerro.[86]

Between 1930 and 1933, the Hayista faction took pains to insist on the international reputation of APRA and the newly founded PAP as an instrument of political manipulation to increase the prestige, and, as a result, bolster the popular support of their political organization. By 1932–1933, this international reputation became increasingly and almost exclusively associated with the figure of a single leader, that of Haya de la Torre. The justification for billing this political figure as "un maestro y un conductor" for all Peruvians became tightly intertwined with the level of sympathy that he was able to rouse internationally, more so than in his capacity to rally the Peruvians around a common collective project.[87] Aprista publications positioned Haya de la Torre as some sort of Peruvian emissary on international matters, suggesting that the widespread outrage his arrest provoked abroad was helping put Peru on the map.[88] These APRA leaders also highlighted the international fame that Haya de la

[84] "Por la libertad de Haya de la Torre," *La Tribuna. En el destierro*, August 1932, p. 2.

[85] "La protesta Argentina" and "Gestiones de los Congresos," in *La Tribuna. En el destierro*, August 1932, p. 3.

[86] "El cablegrama radical," *La Tribuna. En el destierro*, August 1932, p. 3.

[87] "A teacher and conductor." CEN del PAP, *Boletín del Partido Aprista Peruano*, Lima, May 23, 1932.

[88] Ibid.

Torre had secured for himself even before his detention, explaining to Peruvians that his unfair imprisonment was generating international outrage precisely because his intellectual merits had been recognized around the continent beforehand.[89] Alluding to an international public opinion favourable to Hayade la Torre, whether by way of denouncing his recent imprisonment or applauding his past intellectual contributions, bolstered the political legitimacy of this APRA leader. It likewise underscored the political benefits that a PAP placed under his leadership would be able to secure for Peru's democracy.

The reasoning behind the campaign to bring legitimacy back to Haya de la Torre was threefold. First, the PAP and the Peruvian people suffered the same ordeal at the hands of Peruvian authorities – being deprived of basic political rights at best, and enduring unfair persecution at worst. Second, Haya de la Torre commanded respect and galvanized public opinion outside Peru. Third, and *quod errata demonstratum*, a PAP placed under his leadership not only helped defend APRA militants, but it also guaranteed that foreign allies would mobilize to defend the political rights of Peruvian people. What APRA leaders attempted to do, then, was use these positions to build a storyline that could convince their Peruvian audience of one crucial point: Haya de la Torre could garner international support for his persona, the corollary of which was that he was also able to garner international support for his party and for his country.

CONTESTED HOMECOMING

With the rise to power of General Óscar R. Benavides in May 1933, following the assassination of Sánchez Cerro by a presumed Aprista, the situation in Peru finally looked poised to improve for PAP. "There is a general optimism that the reign of terror is over, and that a brighter day is dawning for Peru," stressed one observant close to the Anglo Peruvian college. "Political prisoners are daily being freed, and it is very evident that Benavides' policy is one of tolerance [...]. I believe, and everybody I have spoken to, does, that he is gradually working up to the release of the imprisoned leaders."[90] The handful of APRA leaders who controlled the CEN in Peru held similar hopes. The new government had already

[89] Ibid.
[90] Margaret Rycroft to AMG, Lima, n.d., p. 2, AMGC, Series 3, Box 3, Folder 3.5.

mitigated state repression in Peru. Rumours of a forthcoming political opening were rattling the country.[91]

As a result, the CEN began to plan the return of exiled APRAs to Peru. At first, it only ordered the homecoming of specific leaders. On June 25, 1933, the CEN forwarded a letter to that effect to the APRA leader Arturo Sabroso, who had been living for a while in Valparaiso, Chile. Members of the CEN wanted to repatriate Sabroso in order for him to undertake "una serie de trabajos importantes para el Pap."[92] The nature of these tasks remained unspecified, though given his experience as a labour activist, the CEN most likely assigned him the task of starting to mobilize and organize unions on behalf of the party.[93] Significantly, the CEN stated, as of June 1933, that ordering the return of all APRA exiles would be too hasty at that point in time. The intensity of state repression had certainly decreased in Peru, but respect for all civil liberties had yet to be reinstated and solemnly guaranteed by official authorities. The CEN preferred to handpick the exiled leaders it needed most to start organizing the party anew.[94]

Disagreement surged between the CEN in Peru and a number of APRA exiles regarding the proper tactic to adopt to plan their homecoming. The main point of contention concerned questions of timing. APRA exiles were eager to travel back home. The passage of an Amnesty Law would soon free political prisoners and guarantee the restitution of civil liberties for all citizens of Peru, but for many Apristas this was not necessary to begin coordinating the return of APRA exiles to Peru. On June 27, 1933, one Peruvian Aprista in exile in Valparaiso, Chile, expressed his point of view to Luis Eduardo Enríquez, the leader of the CAP of Santiago, in the

[91] See correspondence of APRA exiles regarding the action of the CEN in Peru in Fondo FLEEC, ENAH, "APRA," 1930–1939.

[92] "A series of important tasks for PAP," letter of Luis Eduardo Enríquez to Arturo Sabroso, Santiago de Chile, June 25, 1933, FLEEC, ENAH, "APRA," 1930–1939.

[93] Sabroso actively participated in the organization of Peruvian textile unions and in international labor organizations as well. He was a major labour activist for the Peruvian APRA Party. Pontificia Universidad Católica del Perú, Centro de documentación de ciencias sociales (hereadter cited as CEDOC), Colección especial Arturo Sabroso Montoya, Biografía, A1, 1–3; Documentos personales, AI, 4 al 6. Two months later Sabroso was named the head of the Secretary of Cooperatives of the Peruvian APRA party. "Comité Ejecutivo Nacional," Lima, August 31, 1933, Magda Portal Papers, Benson Latin American Collection, University of Texas Libraries, the University of Texas at Austin, Box 10, Folder 10.3.

[94] [Anonymous letter], Santiago, June 11, 1933, FLEEC, ENAH, México, "APRA," 1930–1939.

following terms: "Como siempre lo he pensado y como tu dices es necesario que los deportados reingresen al Perú, porque es la única manera de reorganizar nuestras huestes en todos los departamentos. Si a los enemigos les conviene que estemos lejos nosotros debemos darles la contra ingresando."[95] It was neither fair nor sufficient, berated these Apristas, that the CEN selected only a few chosen individuals for return.

That the CEN genuinely worried for the security of its members explains to a certain extent its reluctance to order the return of every APRA exile in June 1933. Another part of the explanation, however, and certainly a crucial one, is to be found in the work of the organization in the making. To better retain control over APRA, the CEN felt compelled to prepare the field to its own advantage before any other influential leader of the movement returned from exile. Handpicking the return of APRA leaders prior to a mass movement back home was an astute move for those who wanted to direct the organization.

When the Benavides government finally passed the Amnesty Law on August 11, 1933, thereby enabling every APRA exile to return to Peru and engage in national politics, the CEN was operational once again. Indeed, PAP had overhauled its program and organizational structure between the months of June and August of 1933. As evidenced by the chart finalized on August 31, 1933, detailing the composition of the new National Executive Committee of the Peruvian APRA Party, the organization of the party was firmly grounded with Haya de la Torre at the head, who, free at last, oversaw the entire committee in his role as general secretary of the party. A team of one secretary and one sub-secretary supervised the respective twenty ministries (*secretarias*) that formed the CEN, leading up to a total of forty-four members who were in charge of the direction of PAP (this number included the general secretary, Víctor Raúl Haya de la Torre, the sub-general secretary, Felipe Destefano, the national secretary, Manuel Arévalo, and finally the treasurer of the party, Manuel Pérez León).[96] This reorganization became possible as a result of

[95] "As I have always thought and as you say, it is necessary for the deported to return to Peru, because it is the only way to reorganize our troops in all departments. If it suits the enemies that we are far away, me must counter them by entering," unknown author to Luis Eduardo Enríquez, Valparaíso, Chile, June 27, 1933, FLEEC, ENAH, México, "APRA," 1930–1939.

[96] "Comité Ejecutivo Nacional," Lima, August 31, 1933, Magda Portal Papers, Benson Latin American Collection, University of Texas Libraries, the University of Texas at Austin, Box 10, Folder 10.3.

the symbolic power that PAP had acquired abroad through the intermediary of one symbol, the APRA leader Víctor Raúl Haya de la Torre.

CONCLUSION

Chapter 4 shows that the Hayista faction built its legitimacy in the early 1930s by way of embracing a democratic discourse that associated PAP with international connections and increasingly, by 1932–1933, with the fame from which the APRA leader Víctor Raúl Haya de la Torre benefited abroad. Publicizing these tales of international solidarity with this figure helped those who manned the executive committee of the party assert their control over the meaning of *Aprismo*. As such, the 1932–1933 international solidarity campaign in favour of Haya de la Torre helped secure the dominion of the Hayista faction over PAP by August 1933 and the short-lived return of democracy to Peru. APRA leaders staffing the CEN wagered on the publicity that international public opinion could have for their organization. They looked toward the international scene to justify the importance of APRA in Peru. More importantly, the CEN displayed an apparatus of political symbols linked to the figure of Haya de la Torre to validate its leadership of the party. Haya de la Torre as an intellectual and a political figure became central to any strategy that aimed at courting international public opinion. His capacity to transcend a singular Peruvian identity made him a particularly powerful symbol throughout Latin America. Both his image and his life story were easily and extensively appropriated by different groups of actors and versions of the narrative began to proliferate across borders.

As Chapter 4 makes clear, past and current experiences of exile continued to provide political opportunities for the survival of APRA well beyond its foundational years in the 1920s. In the early 1930s, part of APRA's success in building local support for its national-popular agenda was very much entangled, both in discourse and in practice, with its deep-rooted internationalism. It is not a coincidence that the rise of PAP as a populist movement in Peru was concomitant with the growth of its international solidarity networks. The substantial traction that APRA was able to gather abroad, as an anti-imperialist and moderate leftist movement praised for its advocacy of Latin American sovereignty, became a key political asset for persecuted Apristas. Another important outcome of APRA's recurring use of foreign allies and exile to ensure the political survival of PAP was that it became impossible for these leaders to think of Peruvian politics without engaging in dialogue with international actors. This continued to be the case throughout the 1930s and in the early 1940s, as shown in the next chapter. Courting international public opinion and foreign allies became the prime strategy favoured by the APRA community to ensure its political survival in Peru.

5

Transnational Solidarity Networks in the Era of the Catacombs, 1933–1939

The consolidation of the Peruvian APRA party (PAP) as a populist force in Peru during the 1930s and early-to-mid 1940s, took place amidst recurrent waves of political repression. The period of political opening that ensued from the passage of the Amnesty Law in August 1933 began to wane by January of the following year. In the face of growing social unrest across the country, the Benavides government resumed persecution against labour organizations and political opponents, cracking down on APRA leaders with particular resolve. PAP's activities were once more restricted and closely monitored, and eventually they were banned altogether. Things took a turn for the worse toward the end of 1934. When the Benavides government cancelled the holding of the parliamentary elections that were scheduled to take place in the spring of 1934, different factions of PAP found themselves exasperated with the impossibility of ever participating openly in Peruvian politics. As a result, they reverted to violence to express their political will and launched a series of uprisings on November 25, 1934, in the departments of Lima, Ayacucho, Huancayo, and Huancavelica.[1] But the party did not have sufficient

Extracts from Chapter 5 first appeared in Geneviève Dorais, "Missionary Critiques of Empire, 1920–1932: Between Interventionism and Anti-Imperilaism," *The International History Review*, 39: 3 (2017): 377–403, DOI: 10. 1080/07075332.2016. 1230767. Visit the Journa;s' website: www.tandfonline.com/.

[1] Nelson Manrique, "*¡Usted Fue Aprista! Bases para una historia critica del APRA*," Lima: Fondo editorial PUCP, 2009, pp. 99–100.

means to sustain its insurrectionary line: a combination of poor planning and inexperience led to a complete fiasco.[2]

These failed rebellions of November 1934 marked an important tipping-point in the history of *Aprismo*. PAP relapsed into full outlawry shortly thereafter. APRA militants were soon imprisoned or sent into exile. As for those who remained in Peru, they looked for hiding places and quickly retreated into underground activity. It took eleven more years before PAP retrieved legal status and was authorized to openly participate again in Peruvian politics. This new spate of repression marked the beginning of what has come to be known in the Aprista lore as the "Era of the catacombs." This expression, especially used by the historians and activists of APRA, describes the historical period that spanned the years from 1934 to 1945, during which APRA followers in Peru suffered unremitting state persecution, first under the military regime of Oscar R. Benavides (1933–1939), and then under the presidency of civilian Manuel Prado Ugarteche (1939–1945).[3]

As a result of this ongoing state persecution, the question of survival for APRA remained intimately connected with the necessity of finding communities of support abroad. Chapter 5 explores the roles and the workings of these solidarity networks during the 1930s. It shows that throughout this period, the survival of PAP hinged on its capacity to remain connected to the external world. Communities of APRA exiles stationed abroad connected with non-Latin American allies, especially with past Christian and pacifist allies like Anna Melissa Graves, to create and sustain solidarity networks that worked in favour of the persecuted PAP in Peru. Chapter 5 first turns to the role that communities of exiled Apristas adopted to sustain the integrity of their movement in Peru. It then studies the contribution and collaboration of foreign intermediaries

[2] Armando Villanueva and Pablo Macera, *Arrogante Montonero*, Lima: Fondo Editorial del Congreso del Perú, 2011, pp. 113–114; Armando Villanueva and Guillermo Thornlike, *La Gran Persecución, 1932–1956*, Lima: s.n., 2004, pp. 44–52.

[3] The election of José Luis Bustamante y Rivero in 1945 hallmarked an era of democratic hopes in Peru. For the first time since 1931, the head of the Peruvian state was freely elected. In May 1945, the APRA party achieved legal status in Peru and prepared for forthcoming elections. Several Apristas were elected to Congress shortly thereafter. The Peruvian "Democratic Spring," however, was rapidly undermined by a spiral of governmental crises that rocked the country and ultimately led to the return of military and authoritarian rule in October 1948. Harry Kantor, *The Ideology and Program of the Peruvian Aprista Movement*, New York: Octagon Books Inc., 1966. Peter Flindell Klarén, *Peru: Society and Nationhood in the Andes*, New York and Oxford: Oxford University Press, 2000.

and allies of the party and highlights their significance for the cohesion and political survival of APRA in Peru.

EXILES DEFEND APRA ON INTERNATIONAL PLATFORMS

On June 29, 1935, during an interview with agents of the United Press in Buenos Aires, the Peruvian Minister of Foreign Affairs, Carlos Concha, voiced his outrage at the continental campaign of shame that the APRA movement was fronting against the Peruvian government. "No es cierto," Concha told the group of Argentine journalists and foreign correspondents who stood before him, "que el Gobierno peruano haya organizado sin motivo ni justificación una campaña de persecución política contra el Apra."[4] Concha explained how, in contrast to recent allegations from Aprista followers, the use of repressive methods in Peru had become a necessary evil in the face of radical elements unwilling to cooperate. Their lack of respect for the law, despite the passage of the Amnesty Law and the return of civil liberties in August 1933, substantiated his self-absolving narrative: APRA followers had refused from day one, argued Concha, to rally behind Benavides' call for national conciliation.[5] "Se hace, pues, necesario decir de una vez toda la verdad," he stated, thanking his international audience for giving him the opportunity to tell the truth and set things right once and for all.[6] Two short seasons had passed since the return of PAP into full outlawry, and already jostling for public opinion outside Peru was a common feature of the war opposing Apristas to Peruvian authorities.

Throughout the 1930s, the communities of exiled Apristas came to play a crucial role in the defence of the Peruvian APRA on international platforms. They organized protests and published articles in the foreign press that condemned the undemocratic regime of Benavides. From Chile and Argentina to Mexico and the United States through France, anti-Benavides propaganda mushroomed in local newspapers and political flyers, carrying APRA's resentment against national politics, as well as its drive to survive as a thriving political movement in Peru and across the Americas. APRA leaders in exile, as well as those who remained in hiding in Peru, were very much attuned to the necessity to cultivate

[4] "It is not true that the Peruvian Government has organized without reason or justification a campaign of political persecution against APRA." "Hizo declaraciones en Buenos Aires el Canciller peruano Dr. Carlos Concha," *El Comercio*, June 29, 1935, Folder 2, Box 5698, Central Files, Record Group 59 (RG 59), 1930–1939, US National Archives at College Park, College Park, MD (NACP).

[5] Ibid. [6] "It is therefore necessary to tell the whole truth at once," ibid.

public opinion in order to build support both within Peru and, crucially, internationally. The success of this liberation campaign persuaded a large swath of the party leadership that appealing to international public opinion was an efficient strategy for the suppression of state persecution in the homeland.[7] International public opinion, the party leadership concluded, had the power to beget change when used strategically.[8] Thus, as the noose tightened on Apristas in Peru at the end of 1934, wooing international public opinion and censuring Peruvian authorities in the foreign press became the central axis of PAP's political actions.

During the 1930s, Apristas published hundreds of articles and flyers condemning the Benavides government for depriving Peruvian citizens of their constitutional rights, and specifically for exacting state persecution against the APRA party. The communiqué that Víctor Peralta, the imprisoned APRA leader in Peru, addressed to the foreign press on June 12, 1935, exemplifies these attempts to publicly shame the Peruvian authorities in an effort to sway continental public opinion in APRA's favour.[9] Peralta was the Secretary General of the Executive Committee for the Political and Social Prisoners (Secretario General del Comité Ejecutivo de Presos Políticos y Sociales) detained in el Frontón, the infamous detention centre where Apristas were carted off to in Peru.[10] "Hacen ya más de 7 meses," decried Peralta in the communiqué, "que más de 2000 apristas nos encontramos viviendo en el presidio como en los días más negros de la persecución durante el gobierno del Sr. General Luis M. Sánchez Cerro, sin haber cometido otro delito que el exigir se respete nuestro derecho a la ciudadanía."[11] Peralta further condemned the

[7] Hector A. Morey to Jane Addams, Lima, September 21, 1933, Series 3, Box 3, Folder 3.8, AMGC; Luis E. Heysen to Anna Melissa Graves (AMGC), Mèxico, DF, April 27, 1933, SCPC, AMGP (1919–1953), Reel 74.8.

[8] Dr. Giesecke, "Memorandum: The Apra Party from Day to Day," August 28, 1933, p. 1, Folder 4, Box 4696, RG 59, 1930–1939, NACP.

[9] Víctor Peralta, Secretario General, El Comité de Presos Políticos – Sociales recluidos en El Frontón, "A todas las organizaciones revolucionarias y conciencias libres de Indo América y del Mundo," El Frontón, June 12, 1935, Pontificia Universidad Católica del Perú, Centro de documentación de ciencias sociales (CEDOC), Colección especial Arturo Sabroso Montoya, Correspondencia de LAS y VRHT y ASM: Importantes, B1, 933 al 951.

[10] Guillermo Vegas León, "Las Torturas y los Crímenes de la Isla 'El Frontón'," *Claridad*, Buenos Aires, Ano XVII, num. 324, April 1938. Armando Bazán, *Prisiones junto al mar, novela*, Buenos Aires: Editorial *Claridad*, 1943.

[11] "For more than seven months, more than 2000 Apristas have been living in prison like in the darkest days of persecution under the General Luis M. Sánchez Cerro, without having committed a crime other than demanding respect for our right to citizenship." Peralta, "A todas las organizaciones revolucionarias y conciencias libres de Indo América."

gruesome conditions that political prisoners endured in Peruvian jails. Many of the Aprista prisoners, he noted, were sick and fearing for their lives.[12] By way of this communiqué to the foreign press, Peralta claimed to be launching on behalf of all Aprista prisoners, "nuestro grito de condenación y protesta por el atropello de que somos víctimas," specifically chiding Peruvian authorities for the spate of renewed injustices perpetrated against PAP in Peru.[13]

While evidence points to more attempts from within Peru to engage in this international war of words against the Peruvian military government, APRA exiles in fact bore the lion's share of the organizing work in support of their persecuted peers in Peru. "Que sepan que no abandonamos un instante la vigilancia y que los puestos del destierro son puestos de incesante trabajo aprista," wrote Luis Alberto Sánchez in 1936 to a peer detained in El Frontón, while living in Santiago de Chile.[14] Ironically, the year-long cycle of deportations that came with the return to illegality in 1934–1935 auspiciously positioned APRA with players outside Peru who benefited from freedom of speech and expression. APRA leaders in exile had, therefore, more opportunity to court foreign allies. Deported leaders of the party promptly reinstated exile committees across the American continent. While archival evidence points to the presence of Aprista activists in Ecuador, Panama, Bolivia, Mexico, Chile, Argentina, France, and the United States, the growing scholarship on the transnational APRA has clearly established that three communities of APRA exiles were particularly active during the 1930s in these solidarity campaigns. They were the Comité Aprista de Santiago (CAP of Santiago), the Comité Aprista of Buenos Aires (CAP of Buenos Aires), and the Comité Aprista de México (CAP of Mexico).[15] In these organizations lay the backbone of APRA's international militancy.

12 Ibid.

13 "Our cry of condemnation and protest for the outrage of which we are victims," ibid.

14 "Let them know that we do not abandon our watch for an instant and that the places of exile are places of incessant Aprista work," Luis Alberto Sánchez to Arturo Sabroso, [Santiago de Chile], June 8, 1936, Pontificia Universidad Católica del Perú, Centro de documentación de ciencias sociales (hereafter cited as CEDOC), Colección especial Arturo Sabroso Montoya, Correspondencia de LAS y VRHT y ASM: Importantes, B1, 933 al 951.

15 Leandro Sessa, "Aprismo y apristas en Argentina: Derivas de una experiencia antiimperialista en la 'encrucijada' ideológica y política de los años treinta." Ph.D. Diss., Universidad Nacional de La Plata, 2013," p. 91; Report of Louis G. Dreyfus to Secretary of State, "Recrudescence of APRA activities," Lima, September 7, 1938, and Report of diplomatic staff Steinhardt, "Aprista letter from Mexico as a sample of anti-Benavides propaganda abroad," Peru, April 4, 1938, Folder 1, Box 4697, RG 59, 1930–1939, NACP.

LIFE IN EXILE

Deportation came with its share of challenges, too, especially for the rank-and-file of the party. To begin, those who left Peru never fully escaped the spectre of state persecution. Arrest and deportation occasionally befell them in foreign countries as well.[16] At other times, authorities of the host country intervened and pressured APRA exiles into ceasing their activities against the Peruvian government. After an agent of the Chilean Ministry of Foreign Relations threatened Carlo Alberto Eyzaguirre, Gerardo Alania, Jorge Valverde and Leoncio Muños, four representatives and leaders of APRA who lived in Santiago de Chile, they reportedly agreed to stop their work in July 1935.[17] Also, exile was fraught with all kinds of emotional and material hardships, which eventually drove many to balk and withdraw from political activism. Starting in the mid-1930s, a considerable number of Peruvian apristas who lived in the Chilean capital initiated contact with the Peruvian ambassador to Chile to demand political amnesty. They promised to leave the APRA party and to cease all political activities in exchange for the right to return home.[18]

Various factors explain their defection from APRA. Some, like Gerardo Berrios, had grown disenchanted with their party for never feeling included in it. Berrios was part of the 84 Apristas deported from Peru between December 6, 1934, and August 20, 1935. Eight of them were sent to Ecuador, 16 to Panama, and 60, including Berrios, to Chile.[19] Berrios told the Peruvian ambassador to Chile in January 1935 that he had joined APRA because he wanted to change things and make a difference for his country. But, to his dismay, the party leadership in the CAP of Santiago never agreed to give him any substantial role or responsibility. In Chile, Berrios was left without any means of subsistence

[16] A pact of mutual assistance to better fight Communism in their respective countries was for example designed between Peru, Chile, and Argentina in the course of 1933. [Peruvian ambassador to Chile,] "Adhesión de Chile al Convenio peruano argentino sobre el comunismo," Santiago de Chile, June 13, 1933, Archivo Central del Ministerio de Relaciones Exteriores, Perú, Oficios de Chile, 5-4-A, 1933.

[17] [Peruvian ambassador to Chile], "Notificación a los lideres apristas," Santiago de Chile, August 5, 1935, Archivo Central del Ministerio de Relaciones Exteriores, Perú, Oficios de Chile, 5-4-A, 1935.

[18] [Peruvian ambassador to Chile], "Deportados políticos," Santiago de Chile, January 2, 1935, Ministerio de Relaciones Exteriores, Archivo Central, Oficios de Chile, 5-4-A, 1935. See also for more examples Archivo Central del Ministerio de Relaciones Exteriores, Perú, Oficios de Chile, 5-4-A, 1936.

[19] "Relación de deportados políticos," Lima, 11 de noviembre de 1935, Archivo General del la Nación, Lima (hereafter cited as AGN), Ministerio de Interior, Dirección de gobierno, Prefectura de Lima, Presos Políticos y Sociales, Legajo 3.9.5.1.15.1.14.7 (1932–1942).

and with nothing to do in terms of political activity. By January 1935, Berrios decided he had had enough of *Aprismo* and was ready to return home.[20] Many rank-and-file members of APRA were similarly left on their own, without a job or enough money to support themselves, "sin tener ni siquiera como alimentarse, ni donde alojarse," highlighted a report penned by the Peruvian ambassador to Chile on January 11, 1935.[21] For Pedro R. Iraola, family obligations convinced him to let go of APRA. He solicited Peruvian authorities in Chile in January 1936 for the right to travel back to Lima to take care of his sick mother.[22]

In contrast, those who manned the committees and occupied positions of power within APRA's exiled chapters were usually quick to acknowledge their favourable circumstances compared to those of their peers back home. In exile, most leaders of the party lived comfortable and generally enviable lives, away from the threat of persecution that Apristas in Peru suffered daily. Leaders like Luis Alberto Sánchez had time and access to resources, enabling them to develop prolific and internationally famed careers as men of letters. "Con ellos," promised – somewhat guiltily – Sánchez to his peers in prison, "en su dolor, que es solo angustia en nosotros los privilegiados del exterior."[23] Many APRA leaders felt compelled to compensate for this life of privilege with a steadfast level of activism in support of the Peruvian APRA party.[24] Others were simply following the instructions they received from the party leadership. Yet all worked together to defend the cause of APRA in an attempt to retrieve their legal rights in Peru.[25]

20 [Peruvian ambassador in Chile], "Solicitud de Gerardo Berrios," Santiago de Chile, January 11, 1935, Archivo Central del Ministerio de Relaciones Exteriores, Perú, Oficios de Chile, 5-4-A, 1935.

21 "Without having anything to eat, or a place to stay." [Peruvian ambassador to Chile], "Solicitud de dos deportados," Santiago de Chile, January 11, 1935, Archivo Central del Ministerio de Relaciones Exteriores, Perú, Oficios de Chile, 5-4-A, 1935. For more similar cases see Archivo Central del Ministerio de Relaciones Exteriores, Perú, Oficios de Chile, 5-4-A, in 1934, 1935, and 1936.

22 [Peruvian ambassador to Chile], "Deportado Pedro R. Iraola," Santiago de Chile, January 17, 1936, Archivo Central del Ministerio de Relaciones Exteriores, Perú, Oficios de Chile, 5-4-A, 1936.

23 "With them, feeling their pain, which is only anguish in us, the privileged in exile," Luis Alberto Sánchez to Arturo Sabroso, [Santiago de Chile], June 8, 1936, Pontificia Universidad Católica del Perú, Centro de documentación de ciencias sociales (CEDOC), Colección especial Arturo Sabroso Montoya, Correspondencia de LAS y VRHT y ASM: Importantes, B1, 933 al 951.

24 Alfredo Saco, "Nuestros Presos," *Trinchera Aprista*, Mexico City, November, 1937, p. 1.

25 Ricardo Melgar Bao, *Redes e imaginario del exilio en México* y América Latina: 1934–1940, Argentina: LibrosenRed, 2003, p. 99.

SHAMING THE BENAVIDES GOVERNMENT

A large part of APRA exiles' activism involved penning opinion and information pieces and organizing public protests in an effort to arouse sympathy for the APRA movement in international forums. Consider the virulent attack that the General Secretary of the CAP of Santiago, Alberto Grieve Madge, fired off against the Peruvian authorities in the pages of *La Opinión* on December 5, 1934. "Ni elecciones, ni garantías, ni prensa: solo persecuciones, prisiones y arbitrariedades," read the subtitle of his diatribe. Alberto Grieve Madge pilloried the so-called "democratic" regime of general Benavides, which lived and governed, he stated, with respect for neither the Constitution nor the Peruvian laws. "Se ha atropellado a los candidatos, se les ha perseguido, y por último, se conciben planes para eliminarlos," stressed another section, in reference to the twenty-three Aprista congressmen ousted by Sánchez Cerro in 1932 who had yet to be reinstated under Benavides.[26] APRA leaders continued to disseminate anti-Benavides propaganda in the Chilean press all through the 1930s and early 1940s. Their contributions appeared in *La Opinión*, *Hoy*, *El Diario Ilustrado*, *Tierra*, *El Mercurio*, *La Nación*, *La Hora*, and *Trabajo*.[27] They also used public conferences to openly condemn the Peruvian authorities and disturbed the peaceful running of diplomatic events to attract attention to their cause.[28]

In similar fashion, the CAP of Buenos Aires customarily released press communiqués in the Argentinean press or disseminated political leaflets to denounce the injustices that PAP suffered in Peru. Toward the late 1930s, the *Boletín Aprista* served as a mouthpiece for the CAP of Buenos Aires, where a handful of leaders broadcasted political views and made

[26] "No elections, no rights, no press: only persecution, prisons and arbitrary rule." "Candidates have been treated with contempt, persecuted, and finally plans are being conceived to eliminate them," Alberto Grieve Madge, "Comunicado de Prensa del Comité Aprista Peruano," *La Opinión*, December 5, 1934.

[27] Archivo Central del Ministerio de Relaciones Exteriores, Perú, Oficios de Chile, 5-4-A, 1934, 5-4-A, 1936, 5-4-A, 1937, 5-4-A, 1938, 5-4-A, 1939.

[28] Report of Pedro Irigoyen to Señor Ministro de Estado en el Despacho de Relaciones Exteriores, "Manifestaciones hostiles," Santiago de Chile, October 25, 1935, Archivo Central del Ministerio de Relaciones Exteriores, Perú, Oficios de Chile, 5-4-A, 1935. "Actuación aprista en la Universidad de Chile," Santiago, 2 de junio de 1937, Archivo Central del Ministerio de Relaciones Exteriores, Perú, Oficios de Chile, 5-4-A, 1937; Carlos Concha, "Manifestación aprista contra el Dr. Marañon," Santiago, March 24, 1937, Archivo Central del Ministerio de Relaciones Exteriores, Perú, Oficios de Chile, 5-4-A, 1937.

information on Peru available to APRA followers in Argentina.[29] In its third issue, dated March 4, 1937, *Boletín Aprista* indicted Peruvian authorities for the loss of the APRA leader Manuel Arévalo. His execution three weeks earlier had allegedly followed a week-long cycle of torture and abuse. The troubling circumstances surrounding Arévalo's death had left Aprista factions across the board blazing with anger and indignation. They shared these feelings with the continental public.[30]

From their location in the Mexican capital, members of the CAP of México (officially reinstated in 1937) soon undertook an intense labour of promotion in favour of Peruvian and continental *Aprismo*. In the late 1920s the community of APRA exiles in Mexico City was impressed, and deeply influenced, by the thriving post-revolutionary scene they found in the Mexican capital. By the mid-to-late 1930s they were benefiting from the open-door policy toward political refugees afforded by the presidency of Lázaro Cárdenas (1934–1940).[31] Like its sister committees in Chile and Argentina, the CAP of Mexico engaged in the production of political propaganda that chastised the Benavides government. It did so by publishing articles in Mexican newspapers and magazines, such as the *Excélsior* and *Hoy*, which defended the political ideas of APRA and contributed to portraying Peruvian Apristas as victims of an unfair and cruel regime.[32] To be sure, Apristas in Mexico also capitalized on their Mexican mouthpiece, *Trinchera Aprista*, to report on the various forms of abuses and violations that Apristas were subjected to in Peru. Like their peers in Chile and Argentina, their attacks followed a basic two-prong discursive strategy: that of shaming Peruvian authorities and advocating the return of individual liberties in Peru on one side, while on the other extolling the heroism and resilience of Aprista militancy.[33]

29 Report from Alexander W. Weddell to Secretary of State in Washington DC, "Activities in Buenos Aires of the Peruvian Aprista Party," Buenos Aires, September 18, 1936, Folder 3, Box 5698, RG 59, 1930–1939, NACP. "Arevalo asesinado," in *Boletín Aprista*, Buenos Aires, March 4, 1937, no. 3, p. 2, AMGC, Box 3, Folder 3.8, Archives of Labor and Urban Affairs, Wayne State University.

30 "Arevalo asesinado."

31 Melgar Bao, *Redes e imaginario del exilio en México*, p. 36. Leading members of this committee in the mid-to-late 1930s included Guillermo Vaga León, Fernando León de Vivero, Alfredo Miro Quesada, José Bernando Goyburu, Carlos J. Meltor, Felipe Cossío del Polmar, Luis Eduardo Enríquez Cabrera (starting in 1939), Moisés Ochoa Campos, and César H. Lanegra.

32 Melgar Bao, *Redes e imaginario del exilio en México*.

33 "Cruces, cruces y más cruces…," *Trinchera Aprista: Órgano del Comité Aprista de México*, México, October 1937, p. 2; Alfredo Saco, "Nuestros Presos," *Trinchera*

Though little is still known about the types of Aprista activism in the United States, pieces of evidence found in archives point to a considerable level of activity. In 1938, the diplomatic staff of the US embassy in Peru noted the increasing amount of anti-Benavides propaganda coming from Mexico and the United States, and California in particular.[34] *Trinchera Aprista* likewise reported on the growing activities of the Comité Aprista de California between 1937 and 1938.[35] We also know that Aprista exiles published in US newspapers *La Prensa* and *La Nueva Democracia*, both based in New York. Finally, archival evidence points to Aprista militants in France playing a role in channelling Aprista communiqués to European newspapers and allies stationed in Europe.[36]

BROADCASTING POPULAR SUPPORT

No matter how finely crafted, indictments of the political situation in Peru could do little to attract sympathy from abroad without first convincing international public opinion that the PAP did not deserve the all-out repression it suffered back home. To that effect, in addition to shaming Peruvian authorities, the articles and editorials that Apristas in exile disseminated across the continent took pains to depict their political movement as a paragon of democracy in Peru and, critically, across the Americas as well. Alberto Grieve Madge's 1936 account of state persecution in Peru illustrates the meticulous portrayal of APRA as undeserving of its current fate. Faced with the Peruvian government's incapacity to detain "el triunfo aplastante del aprismo" in Peru, argued Magde before a Chilean readership, *civilista* forces had found no better remedy than to eliminate "a los candidatos del pueblo." The use of attributes like "candidates of the people," as statements, which implied that there was an intimate bond between APRA and the "mayorías

Aprista, México, November 1937, p. 1; Juan Torres, "Benavides: Sapo con galones," *Trinchera Aprista*, Mexico City, March 1938, p. 8, 10.

34 Report of diplomatic staff Steinhardt, "Aprista letter from Mexico as a sample of anti-Benavides propaganda abroad," Peru, April 4, 1938; Report of Louis G. Dreyfus to Secretary of State, "Recrudescence of APRA activities," Lima, September 7, 1938; Folder 1, Box 4697, Recored Group (RG59), 1930–1939, National Archivews at College Park, MD (NACP).

35 The CAP of California was headed in 1937–1938 by the Peruvian exile Alejandro Carrillo Rocha. See "No hay que ir más lejos…," *Trinchera Aprista*, no. 4, México, January 1938, p. 4.

36 V. Delande, Secretario General, Comité de Paris, Partido Aprista Peruano, Paris, July 18, 1935, AMGC, Box 3, Folder 3.9.

ciudadanas" in Peru, was deliberate and carefully laid out.[37] As prisons overflowed with political prisoners and as attempts against the lives of APRA leaders continued to soar, crafting associations between the notion of popular support and the PAP gave the movement an air of legitimacy.

This political strategy not only affected the way that APRA portrayed its movement in Peru and abroad. It also significantly affected how the scholarship on APRA has reported the rise of this populist party, by regularly using as primary source material the political propaganda that APRA leaders in exile produced in their organization. Up until the early 1960s, Peruvians produced the bulk of Aprista scholarship. These works either correspond to Aprista celebrations of the group's historical mission and leader, Víctor Raúl Haya de la Torre, or, contrastingly, disparage the latter and APRA's political program. By the late 1970s, North American scholars had in turn produced a number of analyses on APRA that fed into classic literature on Latin American mass organizations which emphasized the political awakening of the popular and middle sectors in the region. These studies largely brought into focus, and usually praised, the reformist and democratic character of post-Second World War APRA. Yet by giving prominent attention to APRA's doctrine and discursive frames of analysis, early North American studies regularly ended up reproducing official Aprista histories.[38] These studies failed to contextualize the discursive production of a party that needed to appear strong in the face of recurrent persecution. They tend to take these claims at face value, rather than attempting to bring the complex origins from which they stem to light. One important, if controversial, conclusion to be drawn from this reasoning is to suggest that APRA's scholarly fame as a major populist Latin American movement was in fact, to at least some degree, a product of its own making. Political survival in Peru became so

[37] "The overwhelming triumph of aprismo." "the people's candidates." "citizens' majorities," Alberto Grieve Madge, "Comunicado de Prensa del Comité Aprista Peruano."

[38] Liisa North, "The Peruvian Aprista Party and Haya de la Torre: Myths and Realities," *Journal of Interamerican Studies and World Affairs*, 17: 2 (May, 1975): 245–253; Harry Kantor, *The Ideology and Program of the Peruvian Aprista Movement*, New York: Octagon Books Inc., 1966 (1953); Frederick B. Pike, "The Old and the New APRA in Peru: Myth and Reality," *Inter-American Economic Affairs*, 18 (Autumn, 1964): 3–45; Grant Hilliker, *The Politics of Reform in Peru: The Aprista and Other Mass Parties of Latin America*, Baltimore: Johns Hopkins Press, 1971; Robert J. Alexander, *Aprismo: The Ideas and Doctrines of Victor Raul Haya de la Torre*, Kent: Kent State University Press, 1973.

closely intertwined with the necessity of a strong casting internationally that it affected the political writings and interpretations of Apristas.

Indeed, the need to appear strong in the face of state persecution partly explains the care with which Aprista propaganda underscored the strong popular support that the APRA enjoyed in Peru and internationally. "En todo el Continente no se oye más que un clamor de indignada protesta," highlighted Juan Torrente in 1938 in *Trinchera Aprista*, suggesting that continental outrage against the crimes exacted by Benavides in Peru was rocking the Americas.[39] Similarly, the CAP of Buenos Aires touted the assassination of Manuel Arévalo in 1937 as an event that bore meaning not only for Peru but also for the democratic forces of the continent, suggesting that "toda la Prensa libre de América, ha unido su voz de protesta a la nuestra, ante el desborde de la sañuda persecución que el tirano Benavides, desata implacablemente contra el partido del pueblo."[40] To better attract attention to the precarious situation of the APRA party in Peru, stirring compassion by insisting on the democratic nature of this organization quickly became crucial in these international forums.

According to sociologists Margaret Keck and Kathryn Sikkink, informational politics are the process through which non-state actors engage in a transnational advocacy campaign try to gain power by providing alternative sources of information. These actors "provide information that would not otherwise be available, from sources that might not otherwise be heard, and they must make this information comprehensible and useful to activists and publics who may be geographically and/or socially distant."[41] As such, engaging in informational politics outside Peru enabled PAP to destabilize the narrative monopoly that Peruvian authorities and the traditional elites associated with *civilismo* tried to enforce across Peru and the American continent. It offered alternative channels of information whose stories contrasted greatly with those disseminated in Peru by the

39 "All over the continent you hear nothing but a single cry of outraged protest." Juan Torrente, "Benavides: Sapo con galones," *Trinchera Aprista*, México, March 1938, pp. 8, 10.

40 "The entire free press of America has joined its voice of protest to ours, before the vicious persecution that the tyrant Benavides is implacably unleashing against the people's party." "Arevalo asesinado," in *Boletín Aprista*, Buenos Aires, March 4, 1937, no. 3, p. 2, AMGC, Box 3, Folder 3.8, Archives of Labor and Urban Affairs, Wayne State University.

41 Margaret E. Keck and Kathryn Sikkink, *Activists Beyond Borders: Advocacy Networks in International Politics*, Ithaca and London: Cornell University Press, 1998, pp. 18–19.

civilista press like *El Comercio*, the sworn enemy of PAP, and in the Americas by diplomats and government spokesmen. It likewise aimed to court democratic allies outside Peru, in the hopes that the latter group would mediate on its behalf and persuade governmental forces to reinstate civil liberties in the country.

To achieve this goal, the Aprista committees crafted their diatribes in the foreign press around two fundamental premises. First, they laid bare the inconsistencies of the Peruvian authorities before an international audience. This implied lifting the veil on the dysfunctional state of democracy in Peru, while in turn taking pains to compare this precarious national condition with the deceitful democratic label afforded to the Benavides regime. A spade had to be called a spade, pleaded these articles: the Benavides military regime couldn't be farther from democratic, and APRA exiles were poised to set the record straight. Second, APRA exiles shamed the Peruvian authorities for exacting state persecution against Apristas, but also for depriving, more broadly, Peruvian citizens of their most basic constitutional rights. They likewise took pains to convince their international audiences that APRA only used pacifist and democratic channels to lead its fight against governing authorities, and, moreover, that it garnered the favour of public opinion both in Peru and across the Americas.

GOVERNMENTAL RESPONSES

Peruvian authorities did not remain indifferent to the attacks that communities of APRA exiles disseminated in the foreign press. Representatives of the Peruvian state felt the need to counter and respond to these charges before international audiences. Obviously, shaming the authorities wasn't enough to restore constitutional guarantees, as PAP remained outlawed until 1945. But, in the face of a transnational campaign of moral shaming, Peruvian authorities did feel enough pressure to heed the situation and attempt to downplay the claims of repeated human rights violations. In short, they addressed these claims not by changing their behaviour, but by trying to suppress the circulation of such narratives. They did so via two strategies. First, Peruvian authorities monitored the production of APRA propaganda not only in Peru but abroad as well, mainly through the work of Peruvian diplomats established in foreign countries. They tried to thwart the production of this propaganda. Outside Peru, they also published anti-aprista propaganda that sought to harm the legitimacy of the movement and banned foreign journals and magazines – like the Chilean *Hoy* and the Argentinean *Claridad* – that were favourable to the cause of APRA from circulating in Peru.[42]

Second, Peruvian authorities put official emissaries in charge of redressing the international image of Peru. In the speech that Concha gave to representatives of the foreign press on June 29, 1935, cited earlier in this chapter, persecution in Peru looked more like a measure of last resort than a deliberate instrument of terror. According to the Peruvian officials, persecuting the government's critics, especially APRA, was regrettable, but nevertheless necessary to counter a group poised to "subvertir el orden publico" and "perturbar la paz social" in Peru.[43] A false premise framed Concha's reasoning: either constitutional guarantee with national mayhem, or exceptions to the rule of law with the promise of social peace. As Haya de la Torre put it four years later, the long-running debate in which order and law fought for preeminence had no place in functioning democracies. A democratic government, he correctly argued, simply knew how to maintain social order within the confines of the law.[44]

Interestingly, in 1935, the US ambassador Fred Morris Dearing concurred with Carlos Concha, not with APRA's reasoning. To be sure, he neither supported nor vindicated the Benavides government's use of repressive measures against APRA. But Dearing did censure Apristas for shaming the Benavides government in international publications. In the Peruvian Spring of 1935, similarly to the Peruvian Minister of Foreign Affairs, Dearing anticipated nothing good for a political party whose strategies of survival involved doing, he stated, "everything possible from refuges abroad to discredit Peru and the present administration."[45] His critique carried the insinuation that Apristas should focus exclusively on

[42] "No. 45, Folletos sobre el 'Apra'," Santiago de Chile, 18 April, 1932, Archivo Central del Ministerio de Relaciones Exteriores, Perú, Oficios de Chile, 5-4-A, 1932; Sessa, "Aprismo y apristas en Argentina…," pp. 98, 112–113. Consult reports that the Peruvian ambassador in Chile sent to the Ministry of Foreign Relations in 1936: "Publicación en la Revista 'Hoy'," Santiago de Chile, January 7, 1936; "Publicación sobre el Perú en la Revista 'Hoy'," Santiago, March 4, 1936; "Editorial de 'Hoy'," Santiago, July 31 1936; "Recorte de la revista 'Hoy' – Luis Alberto Sánchez," Santiago, October 3, 1936. Archivo Central del Ministerio de Relaciones Exteriores, Perú, Oficios de Chile, 5-4-A, 1936.

[43] "Subvert public order"; "disturb social peace." "Hizo declaraciones en Buenos Aires el Canciller peruano Dr. Carlos Concha," *El Comercio*, June 29, 1935, Folder 2, Box 5698, RG 59, 1930-1939, NACP.

[44] Víctor Raúl Haya de la Torre, "El Jefe del partido responde al General Benavides," Lima, January 1939, p. 7, Folder 1, Box 4697, RG 59, 1930–1939, NACP.

[45] Report of Fred Morris Dearing to Secretary of State, Lima, September 29, 1935, p. 4, Folder 2, Box 5698, RG 59, 1930–1939, NACP.

national politics and limit themselves to organizing their movement in Peru rather than continentally. Dearing maintained that, unless its enemies decided to cobble together a coalition of conservative factions, the PAP would most certainly win the presidential election scheduled to take place the following year.[46] Of course, the accuracy of such a hunch was contingent on the PAP achieving legal status. It also depended on the implicit faith that the ability to exercise political rights and to participate in free and open elections would necessarily accompany the return of civil liberties in Peru, a faith which, rightly so, APRA leaders were nowhere near sharing. In fact, as we will continue to see in this and the following chapters, the more difficult it was to organize their movement in Peru in the 1930s and early 1940s, the more Aprista leaders laboured to expand their movement abroad, and the more they worked to strengthen their maximum program for the Americas.

COURTING FOREIGN ALLIES

Part of the reason why the communities of exiled Apristas successfully drew the attention of international public opinion to their cause is because many foreign allies worked in tandem with them to spearhead their transnational shaming campaign against the military rule of Benavides. The political and intellectual community revolving around the Argentinean cultural magazine *Claridad*, for example, was particularly proactive in spearheading international solidarity campaigns in favour of major Peruvian APRA leaders like Magda Portal and Serafín Delmar.[47] Thanks to the intense organizing work of Apristas in Chile, Argentina and Mexico, men and women of letters from all over Latin America joined their voices in protest at the undemocratic regime of Benavides. So did a number of key allies from the United States, which contributed toward the expansion of the scope of APRA's solidarity networks following the transnational advocacy campaign in favour of Haya de la Torre in 1932–1933.

Roger Baldwin, chairman of the International Committee for Political Prisoners, was first acquainted with the APRA movement in 1932, when

[46] Ibid.

[47] *Por la libertad de Serafín Delmar. Aspectos de su vida y su obra*, Buenos Aires, Editorial *Claridad*, 1936; *Magda Portal. Su Vida y su obra*, Buenos Aires, Editorial *Claridad*, 1935.

he was approached to partake in the solidarity movement with Haya de la Torre. This committee continued thereafter to monitor the Peruvian authorities and to side with APRA whenever asked to.[48] Upon Luis Alberto Sánchez's request, the International Committee for Political Prisoners sent a petition to the Peruvian Minister to the United States in July 1936 which censured the undemocratic proceedings underway in Peru in view of the forthcoming elections.[49] "As a committee of representative Americans we are shocked by the apparently authentic accounts of the arrests of over 3,000 prisoners, none of whom have had as yet the benefit of a legal trial," stated the document. Members of the committee specifically condemned the arbitrary arrests of Apristas in Peru "for purely political reasons." They furthermore decried cases of torture and ill-treatment in detention to which Aprista prisoners were allegedly subjected to, urging Peruvian authorities to immediately halt political persecution and to act "in accordance with the accepted practice of democratic countries."[50] Baldwin personally sent this petition to Rolland in Switzerland, where he lived at the time, in the hopes that the latter would sign and circulate it.[51]

While the main connection between US solidarity activists and APRA had thus far primarily been confined to Haya de la Torre, the former group was increasingly in touch with different APRA leaders. They began to adapt their political discourses in international publications to praise and defend not only Haya de la Torre but the APRA party as a whole. To be sure, Haya de la Torre continued to attract sympathy from these foreign allies. In 1936, Romain Rolland sent a number of protests to

[48] Roger Baldwin was for example amongst those from the Inter-American Association for Democracy and Freedom who, in 1953, spearheaded yet another solidarity movement with Haya de la Torre. Frances R. Grant, Norman Thomas, Roger Baldwin, Clarence Senior, Ernst Schwarz, Robert Alexander and Francine Unlavy S. Levitas, "To Free Haya de la Torre. United States' Efforts to Obtain Safe Conduct for Peruvian Urged," *The New York Times*, December 15, 1953, Inter-American Association for Democracy and Freedom, Letter to the editors of *The New York Times*, *The New York Times*, December 15, 1953, Box 89, Folder 12, BDWP, 1903–1999, Hoover Institution Archives

[49] Roger Balwin to Romain Rolland, July 15, 1936, BNF, Fonds Romain Rolland, NAF 28400.

[50] [The international Committee for Political Prisoners] to Don Manuel de Freyre y Santander, Peruvian Minister to the United States, July 15, 1936, BNF, Fonds Romain Rolland, NAF 28400.

[51] Roger Balwin to Romain Rolland, July 15, 1936, BNF, Fonds Romain Rolland, NAF 28400.

President Benavides in an effort to specifically protect the life of this APRA leader (at the time in hiding in Lima and once more threatened by authorities).[52] Shortly afterward, Luis Alberto Sánchez communicated with Anna Melissa Graves to enquire whether she could join Rolland's initiative: "Una intervención en el sentido de cablegrafiar continuamente al presidente Benavides interesándose por la vida de Haya," he pleaded in a letter dated May 13, 1937, "será una manera eficaz de salvaguardarla. Ojala tome Ud. Parte en ello."[53] Graves took part in this solidarity protest and in others as well, which suggests that the support of foreign allies became more inclusive of other APRA players. Graves helped to free Magda Portal from prison in 1936 by being personally in touch with Francisco García Calderón, the Peruvian ambassador to France, who was renown to hold sway over President Benavides.[54] In 1937, she attempted to foster support in her own solidarity networks for the liberation of Agustín Haya de la Torre, Víctor Raúl's brother and also a prominent APRA leader.[55]

APRA leaders in exile very proactively sought out this international support. They became quite adept at disseminating the information on Peru they were able to collect from their peers back home to key foreign actors and encouraging them to join them in the defence of APRA. Furthermore, APRA leaders in Peru also efficiently mobilized to court foreign allies. When they heard that foreign journalists were in town, Apristas in hiding in Lima usually found a way to dodge police surveillance to greet them.[56] They organized clandestine meetings, during which they exposed in a favourable light their program and their political objectives, expressing their hopes that foreign journalists would return

52 Luis Alberto Sánchez to Graves, Santiago de Chile, May 13, 1937, SCPC, AMGP, Reel 74.8.

53 "An intervention in the sense of continuously cabled President Benavides taking an interest in Haya's life will be an effective way to save it. Hopefully you take part in it." Sánchez to Graves, Santiago de Chile, May 13, 1937, SCPC, AMGP, Reel 74.8.

54 Graves to Magda Portal, Geneva, April 18, 1936, Magda Portal Papers, Benson Latin American Collection, University of Texas Libraries, the University of Texas at Austin, Box1, Folder 2.

55 Alberto Ulloa to Graves, French Line, S.S. Île de France, October 21, 1937, Reel 74.8, SCPC, AMGP.

56 Prefectura del Departamento de Lima, Sección Orden Político, [Testimonio de Dn. Jorge Eliseo Idiaquez Rios], Lima, September 22, 1939, p. 2, AGN, Perú, Ministerio de Interior, Dirección de gobierno, Prefectura de Lima, Presos Políticos y Sociales, Legajo 3.9.5.1.15.1.14.7 (1932–1942); Carleton Beals, "The Rise of Haya de la Torre," *Foreign Affairs*, 13:2 (1935): 242. Harry Kantor, *The Ideology and Program of the Peruvian Aprista Movement*, p. 139.

home, publicly embrace their cause, and denounce the lack of democracy in Peru. "The Apristas lose no opportunity to state their case, both at home and abroad," remarked Carleton Beals in 1935, following a trip he had recently taken to Peru.[57]

Yet throughout the 1930s, for lack of a better option, letter-writing and sweet-talking remained APRA's prime political weapons. Having few recourses at hand but pen and paper, and occasional access to a typewriter as well, Apristas used the power of words and flattery to court those they needed most. The many letters that APRA leaders sent to Graves reveal that they recurrently and very gracefully complimented their allies, either for the many personal virtues they claimed to see in them or for their political commitments or both. They likewise patiently pandered to their respective emotional quirks, especially to Graves' bad temper, since with these mood changes also came support for their cause. "I am sure all the apristas love you for your activity throughout Europe and the States," assured, for example, Enrique Rojas, an APRA leader in exile in Argentina, in a letter he wrote to Graves in early January 1936.[58] "We frecuently [*sic*] remember you as one of the best friends we have abroad," stated the Aprista Eduardo Goicochea in a letter he wrote to Graves in June 1934.[59] Graves continued to be courted by Apristas throughout the 1930s as she maintained her dogged support for this political organization.

INFORMATION CONVEYOR

In addition to helping organize solidarity campaigns in favour of imprisoned APRA leaders, US intermediaries also assisted in the assembly and upkeep of channels of underground communication. Having access to intermediaries that were able to connect the Apristas in Peru amongst themselves and with the Peruvian population on one side and the communities of Apristas in exile on the other, was of paramount importance for the cohesion, let alone the survival, of the APRA movement. For one, the context of constant persecution in the 1930s caused many problems of coordination for the organization. Party leaders attempted to work together from the haven of dispersed groups in exile or from prison in

[57] Beals, "The Rise of Haya de la Torre," p. 242.

[58] Enrique Rojas to Graves, Buenos Aires, January 7, 1936, SCPC, AMGP, Reel 74.8.

[59] Letter from Eduardo Goicochea to Graves, Lima, June 1934; AMGC, Series 3, Box 3, Folder 3.9.

Peru. Interrupted correspondence found in archives and letters from uninformed party leaders, eager to receive fresh news from Peru, show that the burden of distance and outlawry foiled proper communication in the movement throughout the decade and beyond. Apristas needed help from external intermediaries to stay in touch with one another and to receive fresh news from Peru.

This reliance on external allies for communication partly explains why the number of Aprista correspondents with Graves swelled in the 1930s. During the 1920s, in addition to Haya de la Torre, Graves was in sporadic contact with a handful of APRA leaders only: Eduardo Goicochea, Manuel Cox, and Luis Heysen. By 1935, Graves regularly wrote and exchanged letters with some of the most prominent leaders of APRA at the time, including Magda Portal, Enrique Rojas, Felipe Cossío del Polmar, Luis Alberto Sanchez, Manuel Seoane, Manuel Vasquez Díaz, and Alberto Hidalgo. By the mid-1930s, Graves had become a go-to reference for anybody close to the movement who lived abroad and wanted to be kept abreast of the latest developments in Peru. "Le agradecería infinitamente si me pudiese dar noticias del Apra, pues yo carezco en absoluto de ellas," Luis Dorich Torres wrote to Graves from Paris, France, on May 6, 1938. Though Dorich's affiliation to the APRA party remains open to question, his letter to Graves makes clear that he craved news from Peru and APRA's political project, and that Dorich knew that Graves was an important player to contact to learn more about the state of the APRA movement.[60] APRA leaders used Graves' access to information to their own benefit. In their letters to Graves in the mid-1930s, Apristas like Enrique Rojas and Manuel Seoane showed eagerness to hear about the political situation in Peru. "Let me here of you soon," Rojas wrote to Graves in November 1936, "with your opinion on the Peruvian situation as well as that of any Peruvian you have the opportunity of hearing."[61] In January 1935, Seoane wrote to Graves to scrape any piece of information he could about Haya de la Torre's (he was then hiding in the Peruvian capital) situation.[62]

Because of state censorship, Apristas also needed help from external allies to disseminate and circulate their political material. Bergel has

[60] "I would be infinitely grateful if you could give me some news of APRA, since I don't have any at all," Luis Dorich T. to Graves, Paris, May 5, 1938, SCPC, AMGP, Reel 74.8.

[61] Rojas to Graves, Buenos Aires, November 14, 1936, SCPC, AMGP, Reel 74.8.

[62] Manuel Seoane to Graves, Montevideo, January 30, 1935, SCPC, AMGP, Reel 74.8; Rojas to Graves, Buenos Aires, March 8, 1935, SPCP, AMGP, Reel 74.8.

examined the contribution of young *canillistas*, or newsboys, to help the APRA party shun censorship and disseminate its newspapers to the largest possible audience in Peru.[63] Another important group of intermediaries were family members. For example, Haya de la Torre's sister visited him weekly during his detention in 1932–1933 and she took pains to keep the rest of the community abreast of his moods and physical health.[64] Children of imprisoned APRA leaders sometimes transported, without having a clear understanding of what they were doing, hidden letters and other forbidden material in their clothes and bodies when they visited a parent in prison. Since young children were usually dispensed from the mandatory body search, the party occasionally used them as messengers to communicate with Apristas in prison.[65] Foreign diplomats favourable to the cause of APRA also helped forward letters and material from one community to another from time to time. In 1932, Peruvian authorities accused the Mexican ambassador to Peru, Juan B. Cabral, of smuggling APRA propaganda into Peru by way of diplomatic suitcases.[66] Although Cabral vehemently denied this allegation, evidence in the work of historian Ricardo Melgar Bao suggests that Mexican diplomats similarly assisted APRA on more than one occasion in the 1930s.[67]

Another addition to this list is the group of Christian intermediaries. During most of the 1930s, the small community of Christian missionaries to Peru, who revolved around the Colegio Anglo-Peruano, continued to play a crucial role in connecting APRA leaders in prison with their political community inside and outside the country. The letters that Graves exchanged throughout the 1930s with Margaret Rycroft and Maria Rosa Ribeiro and her son, Samuel Ribeiro Ibáñez, all members of the Protestant community in Lima, as well as with a growing number of APRA leaders, enable us to map out the extent of this support via two main branches.[68]

[63] Martín Bergel, "De canillitas a militantes. Los niños y la circulación de materiales impresos en el proceso de popularización del Partido Aprista Peruano (1930–1945)," *Iberoamericana*, XV: 60 (2015): 101–115.

[64] Rycroft to Graves, Lima, 11 June 1932; Rycroft to Graves, Lima, 21 July 1932; Rycroft to Graves, Lima, September 5, 1932, AMGC, Series 3, Box 3, folder 3.5.

[65] Bergel, "De canillitas a militantes."

[66] "El entredicho peruano-mejicano," *La Gaceta*, Tucumán, May 18 1932, III-1-1-(1), Archivo Histórico de la Secretaria de Relaciones Exteriores, México.

[67] Melgar Bao, *Redes e imaginario del exilio en México y América Latina.*

[68] These leaders included Magda Portal, Enrique Rojas, Felipe Cossio del Polmar, Luis Alberto Sanchez, Manuel Seoane, Manuel Vasquez Díaz, and Alberto Hidalgo.

First, Graves' correspondence reveals that Christian intermediaries helped to circulate Aprista propaganda and other types of censored material (such as correspondence) inside and outside Peru. Thanks to her relations with Protestants in Peru, Graves was able to collect information about Peruvian affairs, which she then disseminated across different communities of exile. All scrambled to gather as much news as they could about the situation in the country, through correspondence by party members in hiding in Peru, foreign newspapers, or even at times hearsay, Graves included. These actors took pains to exchange this information within their respective networks, with specific individuals like Graves serving as the hub around which information passed.

Two informants in Peru were particularly useful to Graves and the APRA community in exile. The first was Margaret Rycroft, a Protestant missionary to Peru who helped direct the Colegio Anglo-Peruano with her husband and the director of the institution between 1922 and 1940, W. Stanley Rycroft. Graves and Rycroft had met during her stay in Peru back in 1922. In the early-to-mid-1930s, Rycroft regularly wrote to Graves to report on the political situation. Her letters to Graves provided detailed accounts of the persecution of the APRA party, with specific details regarding Haya de la Torre's activities. Graves requested that Rycroft keep her updated with the whereabouts of "her boy."[69] From their correspondence, we learn that Graves forwarded letters addressed to Haya de la Torre – and other APRA leaders as well – to Rycroft, who proceeded to distribute her letters to Apristas in hiding in Lima.

The other informant was Maria Rosa Ribeiro, a Peruvian Methodist and a staunch supporter of the APRA movement, with whom Graves began to correspond in February 1934 following Rycroft's recommendation. Ribeiro was particularly useful to Graves, and not just because she knew the whereabouts of party leaders in hiding in Peru. Archival evidence also suggests that she was in regular contact with several of them. Ribeiro sporadically wrote to Graves between 1934 and 1939. Her letters contained detailed accounts of the political situation in Peru and of the fate of the APRA party. Rycroft and Ribeiro were also in touch with one another and seem to have tried to coordinate their actions so as to assist the APRA against the "tyrannical" and "dishonest" Peruvian government.[70] Both used their connections in Peru to gather news about those

[69] Margaret Rycroft to Graves, [Lima], 9 March 1932; Margaret Rycroft to Graves, Miraflores, March 11, 1932, AMGC, Series 3, Box 3, Folder 3.5.

[70] Rycroft to Graves, [Lima], March 9, 1932, AMGC, Series 3, Box 3, Folder 3.5.

in hiding in Lima and to forward the correspondence sent by Graves to Haya de la Torre and others in the party. Rycroft and Ribeiro also served, via Graves, as intermediaries, forwarding letters penned by Apristas in prison or in hiding to contacts outside Peru.[71]

Second, Christian intermediaries in Peru likewise sent APRA members books and political material they wanted them to read in hiding or in prison. Confronted with scant resources and difficult communication avenues in diasporic networks, many APRA leaders initiated contact with Graves in the early-to-mid-1930s with specific requests and demands for favours. Some asked for books, publications and political material that were otherwise difficult to access while suffering persecution in Peru or trying to get by with the scant resources afforded by life in exile.[72] "Please send me any journal or book you have at hand," Enrique Rojas, the secretary of press and propaganda of the CAP of Buenos Aires, wrote to Graves on August 17, 1935. In January 1934, Eduardo Goicochea, the General Secretary of the Aprista Medical Syndicate, asked Graves to send from Brazil, where she travelled at the time, governmental brochures on the subjects of public sanitation, hospitals, and health cooperatives and all the publications that she could find issued by renown Brazilian state institutes.[73] Goicochea, who then resided in Peru, craved access to foreign literature to help define the party's orientation on questions of public health.[74] Magda Portal enthusiastically welcomed the letters and the books that Graves sent to her during her stay in a Peruvian prison in 1935. Portal asked for more, as they helped fight the solitude of her detention and helped to develop her political thinking.[75]

Graves complied with APRA leaders' demands, sending along the material they requested, or else carefully choosing which information she thought would help them understand the virtue of absolute

[71] Rycroft to Graves, Lima, March 26, 1932; Rycroft to Graves, [Lima], 5 April 1932; Rycroft to Graves, Lima, September 5, 1932, AMGC, Series 3, Box 3, Folder 3.5. For an example of letters penned by Apristas, which left Peru thanks to the intermediary of Margaret Rycroft, see AMGC, Series 3, Box 3, Folder 3.8.

[72] Enrique Rojas to Graves, Buenos Aires, October 22, 1934, SCPC, AMGP, Reel 74.8.

[73] Eduardo Goicochea to Graves, Lima, January 17, 1934; Goicochea to Graves, Lima, March 16, 1934; AMGP, Series 3, Box 3, Folder 3.9.

[74] Goicochea to Graves, Lima, March 29, 1934; AMGP, 1921–1948, Series 3, Box 3, Folder 3.9.

[75] Portal to Graves, St. Tomas, October 10, 1935, Graves to Portal, Geneva, September 10, 1935, Graves to Portal, [Geneva?], November 17, 1935, Magda Portal Papers, Benson Latin American Collection, University of Texas Libraries, the University of Texas at Austin, Box 1, Folder 1.

pacifism.[76] This point is crucial to understand Graves' commitment to supporting the APRA. Graves was a very stubborn woman. She was as determined in the 1930s to orient APRA's envisioned revolution for Peru and the Americas toward pacifism as she had been when shaping Haya de la Torre's political trajectory in the previous decade. As a result, Graves happily engaged with APRA leaders who asked for her assistance because doing so gave her the opportunity to influence them. For example, Graves sent APRA leaders in exile books like *The Conquest of Violence*, by Bart de Ligt, which studied the practice and theory of non-violence, as well as US magazines like *the New Leader*, which dovetailed with her liberal and anti-communist positions.[77] She also forwarded her own publications on pacifism, including "I Have Tried to Think," "Hate-Mongers Again," and "Some of the Causes of war and some ways of making those causes less potent."[78] When Apristas confessed to having a hard time reading the material she sent in English, Graves then wrote long and detailed letters in Spanish to party leaders, either in exile or in prison in Peru, encouraging them to advance their agenda of Latin American solidarity, rather than Peruvian nationalism, to the forefront of their current fight. Over and above everything else, she urged them to cling to absolute pacifism in their fight against Peruvian authorities.[79]

Other important and recurrent demands involved asking intermediaries like Graves to distribute APRA's political material to their own networks. APRA leaders customarily shipped their latest work to Graves in the hopes that she might help promote APRA's ideas to her own contacts. To that end, in October 1935, Luis Alberto Sánchez sent Graves his latest publication, *Vida y pasión de la cultural en América*. "Tal vez podría interesar a otras personas que [carecen] de un panorama de nuestra América," Sánchez hinted.[80] This request for international

[76] See letters of Goicochea to Graves from January 17, 1934 to November 14, 1934 in AMGP, Series 3, Box 3, Folder 3.9; Graves to [Ribeiro?], Geneva, November 19, 1935, Magda Portal Papers, Benson Latin American Collection, University of Texas Libraries, the University of Texas at Austin, Box1, Folder 1.

[77] Rojas to Graves, Buenos Aires, June 23, 1936; Rojas to Graves, Buenos Aires, September 8, 1938; SCPC, AMGP, Reel 74.8; SCPC, AMGP, Reel 74.8; Graves to [Ribeiro?], Geneva, November 19, 1935, Magda Portal Papers, Benson Latin American Collection, University of Texas Libraries, the University of Texas at Austin, Box1, Folder 1.

[78] Dorich to Graves, Paris, May 5, 1938, SCPC, AMGP, Reel 74.8.

[79] Graves to Portal, [Geneva?] November 17, 1935; Portal to Graves, Santo Tomas, January 16, 1936, MPP, Benson Latin American Collection, Box1, Folder 1; Dorich to Graves, Paris, May 5, 1938, SCPC, AMGP, Reel 74.8.

[80] "Perhaps it might interest other people who [lack] an overview of our America." Sánchez to Graves, Santiago, October 28, 1935, SCPC, AMGP, Reel 74.8.

publicity was not exceptional. When in 1934 Rojas learned from an Argentine peer that Graves was about to travel to Río de Janeiro, Brazil, he jumped on the chance and sent a letter of introduction along with ten copies of the edition of the *APRA* magazine published outside Peru. "Hemos de agradecerle la distribución de esos ejemplares," Rojas wrote to Graves on May 28, 1934, "a fin de que muchos brasileros puedan ir enterándose de nuestro movimiento y decidan formar un Comité allí."[81] Furthermore, the letters and packages that Rycroft and Graves exchanged with one another sometimes contained party propaganda such as copies of *La Tribuna* or *El APRA*, which Graves wanted to read and disseminate in her networks.[82]

SPREADING APRISTA IDEAS IN THE UNITED STATES

Scholars have marvelled at APRA's continental presence, which in many ways reflects the success of APRA's transnational organizing efforts. What is less known about the history of APRA as transnational movement, however, is that APRA leaders took pains to disseminate their ideas and their attacks against Peruvian authorities not only to Latin America but throughout the United Sates as well. Specifically, the promotion and circulation of APRA's ideas north of the Río Grande was facilitated by the assistance of foreign allies who published and promoted the ideas of APRA in US publications. This helped APRA gain a continental presence both south and north of the Río Grande.

Liberals like Earle K. James, the *New York Times* correspondent to South America, and Carleton Beals, a writer-activist devoted to bettering Latin America –US relations, enthusiastically reported on the Peruvian APRA party in the US press. In a 1934 piece which appeared in *Current History*, James extolled the nationalist program of the Peruvian APRA party. He carefully and positively reviewed the program's many features, from the need to better incorporate the Indigenous population of Peru into the Peruvian nation to the proposed industrialization of the country, to the recovery from foreign interests of key economic sectors. Interestingly, as he argued that APRA's objective to "peruvianize Peru" was a good thing, he drew implicit parallels between APRA's demands

[81] "We thank you for distributing these copies, so that many Brazilians can learn about our movement and decide to form a committee there." Rojas to Graves, Buenos Aires, May 28, 1934, SCPC, AMGP, Reel 74.8.

[82] Rycroft to Graves, Lima, July 19, 1932, AMGC, Series 3, Box 3, Folder 3.5.

that the Peruvian state intervene more forcefully in the economy of the country, especially needed to better the fate of the "oppressed and exploited," and the provisions of the newly passed New Deal increasing state intervention in the US economy.[83]

APRA's continental program also drew praise from these actors. In 1935, James opined in*Times* article that the continental APRA was a "vital force in South America today," for it coherently combined influences from different American cultures and traditions in its groundbreaking attempt "to envisage a State that will crystallize the age-old aspirations of security combined with liberty."[84] Carleton Beals argued that same year that "to understand the Apra movement and its leadership is to understand the probable evolution of Latin America in the years ahead."[85] In the face of the "impending political crises," which he correctly presaged would soon affect economic and political relations in the Western Hemisphere, Beals suggested that the APRA movement provided no less than "the key to Latin American developments for the next few decades." In addition to praising "its remarkable discipline and remarkable leadership," Beals was particularly enthused about APRA's ability to harmonize different class interests and to promote social justice without rejecting capitalist property.[86]

Throughout the 1930s, Christian social activists also published and promoted APRA's ideas in publications that appeared in the United States. In 1932, John A. Mackay, as we have seen, used *The Other Spanish Christ* to publish a very positive appraisal of the leadership of Peruvian politician Haya de la Torre as well as the APRA party this leader commanded in Peru.[87] For his part, Stanley Rycroft extolled the attempts made by Luis Alberto Sánchez to construe a universal American civilization inclusive of its many parts, not just its Latin component.[88] Samuel G. Inman, the secretary of the Committee of Cooperation in Latin America (CCLA), wrote articles and published books that highlighted

[83] [Translation is mine] Earle K. James, "El llamado del Aprismo a la América Latina," translated in Spanish and reproduced from *Current History* in *APRA: Revista Aprista*, Buenos Aires, January 1935, no. 9, pp. 13–14.

[84] Earle K. James, "South America Advances," *The New York Times*, New York, January 20, 1935, p. XX3.

[85] Carleton Beals, "The Rise of Haya de la Torre," pp. 236–246. Beals, *America South*, Philadelphia, New York: Lippincot Company, 1937.

[86] Beals, "The Rise of Haya de la Torre," p. 246.

[87] Mackay, *The Other Spanish Christ*, 193–198.

[88] W. Stanley Rycroft, *On this Foundation. The Evangelical Witness in Latin America*, New York: Friendship Press, 1942, p. 10.

the significance of APRA's democratic and revolutionary nature for the Americas.[89] Furthermore, Inman sat on the editorial board of *La Nueva Democracia*, a New York-based monthly review and mouthpiece of the CCLA, which came to play an important role throughout the 1930s and early 1940s, advocating the views of APRA thinkers within its Christian readership in both the United States and Latin America.

La Nueva Democracia covered continental affairs from a Christian point of view. Since its foundation in the mid-1920s, this publication had served as a coveted platform for debates between thinkers, clerical and lay alike, from all over the Western Hemisphere.[90] *La Nueva Democracia* was distributed in the United States as well as in Latin America, reaching an influential and transnational audience (it had one limitation: its articles were all in Spanish). Thus, its very format contributed to the construction and, arguably, the imagination as well, of a Hispanophone community in the Americas. Significantly, and from the very beginning, this monthly review published articles that censured US foreign policy toward Latin America. Its editorial board wanted their magazine to voice "the spirit of appreciation of the liberal North American movement against imperialism."[91] This commitment to fight US imperialism helps explain why many renowned Latin American anti-imperialists, including Apristas, published in the pages of *La Nueva Democracia* throughout the 1920s and beyond.[92]

Significantly, this monthly review regularly advertised in the 1930s the latest *Aprista* publications in its "New Arrivals" section. One 1934 article even suggested a list of books that aimed to introduce the political project of APRA to a US and Latin American public. This list included the classics *Política Aprista* and *En Torno al Imperialismo*, respectively authored by

89 Samuel G. Inman, "América Revolucionaria," *La Nueva Democracia*, New York, February 25, 1933, p. 15; Inman, *Latin America, Its Place in World Life*, Chicago: Willet, Clark, 1937.

90 Rosa del Carmen Bruno-Jofre, "Social Gospel, the Committee on Cooperation in Latin America, and the APRA: The Case of the American Methodist Mission, 1920–1930," *Canadian Journal of Latin American and Caribbean Studies/Revue canadienne des études latino-américaines et caraïbes*, 9: 18 (1984): 80; Kenneth Flint Woods, "Samuel Guy Inman – His Role in the Evolution of Inter-American Cooperation," Ph.D. Diss., The American University, 1962, pp. 95–98.

91 Virginia S. Williams, *Radical Journalists, Generalist Intellectuals, and U.S.-Latin American Relations*, Lewiston, NY: The Edwin Mellen Press, 2001, p. 58.

92 Geneviève Dorais, "Missionary Critiques of Empire, 1920–1932: Between Interventionism and Anti-Imperialism," *International History Review*, 39: 3 (2017): 377–403.

APRA leaders Haya de la Torre and Carlos Manuel Cox, whose contents included criticism of US imperialism. "Read the following books so that you can stay informed about this extraordinary movement that progressed in recent years, particularly in Peru," advised a note on top of the reading list.[93] Book reviews similarly highlighted the value of APRA's program, not just for Peru but also for the entire American continent.[94] The editors of *La Nueva Democracia* also authored several articles that openly advanced the cause of APRA. They suggested that the APRA movement sparked interest not only in Latin America but throughout the United States as well, calling the attention of everybody who was interested in the fate of the "New World."[95]

In addition to advertising the work of prominent Aprista intellectuals, the editorial board of *La Nueva Democracia* was also committed to publishing their writings. The renown APRA leader Luis Alberto Sánchez, for example, disseminated in *La Nueva Democracia* the views of his political organization.[96] Some of his articles condemned the United States for having confined the countries of Indo-América to a subsidiary role in the global economy, presaging in many ways the touchstone argument of Dependency theory.[97] Others celebrated the authenticity and originality of the Mexican Revolution (1910–1920), or else highlighted the recent surge in Latin America of a 'mystical, messianic generation' in response to the material and spiritual crisis that afflicted the postwar world. Sánchez praised this new generation for being able to think for itself and by itself.[98] Whether they took the form of attacks on

[93] "Qué es el aprismo? ¿Cuáles son sus propósitos? ¿Quiénes son sus apóstoles?," *La Nueva Democracia*, May 25, 1934, 20; [n.d], *La Nueva Democracia*, New York, December 1, 1922, p. 20.

[94] Augusto Arias, "¿A Dónde va Indoamérica?," *La Nueva Democracia*, New York, February 1, 1936, p. 15.

[95] Alberto Rembao, "Editorial," *La Nueva Democracia*, New York, March 1, 1936, p. 13; Ben Ossa, "Páginas de Fuego y Devoción," *La Nueva Democracia*, New York, April, 1, 1935, p. 9.

[96] Luis Alberto Sánchez, "El Anti-Rodó," *La Nueva Democracia*, New York, January 25, 1934, 14; "La Mística de la Nueva América," *La Nueva Democracia*, New York, October 25, 1934, 11; "Desesperación y Exasperación En la Juventud Indoamericana," *La Nueva Democracia*, New York, January 1, 1935, 24; "Bolivarismo, Monroísmo y Aprismo," *La Nueva Democracia*, New York, March 1, 1935, 8; "Religión no es Adversaria de Acción," *La Nueva Democracia*, New York, April 1, 1935, 18.

[97] Luis Alberto Sánchez, "Para Que el Interamericanismo Sea… El Problema Esencial de Nuestra América," *La Nueva Democracia*, New York, January 25, 1942, 11.

[98] Luis Alberto Sánchez, "El Anti-Rodó," *La Nueva Democracia*, New York, January 25, 1934, 14.

US imperialism or appraisals of Latin American achievements, Sánchez's pieces all converged on a plea in favour of improved and more just relations between the United States and its southern neighbours. They also asserted the genuine and 'intensely' anti-imperialist nature of the APRA party.[99]

Several more APRA leaders appeared in the pages of *La Nueva Democracia*. Julian Petrovick, Manuel Seoane, and Luis Heysen, for example, wrote about either their commitment to democracy and anti-imperialism or the specifics of APRA's program, or both.[100] They presented the doctrinal tenants of APRA in a simple fashion, bringing forth the importance for semi-colonial countries in Latin America of rooting their anti-imperialist struggles in nationalism rather than socialism or communism.[101] Moreover, Apristas who wrote in *La Nueva Democracia* took pains to dissociate rigid, therefore objectionable, Marxist dogmas from APRA's dialectical Marxism, a philosophical position Aprista ideologues claimed to adopt to help them reveal the singularity of the American continent rather than to prepare for a class war they did not believe in. Apristas rejected Marxism the moment it either became a "dogma inmóvil" or was appropriated, like they argued it was in communism, "como ortodoxia congelada."[102]

CONCLUSION

The deportation of party leaders in the early 1930s took a toll on the coordination of the APRA party in Peru, leaving for example many rank-and-file members without clear instruction regarding what to do or prioritize next. But, as Chapter 5 showed, it also paradoxically gifted their movement with political opportunities that were impossible to leverage otherwise. In exile, APRA leaders were free to come and go as they pleased. Resources sometimes ran scant, but they were able to resume

[99] Luis Alberto Sánchez, "Bolivarismo, Monroísmo y Aprismo," *La Nueva Democracia*, New York, March 1, 1935, p. 8.

[100] Manuel Seoane, "Socialismo, Nacionalismo, Aprismo," *La Nueva Democracia*, New York, July 1, 1935, p. 18; Julian Petrovick, "Aprismo y Democracia," *La Nueva Democracia*, New York, December 25, 1934, p. 11; Luis Heysen, "Restauración Vital," *La Nueva Democracia*, New York, August 1, 1936, p. 25.

[101] Manuel Seoane, "Socialismo, Nacionalismo, Aprismo," *La Nueva Democracia*, New York, July 1, 1935, p. 18.

[102] "Immobile dogma"; "like a frozen orthodoxy," Luis Pachacuteck, "El Llamado del Apra a la América Latina," *La Nueva Democracia*, New York, January 1, 1935, p. 14.

their political work without having to circumvent censorship, let alone fear for their lives. As a result, party members in hiding in Peru largely relied on the propaganda work of their peers abroad to educate people about what was going on in their country. They hoped to expose the dictatorial nature of the Peruvian government, and more importantly they did everything they could to draw the attention of public opinion to the plight that the APRA party was suffering at the time. This helped to nudge APRA away from its earlier radical positions and engage with democracy in the mid-to-late 1930s, through the prism of individual and civil liberty.

Chapter 5 also highlighted the key role that foreign allies, specifically Christian intermediaries like Anna Melissa Graves, continued to play in securing the survival of the PAP during the 1930s. Christian intermediaries were not alone in this task, but they had one advantage over other clandestine networks which made them particularly valuable for *Apristas* in the midst of persecution: they had access to resources and publicity abroad. APRA leaders in prison in Peru, and especially those stationed abroad, learned to use this help to get access to material and to disseminate their ideas throughout the rest of the Americas. These US anti-imperialists and Christian intermediaries assisted APRA in a number of ways: they participated in solidarity campaigns with imprisoned leaders of the party; they helped circulate propaganda and other types of censored material (such as correspondence) inside and outside Peru; they published and promoted the ideas of APRA in US publications, thereby helping APRA gain a continental presence both south and north of the Río Grande; and they likewise sent to APRA members books and political material they wanted them to read in hiding or in prison. APRA's reliance on foreign allies to attract the favour of international public opinion continued to affect its ideological production well into the early 1940s, as further detailed in the next chapter.

6

Indo-América Looks North: Foreign Allies and the Inter-American Community, 1933–1945

"There does not seem to be any one place [...] where the Aprista ideology has been synthesized and made available to those interested in finding out what it is," the political scientist Harry Kantor once surmised about the fragmented nature of APRA's ideological production in the first half of the twentieth century.[1] A quick look at the hundreds of articles, pamphlets, and edited collections produced by Apristas before the return of democracy in Peru in 1945 suffices to prove Kantor right. This was especially the case with Indo-América, the name that APRA officially gave to its maximum program, or program for all Latin America.[2] The resilience of this project as an ideological utopia of continental solidarity and as a political weapon for anti-imperialist resistance relied on a surprising ideological malleability. The concept of Indo-América, as this chapter details, proved adaptable to changing circumstances and experiences.

Scholars have focused on the international scene to shed better light on APRA's changing ideological positions. They advance that the Good Neighbor policy (1933), first, then the Second World War shortly thereafter, are responsible for softening APRA's initial attacks against the United States. They highlight, correctly so, that Nazism replaced the United States as the greatest imperialist threat in Aprista's political doctrine. "The war," stresses one prominent scholar of APRA, "also led the

[1] Harry Kantor, *The Ideology and Program of the Peruvian Aprista Movement*, New York: Octagon Books, 1966, p. 22.

[2] For an overview of this fragmented production see Alfredo Saco, "Aprista Bibliography," *The Hispanic American Historical Review*, 23: 3 (1943): 555–585.

Apristas to accentuate the democratic features of their program."[3] To be sure, the growing perils of Nazi and Fascist intervention in Latin America did affect how APRA came to envision its call for continental solidarity. In fact, these fears affected the construction of Latin American identity in intellectual circles throughout the Southern Hemisphere. Some leftists and radicals even reinvested the concept of Hispano-America to oppose the rise of European fascism. They momentarily reclaimed Hispanic culture as the basis for an imagined continental community that stood in solidarity with the Second Spanish Republic against rebel conservative factions.[4] By the late 1930s, Apristas similarly demanded a revision of the maximum (or continental) program in a way that would adapt its anti-imperialist claims before the rise of Fascist threats worldwide.[5]

Not everybody in the party celebrated this flexibility. With hindsight, many Apristas condemned the changes that underpinned the ideological evolution of APRA toward the right of the political spectrum, and that of its Indo-American project of hemispheric unity in particular. The most disillusioned left the PAP in the 1940s and 1950s and attacked the party leadership for betraying APRA's foundational anti-imperialist principles of the 1920s.[6]

Historians of Peru have partly absorbed and replicated these critiques, suggesting that APRA's ideological change from the radical left to a moderate populist right were due to Víctor Raúl Haya de la Torre's insatiable thirst for power. His cunning pragmatism, argue these

[3] Kantor, *The Ideology and Program of the Peruvian Aprista Movement*, p. 98.

[4] This progressive remodelling of Hispanoamericanismo came to a halt with the rise to power of Francisco Franco in 1939. Alexandra Pita Gonzalez, "La discutida identidad latinoamericana: Debates en el Repertorio Americano, 1938–1945," in Aimer Granados García and Carlos Marichal (eds), *Construcción de las identidades latinoamericanas*, México, DF: El Colegio de México, 2004, pp. 241–265.

[5] [Peruvian Aprista], Santiago de Chile, December 8, 1938, Fondo Luis Eduardo Enríquez Cabrera (hereafter cited as FLEEC), ENAH, México, "APRA," 1930–1939.

[6] APRA enemies and defectors published many critiques, from both left and right ends of the political spectrum, to render public what they deemed deceitful manoeuvres within this movement. These often included open and abrupt rupture from APRA. See Mariano Valderrama, "La evolución ideológica del APRA, 1924–1962," in *El APRA: Un camino de esperanzas y frustraciones*, in Mariano Valderrama, Jorge Chullen, Nicolás Lynch and Carlos Malpica, Lima: Ediciones El Gallo Rojo, 1980; Hernando Aguirre Gamio, *Liquidación histórica del APRA y del Colonialismo Neoliberal*, Lima: Ediciones Debate, 1962; Alberto Hernández Urbina, *Los partidos y la crisis del Apra*, Lima: Ediciones Raíz, 1956; Magda Portal, *La Trampa*, Lima: Ediciones Raíz, 1956; Portal, *¿Quienes traicionaron al pueblo?*, Lima: Ediciones Raíz, 1950; Alberto Hidalgo, *Por qué renuncié al Apra*, Buenos Aires: Imprenta Leomir, 1954; Luis Eduardo Enríquez Cabrera, *Haya de la Torre, la estafa política más grande de América*, Lima: Ediciones del Pacifico, 1951.

Peruvian-centric studies, led Haya de la Torre to change the APRA doctrine whenever he deemed it necessary to serve his political ends. This APRA leader was indeed a pragmatic and savvy political figurehead whose instincts led him to compromise on numerous occasions. Yet by insisting on the personal attributes of a single APRA leader rather than interrogating the collective dynamics that underpinned the ideological production of APRA, these studies fail to weigh the impact of persecution and exile, and the political struggles for survival that these experiences brought to bear on the many meanings of APRA's project of hemispheric unity.[7] Imagining Indo-América altogether as a vindication of Latin American sovereignty and of democracy and social justice for the Americas was not the project of a single individual; it stemmed from the fragmented experiences of dispersed networks of anti-imperialist activists desperate to retrieve basic political liberties in their home country.

Chapter 6 focuses on the evolution of APRA's maximum program for all Latin America during the 1930s and 1940s in light of these analytical premises. It suggests that Apristas' reasons to develop and hold on to their continental program during the 1930s and 1940s were not merely ideological, but also political. This chapter analyzes specifically the impacts that APRA's engagement with transnational solidarity networks had on the evolution of its ideology, particularly that of its project of hemispheric and anti-imperialist unity. While scholars usually advance that APRA's interest for its continental project waned after it turned into a national party in the early 1930s, Chapter 6 suggests that, quite to the contrary, it is during the 1930s and early-1940s that APRA consolidated the concept of Indo-América and propelled it to the centre-stage of its political doctrine. Recurrent state persecution against PAP, combined with APRA's innovative political strategies in exile, contributed to building an Indo-American project based on the defence of political rights and democracy rather than the bulwark against US imperialism that APRA's continental program originally asserted in the 1920s. It similarly curbed its advocacy of social justice in Peru and focused ever more forcefully on the defense of civil liberties.

To fully appreciate these ideological changes in APRA's program, Chapter 6 contends that preserving in its doctrine a call for Latin

[7] One exception is the study of Carlos Aguirre on the experience of imprisonment in the APRA movement. See Carlos Aguirre, "Hombres y rejas. El APRA en prisión, 1932–1945," *Bulletin de l'Institut français d'études andines*, 43: 1 (2014), http://journals.openedition.org/bifea/4234.

American solidarity, which Apristas came to bill ever more regularly with Indo-American solidarity on one side and associate ever more closely with a democratic inter-American order on the other, offered tangible political and personal opportunities to those who ran the high command of APRA. By the 1940s Indo-América, APRA's celebrated vision for Latin American unity, turned into a political instrument in the service of the Hayista faction. Ambiguity and adaptability, as we shall see, explain part of Indo-América's ideological power, but also the tensions and contradictions that nestled within it.

TRANSNATIONAL SOLIDARITY CAMPAIGNS AND INDO-AMÉRICA

The rise of Indo-América as a new hemispheric consciousness in APRA during the 1920s and early 1930s was embedded as much in the legacy of anti-imperialist struggles against an aggressive US foreign policy as in the lived experience of exile and the struggles for political survival following the return to the homeland. Yet the ideological consolidation of Indo-América as a political project, one of anti-imperialist resistance and hemispheric unity, happened most decisively from exile during the 1930s and the early 1940s, a period of recurrent persecution against Apristas in Peru. Surprisingly, few scholars have underscored the odd correspondence during that period between APRA's moment of most fervent ideological production, on one side, and the moment of fiercest censure and persecution recalled by the history of the party, on the other.[8] This correspondence, however, was not a coincidence. Rather, the production of Indo-América as a political concept of anti-colonial resistance and Latin American solidarity, which took place during that period, was closely entwined with the transnational solidarity campaigns that Aprista exiles organized to stop persecution in Peru.

Social scientists have studied how advocacy groups that want to successfully externalize a specific agenda when their demands are blocked at the national level do so by turning this agenda into universal claims. For these advocacy groups, the strategy of extending the appeal of local

[8] Martín Bergel is one exception to this general blind spot. See Martín Bergel, "Populismo y cultura impresa. La clandestinidad literaria en los años de formación del Partido Aprista Peruano," *Ipotesis*, 17: 2 (2013): 135–146; Bergel, "De canillitas a militantes. Los niños y la circulación de materiales impresos en el proceso de popularización del Partido Aprista Peruano (1930–1945)," *Iberoamericana*, 15: 60 (2015): 101–115.

demands seeks to interest international allies that would otherwise feel disengaged from their cause.[9] To ensure the political survival of APRA, the Hayista faction and its widespread networks of exiled Aprista activists put forth a defensive strategy that worked precisely along these lines. Within APRA's five-point maximum program lay Indo-Americans' best defence against foreign oppressors and the only path toward their liberation.[10] At least this is the message that Apristas, who painstakingly portrayed abroad their organization as working for the rest of the continent, wanted to convey. Apristas, in short, used Indo-América as a way to universalize their demands in the context of local repression.

Consider for example the communiqué that the APRA leader Víctor Peralta wrote in June 1935 in an attempt to alert continental public opinion to the persecution that Apristas endured in Peru. Peralta was at the time incarcerated in El Frontón, a detention centre located off the coast of the Peruvian capital which was infamous for its brutality toward inmates.[11] Interestingly, his cry for help was specifically addressed to those Peralta called his "Indo-American brothers."[12] Peralta explained that because freedoms of expression didn't exist in Peru, Apristas had to resort to the outside world to be heard; they had to bring their appeal before "todas las organizaciones revolucionarias y conciencias libres de Indo América y del Mundo."[13] Peralta requested solidarity of action in the face of the injustices that Apristas endured in Peru on account of their ongoing activism, not only for Peruvian democracy and social justice but also in support of the oppressed people of the continent.

Because of APRA's commitment toward Indo-América, reasoned Peralta, the fate of Apristas in Peru should be the concern of all Indo-

[9] Sydney Tarrow, *The New Transnational Activism*, New York: Cambridge University Press, 2005.

[10] Fernando León de Vivero, *Avance del imperialismo fascista en Perú*, México: Editorial Trinchera Aprista, 1938, p. 38.

[11] The nightmare of El Frontón rankles more than any other jail in the Aprista *martirologio*. For examples of testimonies and memories that dealt with this prison consult: Guillermo Vegas León, "Las Torturas y los Crímenes de la Isla 'El Frontón'," *Claridad*, Buenos Aires, Ano XVII, num. 324, April 1938; Armando Bázan, *Prisiones junto al mar, novela*, Buenos Aires: Editorial *Claridad*, 1943.

[12] Víctor Peralta, Secretario General, El Comité de Presos Políticos – Sociales recluidos en El Frontón, "A todas las organizaciones revolucionarias y conciencias libres de Indo América y del Mundo," El Frontón, June 12, 1935, Pontificia Universidad Católica del Perú, CEDOC, Colección especial Arturo Sabroso Montoya, Correspondencia de LAS y VRHT y ASM: Importantes, B1, 933 al 951.

[13] "All the revolutionary organizations and free consciences in Indo América and the world," ibid.

Americans. "Nosotros sabemos que nuestros hermanos de Indo América, por cuya unión política y económica luchamos," he wrote, "sabrán en estos momentos de tragedia peruana recoger el S.O.S. de nuestros hogares en abandono, no para enviarnos sus barcos mercantes con cargamento de víveres como suele hacerse para auxiliar a las victimas de los terremotos, sino para mandarnos sus cruceros de guerra cargados de su protesta enérgica." What Apristas wanted, he claimed, was to hear "el rugido de nuestros hermanos explotados de América India."[14] Nowhere in this letter did Peralta call for Indigenous solidarity to oppose creole oligarchy. Nor did any references refer to the rights of the Indigenous peoples in Peru or Native Americans elsewhere in the Americas. The references to América "India" and Indo-América that dotted Peralta's communiqué alluded exclusively to APRA's fight for political and economic Latin American sovereignty.

That Peralta used Indo-América as a political instrument to advance the cause of APRA internationally, and that he did so without references to Indigenous agency, was all but exceptional. For one, despite earlier, if superficial references to a common Latin American indigenous legacy, from the mid-1930s onward, the concept of Indo-América more accurately referred to APRA's project of hemispheric unity for Latin American sovereignty and democracy rather than an alleged utopia of Indigenous resistance in the Americas. Apristas praised José Vasconcelos' approach to the ideal of a mixed race in the Americas, "el primer caso de raza positivamente universal," and imported his racial mysticism into their continental designs.[15] As a result, while APRA's domestic program sought solutions to integrate the Indigenous population of Peru into the nation-state, at the continental level Apristas expanded beyond essentialist definitions of who were Indigenous actors and what constituted indigeneity.[16] "No necesitamos tener predominio de sangre india, española o

[14] "We know that our brothers from Indo América, for whose political and economic union we fight, will know in these moments of Peruvian tragedy to listen to the S.O.S. sent from our abandoned homes. They will not send us their merchant shops with food shipments, as is usually done to help the victims of earthquakes, but their war cruisers loaded with their energetic protest." "The roar of our exploited brothers from India America," Peralta, "A todas las organizaciones revolucionarias y conciencias libres de Indo América."

[15] "The first truly universal race." "Hispanoamericanismo… Latinoamericanismo… Indoamericanismo…" *Trinchera Aprista*, México, DF, Year 1, no. 2, 1937, p. 2. Victor Raul Haya de la Torre, p. 10.

[16] Víctor Raúl Haya de la Torre, "El problema del Indio," *Construyendo el aprismo*, Buenos Aires, *Claridad*, 1933, pp. 104–113; Alfredo Saco, *Programa agrario del*

italiana para sentir y pensar como indoamericanos," claimed exiled Apristas in 1937, for they trusted that the "nuevo espíritu iniciado en América" forced itself upon those who lived in Indo-América.[17] This telluric framing of indigeneity claimed to be inclusive of everyone in Latin America, but in fact it rested on APRA's capacity to de-racialize Indigenous references in its continental program. This approach to Indo-América from the 1930s onward presented one important advantage for the persecuted APRA: it made its vision for hemispheric unity more malleable in the face of international public opinion.

By the mid-1930s, the telluric use of Indo-América as an imagined continental community had become ubiquitous in the transnational solidarity campaigns put forth by Aprista exiles. If publicizing the support that APRA was able to garner from Indo-American allies was crucial to bolster APRA's legitimacy before Peruvians, as seen in previous chapters, the reverse was also true. Courting foreign allies similarly forced on Apristas the necessity to show that their organization was working for all Latin Americans – which many in the party came to bill Indo-Americans, though not exclusively – not just for the Peruvian people. This organizing strategy incited the upholding of their maximum program despite the focus given to the Peruvian scene. It also confirmed that Indo-América was the reality of all, stressed Apristas. And APRA proposed not only to unveil this Indo-American reality, but also to theorize it for them.

One way to do so was by framing the social and political problems that were plaguing Peru as a cautionary tale for the rest of Indo-América. For example, as publicizing abroad the persecution of Peruvian Apristas turned into a core objective of APRA's continental diffusion in the 1930s and 1940s, Apristas began to accompany these descriptions of violence not only with calls for Latin American solidarity to protect PAP, but also with implicit warnings against the imminent dangers Latin Americans similarly faced. In these accounts, Apristas' suffering in Peru and exile hung over Indo-América like the sword of Damocles.[18]

aprismo, Lima: Ediciones populares, 1946; Luis Alberto Sánchez, "On the Problem of the Indian in South America," *The Journal of Negro Education*, 10: 3 (1941), pp. 493–503.

17 "We do not need to have a greater amount of Indian, Spanish or Italian blood to feel and think like Indo-Americans"; "new American spirit." "Hispanoamericanismo... Latinoamericanismo... Indoamericanismo..." *Trinchera Aprista*, México, D.F., Year 1, no. 2, 1937, p. 2.

18 Alfredo Saco Miro Quesada, *Difusión continental del aprismo*, Lima: Okura Editores, 1986, p. viii. Comité Aprista de México, *¡Partidos de frente único para Indoamérica!*, Colección, *Trinchera Aprista*, México, DF, 1938, pp. 25–33.

Apristas' efforts to highlight in their maximum program the ways in which Peru's historical development was the same as that of other Latin American countries further reinforced these forewarnings. Problems faced by Peru, advocated Apristas, were problems Indo-América faced as well.[19]

As the previous section details, this argument was vividly portrayed in the analyses that Aprista exiles wrote on the concurrent threats of imperialist and Fascist penetrations of the Americas in the mid-to-late 1930s. They argued that Peru's intimate experience with foreign imperialism yielded important lessons for the rest of the continent. "La penetración fascista en Indoamérica es un hecho que nadie puede negar," the Aprista José de Goyburu noted in the prologue to *Avance del imperialismo fascista en el Perú*. "El estudio que el compañero doctor Fernando León de Vivero hace de la penetración italiana, alemana y japonesa en el Perú," he stated, "así nos lo demuestra."[20] In the 1930s, APRA's transnational advocacy campaign for the return of democracy in Peru increasingly associated Peruvian president Benavides with fascism, rather than presenting him as a pawn of US imperialism as they did previously. A Fascist regime supported by a small oligarchic minority had taken over Peru, argued Apristas by the late 1930s. Their political analyses, which committees in exile took pains to circulate broadly in Latin America and in the United States, repeatedly touted the repressive rule of the Benavides government as evidence of the growing advances of fascism in the Americas.[21]

Apristas presented their democratic and revolutionary program as the only viable way to save the middle classes in the Americas from Fascist ideas. "El camino para detener el avance fascista en Indoamérica es el aprismo," advanced one APRA leader in 1938.[22] "En los momentos que la Europa Fachista [*sic*] provoca a una guerra, que será desvastadora

[19] "También en Cuba el Frente Único de Clases Explotadas," *Trinchera Aprista*, no. 4, México, DF, January 1938, p. 7.

[20] "The fascist penetration in Indo-América is a fact that no one can deny." "The study of our colleague Dr. Fernando León de Vivero makes of the Italian, German and Japanese penetration in Peru shows this to us." José de Goyburu, in Fernando León de Vivero, *Avance del imperialismo fascista en el Perú*, México, DF: Editorial Trinchera Aprista, 1938, p. 5.

[21] De Vivero, *Avance del imperialismo fascista en el Perú*; [Magda Portal], "Frente Popular a las izquierdas de América," Lima (en la persecución), October 1935, Magda Portal Papers, Benson Latin American Collection, University of Texas Libraries, the University of Texas at Austin, Box 3, Folder 35; Magda Portal, "El derecho de asilo, Institución Indoamericana," Buenos Aires, August 17, 1939.

[22] "The way to stop the fascist advance in Indo-América is APRA," Víctor Raúl Haya de la Torre, in León de Vivero, *Avance del imperialismo fascista en el Perú*, p. 3.

[*sic*]," wrote another, "Indoamérica quedara como preciosa reserva de cultura y civilización, si las izquierdas de todos los países de Indoamérica se unifican con programas que miren y defiendan a las grandes mayorías explotadas, en frente únicos, contra el imperialismo, el fachismo y las tiranía nacionales."[23] Even when the civilian Manuel Prado Ugarteche rose to power in Peru in 1939, Apristas continued to rebuke Peruvian authorities at home and abroad for being Fascist and contrary to the true Indo-American ideals of democracy and civil liberty.[24]

The work of imagining Indo-América during the 1930s and 1940s remained mostly the prerogative of APRA leaders in exile. The space of exile was particularly propitious, if not mandatory according to Aprista exiles, to originally reflect upon the changing realities of Indo-América.[25] In effect, with the notable exceptions of Haya de la Torre and Antenor Orrego, the Apristas who stayed in Peru between 1934 and 1945 were either too consumed by national politics and by the need to efficiently organize political action in the midst of state persecution, or too remote from the continental scene to seriously engage with the production of political analysis on the fate of Indo-América.[26]

As a result, a rich intellectual production on the meaning and ambitions of APRA's vision of hemispheric unity only saw light outside Peru. The communities of Peruvian Apristas exiled in Chile, Argentina, and Mexico produced the brunt of this political work. They disseminated

[23] "Whenever fascist Europe might provoke a war, which will be devastating, Indo-América will remain as a precious reserve of culture and civilization as long as the left of all Indo-American countries unify with programs that defend and attend to the great exploited majorities, in united fronts, against imperialism, fascism and national tyranny," "Editorial," *Trinchera Aprista, Órgano del Comité Aprista de México*, México, D.F. October 1937, p. 1.

[24] Andrés Townsend Ezcurra to Magda Portal, Buenos Aires, Argentine, October 14, 1941, Magda Portal Papers, Benson Latin American Collection, University of Texas Libraries, the University of Texas at Austin, Box1, Folder 5. Several reports by the US diplomatic staff detail the activities that the community of Aprista exiles in New York were conducting amongst democratic circles and governmental spheres to censure the Prado regime and to demand the return of democracy in Peru. See Jefferson Patterson, First Secretary of Embassy in Lima, to the Secretary of State, Lima, August 13, 1941, "Use by the Aprista party of excerpts from Fr. Hubert Herring's book 'Good Neigbors', p. 2, Folder 4, Box 4346, Central Files, Record Group (RG59), 1940–1944, US National Archives at College Park, College Park, MD (NACP).

[25] Gabriel del Mazo to Magda Portal, May 26, 1940, Magda Portal Papers, Benson Latin American Collection, University of Texas Libraries, the University of Texas at Austin, Box1, Folder 4.

[26] Antenor Orrego, *Pueblo-Continente; ensayos para una interpretación de la América latina*, Buenos Aires: Ediciones Continente, 1957.

Indo-American knowledge across the hemisphere by way of their publications in exile, such as *Trinchera Aprista* in Mexico and the *Boletín Aprista* in Argentina. The Comité Aprista of Santiago (CAP of Santiago) played a crucial part in the upkeep of APRA's maximum program throughout the 1930s and 1940s. Chile's long period of stable democracy between 1932 and 1973, in effect, provided Apristas exiled in that country with a safe haven from where they produced political propaganda and worked to spread the Aprista doctrine across the continent. It is in Chile that the Hayista faction, with the Ercilla press, published its most cited work on Indo-América.[27] Smaller and lesser-known communities of Aprista exiles in the United States also worked to produce and disseminate political knowledge on Indo-América in North America, notably in the booming Hispanic press in the United States.

Nevertheless, given the extent of the public opinion campaigns, it was important for Aprista ideologues in exile to maintain a serious dialogue between Peru and the rest of the continental scene. Consequently, even when publication topics aimed directly at Peru – and because these publications appeared outside Peru – Apristas took pains to justify their publications and ideas before a foreign, Indo-American audience. They carefully explained the continental relevance of their Peruvian-centric studies by highlighting the economic and political lessons that their publications could yield to "Nuestra América."[28] Significantly, then, even in the cases where analyses focused on Peru, Apristas always included an introductory section to prove the relevance of these studies to the rest of the Americas. The work on Indo-América that APRA leaders and ideologues were conducting outside Peru evidenced the commitment of APRA to working for the redemption not only of the Peruvian people but also of all citizens of the Americas.

As Apristas used Peru to educate their Latin American peers about the dangers to which the Southern Hemisphere was exposed, they also

[27] Víctor Raúl Haya de la Torre and Luis Alberto Sánchez, *Correspondencia, Tomo 1, 1924–1951*, Lima: Mosca Azul Editores, 1982; Iñigo García-Bryce, *Haya de la Torre and the Pursuit of Power in Twentieth-Century Peru and Latin America*, Chapel Hill: The University of North Carolina Press, 2018, pp. 188–189; One of the best portrayals of this community of APRA exiles to this day appears in Juan Manuel Reveco del Villar, "Influencia del APRA en el partido socialista de Chile," in Juan Manuel Reveco *et al.*, *Vida y Obra de Víctor Raúl Haya de la Torre*, Segundo Concurso Latinoamericano, Lima: Instituto Cambio y Desarrollo, 2006, pp. 19–134.

[28] "Our America." Carlos Manuel Cox, "Prologo," in Pedro E. Muñiz, *Penetración Imperialista (Minería y Aprismo)*, Santiago de Chile: Ediciones Ercilla, 1935, pp. 5, 5–11.

assiduously framed themselves as champions of Indo-América. Their political writings portrayed Apristas as expert-interpreters, who were able to translate what they saw happening in Peru for the larger benefit of the Latin American people.[29] Prologues added to Peruvian-centric analyses boasted about the continental commitment of Aprista authors, introducing them to readers as devout Indo-American thinkers and activists. The Aprista Pedro E. Muñiz had dedicated his life with absolute abnegation, assured the APRA leader Carlos Manuel Cox in one such prologue, "a la causa de la redención de las mayorías productoras de nuestra América."[30] Cox defined *Aprismo* as a constructive and serious political movement of continental dimensions, fully able to "conducir a los pueblos y naciones oprimidos de América, a la ansiada meta de progreso, bienestar, soberanía e independencia económica."[31]

Though the study that Cox was then introducing focused primarily on the Peruvian national context, his presentation hoped to convince readers outside Peru that APRA also worked for their benefit. At other times, book prefaces reprinted excerpts from European and US allies who praised Apristas' help in bringing to light the problems of the Americas.[32] Likewise, biographical notes introducing APRA leaders outside Peru stressed the ideological contributions they were making to the anti-imperialist struggle against foreign powers and oligarchic minorities and for the liberation of the Americas. A 1935 publication dedicated to the work and life of the APRA leader Magda Portal, which appeared in Buenos Aires, Argentina, thus enthused about the significance of her activism for the "independencia integral" of "nuestra América." "Su tenacidad en la brega, su esclarecida mentalidad, su fidelidad inquebrantable," added the book's editors about Portal's remarkable qualities, which served as a model for men and women "en todo el continente."[33]

Because Apristas appealed to continental public opinion as a means to retrieve personal liberties and basic political rights in Peru, the concept of

[29] APRA, ¿Qué es el Aprismo?, *APRA: Revista Aprista*, Year II, no 9, January 1935, p. 2.

[30] "For the redemption of the working majority in our America." Cox, "Prologo," p. 9.

[31] "lead the oppressed peoples and nations of America to the desired goal of progress, well-being, sovereignty and economic independence," ibid., p. 6.

[32] Editorial Ercilla, *¿A dónde va Indoamerica?*, Santiago de Chile: Editorial Ercilla, 1935, p. 1.

[33] "Intrinsic independence"; "our America." "Her tenacity in the struggle, her enlightenmed mentality, her unshakable fidelity"; "across the whole continent." "Apuntes Biográficos sobre Magda Portal," *Magda Portal: Su vida y su obra*, Editorial *Claridad*, Buenos Aires, 1935, p. 3.

Indo-América had to evolve as a political project that catered not only to Peruvians, but also to Latin Americans across the Americas. This helps to explain why the first attempt to ideologically consolidate the meaning of Indo-América came in 1935 in the form of a book, titled *¿A donde va Indoamérica?* This publication claimed to be the first official work to introduce the concept of APRA's Indo-América to a non-Peruvian audience. The editors state in the preface that this was a mandatory read for anybody on the continent who wanted to gain awareness of the Indo-American realities and problems; "con ojos propios," they stressed, without a "nieblas europeizantes."[34] However, far from being the ultimate Indo-American handbook, as implied by the Apristas responsible for its publication, *¿A donde va Indoamérica?* in fact consisted of reproductions of collected essays about the meaning and future of the Americas that Haya de la Torre had authored between late 1928 and 1931, a period in which the use of Indo-América by Apristas was still scarce and ill-defined. Yet the value of this book should be assessed in light of its political significance rather than its ideological contributions. The entanglement between the ideological production of Indo-América on one side, and APRA's political activism abroad on the other, stemmed from the necessity to advocate for the return of democracy in Peru.

RAPPROCHEMENT BETWEEN INDO-AMÉRICA AND NORTH AMERICA

APRA's call for continental unity always was, and stayed, at the core of its political program from its foundation onward. Yet the justifications Apristas gave for imagining a regional alliance against foreign enemies changed over time. Not everybody in Latin America understood this shift at first, let alone the nature of APRA's anti-imperialist project of hemispheric unity. Many contemporary critiques of APRA's *Indoamericanismo*, for instance, scorned the concept for failing to represent Latin America's racial and ethnic diversity. "¿Por qué indoamericano?" asked one such opponent, as reported in the pages of *Trinchera Aprista* in 1937; "¿Acaso todos son indios en Sudamérica?"[35] Many

[34] "With their own eyes"; "European filter." Carlos Manuel Cox, Carlos Mosto, Luis López Aliaga, Luis Alberto Sánchez, Samuel Vásquez, Santiago, May 23, 1935, in Haya de la Torre, *¿A dónde va Indoamérica?*, p. 10.

[35] "Why Indo-American?"; "Are we all Indians in South America?" "Hispanoamericanismo… Latinoamericanismo… Indoamericanismo…" *Trinchera Aprista*, México, D,F, Year 1, no. 2, 1937, p. 2.

more pointed toward the incongruity of such a name for a continent that included countries like Argentina, which claimed to have a population of almost exclusive European descent, while others noted the exclusion of people from African descent from the Indo-American appellation.[36]

To these critics Apristas replied with pragmatism. Indo-América was more practical a term than, say, the use of "ibero-lusitano-Franco-Africa-Americanos" to encompass the rich cultural and racial diversity of the American people.[37] Of course Indo-América was never only a practical term or an exclusive anti-imperialist project of hemispheric unity. From the mid-1930s onward, Indo-América as a political concept also came to signal the advent of a new historical period – one in which Latin Americans would finally break with all forms of "colonialismo mental" inherited from past colonial and neocolonial periods.[38] As such, APRA's Indo-América was also an attempt to construct a historical consciousness of continental unity.[39] Problematically, however, the universal appeal for the inclusion of different ethnic and racial backgrounds, which scholars like Luis Arturo Torres Rojo have praised in APRA's Indo-América, relied on its capacity to de-racialize indigeneity. In other words, the success of Indo-América's resilience as an ethos of Latin American and anti-imperialist solidarity during the interwar period and beyond rested *precisely* on disinvesting this political concept of all Indigenous agency.

This was all too clear by the early 1940s. Apristas then advocated the use of Indo-América "not as an exclusive revindication of the Indian, but, on the contrary, as a kind of effective integration of all the demographic components of this part of the globe."[40] Leaders of the Hayista faction came to associate broad psychological characteristics, such as patience,

[36] The erasure of blackness was a common feature of white and mestizo nationalist discourses in early twentieth-century Latin America. For an introduction to the Latin American myth of racial democracy see Paulina L. Alberto and Jesse Hoffnung-Garskof, "'Racial Democracy' and Racial Inclusion: Hemispheric Histories," in Alejandro de la Fuente and George Reid Andrews (eds), *Afro-Latin American Studies. An Introduction*, Cambridge University Press, 2018, p. 264–316.

[37] Víctor Raúl Haya de la Torre, "La cuestión del nombre," (1930), *¿A dónde va Indoamérica?*, Santiago de Chile, Ediciones Ercilla, 1935, p. 33.

[38] APRA, ¿Qué es el Aprismo?, *APRA: Revista Aprista*, Year 2, no. 9, January de 1935, p. 2

[39] Luis Arturo Torres Rojo, "La semántica política de Indoamericana, 1918–1941," in Aimer Granados and Carlos Marichal (eds), Construcción de las identidades latinoamericanas. Ensayos de historial intelectual siglos XIX y XX, México, DF: El Colegio de México, 2004, pp. 207–240.

[40] Luis Alberto Sánchez, "A New Interpretation of the History of America," *The Hispanic American Historical Review*, 23: 3 (1943): 446–448.

resilience, or love for the land with Indigenous subjects in the Americas. This vague framing of indigeneity meant that even predominantly white cities like Buenos Aires, Argentina, Montevideo, Uruguay, and Santiago, Chile, according to Apristas, shared "Indian" features with the Indigenous populations of Latin America.[41] Apristas repeatedly cautioned against misinterpretation of the use of Indo-América; this wasn't a "racist" term that demanded people "'regress' to political and social forms of the pre-colonial period," Luis Alberto Sánchez, one of APRA's main ideologues, stated in a 1943 article published in the *Hispanic American Historical Review*. Neither did it call for a racial war against white people, Apristas claimed. Rather, for white and mestizo Apristas who were close to the Hayista faction, Indo-América aimed to restore the dignity and the economic and moral independence of the people of the continent by way of political unity between its more than twenty republics, while concurrently making overtures to critics of empire from the North.

It isn't surprising, therefore, that APRA's fierce anti-US sentiments, which initially accompanied its anti-imperialist project of hemispheric unity, gave way to more moderate positions vis-à-vis the northern hegemon starting in the mid-to-late 1930s. The inspiration for this program still heavily relied on the five-point platform that Apristas had designed in 1926 as part of the foundational doctrine of their anti-imperialist APRA. As we have seen in Chapter 2, the handful of Peruvian exiles who resided in Paris placed resistance against "yankee imperialism" at the forefront of their priorities. From this principal position four other points ensued, including (1) the political unity of Latin America and (2) the nationalization of land and industry in the region. The APRA also requested in the 1920s (3) the internationalization of the Panama Canal, which at the time was controlled by US authorities, and (4) proclaimed its solidarity with the oppressed people of the world.[42] A decade later the continental program read a bit differently. Apristas had traded the first principal of opposition to US imperialism to opposition to "all imperialisms." The fourth point now demanded the "interamericanization" of the Panama Canal instead of its "internationalization."[43]

[41] Sánchez, "A New Interpretation of the History of America," p. 446. Sánchez, "On the Problem of the Indian in South America."

[42] Víctor Raúl Haya de la Torre, "What is the A.P.R.A.?," *The Labour Monthly*, December 1926, pp. 756–759.

[43] Manuel Vázquez Díaz, *Balance del Aprismo*, Lima: Editorial Rebelión, 1964, pp. 3–8.

These changes reflected APRA's evolving worldviews with regard to Pan-Americanism. The election of Franklin D. Roosevelt to the US presidency in March 1933 certainly had something to do with it. The Roosevelt presidency indeed heralded a period of changes in the conduct of US–Latin American foreign relations. The inauguration of the Good Neighbor Policy on April 12, 1933, which thrust the principles of non-intervention and non-interference to the forefront of US foreign policy in Latin America, had a positive impact on Latin American public opinion toward the United States as well as Washington's Pan-American project. By stating that a "common ideal of mutual helpfulness, sympathetic understanding and spiritual solidarity" traversed the Americas and enshrined ideals of mutual respect and "neighborly cooperation" into the cornerstones of a democratic Western Hemisphere, this US foreign policy signaled the coming of a new era for Pan-Americanism.[44] The contrast with the belligerent positions adopted by previous administrations since 1898 in the conduct of US foreign policy in the Western Hemisphere was striking. Latin American diplomats framed this change of foreign policy in a favourable light. They extolled the recognition of juridical equality this new Pan-Americanism bestowed on nations of the continent as well as the end it put to the Monroe Doctrine. The wave of editorials in the Latin American press reflected a similar sense of relief in the public opinion.[45]

Calls for the need to bring spirituality and friendship in an otherwise commercial and financially driven Pan-Americanism, which Christian intermediaries and APRA sympathizers like Charles Thomson, John A. Mackay, and Samuel G. Inman had been advocating for well over a decade, made their way into this new era of US–Latin American relations.[46] Roosevelt's attention to "the entire material, moral, and spiritual welfare of the people of this hemisphere" contrasted greatly with his predecessors' shaping of Pan-Americanism in light of mere financial and

[44] Franklin D. Roosevelt, "Address on the Occasion of the Celebration of Pan-American Day," Washington, April 12, 1933, Collection "Public Papers and Addresses of Franklin D. Roosevelt," *The American Presidency Project*. URL: www.presidency.ucsb.edu/ws/index.php?pid=14615.

[45] Records of the Department of State Relating to Political Relations of the United States with Other American States (The Monroe Doctrine), 1910–1949, Decimal File 710.11, National Archives Microfilm Publications M1276.

[46] Geneviève Dorais, "Missionary Critiques of Empire, 1920–1932: Between Interventionism and Anti-Imperialism," *International History Review*, 39: 3 (2017): 377–403.

commercial interests.[47] APRA allies felt reassured by this policy and worked to ensure that the Roosevelt administration's actions were in line with these idealist and pro-democratic positions.

Because courting foreign allies was so central to APRA's survival and certainly because many of them were convinced that a combination of domestic reforms from within and inter-American collaboration from without would have the power to keep US imperialism in check, Apristas increasingly presented the United States as a champion of democracy in the Western Hemisphere. The concomitant rise of European fascism confirmed this rapprochement in the 1930s. Before the threat of war and fascism in Europe on one side, and the repeated denial of civil liberties in Peru on the other, the struggle for democracy moved to the foreground of the Indo-American project, leaving many in the movement to wonder what to do with their belligerent positions against the United States. "Si el control yanqui es inconveniente y lesivo para la independencia de una republica latino-americana," reasoned, for example, one APRA ideologue in December 1938, "la implantación de intereses imperialistas japoneses o alemanes en el canal tendrán que ser peor."[48] In the changing global context, the United States was depicted as a desirable lesser evil. Significantly, this fear affected the democratic left in similar ways elsewhere in Latin America, as reported by US diplomats in post in San Salvador, about an editorial appearing in *La Prensa* on the threat of totalitarianism in the Americas. Robert Frazer commented the following to the Secretary of State on February 9, 1938: "It is interesting to note the change in the attitude towards the Monroe Doctrine which, having been considered for decades a menace if not an actual threat to Latin American sovereignty, becomes now, at the first sign of danger from a non-American source, a shield and a defense behind which American democracy may shelter."[49]

[47] Cited in John A. Gronbeck-Tedesco, *Cuba, the United States, and Cultures of the Transnational Left, 1930–1975*, New York: Cambridge University Press, 2015, p. 89.

[48] "If Yankee control is inconvenient and harmful to the independence of Latin American republics, the implantation of Japanese or German imperialist interests in the canal would be much worse." [Peruvian Aprista], Santiago de Chile, December 8, 1938, FLEEC, ENAH, México, "APRA," 1930–1939.

[49] Robert Frazer to Secretary of State [Welles], San Salvador, February 9, 1938, National Archives Microfilm Publication, Microfilm Publication M1276, Records of the Department of State Relating to Political Relations of the United States with Other American States (The Monroe Doctrine), 1910–1949, Decimal File 710.11, Roll 16, 710.11/2221-2400.

Yet anti-Fascist unity never inspired Apristas to bow before US interests like obedient wards. On the contrary, the rapprochement between the APRA and the United States was never a linear, let alone ineluctable process. Despite what scholars often suggest, Apristas did not altogether abandon their anti-US positions following the inauguration of the Good Neighbor policy. One year after the Good Neighbor Policy, most Apristas in fact continued to hold straightforward anti-US positions in their approach to economic imperialism. "Frente al gran peligro del coloso del norte," noted the APRA leader Oscar Herrera in a 1934 analysis for the *APRA: Revista Aprista*, "las pequeñas diferencias desaparecen en significación y es deber de la hora aunar la defensa."[50] Even when, four years later, Apristas relinquished their most aggressive attacks against the northern giant, their writings suggest that they stayed wary of US influence well into the 1940s. The article that Haya de la Torre wrote in August 1938, "El Buen Vecino. ¿Garantía definitiva?," which appeared in Chilean, Mexican, and US publications, tackled the conundrum of trying to envision the future of Indo-América in relation to its most imminent dangers.[51] In this article, Haya de la Torre ponders the position that Indo-Americans had to adopt vis-à-vis the United States now that the Americas faced a more scary threat: European Fascism.

Apristas' conclusions on the question were prudent. They favoured a rapprochement with the United States, but they remained aware of the possible caveats of cooperation between Indo-América and North America.[52] Particularly worrisome for Apristas was the temporary nature of Roosevelt's foreign policy. They claimed to trust the good faith of Roosevelt's administration, but they knew only too well that the Good Neighbor policy represented the policy of only one, non-permanent US administration. As a result, they viewed in Roosevelt's promise of improved Latin America–US relations a guarantee of security for Indo-

[50] "Faced with the great danger of the northern colossus, our small differences lose their significance and it is our duty to join in defense." Oscar Herrera, "Nacionalismo Continental," *APRA: Revista Aprista*, Buenos Aires, 2, May 9, 1934, p. 5.

[51] "The Good Neighbor. A Definitive Guarantee?" It appeared in August 1938 in Chile, Mexico, and the United States in the following publications: *Aurora de Chile*, Santiago, Chile, *Trinchera Aprista*, México DF, Mexico, and *La Nueva Democracia*, New York, United States.

[52] Víctor Raúl Haya de la Torre, "El "Buen Vecino" ¿Garantía Definitiva?," *Aurora de Chile*, Santiago, Chile, August 17, 1938, National Archives Microfilm Publication, Microfilm Publication M1276, Records of the Department of State Relating to Political Relations of the United States with Other American States (The Monroe Doctrine), 1910–1949, Decimal File 710.11, Roll 16, 710.11/2221-2400.

América, yet "por lo que la experiencia histórica nos demuestra," Haya de la Torre noted, this guarantee of security was unstable and most likely all too ephemeral. "Se trata solo de una política que puede variar con el cambio de persona o de partido en el Ejecutivo de los Estados Unidos."[53]

Apristas benefited from the growing climate of fear within the US political elite vis-à-vis the safeguard of liberal democracy in the Western Hemisphere. Yet they never hurriedly ran toward the United States. On the contrary, they argued that an alliance against the "Internacional Negra" should never devolve into "nuestra sumisa e irrestringida unión con el 'buen vecino' poderoso."[54] Apristas still forcefully opposed US-led Pan-Americanism. They proposed instead to build a coalition of democratic forces between the people of the Americas. They called this front the Democratic Front North-Indo-American (*Frente Democrático Norte-Indoamericano*), hoping to kill two birds with one stone: competing with the Pan-American Union, while resisting the rise of international fascism by way of continental solidarity. Apristas insisted on the democratic and popular nature of this front:

> Un Frente Norte-Indoamericano contra la Internacional Negra debe ser un Frente de Pueblos. Que sea la Democracia su bandera, pero una Democracia no complaciente con los tiranos en ninguno de los países que el frente anti-fascista comprenda. [...] De allí que el Frente Norte-Indoamericano contra los planes de conquista del Fascismo Internacional Nipón-Europeo debe ser popular. Debe arraigar[se] en las grandes masas nacionales de ambas Américas, debe estar basado en la confianza y en la unidad de acción internacional.[55]

Magda Portal's years of militancy in APRA from the margins of persecution similarly affected her outlook on Indo-América in the late 1930s. She was also inclined to make concessions, and think of alliances with the United States, as evidenced in her essay "La union impossible," which she wrote from exile in Buenos Aires (Argentina) in August 1939. This essay sheds light on what Portal deemed to be profoundly Indo-

[53] "It is a policy that can change depending of the person or party who controls the executive power in the US," Haya de la Torre, "El 'Buen Vecino...'," p. 6.

[54] "The black international." "Our submissive and unrestricted union with the powerful 'good neighbor'," ibid., p. 6.

[55] "A North American Front Against the Black International must be a People's Front. Let Democracy be your banner, but a Democracy not complacent with tyrants in any of the countries included in the anti-fascist front [...] Hence, the North-Indo-American Front against the plans of conquest of the Japanese-European International Fascism must bear a popular nature. It must be rooted in the national masses of both Americas. It must be based on trust and international unity of action," ibid., p. 6.

American as of the late 1930s. Nazism, Fascism, and communism, she argues, opposed the democratic principles that underpinned the independence of the Americas and the project of Simon Bolivar, the nineteenth century creole who fought for the political independence of the Spanish colonies in the Americas. Portal defined anti-imperialism in light of the fundamental, Indo-American principles of democratic liberty and political sovereignty, linking them back to the experience of the nineteenth-century cycles of independence.[56] To keep war against European powers at bay and protect Indo-América, Apristas were willing to envisage an alliance with the United States. Apristas remained wary of the northern power, Portal claimed, but as of January 1940 she also conceded to seeing useful complementarities between South and North America.[57] In the essay she wrote in Chile, in 1940, entitled "Identidad y Diferenciación," Portal first insists on continental differences between North America and South America, but her final argument stresses the complementary of both Americas. On the one hand, Portal takes great pains to describe how two Americas constitute the continent. Pointing to the spiritual and emotional incompatibility between North America and South America, Portal reverted to the arguments advanced years before by the Latin American Modernists. Latin America was spiritual and deep, whereas North America was materialistic and shallow. Only by establishing harmony and balance between Indo-América, the bearer of spiritual progress, and North America, the bearer of material progress, would humanity secure a peaceful future.[58]

The political practice of the past fifteen years of militancy in dialogue with US solidarity activists determined in many ways how they imagined their anti-imperialist project of hemispheric unity. Apristas believed in the people of the Americas and in the democratic forces that resided in grassroots unity. The fact that Apristas never experienced democracy at a national level helps to understand APRA's growing understanding of democracy in light of continental cooperation. Democracy, for Apristas like Haya de la Torre and Magda Poral, came to be attached to the notion of hemispheric unity. The lack of basic political rights in Peru, perhaps more so than the changing world order, provoked important changes in

[56] Magda Portal, "La unión imposible," Buenos Aires, August 2, 1939, p. 1, Magda Portal Papers, Benson Latin American Collection, University of Texas Libraries, the University of Texas at Austin, Box 3, Folder 36.

[57] Portal, "Identidad y Diferenciación," Santiago de Chile, January 1940, Magda Portal Papers, Box 3, Folder 37.

[58] Ibid.

how they were willing and able to imagine their continental program for Latin America, or for the Indo-American community.

GOOD NEIGHBOURS IN A CHANGING INTER-AMERICAN ORDER

In 1936, talk of the upcoming presidential election yielded the hope of an auspicious game change in Peru. Aprista activism intensified abroad in anticipation of these elections. APRA leaders in exile published articles in foreign journals advocating PAP's demands to participate in the forthcoming elections. They also toured South America to give conferences and take part in interviews in which they promoted PAP's electoral program.[59] These efforts were conducted to no avail. The PAP was once more denied the right to participate in Peruvian elections due to charges of being an international organization.[60] When the presidential candidate from the Social Democratic Party – Luis Antonio Eguiguren, whom Apristas supported – appeared to be on the brink of victory, "Benavides canceled the election and remained in power for another three years."[61] Communities of APRA exiles reacted promptly and forcefully to this umpteenth denial of democracy in Peru, disseminating in their mouthpieces and in the foreign press criticism of the Benavides government for refusing to register PAP candidates.[62] Yet what difference could this make? Apristas had persistently censured the gruesome rule of the Benavides government in international publications without result. At the end of 1936, APRA's illegal status still lingered in Peru. The PAP was barred from the normal democratic process. Scores of Peruvian Apristas continued to live in exile. As a result of this impasse, the Hayista faction looked poised to delve deeper into new forms of transnational political activism.[63] Changing global and inter-American

[59] Findley Howard, Legation of the United States of America, to the Secretary of State, Asuncion, April 24, 1936, Folder 3, Box 5698, RG 59, 1930–1939, NACP.

[60] Article 53 of the Peruvian Constitution stated to that effect, "the State does not recognize the legal existence of political parties of international organization, and those who belong thereto cannot exercise any political function." Art. 53, Peruvian Constitution, cited in Report from Alexander W. Weddell to Secretary of State in Washington DC, Buenos Aires, September 18, 1936, Folder 3, Box 5698, RG 59, 1930–1939, NACP.

[61] García-Bryce, *Haya de la Torre and the Pursuit of Power*, pp. 74–75.

[62] Report from Alexander W. Weddell to Secretary of State in Washington D.C., Buenos Aires, September 18, 1936, Folder 3, Box 5698, RG 59, 1930–1939, NACP; Peruvian Ambassador in Chile, "Comunicado Aprista," Santiago de Chile, September 9, 1936, Ministerio de Relaciones Exteriores, Archivo Central, Oficios de Chile, 5-4-A, 1936.

[63] Tarrow, *The New Transnational Activism*, p. 3.

contexts furnished them with new tools to advance APRA's political struggle for the return of democracy in Peru on the international stage.

In the aftermath of the electoral defeat of October 1936, PAP began to feel that backroom negotiations with political authorities and individual networking were no longer the right political strategy to adopt. The thank you letter that Haya de la Torre sent to the French pacifist Romain Rolland in April 1937 expressed more dissatisfaction than it did gratitude regarding his latest intervention before Peruvian authorities.[64] Rolland's gesture was certainly appreciated, but Apristas showed reservations regarding how much sway individual initiatives could hold over authorities in Peru. The Hayista faction realized that letters from renowned intellectuals were not sufficient anymore. Rather, what the party leadership expected from Rolland was his intervention to attract the attention of the League of Nations (LN) to APRA's predicament in Peru. Peruvian Apristas hoped very much that, compelled by international pressure, Benavides would agree to let a "comisión imparcial auspiciada por la SDN" come and visit Peru.[65]

Interestingly, this letter to Rolland reveals that the PAP had already designed a detailed mandate to give to the League of Nations emissaries when they came to Peru. Apristas demanded that international observers direct their attention to the conditions in which political prisoners were being held in Peruvian jails as well as investigate the domestic situation in Peru more broadly. Separating truth from lies in what the Benavides administration showcased in international forums was the mantle the PAP now passed along to international organizations like the LN. "Quisiéramos que alguna vez se deje oír la voz de la SDN a favor de los pueblos oprimidos de América Latina. [...]," Haya de la Torre pleaded on behalf of the Peruvian people. "Quisiéramos que siempre la voz de los hombres libres del viejo Mundo, dejen oír una palabra mas enérgica y más conminatoria [sic] contra los horrores que aquí cometen los grotescos imitadores del fascismo europeo."[66] Touting domestic affairs in Peru, and particularly state repression against PAP, as a case of continental

[64] Víctor Raúl Haya de la Torre to Romain Rolland, Incahuasi, Peru, April 23, 1937, AMGC, Box 3, Folder 3.10, Archives of Labor and Urban Affairs, Wayne State University.

[65] Ibid.

[66] "We would like the voice of the SDN to be hear in favor of the oppressed peoples of Latin America. [...] We would like to hear a more energetic and comminatory protest from the voices of the free men of the old world against the horrors that the grotesque imitators of European fascism are here committing," ibid.

responsibility to resist Fascist intervention had by then fully entered the movement's repertoire of political action. Moreover, the mounting threat of Fascist imperialism in Europe furnished the PAP with the prospects of worldwide moral concern: "¿Podremos esperar de Ud.," Haya de la Torre asked Rolland, "y de todos los hombres libres de Francia y Europa, la ayuda moral que necesitamos para defender al pueblo peruano?"[67]

More importantly still, renewed denial of democracy in Peru in September of 1936 took place against a backdrop of Inter-American developments anchored ever more firmly in the hemispheric principles of peace and democracy. By the end of the decade, the rise and consolidation of European Fascism and Nazism on one side and the clear and present threat of a conflict with the Axis powers on the other, encouraged further changes in APRA's maximum program. The Spanish Civil War of 1936–1937 had appeared for many in the Americas, including Apristas, to be a kind of last-call for the preservation of democratic principles in the Western Hemisphere. The havoc this war brought about in Europe was a foil for precisely what Inter-American diplomats wanted to avoid at all cost. Specifically, the Roosevelt administration became increasingly wary of Nazi plans for Latin America. Latin American diplomats communicated directly with Summer Wells from the State Department to warn the United States against the rise of fascism in Latin America. US informants to South America similarly reported on the dangers of Nazi conspiracy in the region.[68]

These world events bolstered the diplomatic legitimacy of the Good Neighbor Policy and called for its expansion to the whole continent.[69] Discussions held at the Buenos Aires (1936) and the Lima (1938) Inter-American conferences signalled hemispheric security efforts and confirmed unity of action in the face of European Fascism.[70] The holding of the VIII Inter-American Conference in Lima by the end of 1938 constituted a golden opportunity for an APRA leadership in search for fresh ways to attract international attention to its cause. The Hayista faction

[67] Ibid.

[68] Andreu Espasa, "'Suppose they were to Do it in Mexico': The Spanish Embargo and Its Influence on Roosevelts' Good Neighbor Policy," *The International History Review*, 40: 4 (2018): 784–785.

[69] Donald Marquand Dozer, *Are We Good Neighbor? Three Decades of Inter-American Relations 1930–1960*, Gainesville: University of Florida Press, 1961, pp. 38, 42–44.

[70] Dozer, *Are We Good Neighbor?* Martin Sicker, *The Geopolitics of Security in the Americas: Hemispheric Denial from Monroe to Clinton*, Westport and London: Praeger, 2002.

was poised to use this event to promote the cause of PAP internationally. To do so, APRA leaders devoted time and energy months in advance to muster forces and prepare a sound plan of attack, coordinating lines of combat between the National Executive Committee (CEN) of the party and other committees in exile abroad, those of Chile and Mexico in particular. The Hayista faction trusted that the Lima Conference represented the best assets in a bid to revive the transnational campaign they had been spearheading for the past four years.

In October of 1938, two months before it took place, the CEN in Peru confirmed that it was ready to stage its offensive at the Lima Conference.[71] APRA leaders placed confidence in the plan of attack prepared in view of the forthcoming event. They hoped that a combination of forceful propaganda circulating in Peru and external pressure from Latin American delegates might induce the Peruvian authorities to "free a large number of political prisoners at the time of the Pan American Conference."[72] A first wave of propaganda was published in exile and before the conference took place in Lima. Starting in the summer of that year, APRA exiles in Chile and Mexico worked to convince Inter-American foreign emissaries to take up the case of the PAP as a symbol of anti-Fascist unity in Peru, and, more broadly speaking, address what had gone wrong with democratic governments in the Americas. This strategy aimed to influence public opinion abroad through the sway of social movements and prepare those in Peru by way of propaganda.[73] Reporting on the growing continental solidarity that organized in favour of APRA, their writing argued that "intimidated by continental condemnation," and also very "conscious of the pressure being brought to bear," Peruvian authorities were now searching for ways to dodge the demands "of the civilized world."[74]

[71] Correspondence from CAP de Santiago to Secretario General del CAP de México, Santiago, October 12, 1938, FLEEC, ENAH, México.

[72] W.P.C. "Memorandum for Mr. Dreyfus," Lima, September 7, 1938, in Report of Louis G. Dreyfus to Secretary of State, "Haya de la Torre, Aprista leader," Lima, September 8, 1938, Folder 1, Box 4697, RG 59, 1930–1939, NACP.

[73] Primary sources: Report of Louis G. Dreyfus to Secretary of State, Despatch No. 635, Lima, September 7, 1938, Folder 1, Box 4697, RG 59, 1930-1939, NACP. [Aprista political flyer, 1938,] as cited in report of Louis G. Dreyfus to Secretary of State, Despatch No. 635, Lima, September 7, 1938, Folder 1, Box 4697, RG 59, 1930–1939, NACP.

[74] [Aprista political flyer, 1938,] as cited in report of Louis G. Dreyfus to Secretary of State, Despatch No. 635, Lima, September 7, 1938, Folder 1, Box 4697, RG 59, 1930-1939, NACP.

The ways in which they couched their requests also show that Apristas knew how to play with the desire of Roosevelt to frame himself as the champion of democracy in the Western hemisphere and as a friend to Latin America. "It is well known that President Roosevelt has always condemned usurpers and tyrants," stressed the September issue of APRA's clandestine publication *Cuaderno Aprista*. "No one is ignorant of the fact that the great Yankee democrat, freely elected and reelected by millions of his fellow-citizens, abominates all those who seize the power of government by artifice and by force, to become the hangmen (executioners) of their peoples."[75] Apristas took Roosevelt at his words when he promised democracy and security to the Western Hemisphere. They demanded that the US president respect the principles of peace and democracy in the Americas that were ratified at the 1936 and 1938 Inter-American conferences. APRA leader Alberto Grieve Madge travelled to New York City in August 1938 to the Segundo Congreso de la Juventud por la Paz. There, he took the floor to denounce the lack of respect for the most "elementales derechos democráticos del pueblo" and to publicize APRA's position: "Nosotros recogimos las palabras del Presidente Roosevelt en Buenos Aires durante la Conferencia Interamericana en diciembre de 1936," he noted, astutely adding shortly afterward that "Las reiteradas expresiones del mandatario norteamaericano conducen a suponer que atentan contra la paz interna y constituyen una amenaza para la paz internacional los gobiernos americanos que se divorcian de la democracia."[76]

Apristas criticized the lack of international mobilization for PAP by requesting that the word of the US president and the principles of democracy enshrined in the inter-American order be respected. These democratic principles provided Apristas with a discourse of intervention based on the legitimacy of the growing inter-american order. They denounced Pan-Americanism on one hand, while using Inter-American institutions

[75] Mariano Yupanky K. "President Roosevelt Will Not Come to Peru," *Cuaderno Aprista*, no. 15, September, 1938, informal translation in Report of Louis G. Dreyfus to Secretary of State, Despatch No. 635, Lima, September 7, 1938, Folder 1, Box 4697, RG 59, 1930–1939, NACP.

[76] "The most basic democratic rights of the people"; "We are here using the words of President Roosevelt in Buenos Aires during the Inter-American Conference in December 1936"; "These repeated expressions by the North American president lead us to suppose that the American governments that reject democracy are threatening internal peace and constitute a threat to international peace," Alberto Grieve Magde, cited in "Hispanomaérica representada en el Congreso Mundial de la Juventud," *La Prensa*, San Antonio, August 20, 1938, p. 5.

on the other to demand intervention in Peru to impose democracy. Their activism at the Lima Conference, then, aimed to prepare the ground in favour of APRA by mobilizing public opinion and working to sway foreign delegates to Lima or exert direct pressure on Roosevelt to reinstate civil liberty in Peru.[77] This brings us back to the recurrent tension between internationalism and nationalism in the growth of APRA during the interwar period. By the late 1930s, Apristas forthrightly demanded foreign intervention in order to halt the non-democratic regime in Peru and restore civil liberties in their country.[78] Significantly, these claims were voiced not only to non-state US actors, as we have seen in previous chapters, but also to foreign diplomats and state representatives.

The recrudescence of aprista activities on the eve of the Lima Conference was so intense, it attracted comments from diplomatic agents. One US report summarized: "Minister for Foreign Affairs informs of an increasing amount of Aprista propaganda reaching Peru by mail from Mexico and United States. Aprista representatives gathering at Labor Conference in Mexico City and will do anything to annoy Peruvian Government during Inter-American Conference in Lima."[79] These two communities of Aprista exiles prepared political material that specifically aimed to inform the delegations attending the Inter-American conference in Lima about the situation of repression that prevailed in the country at that time.[80]

The other wave of propaganda happened during the conference. The PAP deployed every effort to court the flock of journalists who had just converged in the Peruvian capital. APRA leaders met with foreign correspondents and official delegates from Chile, Mexico, Cuba and the United States, within the precincts of Incahuasi, the name given to the hiding place of Haya de la Torre in Peru.[81] Aprista prisoners, in turn, conducted

[77] CAP de Santiago to Secretario General del CAP de México, Santiago, October 21, 1938, FLEEC, ENAH, México; CAP de Santiago to Secretario General del CAP de México, Santiago, November 9, 1938, FLEEC, ENAH, México. CAP de Santiago to c. Alfredo Saco Miro Quesada, Secretario General del CAP de México, Santiago, November 30, 1938, FLEEC, ENAH, México.

[78] Portal, "Libertad en Expresión. Para "LA VOZ DEL INTERIOR," Buenos Aires, July 23, 1939, p. 1, Magda Portal Papers, Benson Latin American Collection, University of Texas Libraries, the University of Texas at Austin, Box 3, Folder 36.

[79] Louis G. Dreyfus to Secretary of State, "A.P.R.A. activities," Lima, September 7, 1938, Folder 1, Box 4697, RG 59, 1930–1939, NACP.

[80] Comité Aprista de México, *El aprismo frente a la VIII Conferencia Panamericana*, México, editorial Manuel Arévalo, 1938; Saco, "Aprista Bibliography."

[81] Prefectura del Departamento de Lima, Sección Orden Político, [Testimonio de Dn. Jorge Eliseo Idiaquez Rios], Lima, September 22, 1939, p. 2, Archivo General de la Nación,

a hunger strike for the duration of the Inter-American conference. They also clandestinely forwarded to international allies, often by way of their loved ones and other Peruvian allies, detailed descriptions of the detention conditions they were subjected to, hoping to have international observers corroborate the horror stories listed in their accounts.[82] "Hay quienes ponen en duda nuestras afirmaciones!" the wife of an Aprista prisoner told Mexican delegate Esperanza Balmaceda de Josefe on 10 December 1938.[83] "Vaya los Delegados a las prisiones y demanden la presencia de los presos," she wrote to Balmaceda de Josefe. "Sus revelaciones fieles les demostrarán pasajes dantescos del 'Infierno Verde'."[84]

Foreign delegates to the Lima Conference bore one quality deemed essential for Apristas: they embodied political capital internationally. As mentioned earlier, the holding of the Buenos Aires Conference in 1936 sanctioned the growth of an Inter-American system oriented toward ideals of democracy deeply rooted in concepts of continental security. As such, members of the delegations who traveled to Lima in 1938 to further the development of this regional order represented the "noblest of democratic ideals" for those truly committed to advancing the development of a democratic Western Hemisphere.[85] The delegates to the Lima Conference's symbolic power for the Americas as a whole added leverage to the type of work and interventions that these delegates would engage in upon returning in their respective countries. This explains why Apristas were willing to adapt their maximum program in a way that opened a venue for collaboration with Inter-American institutions. If it made sense ideologically, for the threat of Fascism felt impending, adapting Indo-América in a way that positioned APRA against communism and Fascism, reinforced, politically, its struggles to advance the return of democracy in Peru. The Inter-American institutions furnished the Hayista faction with new tools to promote internationally APRA's political struggles for the return of democracy in Peru.

Perú, AGN, Ministerio de Interior, Dirección de gobierno, Prefectura de Lima, Presos Políticos y Sociales, Legajo 3.9.5.1.15.1.14.7 (1932–1942).

82 [Unknown author] to Sra. Esperanza Balmaceda de Josefe, Lima, December 10, 1938, Pontificia Universidad Católica del Perú, CEDOC, Colección especial Arturo Sabroso Montoya, Cartas personales, AI, 7 al 11.

83 "Some people question our statements!" Ibid.

84 "The delegates must go to the prisons and speak with the prisoners." "Their testimonies will reveal to you Dantean passages from the 'Green Hell'," ibid.

85 Ibid.

INTERNATIONALISM VS NATIONALISM

By 1938, however, disagreements about how best to defend PAP and fight to retrieve basic political liberties in Peru were rife within the movement. Those who believed in Indo-América did not always agree on how to write about it. Correspondence between APRA leaders in exile and in hiding in Peru opens a window on the lack of unanimity within the party regarding Indo-América's role and place in the Aprista doctrine. The internationalism of the Hayista faction, together with its insistence on APRA's maximum program, provoked resentment among sections of the party leadership. Many deemed it was time for PAP to focus its energy back on Peru rather than Indo-América. Meanwhile, APRA leaders and close allies of the Hayista faction residing outside Peru faulted Haya de la Torre for the lack of foresight in his new designs for Indo-América. "Su concepción continentalista parece como relegada, luego de lo que hubiera sido impulsión de juventud," stressed the Argentine Gabriel del Mazo in his correspondence with the APRA leader Magda Portal in 1940.[86] Portal had by then managed to escape to Argentina and then Chile, where she took residency in November 1939 and began working with the community of Aprista exiles established in the Chilean capital. She agreed with del Mazo. Both blamed Haya de la Torre for obstinately refusing to leave Peru. Portal argued that Haya de la Torre's prolonged isolation in Peru, and his implication in trivial party matters, caused him to lose touch with larger continental realities. In turn, del Mazo suggested that exile bestowed on intellectuals and political activists the experiences and stimulation necessary to reflect originally upon the Americas. Their verdict was unequivocal: Haya de la Torre's prolonged confinement in Peru had made him lose touch with continental developments.[87] Indo-América endured in APRA with different meanings, changing forms and premises depending on where or with whom one reflected upon its nature.

By the fall of 1937, the Hayista faction's insistence on focusing on the international scene reverted to inter-American platforms to lead its battle for civil liberties. The struggle to exist as a political party in Peru depended on Indo-América, both as a concept and as a practice of political solidarity and support from other Indo-American countries.

[86] "His continentalist perspective seems to be relegated to something close to a youth impulse." Gabriel del Mazo to Magda Portal, May 26, 1940, Magda Portal Papers, Box 1, Folder 4.

[87] Ibid.

But a new electoral cycle in Peru concurrently resuscitated the hopes of democratic participation at the national level. As a result of the Hayista faction's failure to retrieve civil liberties by appealing to the continental scene, a crisis of leadership in APRA burst into the open in 1939–1940.

Part of the party leadership in Peru reproached Haya de la Torre for this defeat. In the course of 1939, plans emerged to remove him and declare the Aprista Alfonso Vasquez Lapeyre as leader of the PAP in his stead. Vásquez Lapeyre's plot to overthrow Haya de la Torre came to fruition in August of that year. The internal coup began with the takeover of the *Tribuna*, the official mouthpiece of APRA in Peru, on August 24, 1939. Vásquez Lapeyre addressed an editorial to his "compañeros de toda la republica," in which he declared himself the Secretary General of the PAP and announced that he was from now on the person in charge of the party. "Ha querido el destino que recaiga en mi," he wrote, "modesto militante, la responsabilidad de conducir a buen puerto la gloriosa nave aprista. Izo, pues, el pabellón de la armonía, de la abnegación y de la sinceridad, seguro de que nadie osara arriarla jamás."[88] Vásquez Lapeyre asked for the cooperation of the Aprista masses. He also included references to persecution and exile in recognition of the suffering of APRA militants. One can feel in his discourse the need to assert his authority as the new leader of APRA.[89]

This crisis of leadership casts a spotlight on a series of conundrums the party had to face: Who was in the best position to fight to restore full individual liberties to Peruvian Apristas: Apristas in Peru or their peers in exile? What was the best way to do so? Participate from within the national scene, with perhaps the price of compromise with national enemies? Or use Indo-American solidarities as a way to exert pressure on the Peruvian government? In the latter case another compromise would be necessary, that of curtailing APRA's aggressive attacks against the US government and, as a corollary, moderating their initial critiques of structural inequalities in the Americas. What would be gained and what would be lost from these contrasting positions?

[88] "Companions from all over the republic." "Fate has wanted that I, a modest activist, be given the responsibility of bringing the glorious Aprista movement to fruition. So I hoist the flag of harmony, self-denial, and sincerity, certain that no one would ever dare to bring it down." Alfonso Vásquez Lapeyre, "El Secretario General del P.A.P. se dirige a su compañeros de toda la república," La Tribuna, Lima, Edicion Extraordinaria, August 24, 1939, *La Tribuna: Diario Popular de todo el Perú*, Edicion Extraordinaria, Lima, Thursday August 24, 1939, p. 3, Biblioteca Nacional del Perú, Hemeroteca Nacional.

[89] Ibid., p. 3.

For Apristas who supported Vásquez Lapeyre, the answer to these questions lay in the national scene. Calls to focus the organizing efforts of the party on Peru rather than on Indo-América began to emerge in the previous year. Consider, for example, the letter that one Aprista exile in Santiago de Chile wrote to the Aprista Committee of Mexico on December 8, 1938. This document highlights a degree of discontent regarding the overwhelming attention granted to the international scene. In what follows, the author argues that the APRA movement had to refocus its attention onto Peru:

> En cuanto al actual programa máximo del Partido una simple relectura de mi proposición demostrara que yo no quiero eliminarlo ni siquiera restarle su importancia intrínseca, sino simplemente trasladar el acento de la actividad doctrinaria y la literatura aprista de lo internacional a lo nacional. Es decir intensificar más, mucho más, su nacionalismo y poner en segundo término su acción internacional.[90]

Alfonso Vasquez Lapeyre dovetailed with this position. He promised to focus on the national scene and to act so as to restore civil liberties in Peru as soon as possible. The group that ousted the Haya de la Torre clique was tired of the party's illegal status, from which nothing could be done for the masses of Peru, it argued. Moreover, the forthcoming national elections seemed to offer a perfect opportunity to retrieve civil liberties and act within the national political scene.[91] They promoted peace and cooperation rather than confrontation with the enemy and insisted on the nationalist and democratic nature of the PAP.[92] The PAP is for Peru, stressed Vasquez Lapeyre, blaming the previous leadership for having forgotten this fact and for "un minúsculo grupo de exaltados sin función en el Partido, sin visión y sin entraña."[93]

[90] "Regarding the current maximum program of the Party, a simple review of my proposal will show that I do not want to eliminate it or even reduce its intrinsic importance, but simply to transfer the accent of doctrinal activity and Aprista literature from the international to the national. That is, to intensify more, much more, your nationalism and put your international action in the background," Unidentified APRA exile in Chile to the Aprista Committee in México, Santiago, December 8, 1938, FLEEC, ENAH, México.

[91] "La Tribuna," *La Tribuna: Diario Popular de todo el Perú*, Lima, August 31 1939, p. 4.

[92] Partido Aprista Peruano, "Manifiesto del Partido Aprista Peruano a la Nación," *La Tribuna: Diario Popular de todo el Perú*, Lima, Thursday August 24, 1939, p. 2.

[93] "A tiny group of exalted Apristas without function in the party, without vision and without guts," Alfonso Vasquez Lapeyre, "El secretario general del comité ejecutivo nacional a todos los miembros del partido," *La Tribuna: Diario Popular de todo el Perú*, Lima, August 31, 1939, p. 3.

On October 10, 1939, three days before the release of the tenth issue of *La Tribuna* under the control of the Vásquez Lapeyre faction, a small pamphlet from *La Tribuna*, subtitled "edición clandestina de protesta" appeared. The format of this clandestine publication differed from the official version of *La Tribuna*. It was smaller and showed that the Hayista faction had access to less resources to publish the journal it used to control. APRA leaders in exile, including Arturo Sabroso Montoya and Luis Heysen, were in communication with Haya de la Torre in Peru in order to address the situation.[94]

The Hayista faction would not relinquish the party leadership without a fight. It rapidly organized in order to regain its authority inside Peru. Communities of Aprista exiles wrote petitions and sent out messages of solidarity in Peru in which they confirmed their allegiance to the leadership of Haya de la Torre. They likewise censured the new National Executive Committee that claimed to be organizing PAP henceforth. Furthermore, the editorial staff of the Editorial Ercilla, in Chile, sent a note to Peru in August 1939, condemning the recent take over of *La Tribuna*. Another party document signed by over ninety Aprista exiles argued that this was a fraud, reiterating their faith in an APRA movement united under the leadership of Haya de la Torre:

> Ante la audaz tentativa de sorprender a la opinión publica con la formación de un pretendido Comité Ejecutivo Nacional, y con el uso ilegitimo del órgano oficial del Partido, "LA TRIBUNA," los desterrados apristas residentes en Chile, protestamos publica y enérgicamente, condenando todo intento divisionista, reiterando nuestra absoluta adhesión al Jefe del Partido, Haya de la Torre, y al Comité Nacional de Acción, y declarando nuestro inquebrantable propósito de mantener y defender la férrea unidad del aprismo.[95]

Another form of mobilization took form in print. The Hayista fraction attempted to publicize within Peru its most recent doctrinal work abroad.

[94] "Underground protest edition," Letter of Luis Heysen to Víctor Raúl Haya de la Torre, August 29, 1939; Letter of Arturo Sabroso Montoya to Víctor Raúl Haya de la Torre, 7 Diciembre 1939; Pontificia Universidad Católica del Perú, CEDOC, Caso Vásquez-Lapeyre, Cartas de VRHT Y ASM: Importantes, B1, 952 al 975.

[95] "Before the audacious attempt to surprise the public opinion with the formation of an alleged National Executive Committee, and with the illegitimate use of the official organ of the Party, 'LA TRIBUNA', we, the exiled Apristas residing in Chile, publicly and energetically protest and condemn any attempt at division. We reiterate our absolute support of the party leader, Haya de la Torre, and of the National Action Committee, and we confirm our unwavering intention to maintain and defend the strong unity of Aprismo." Santiago, August 1939, Pontificia Universidad Católica del Perú, CEDOC, Caso Vásquez-Lapeyre, Cartas de VRHT Y ASM: Importantes, B1, 952 al 975.

It announced, for example, that new books were to reach Lima shortly, and invited every party follower who wanted to read them to contact the National Secretary of Culture (Secretario Nacional de cultura). The authors of these books were APRA ideologues we are by now familiar with, as you can see in the following statement: "Todos los cc. Que quieran recibir obras de Haya de la Torre, Antenor Orrego, Luis Alberto Sánchez, Juan y Manuel Seoane, Ciro Alegría, Cossio del Pomar, Pedro E. Muñiz, etc., que tanta resonancia han hallado en Indoamérica podrán recibirlas pidiéndolas al Secretario Nal. De Cultura."[96] It was important to highlight, as they had in the past, the relation between these ideologues and the rest of Indo-América. These efforts to reassert to the rank and file members of the party the legitimacy of the APRA leaders who manned the Hayista faction suggested that Aprista exiles, the foreign press, and regional Aprista forces from all over Peru supported them.

By February 1940, the Hayista faction had recovered the party leadership, illustrated by the control it resumed over *La Tribuna*. References to the outside world immediately returned to its pages, as all references to "Indo-América" had disappeared since the takeover in August 1939. The celebrations for Haya de la Torre's birthday described in the February 29, 1940 issue suggested that APRA exiles and the international community rejoiced at these festivities. Internationally, it publicized the solidarity of APRA exiles with the leadership of Haya de la Torre: "Los desterrados apristas en Chile, Nueva York, México, Buenos Aires y La Paz se reunieron en grandes asambleas la noche del 21 para esperar el 22 de febrero. Se pronunciaron discursos de saludo a Haya de la Torre."[97]

APRA leaders also returned to international allies as a means to gain legality in Peru. Thanks to connections with foreign allies, the current CEN was now in position of power to ask that foreign governments intervene by requesting that civil liberties be restored in Peru.[98] The

[96] "Those who want to receive works by Haya de la Torre, Antenor Orrego, Luis Alberto Sánchez, Juan and Manuel Seoane, Ciro Alegría, Cossio del Pomar, Pedro E. Muñiz, etc., which have had so much impact in Indo-América, may receive them by requesting them from the Secretary of culture," "Libros apristas," *La Tribuna: Órgano Clandestino del PAP*, March 6, 1940, p. 1.

[97] "Aprista exiles in Chile, New York, Mexico, Buenos Aires and La Paz met in large assemblies on the night of February 21 to wait for February 22. They made speeches of greeting to Haya de la Torre." 2. "NOTICIARIO APRISTA," *La Tribuna: Órgano Clandestino del PAP*, February 29, 1940, p. 4.

[98] Luis Alberto Sánchez, "Una carta de Luis Alberto Sánchez Al Presidente de la Cámara de Diputados de Chile," *La Tribuna: Órgano Clandestino del PAP*, March 6, 1940, p. 4.

Hayista faction claimed to serve as the only legitimate intermediary to the outside world and to allegedly powerful allies.

This episode of contested leadership provides a privileged view of the political intrigues and divisions that ran through the PAP in 1939–1940. These political intrigues in turn show how difficult betrayals were at a personal level. They give access to details that shed light on how internal political debates were pursued within intimate spheres, including how longtime friends and colleagues tried to exert power over one another.[99] Archival documents help to identify the role that communities of exiles played when the legitimacy of one leader was being questioned. This crisis of leadership points to the crucial question of legitimacy within the APRA movement. Securing legitimacy, these moments reveal, was part of the everyday struggle as well. Outlawed, the PAP received no institutional legitimacy from anyone – no state, no governmental apparatus, no democratic system, and no open party politics. Its only legitimacy derived from transnational networks of peers, activists, comrades, and colleagues.

Significantly, once the Hayista faction retrieved power within the PAP, it returned ever more firmly to internationalism and to Indo-América's project as a bulwark against the advance of facism in the Americas. The Hayista faction had to maintain its hold of the continental project for pragmatic and political reasons. The adaptation of Indo-América, as seen in this chapter, came about as a result of the Hayista faction's use of the maximum program to attract international public attention and to legitimize its power internally in the PAP. Local struggles and party politics contributed to a great extent to bringing forward the internationalist character of APRA's approach to democracy, social justice, and continental solidarity. In effect, the global world order cannot explain in and of itself the ideological changes that underpinned the maximum program of this anti-imperialist movement. Rather, the need to resist recurrent state persecution and to survive politically played as much of a role, if not more, in making sure that Indo-América would survive in the Aprista doctrine beyond the foundational years.

PRESSURING ROOSEVELT INTO THE 1940S

APRA's focus on Fascist imperialism rather than US imperialism helped to solve a growing paradox in their movement. Apristas walked a

[99] See letters from 1939 through 1941, Pontificia Universidad Católica del Perú, CEDOC, Caso Vásquez-Lapeyre, Cartas de VRHT Y ASM: Importantes, B1, 952 al 975.

tightrope between their anti-imperialist theses, which rejected foreign intervention and established the sovereignty of Indo-America nations on one side, and their repeated demands that the continental democratic community intervene in Peru's domestic affairs on the other. Direct pleas for US intervention to help restore and safeguard democracy in Peru and protect Latin America from dictatorial rules peppered their political writings from the late 1930s onward. Sometimes these pleas were indirect and aimed at a democratic US public. In a reflection authored in 1941 on the Indigenous question in South America, entitled "Racial Minorities and the Present International Crisis," Luis Alberto Sánchez underscores the need for US subjects to implicate themselves in the current problems of Peru. Because foreign capitals had amply benefited from the economic exploitation of Indo-América, advanced Sánchez in an intricate argument, it was to the foreign capital's advantage to protect these benefits by making sure that totalitarianism did not make more headway in Indo-América. It was the foreign capital's responsibility "to fulfill a human task and for its own advantage," noted Sanchez, to act not as an obstacle "but rather an inducement in the task of obtaining effectiveness of the democratic regime in each of the American countries." The conclusion was unequivocal. "To give real life to democracy, is to start democracy among us," concluded Sanchez. "Anything else would be to serve, today or tomorrow, the aggressive and sullen force of totalitarianism."[100] Between this command and an explicit invitation for US capitalists to intervene in Latin America and dethrone dictatorships there was but a step.

At other times APRA leaders demanded US intervention in Peruvian affairs much more explicitly. Correspondence between leaders in exile showcases that Apristas enthusiastically welcomed, and even sought, Roosevelt's pressure on Peruvian authorities, as revealed in the letters of the Aprista Andrés Townsend Eszurra to Portal: "Muy bien la carta de Ciro y acorde con tu estimación de 'que la publicidad y no la reserva ayudan a la causa de Juan y Serafín," he wrote on October 14, 1941.

> Es también la opinión de Víctor Raúl, quien en carta de hace pocos días me dice que la carta de Palacios tuvo 'efectos fulminantes' [...]. Parece que la presión de Roosevelt sobre Prado es mucha y hasta me adelanta que podría llegar a entrañar nuestra 'ingerencia [sic] en el gobierno'. Ojala el golpe panameño tenga eco en el Perú y Prado aprenda la lección... o no la aprenda y lo echen.[101]

[100] Sánchez, "On the Problem of the Indian in South America," p. 503.

[101] "Ciro's letter was very good and agrees with your assessment that 'advertising and not reservation help the cause of Juan and Serafín." "It is also the opinion of Victor Raul,

APRA leader and labour organizer Arturo Sabroso Montoya directly wrote to the US Vice-President Henry Wallace on April 12, 1943, in an effort, he claims, to establish relationships between democratic forces of the Americas. In his letter to Wallace, Sabroso described the workers of Peru as the bearers of democracy in the Western Hemisphere who were pleading for a rapprochement between continental allies who were democrats in the face of foreign, non-American Fascist regimes. Significantly, Sabroso's letter put Roosevelt on par with heroes of Latin American independence as a symbol of the forefathers of democracy in the Americas. "Como salutación mas genérica al pueblo todo de los Estados Unidos, cumplimentamos fervorosamente al ilustre Presidente Franklin Delano Roosevelt," Sabroso noted as an introductory note, "cuyo nombre ya resuena en nuestros hogares como el de los grandes conductores democráticos del presente, y en el futuro quedara grabado por la Historia, como lo esta el de Bolívar, Juárez, y demás próceres de nuestra primera independencia."[102] Though he perhaps truly believed in the virtues of these political actors, it is crucial here to bear in mind that this APRA leader was strategically appealing to figures of power to gain more clout for his outlawed movement.[103] Adapting Aprista discourse in a way that pointed to common agendas between them and the allies they courted was a necessary means to an end. Here, my study shows that we need to study the specific political strategies that affected the types of political discourse and that were, at times, vehemently condemned within the rank and file of the Aprista group.

APRA's rapprochement with the United States suggests that the growth of wartime pro-US sentiments in the Latin American left were a result not only of the fear of Fascism but also of direct political gains the

who in a letter a few days ago told me that Palacios' letter had 'withing effects' [...]. It looks like Roosevelt's pressure on Prado is great and he even anticipates that it could involve our 'implication in the government'. I hope the Panamanian coup has an echo in Peru and Prado learns the lesson... or does not learn it and they throw him out." Andrés Townsend Ezcurra to Magda Portal, Buenos Aires, Argentine, October 14, 1941, Magda Portal Papers, Box 1, Folder 5.

102 "As a general salutation to the people of the United States, we fervently compliment the illustrious President Franklin Delano Roosevelt, whose name resonates in our homes as one of the great democratic leaders of our times. He'll be recorded by history in the future, like were Bolivar, Juarez, and other heroes of our first independence." Arturo Sabroso Montoya to Henry Wallace, "Mensaje al senor Henry Wallace," April 12, 1943, Pontificia Universidad Católica del Perú, CEDOC, Colección especial Arturo Sabroso Montoya, F.T.T.P. Asuntos Internacionales, C3, 2033 al 2039.

103 Manuel Seoane, "If I Were Nelson Rockefeller," 1943, pp. 312–318, SCPC, Peoples Mandate Committee (US), Box 21, Rockefeller, Mr. Nelson A.

left could make by engaging with the inter-American order. Scholars who study the international history of the Western Hemisphere have recently begun to re-conceptualize the Pan-American order by taking into account the role that Latin American diplomats played in the development of inter-American relations.[104] Part of the left, such as the APRA movement in Peru, also attempted to use these new platforms to advance their agenda back home. Certainly, this can also explain why Indo-América was less rigid as a concept than other points of the Aprista program. At first, in the 1920s, the meaning of APRA's imagined continental community evolved because it occurred in a moment of sheer creation. It then continued to evolve in the 1930s, this time partly because this concept had to remain flexible as Apristas sought to justify their international pleas for help. They needed to construct a sense of belonging between continental actors and the APRA movement. In fact, this is crucial to understanding the rise of Indo-América as a bulwark against Fascism as well as this project's lack of interest, in the end, in the Indigenous peoples of the Americas. It would be hard to claim that the changing international order had nothing to do with it. But even more significant was what Indo-América and Latin American solidarity represented a political instrument for Apristas to gather supporters and defend their political organization back home. And the truth is, it worked. Many allies established dialogues with Apristas in the late 1930s to early 1940s, precisely because they viewed them as either allies in the fight against fascism or paragons of democracy in the Western Hemisphere, or both.[105]

CONCLUSION

The repressive political context in Peru deeply affected APRA's ideological production on Indo-América. One significant consequence of the

[104] See for example: Mark Petersen and Carsten-Andreas Schulz, "Setting the Regional Agenda: A Critique of Posthegemonic Regionalism," *Latin American politics and Society*, 60: 1 (2018): 102–127; Petersen "'The Vanguard of Pan-Americanism': Chile and Inter-American Multilateralism in the Early Twentieth Century," in Juan Pablo Scarfi and Andrew R. Tillman (eds), Cooperation and Hegemony in US–Latin American Relations: Revisiting the Western Hemisphere Idea, New York: Palgrave Macmillan, 2016, pp. 111–137; Scarfi, *The Hidden History of International Law in the Americas*; Scarfi and Tillman, *Cooperation and Hegemony in US-Latin American Relations*: Revisiting the Western Hemisphere Idea, New York: Palgrave Macmillan, 2016.

[105] Solidaridad Internacional Antifascista to Magda Portal, "Fecha: 17/3/1939. Secretario nacional de solidaridad internacional antifascista de la argentina," Buenos Aires, March 17, 1939, Magda Portal Papers, Box 1, Folder 3.

experience of persecution and exile is that Apristas were engaged in a creative process that required them to constantly coax foreign allies. They wanted solidarity activists, and, starting in the late-1930s, state representatives as well, to defend their cause in international forums and supply resources for their movement. Because Apristas needed to appeal to continental public opinion in an attempt to retrieve basic political rights in Peru, Indo-América had to remain alive as a project able to sustain anti-imperialist aspirations for the continent at large. It also increasingly had to be framed as a symbol of democracy, anti-communism, and anti-fascism in the Western Hemisphere for APRA to receive the international support it was seeking. Calling attention to the notion of Indo-American unity and Latin American solidarity, in other words, empowered Peruvian Apristas to formulate a line of defence that extended beyond the purview of the nation-state.

Central in PAP's political struggle during the 1930s and 1940s was the capacity to appeal to international democratic forces and to representatives of free speech in Indo-América. In APRA's political writings, the political climate in Peru portended what risked happening in Indo-América if the left failed to mobilize against foreign imperialism and oligarchic minorities. APRA exiles prided themselves on having been able to analyze the problems of the Latin American continent. They claimed to be equally aware of their political responsibility vis-à-vis their peers abroad. Even when reflecting upon Peruvian issues, therefore, Aprista ideologues did so in a way that stressed the relevance these questions had for the larger Indo-American scene.

It is from this vantage point that we must approach the evolution of the Indo-American project from the mid-1930s to early-1940s rather than by way of exclusive discursive analyses. Without granting attention to the political processes that undergirded APRA's ideological changes, in effect, we risk providing a seamless historical narrative where fragments and contingencies prevailed. Neither the inauguration of the Good Neighbor Policy in 1933, nor the advent of the Second World War six years later can in and of themselves satisfactorily establish a causal relationship between the international context and APRA's changing political discourse, for these approaches fail to understand the intricate interplay between the local scene and the global context in fashioning one of Latin America's most important and enduring projects of hemispheric unity. APRA did not move to the right of the political spectrum or abandon its vindication of Indigenous groups – however superficial they were in the first place – because of international events. Nor did it as a result of the betrayal of its foundational principles in exile once Apristas returned to Peru. Rather, we should envision the ideological and evolutionary changes in APRA not as a linear process but as a mosaic of contested ideas and visions rooted in the connections between the local and the global. We must likewise reckon with the fact that US historical actors participated in shaping the development of APRA's anti-imperialism from the start, and even before its founders in fact officially established their political movement in the mid-to-late 1920s.

Conclusion

APRA means different things to different actors. During the period under study in this book, *Aprismo* alternately designated a revolutionary social movement, a left-wing reformist national party, an anti-imperialist and anti-oligarchic doctrine, and an alternative to communism in the Southern Hemisphere. For many Aprista followers in Peru it even came to signify a moral code of conduct and a unique, holistic way of being. One reason that explains this array of definitions is that the revolutionary ideology of APRA was in fact an encompassing and malleable mantle that sutured together disparate ideological tendencies.[1] At its beginnings, the APRA argued that Latin American countries had to come together and unite as a means to better expose and resist US imperialism. APRA's anti-imperialism was rooted in Latin American nationalism. Starting at the turn of the century, the advance of North American capital in Latin America and the repeated interventions by the US marines in Central America and the Caribbean (ostensibly in the name of law and order but really to protect US business interests abroad) left a strong legacy of anti-Americanism in the region.[2] Apristas, like many of their contemporaries, censured

[1] For a positive assessment of these ideological changes see Roy Soto Rivera, *Aprismo y antimperialismo*, Arequipa: Editorial Mirando, 1970. For a negative assessment see Mariano Valderrama, "La evolución ideológica del APRA 1924–1962," in Mariano Valderrama, Jorge Chullen, Nicolás Lynch and Carlos Malpica, *El APRA: Un camino de esperanzas y frustraciones*, Lima: Ediciones el Gallo Rojo, 1980, pp. 1–98.

[2] In 1904, the Roosevelt Corollary to the Monroe Doctrine turned a defensive dictum contained in the Monroe Doctrine (1823) into an aggressive policy of US supremacy in the region. This aggressive foreign policy lasted until the promulgation of the Good Neighbor Policy in 1933 sought to curb some of Washington's fiercest expansionist policies.

Washington's expansionist policies in the Western Hemisphere.[3] The revolutionary outbursts in Mexico (1910) and Russia (1917) also contributed to shaping the Aprista doctrine, or *Aprismo*. They yielded the promise of social change and made the young founders of APRA dream of emancipated nations and fairer societies.[4]

Although the APRA party did not achieve national power until 1985, under the leadership of the young and dynamic Alan García, decades of popular support and influence in Congress positioned the party at the head of ongoing struggles to forge an inclusive Peruvian state during most of the past century. Yet by the time García took office, the APRA looked quite different than it did during the period under study in this book. From the 1920s radical anti-imperialist movement to the 1930s and 1940s Peruvian leftist and nationalist party, the APRA ended up forging alliances with Peruvian conservative elites in the 1950s and 1960s. By the 1970s, following a wave a defection in the party, the APRA struggled to maintain relevance: the reformist military government of Juan Velasco Alvarado (1968–1975) implemented much of the APRA programs' social demands. To this day, it is Velasco – not APRA – who Peruvians remember as the agent who first attempted to incorporate all Peruvians in the nation.[5] So when an Aprista finally took hold of the presidency in the mid-1980s, the stakes ran high for party members. That García had run on a bold social-democratic platform in the midst of an acute economic crisis and of the Shining Path's violent insurrection made his rise to power all the more significant for leftist observers as well. Unfortunately, after a few years of successful policies and high approval rates in Peru, García's

Serge Ricard, "The Roosevelt Corollary," *Presidential Studies Quarterly*, 36: 1 (March 2006): 17–26. Edward S. Kaplan, *U.S. Imperialism in Latin America, Bryan's Challenges and Contributions, 1900–1920*, Westport and London: Greenwood Press, 1998.

[3] These anti-US sentiments were influenced but not determined by the expansion of international Communism following the creation of the Comintern in 1919. Jeffrey L. Klaiber, "The Non-Communist Left in Latin America," *Journal of the History of Ideas*, 32: 4 (October–December, 1971), p. 607.

[4] Pablo Yankelevich, "La revolución Mexicana en el debate político latinoamericano: Ingenieros, Palacios, Haya de la Torre y Mariategui," *Cuadernos Americanos*, 3: 11 (May 2005): 161–186.

[5] A large scholarly production has debated about the nature of the Velasco regime and the extent of his nationalist reforms. See for example Juan Martín Sánchez, *La Revolución Peruana: Ideología y practica de un gobierno militar, 1968-1975*, Sevilla: Universidad de Sevilla, 2002; Abraham F. Lowenthal and Cynthia McClintock (ed.), *The Peruvian Experiment Reconsidered*, Princeton: Princeton University Press, 1983.

first term in office ended in disaster.[6] By the time he left office in 1990, only 6 per cent of Peruvians approved of him.[7] That isn't surprising. García was then embroiled in corruption scandals, the country was mired in a policymaking crisis, and the economy was collapsing under hyperinflation. There seemed nothing left to be saved of APRA. As Daniel Alarcón bluntly notes: "[García's] reputation as the bright young hope of the Latin-American left had been destroyed."[8]

Many critics have chastised in hindsight the conservative drift of the party's program. These critics suppose that over the course of the past century, APRA's political agenda has followed a left-wing to right-wing linear, inexorable progression. In these accounts, the social-democratic agenda of Alan García's first period in office (1985–1990) appears as an awkward parenthesis – the exception to the rule. And effectively, the neoliberal policies that characterized his second presidential term (2006–2011) appear to prove these critics correct. In a 2011 publication, García openly parted with the party's social-democrat tradition by defining democracy in terms of consumer rights and market opportunities. García's *Contra el temor económico: Creer en el Perú* argues that the pursuit of a neoliberal political agenda will bring Peru into modernity and help solve its social problems. As a result, García let go of the Indo-American dream, enthusiastically promoting *La Alianza del Pacifico* (Chile, Peru, Colombia Mexico, Panama) instead as the best plan for regional integration.[9] In the 2010s, the expansion of free-trade markets was driving García's internationalism, not the necessity of Latin American solidarity, much less resistance to foreign imperialism.[10]

Nevertheless, the left-wing versus right-wing debate is too simplistic to capture the full complexity behind APRA's ideological disagreements and evolution over time, mainly because it focuses exclusively on the national scene to explain these transformations. *Journey to Indo-América* deepens our comprehension of APRA's ideological production by exploring the

[6] Martín Tanaka, "El giro del APRA y de Alan García," *Nueva Sociedad*, 217 (2008), ISSN: 0251-3552, www.nuso.org; Carol Graham, *Peru's APRA: Parties, Politics, and the Elusive Quest for Democracy*, Boulder: L. Rienner Publishers, 1992, p. 99–170.

[7] Daniel Alarcón, "What Led Peru's Former President to Take His Own Life?," *The New Yorker*, July 1, 2019, www.newyorker.com/magazine/2019/07/08/what-led-perus-former-president-to-take-his-own-life.

[8] Ibid.

[9] Alan García, *Contra el temor económico: Creer en el Perú*, Lima: Planeta, 2011.

[10] Alan García took his life in April 2019. For a detailed contextualization of his dramatic death in the midst of a corruption scandal consult Daniel Alarcón, "What Led Peru's Former President to Take His Own Life?"

context in which APRA's project of hemispheric unity first came to life and evolved thereafter.

Drawing on original research in underutilized archives in the United States, France, Mexico, and Peru, this book reconfigures APRA history as transnational and hemispheric history. By tracing the journey that underpinned the creation and development of Indo-América, first as a cultural hemispheric consciousness in the 1920s, then as a political hemispheric project beginning in the 1930s, *Journey to Indo-América* reveals the worlds of transnational radical activism that carried this project through the wheel of time. This book seeks to understand better the evolution of Indo-América through an innovative approach that enabled me to tell an untold story about APRA. To do so, I shift the analytical gaze away from exclusive Peruvian politics to pay attention to the global connections that underlay the history of this Latin American anti-imperialist movement. I also shift the analytical gaze away from either undying tales of betrayal or celebrations of a legendary and uncontested leader, Víctor Raúl Haya de la Torre, and focus my attention instead on the radical worlds that fostered the emergence and evolution of APRA during the interwar period. Probing, on the one hand, the experience of life in exile as a culturally and politically innovative diaspora of anti-imperialist thinkers, while granting attention, on the other, to life rooted in Peru, illuminates APRA's project of social inclusion and the radical militancy of its founders. Doing so also puts on display the limiting factors that contributed to moderating APRA's radical critiques of empire in later years. A yearning for an anti-oligarchic state in Peru, and in the Latin American (or Indo-American) republics more broadly, took root in the exchanged desires and sensibilities that defined interwar communities of exiles, bohemians, and activists in key cities in the Americas and Europe.

While the scope of this study is limited to the early experience of APRA, and thus cannot explain in full the ideological transition of this movement over the full course of the past century, it sheds new light on the initial transformation of APRA, the period in which many critical accounts locate the beginning of APRA's tergiversations. Understanding how and why Apristas came to imagine Indo-América during the interwar period as they battled for the return of democracy in Peru on one side, while navigating and using, on the other, a heteroclite web of transnational solidarity networks to help them withstand state persecution, contributes to shedding new light on what happened.

As a result, a central endeavour of this book is to historicize the workings of transnational solidarity networks that assisted the development of APRA as a persecuted political group. To do so, I highlight the role that North American and European allies adopted for the Aprista solidarity networks during the interwar period. Foreign intermediaries like Anna Melissa Graves and John A. Mackay contributed to assuring the political vitality and collective integrity of APRA in the face of recurrent state persecution.[11] The impact that these actors had on public opinion outside Peru as well as the pressure that they exerted on Peruvian state actors helped the APRA fight political repression. It likewise contributed to gathering international supporters to APRA's cause, and specifically to a moderate, democratic and anti-communist APRA placed under the headship of the Hayista faction. Starting in the early 1920s, Christian pacifist actors and solidarity activists tapped into home-based networks to bolster international awareness of the student leader Víctor Raúl Haya de la Torre, and to attract attention more broadly to the Reform-minded university students' project of moral regeneration for Peru. As APRA developed, and as its political project crystallized, the support of these foreign actors changed in nature but remained strong nevertheless. The emotional weight of their early friendships in exile gradually developed to form stable political alliances where parties engaged on an equal footing with one another. In the early 1930s, Mackay and Graves used their respective international contacts to advocate in favour of APRA. They published favourable reviews of the movement and readily celebrated the work of an anti-communist and anti-imperialist APRA in the Western Hemisphere.

The formation of friendships between the *Reformista* generation of Latin American university students and Christian missionaries and internationalist pacifists reveals an important dimension of the worlds of radical activism that foregrounded the initial formation of Indo-América. In a world shaken by the recent experience of World War I, where once solid points of reference went adrift in a sea of despair, shared disillusions and hopes proved more important than common ideological ground to engage in alliances. For both North American Christian pacifists and Latin American leftist activists, as we have seen, the Americas stood as a utopian geography where civilization might rise again, and be saved.

[11] I am indebted to the work of Daviken Studnicki-Gizbert on the Portuguese Atlantic diaspora between the fifteenth and seventeenth centuries for thinking of the concepts of "political vitality" and "collective integrity." See Daviken Studnicki-Gizbert *A Nation Upon the Ocean Sea: Portugal's Atlantic Diaspora and the Crisis of the Spanish Empire, 1492–1640*, New York: Oxford University Press, 2007.

In addition to the social connections made necessary by political despair, these alliances were sustained by similar ideologies. These groups shared the same aversion to positivist and materialist philosophies. They were also distrustful of the nation-state as an inclusive and emancipatory form of human organization. These North American, European, and Latin American radicals recognized each other as dreamers who were willing to give their lives to the service of a higher cause. And although this "higher cause" was still ill defined at the beginning of the 1920s, these historical protagonists were equally convinced of one thing: the necessity to rethink the future of the Americas was tantamount to solving the problems that plagued the postwar Western World.

The Cuban José Martí is one of the first intellectuals to have foreseen and clearly expressed the danger that US expansion represented for Latin American republics. To this day, Martí is praised for having interpreted the struggle for national liberation in nineteenth-century Cuba as a way to gain political independence from Spain as well as to contain the advance of US imperialism in the region. His anti-colonial thoughts are reflected in what he called "Our America," a vision of hemispheric unity free from US oppression, which furthermore boasted the Indigenous and African origins of Latin America.[12] The following generation of anti-imperialist thinkers in Latin America walked in his footsteps. Though initiated through the earlier work of Simon Bolívar and José Martí, the forefathers of continental nationalism, the rise of hemispheric consciousness progressed most definitely as young APRA members travelled back and forth between Peru and places of exile. This generation had inherited from their forefathers a commitment toward hemispheric solidarity as well as the resolve to imagine the Americas in new ways. While their ability to do so was all but certain in the late 1910s, the experience of exile, beginning in the 1920s, triggered in them a capacity for original creation regarding the future of the Americas.

Studying what exile entailed for young APRA members at this personal and intimate level, therefore, helps to illuminate how new knowledge on the Americas emerged in the 1920s. Before they were able to conceive differently of collective identities, the student activists and radical poets who began to imagine Indo-América and who built the anti-imperialist APRA had to realign, first, how they approached and conceived of their own individual identity. Apristas, or soon-to-be Apristas, I argue, had to

[12] Roberto Fernández Retamar (ed.), *Cuba, Nuestra América, Los Estados Unidos, por José Martí*, México: Siglo veintiuno editores, 1973.

come of age individually before they could come of age as a group. The lived experience of exile both prompted and assisted these respective experiences of personal emancipation. Whether it was feelings of alienation from the homeland or feelings of bliss in the face of new possibilities, these emotions intensified the connection that many of them developed with radical communities abroad. In both cases, intellectual engagement was intimately intertwined with the emotional weight that came with group dynamics (or the lack thereof) particular to life in exile. The lived experience of exile enabled this generation of anti-imperialist thinkers to produce original political knowledge on Latin American unity. Importantly, because in exile alliances were crucial to secure access to rare resources, the need to compromise on certain ideals in order to insure political survival also positioned the ideal of collaboration at the forefront of their work.

This ideal of collaboration offered resiliency to APRA throughout the 1920s. Collaboration prompted a series of cultural and intellectual exchanges regarding the future of the Americas rather than yielding clearly defined ideologies. Before the new cultural consciousnesses of the 1920s crystallized into firm political positions in the following decade, in effect, the pursuit of hemispheric unity in the Americas continued to be paramount. It surpassed the need to closely identify with communism, socialism, or nationalist anti-imperialism, not only because these movements were still in formation at the time but also because they all advocated the same end-point: the nation-state had to be re-imagined entirely if humanity was to survive. Furthermore, this desire to forego the nation-state was only confirmed in APRA by the impossibility of taking an active part in Peruvian politics because of unremitting state persecution. Such a distrust for the nation-state made alliances possible between protagonists, who like Víctor Raúl Haya de la Torre and José Carlos Mariátegui, disagreed over the exact meaning of Indo-América: the latter mattered less than did the intention to imagine Peru and the Americas in new ways. In the 1920s, acknowledging intellectual, political, and tactical differences in the APRA movement did not entail ceasing relations with opposing factions. To the contrary, it was still possible at the time to suspend political and doctrinal disagreements if this meant serving the larger cause of "Nuestra América."

Building from José Martí's utopian vision, the Latin American anti-imperialist left during the interwar period also collaborated with North American non-state actors who similarly pondered projects of continental integration. Some simply wanted more cooperation and more mutual understanding between the people of the Americas. Others objected to Pan-American definitions that exclusively focused on commercial exchange and financial interest. These factions actively sought to envision alternative, more democratic visions of Pan-Americanism. Regardless of their differences, all readily put ideological dissent aside whenever it served their cause best. The growth of solidarity networks between the Peruvian vanguard and foreign allies rested on the shared project of building a new continental utopia. In this scenario, mutual interdependence and the need to gain access to rare resources also helped surpass the inevitability of political factions.

But APRA's reliance on foreign solidarity activists to ensure personal and political survival also came with a price. This strategy resulted over time in moderating Apristas' critiques of US imperialism and global capitalism and limiting the possibilities for social change they first envisioned in the 1920s during their time in exile. These changes were clearly felt in APRA's project of hemispheric unity. While the reliance on allies abroad, including US critiques of empire who peddled a softer anti-imperialism, informed APRA's decision to placate its anti-US sentiments on one side, it nevertheless confirmed APRA's appeal toward regional alliances. As APRA's anti-imperialism lost momentum starting in the mid-1930s, the continental integration project of Indo-América gained in both specificity and notoriety.

This book also highlights the permanence of conflict in APRA. Rather than focusing on the ruptures that have rocked this movement in the course of its history, *Journey to Indo-América* draws attention to the possibilities embedded within conflict. This enables me to probe the question of APRA's leadership with different premises in mind: Víctor Raúl Haya de la Torre, I argue, was not the uncontested leader of APRA as early or as consistently as imagined. The constant internecine strife to determine which faction was in control of the movement had major consequences for the development of APRA's project of hemispheric unity in the 1930s and 1940s. That these battles took place in the midst of unremitting political repression contributed to converting Indo-América, an ill-defined and flexible utopia for the Americas in the 1920s and early 1930s, into a precise instrument of political survival by the 1940s.

Thus, by exploring the group dynamics particular to the transnational APRA and unveiling the symbolic politics that turned Víctor Raúl Haya de la Torre – certainly an important leader in the movement but not the only one – into the only legitimate representative and ideologue of APRA, this book not only helps to decentre the study of *Aprismo*. It in fact tells an entirely different story, one that traces the multifaceted rise of anti-imperialist projects of hemispheric unity in the Americas and reveals the possibilities for social and political transformation that visions for Latin American unity have enabled in the past century, as well as the important limitations and contradictions that nestled within them.

The creation of the Peruvian APRA party (PAP) in October of 1930 marked the onset of a new era for both Apristas and APRA's continental program. Before the promise of a democratic Peru with the fall of Augusto B. Leguía in the Peruvian winter of that year, APRA exiles returned home and began to organize their movement at the national level. The newly founded PAP faced two main challenges. First, APRA leaders in Peru had to homogenize the movement's ideology: they worked to integrate political positions particular to different APRA exiles into a single philosophy of action. Second, APRA leaders needed to translate their anti-imperialist project of hemispheric unity in a way that would be appealing to the Peruvian population. They had to adapt their internationalist prose and put forward a unified proposal that Peruvian people could understand, recognize, and identify with. References to past travels and to the experience of exile in the 1920s proved useful to accomplish these tasks. In this lay the genesis of what soon became the political appeal of Indo-América: if the Americas supported APRA, went the storyline promoted by the Hayista faction, then the Americas would support a Peru placed under the guidance of the Peruvian APRA party.

The legitimacy granted by the experience of exile not only shaped how APRA successfully transitioned into the Peruvian APRA party (PAP) in 1930–1931 from an international movement, it also came to concurrently define the touchstone of APRA's nationalism as well as that of Indo-América as a concept of Latin American resistance and solidarity. I argue that Indo-América as a political project was not consolidated in the heyday of transnational exile in the 1920s. Rather, Indo-América is best understood as a form of universal appeal to which the Hayista faction arrived more definitely in the 1930s to advance a political struggle inside Peru. This book asserts that imagining global communities that reach across national borders can be an effective strategy to press on local demands.[13] Local dynamics, then, often without our knowledge, actually dictate the contours of global utopias.

[13] For a study on this theme see Maurice Demers, *Connected Struggles: Catholics, Nationalists, and Transnational Relations between Mexico and Quebec, 1917–1945*, Montréal and Kingston: McGill-Queen's University Press, 2014.

The return of state persecution in Peru toward the end of 1931 impelled PAP to expand its repertoire of political actions. Facing the impossibility of democratic participation in Peruvian politics, it developed transnational strategies that could assist its political survival in Peru. Paradoxically, this precarious situation helped the Hayista faction to take control of the APRA party by August of 1933. Making use of the symbol of a democratic and internationally famous Víctor Raúl Haya de la Torre served the cause of PAP, and especially that of the Hayista faction, for it had the power to attract international attention onto the exactions suffered by Apristas in Peru. Thus, APRA's associations with the outside world and with Indo-América in particular became ever more tied to the exclusive leadership of the Haysita faction in the movement.

The APRA leaders close to the Hayista faction became very aware of the benefits that transnational networks of solidarity yielded for their political movement as well as their own position within the party. In addition to reinforcing the political legitimacy of APRA leaders in Peru in the early 1930s, exile also assisted the establishment of alliances with foreign actors and the insertion of APRA into transnational networks of solidarity. Being connected to the outside world gave them access to crucial resources, including material and symbolic capital, and thus became of paramount importance to both maintain alliances with foreign actors and to publicize in Peru their international relationships as a sign of authority. This explains why referring to APRA's connection with the rest of Indo-América became central to the Peruvian APRA party's defence strategy in the face of state persecution. The need to foster and maintain alliances with foreign actors shaped the way in which APRA thought of democracy and defined the political knowledge it produced.

Throughout the 1930s and early 1940s, during what the Aprista lore refers to as "the Era of the Catacombs," Peruvian APRA leaders close to Haya de la Torre continued to court potential allies abroad. Engaging in information politics outside Peru proved to be a crucial strategy for the PAP to jeopardize the monopoly that Peruvian authorities maintained over media outlets in Peru. For example, the party spearheaded a transnational campaign of moral shaming against the Benavides government in an attempt to attract supporters to its cause. Communities of APRA exiles played an important role in these campaigns. They produced anti-Benavides propaganda and circulated it outside Peru. They courted foreign allies and advocated on international platforms for the right of PAP to exist as a legitimate political organization. In the articles they wrote, APRA exiles opposed to barbarian Peruvian authorities a civilized public opinion, largely associated with the Americas, which sided with Peruvian Apristas in their censure of dictatorial regimes. PAP was invariably portrayed as a model of democracy for Peru and for Latin America more broadly.

Calling attention to the notion of Latin American, or Indo-American, solidarity empowered Peruvian Apristas to formulate a line of defence that extended beyond the purview of the nation-state. Central to PAP's political struggle, in effect, was an appeal to international democratic forces and to the representatives of free speech in the Americas. One consequence of this strategy, I show, was to put the concept of Indo-América decisively at the forefront of APRA's intellectual production. Social scientists have stressed how advocacy groups that want to externalize a specific agenda, usually when their demands are blocked at the national level, do so by turning this agenda into universal claims that can best appeal to international allies. Because Apristas appealed to continental public opinion as a means to retrieve basic political rights in Peru, it encouraged them to retain internationalist references and their project of hemispheric unity and Indo-American solidarity as one that carried anti-imperialist aspirations, and dreams of democracy by the mid-to-late 1930s, for the continent at large.

To be sure, changes on the international scene affected the way in which APRA ideologues thought of Indo-América. According to historian Greg Grandin, the first phase of US imperialism in Latin America, which had started in the nineteenth century with the Mexican-American war (1846–1848) and continued more brutally still with the Hispano-American war (1898), came to a close in the early 1930s. The declaration of the Good Neighbor policy in 1933, he argues, as well as the experience of the Popular Front shortly after, "dampened the anti-imperialist rhetoric of the Left" in Latin America.[14] As such, APRA's shift toward the right of the political spectrum in the 1930s was part of a larger trend that affected the Latin American left at large. By 1936, Washington had renounced its right to intervene in the region. The promise of friendly relations, after close to a century of US aggression and conceit, had every appearance of sincerity. On the other hand, the Popular Front curbed opposition between communist and socialist parties and enabled a rapprochement between the Latin American left and the United States in the

[14] Greg Grandin, "The Narcissism of Violent Differences," in *Anti-Americanism*, edited by Andrew Ross and Kristin Ross, New York: New York University Press, 2004, p. 20.

face of mounting European Fascism.[15] In many ways, the Popular Front strategy consolidated at a political level what was already conceivable at a cultural level. The communist and socialist parties in Latin America not only came together but they also agreed to align their respective programs of action with those of the United States.

This new world order contributed to moving problems of democracy to the forefront of APRA's Indo-American project. It also encouraged many in the party to pacify their positions vis-à-vis the United States. APRA ideologues began to revise the party's maximum program so as to divert its anti-imperialist attacks onto Fascism and Nazism instead of US imperialism. Cooperation between Indo-América and North America appeared in the mid-1930s onward to be a lesser evil with which to salvage democracy in the Western Hemisphere. Significantly, Indo-América was still couched in anti-imperialist vernacular. The international conjuncture, however, had contributed to transforming the nature of the imperialist threat. Imperialism was now associated with Fascism and totalitarian regimes in Europe rather than Yankee expansionism.

This book expands this argument, thanks to the dialogue I established between local and transnational levels of historical analyses. By evincing the role that local politics in Peru played in shaping definitions of Indo-América in different times and places, my work reveals an important feature of Pan-American visions. It portrays the design of hemispheric unity projects not only as a response in the face of international relations, which to be sure mattered greatly, but also as a result of local demands. *Journey to Indo-América* argues that Indo-América came to be portrayed as a bulwark against the rise of Fascism in Europe not only as a result of world events but also out of the necessity of political survival at the national level. The persecution of the PAP in Peru, combined with APRA's innovative political strategies, greatly contributed to forging a sense of continental solidarity based on the defence of individual political rights and democratic regimes. Starting in the 1930s, references to Indo-América helped the PAP to externalize its domestic demands for democracy by universalizing its cause before an international public opinion.

Furthermore, local party dynamics explain why Indo-América has come to be associated exclusively with the leadership of one faction in the APRA movement. The practice of political survival in the face of recurrent state persecution in Peru favoured the rise of a leader whose

[15] Greg Grandin, *Empire's Workshop, Latin America, the United States, and the Rise of the New Imperialism*, New York: Henry Holt and Company, 2006, pp. 33–39.

fame helped project the APRA onto the world stage; a democratic Indo-América seemed indeed to support Víctor Raúl Haya de la Torre. When Peru's 1945 Democratic Spring announced a return to democracy in the country, Haya de la Torre showed himself ready to engage in national politics and to help build a better Peru. Indo-América hovered by this leader's side, pointing to democratic ideals honed by the weight of past persecution and the prospects of political inclusion and fairer societies.

The moral and radical yearnings that characterized Indo-América in the first half of the twentieth century were progressively subsumed by the demands imposed by the Cold War. As communities of radical Peruvian artists and intellectuals in the 1920s crystallized into political parties the following decade, they learned to restrain their utopian ideals and define more precisely the demands that they advanced in Peruvian politics. Starting in the mid-1930s, and ever more forcefully in the aftermath of the Second World War, the need to survive politically contributed to Indo-American ideologues' shift away from an ideal of democracy based on socio-economic justice, and closer to the ideal of democracy advanced at the time by the United States to counter communism: a liberal democracy based on individual rights and civil liberties.[16]

Not everybody in APRA embraced this conversion. Although internal critiques surged all through the 1940s and the 1950s, it was ultimately the *Convivencia* (1956–1962) that marked for many Apristas the end of the Peruvian APRA as an anti-imperialist party. The "convivencia" government refers to the political alliance that Víctor Raúl Haya de la Torre forged in 1956 with Manuel Prado Ugarteche, a Peruvian politician connected to elements of the national oligarchy in the agro-export sector, in exchange for the PAP's return to legality and the promise to participate in the Peruvian government. Detractors and disillusioned members of APRA argued that their party no longer served the interests of the Peruvian people. According to the party's leftist faction, not only had the PAP, presumably the anti-oligarchic party par excellence in Peru, come to terms with the national oligarchy, but it now defended the interests of these groups by tempering the demands of its labour unions and by supporting bills in congress that served the status quo. The verdict was harsh: "El PAP, sirviendo de instrumento al servicio de los intereses de la oligarquía está defraudando las más caras esperanzas del pueblo del

[16] Greg Grandin, *The Last Colonial Massacre: Latin American in the Cold War*, Chicago and London: The University of Chicago Press, 2004.

Perú," wrote the founders of APRA Rebelde on 10 October 1959.[17] This group of Cuban-inspired militants publicly broke from APRA and founded APRA Rebelde, in their view more attuned to APRA's original revolutionary doctrine. This group vindicated the democratic, anti-oligarchic, and anti-imperialist legacy of the Peruvian APRA party and demanded that the party return to these foundational principles.[18] According to APRA Rebelde, these radical claims could not be limited to the national sphere; they had to come with a call to action to all "Indo-American revolutionaries."[19] This dissident group tapped into APRA's long-standing internationalism, hoping to resuscitate APRA's ethos of Latin American solidarity and resistance in the face of global injustices.

The radical legacy of Indo-América, as a project of hemispheric integration, may not have survived over time in the party's official establishment, but it certainly did in the margins of the movement as well as in the political imaginations of the Latin American left. To be sure, the search for an alternative and non-Western concept capable of challenging "Hispanic America" or "Latin America" did no culminate in the Indo-American project, as this book has made clear. APRA's Indo-América was in the end much more a product of north–south conciliation than of the anti-colonial vindication of Indigenous rights it once claimed to represent. But the work of trying to envision the rebirth of the Americas in new ways nevertheless contributed to nourishing the ethos of continental unity and Latin American solidarity as a catalyst for opposing oligarchic rule and foreign hegemon in the Western Hemisphere. Radical elements from APRA's continental program passed on to subsequent generations in Latin America. These new generations borrowed from APRA's anti-imperialist theses while adding their own visions of social utopias, just as Apristas had inherited from their predecessors dreams of better futures that nestled within the mystique of united geographies.[20]

[17] "La realidad nacional y la línea política de la convivencia," in *Documentos para la historia de la revolución peruana. Del APRA al APRA Rebelde*, Lima: Perugraph Editores, 1980, pp. 93–94.

[18] Ibid., pp. 90–91.

[19] APRA Rebelde, *Indo: Órgano del Comité Aprista Rebelde*, Buenos Aires, 1:1 (1960), p. 12, Pontificia Universidad Católica del Perú, CEDOC, Colección especial Arturo Sabroso Montoya, APRA, BIV, 1364 al 1385.

[20] On the question of transnational radicalism in the Cold War Southern Cone see Aldo Marchesi, *Latin America's Radical Left: Rebellion and Cold War in the Global 1960s*, New York: Cambridge University Press, 2017.

Pan-American visions look nowadays to be primarily linked to either free trade agreements or plans for regional market integration. In the 1980s–1990s, the NAFTA and its economic analogues in the region rose victorious. Neoliberalism seems to have diluted any project of hemispheric unity in the Western Hemisphere into mere prompts for either increased or better commercial relations and financial exchanges. Even regional projects like the MERCOSUR or the ALBA, which claimed to propose alternatives to US neoliberal proposals, primarily sought to consolidate regional economic integration. References to the necessity of cultural, spiritual, and moral collaboration in assisting the pursuit of social justice in the Americas are time and again kept on the backburner of inter-American designs.

These economic dynamics have progressed unabated in the past decade. The twenty-first century is disclosing drastic increases in income inequalities. Democracy recedes, bowing before the commands of a cosmopolitan oligarchy (more commonly referred to as the 1 per cent since September 2011, when Occupy Wall Street set up camp in Zuccotti Park, New York). The new generation of political activists, according to analysts of the so-called "New New Left," are wary of electoral politics and are exploring ways to do politics and think of democracy differently.[21] Activists in the United States, Canada, and elsewhere in Latin America are taking to the streets to voice their demands for participatory democracy and their discontent with a system tailored toward a restricted plutocracy. They are spearheading populist movements, gesturing to the beginning of a new era of mass politics globally.

The clash between a right- and left-wing populism, as presaged by Chantal Mouffe in *For a Left Populism* (2019), looks all the more inevitable today as I write these words in the midst of a global pandemic and the consolidation of the right turn in Latin America, following the Pink Tide spark of the 2000s and early 2010s. As this book studied the extent to which transnational and trans-American solidarity networks contributed to breeding the rise of the Latin American populist moment of 1930–1960, it bears keeping in mind the power that the ethos of Latin American solidarity can bring to political projects of social inclusion and human emancipation. But *Journey to Indo-América* also yields important

[21] Peter Beinart, "The Rise of the New New Left," *The Daily Beat*, September 12, 2013, www.thedailybeast.com/articles/2013/09/12/the-rise-of-the-new-new-left.html.

forewarnings about the limitations that solidarity work can impose on revolutionary moments. Above all, perhaps, it reminds us that activists involved in solidarity work all face obstacles. Whether within their movement or external to it, these obstacles shape these actors' organizing efforts and the limits and possibilities for solidarity and radical thought therein.

Bibliography

ARCHIVES

- Austin, Texas
  - University of Texas Libraries
    - Benson Latin American Collection
      - Magda Portal Papers
      - Microforms
- College Park, Maryland
  - National Archives and Records Administration (NACP)
    - Records of the Department of States
- Detroit, Michigan
  - Wayne State University
    - Archives of Labor and Urban Affairs
    - Anna Melissa Graves Collection (AMGC)
- Lima, Perú
  - Archivo General de la Nación (AGN)
    - Ministerio d\e Interior
  - Archivo del Ministerio de Relaciones Exteriores
    - Oficios de Chile y de México
  - Biblioteca Nacional
    - Colección Hemeroteca
    - Colección Magda Portal
    - Fondo Raúl Porras Barrenechea
  - Pontificia Universidad Católica del Perú
    - Centro de documentación de ciencias sociales (CEDOC)
      - Archivo Arturo Sabroso
      - Archivo del APRA
- Madison, Wisconsin
  - Wisconsin Historical Society Library
    - Microfilm Collection

México City, México
Archivo General de la Nación (AGN)
Dirección General de Investigaciones Políticas y Sociales
Secretaria de Gobernación
Archivo Histórico de la Secretaria de Relaciones Exteriores
Informes Politico de la Legacion de México en el Peru. 1934–1940
Escuela Nacional de Antropología e Historia, México (ENAH)
Fondo Luis Eduardo Enríquez Cabrera (FLEEC)
Paris, France
Archives Nationales de Paris
Ministère de l'Intérieur
Affaire générale de Police
Archives de la Préfecture de Police de Paris
Collections Diverses
Archives du Ministère des Affaires Étrangères, France
Correspondance Politique et Commerciale
Bibliothèque nationale de France (BNF)
Département des Manuscrits (DM)
Fonds Romain Rolland
Philadelphia, Pennsylvania
Presbyterian Historical Society
W. Stanley Rycroft Papers
The United Presbyterian Church in the United States of America
Foreign Missionary Personnel Files
Stanford, California
Stanford University
Hoover Institution Archives
Bertram David Wolfe Papers, 1903–1999 (BDWP)
Jay Lovestone Papers
Swarthmore, Pennsylvania
Swarthmore College, Peace Collection (SCPC)
Anna Melissa Graves Papers, 1919–1953 (AMGP)
Fellowship of Reconciliation Records, 1915, Current
Women's Peace Union, 1921–1940
Women's International League for Peace and Freedom Collection
Washington
US National Archives (USNA)

NEWSPAPERS AND JOURNALS

APRA: Órgano del frente único de trabajadores manuales e intelectuales, Lima
APRA: Revista Aprista, Buenos Aires
Amauta, Lima
Claridad: Órgano de la juventud libre del Perú, Lima
Flechas: Revista Quincenal de Letras, Lima
La Nueva Democracia, New York

La Prensa, New York
La Prensa, San Antonio
La Tribuna, Lima
La Tribuna en exilio, México
Repertorio Americano, San José
The New York Times, New York
Trinchera Aprista, México

PUBLISHED PRIMARY SOURCES

Bazán, Armando. *Prisiones junto al mar, novela*. Buenos Aires: Editorial Claridad, 1943.

Mariátegui y su tiempo. Lima: Empresa Editora Amauta, 1969.

Beals, Carleton. "The Rise of Haya de la Torre." *Foreign Affairs*, 13: 2 (1935): 236–246.

America South. Philadelphia, New York: Lippincot Company, 1937.

Brum, Blanca Luz. *Mi vida. Cartas de amor a Siqueiros*. Santiago de Chile: Editorial Mare Nostrum, 2004.

Comité Aprista de México. *¡Partidos de frente único para Indoamérica!* México: Colección 'Trinchera Aprista, 1938.

El aprismo frente a la VIII Conferencia Panamericana. México: editorial Manuel Arévalo, 1938.

Committee on Cooperation in Latin America. *Christian Work in Latin America: Survey and Occupation and Method Education*. Vol. 1, New York City: The Missionary Education Movement of the United States and Canada (for the Committee on Cooperation in Latin America), 1917.

Regional Conferences in Latin America. New York City: Missionary Education Movement of the United States and Canada, 1917.

"Inception and History of the Congress on Christian Work in Latin America." *Christian Work in Latin America: Survey and Occupation and Method Education*. Vol. 1, New York City: The Missionary Education Movement of the United States and Canada (for the Committee on Cooperation in Latin America), 1917.

Christian Work in South America: Official Report of the Congress on Christian Work in South America, at Montevideo, Uruguay, April, 1925, ed. Robert E. Speer, Samuel G. Inman, and Frank K. Sanders. New York and Chicago: Fleming H. Revell Company, 1925.

"The Report of Commission Eleven on Special Religious Problems in South America," *Christian Work in South America: Official Report of the Congress on Christian Work in South America, at Montevideo, Uruguay, April, 1925*, ed. Robert E. Speer, Samuel G. Inman, and Frank K. Sanders, New York and Chicago: Fleming H. Revell Company, 1925. pp. 295–377.

Directory of Evangelical Missions in Latin America. New York City: Committee on Cooperation in Latin America, 1929.

Cossío del Pomar, Felipe. *Víctor Raúl. Biografía de Haya de la Torre*. México, DF: Editorial Cultura T. G., S. A., 1961.

Cox, Carlos Manuel. *En torno al imperialismo*. Lima: Editorial cooperativa aprista "Atahualpa." 1933.

Documentos para la historia de la revolución peruana. Del APRA al APRA Rebelde. Lima: Perugraph Editores, 1980.

"Prologo," in Pedro E. Muñiz, *Penetración Imperialista (Minería y Aprismo)*, Santiago de Chile: Ediciones Ercilla, 1935, pp. 5, 5–11.

De Vivero, Fernando León. *Avance del imperialismo fascista en Perú*. México: Editorial Trinchera Aprista, 1938.

Del Mazo, Gabriel. "Hace Cuarenta Anos," in *La Reforma Universitaria, Tomo 1: El Movimiento Argentino*. Lima: Universidad Nacional Mayor de San Marcos, (1967?).

La Reforma Universitaria. Tomo 1: El Movimiento Argentino. 3rd ed. Lima: Universidad Nacional Mayor de San Marcos, 1967.

Enríquez Cabrera, Luis Eduardo. *Haya de la Torre, la estafa política más grande de América*. Lima: Ediciones del Pacifico, 1951.

"'La Realidad Nacional y la línea política de la Convivencia.' Moción presentada en la IV Convención del Partido Aprista el 10 de octubre de 1958," in *Documentos para la historia de la revolución peruana. Del APRA al APRA Rebelde*, Lima: Perugraph Editores, 1980, p. 56–108.

Faraday, Wilfred Barnard. *Socialism and the United Free Church of Scotland. A Reply to the Four Pamphlets of the Committee on Social Questions*. Westminster: Anti-Socialist Union of Great Britain, 1911.

Graves, Anna Melissa. *"I Have Tried to Think" and Other Papers*. Baltimore, MD: s.n., n.d.

"Haya de la Torre," *The New Leader*, April 26, 1924.

Haya de la Torre, Víctor Raúl. "What is the A.P.R.A.?" *The Labour Monthly*, December 1926, 756–759.

Por la Emancipación de América Latina. Artículos, Mensajes, Discursos (1923–1927). Buenos Aires: Editor Triunvirato, 1927.

Política Aprista. Lima: Editorial Cooperativa Aprista Atahualpa, 1933.

Construyendo el aprismo. Buenos Aires: Claridad, 1933.

¿A dónde va Indoamérica? Santiago de Chile: Editorial Ercilla, 1935.

La defensa continental. Buenos Aires: Ediciones Problemas de América, 1941.

Espacio-Tiempo-Histórico: Cinco Ensayos y Tres Diálogos. Lima: s.n., 1948.

"El Antiimperialismo y el APRA," in *Obras Completas*, Vol. 4, Lima: Editorial Juan Mejía Baca, 1976–1977.

(1931) "Discurso contra la fraude y la tiranía," in *Antología del pensamiento político de Haya de la Torre*, edited by Andrés Townsend Ezcurra. Lima: Biblioteca Nacional del Perú, 1995, pp. 30–32.

Haya de la Torre, Víctor Raúl and Luis Alberto Sánchez. *Correspondencia, Tomo 1, 1924–1951*. Lima: Mosca Azul Editores, 1982.

Hidalgo, Alberto. *Por qué renuncié al Apra*. Buenos Aires: s.n., 1954.

Hobson, John A. *Imperialism: A Study*. New York: J. Pott and Company, 1902.

Ingenieros, José. *Por la Unión Latino Americana. Discurso pronunciado el 11 de octubre de 1922 ofreciendo el banquete de los Escritores Argentinos en honor de José Vasconcelos*. Buenos Aires: L. J. Rosso y Cia., Impresores, 1922.

Inman, Samuel G. *Ventures in Inter-American Friendship*. New York: Missionary Education Movement of the United States and Canada, 1925.

Problems in Panamericanism. New York: George H. Doran Company, 1925 (1st ed. 1921).

Latin America, Its Place in World Life. Chicago: Willet, Clark, 1937.

Mackay, John A. "Student Life in a South American University." *The Student World*, 13: 3 (July, 1920): 89–97.

Religious Currents in the Intellectual Life of Peru." *Biblical Review Quarterly*, 6: 2 (April 1921): 192–211.

Los Intelectuales y los Nuevos Tiempos. Lima: Librería e Imprenta "El Inca," 1923.

The Other Spanish Christ: A Study in the Spiritual History of Spain and South America, New York: The Macmillian Company, 1932;

Mariátegui, José Carlos. *Correspondencia (1915–1930)*. Lima: Biblioteca Amauta, 1984.

Miro Quesada, Alfredo Saco. *Tiempos de Violencia y Rebeldía*. Lima: OKURA Editores, 1985.

Difusión continental del aprismo. Lima: Okura Editores, 1986.

Mella, Julio Antonio. *¿Qué es el ARPA?* Miraflores: Editorial Educación, 1975 (1st ed. 1928).

Muñiz, Pedro E. *Penetración Imperialista (Minería y Aprismo)*. Santiago de Chile: Ediciones Ercilla, 1935.

Orrego, Antenor. *Pueblo-Continente; ensayos para una interpretación de la América latina*, Buenos Aires: Ediciones Continente, 1957.

Portal, Magda. "El Clero Católico de México Frente a la Revolución," *Indoamérica*, 1: 2 (August 1928): 6.

América latina frente al imperialismo. Lima: Editorial Cahuide, 1931.

Su Vida y su obra, Buenos Aires, Editorial Claridad, 1935.

Por la libertad de Serafín Delmar. Aspectos de su vida y su obra. Buenos Aires: Editorial Claridad, 1936.

¿Quienes traicionaron al pueblo? Lima: Ediciones Raíz 1950.

La Trampa. Lima: Ediciones Raíz, 1956.

Rodo, José Enrique. *Ariel*. México DF, Editorial Calypso, 1948 (1st ed. 1900).

Roosevelt, Franklin D. "Address on the Occasion of the Celebration of Pan-American Day, Washington." Washington, April 12, 1933. Collection "Public Papers and Addresses of Franklin D. Roosevelt." Online by Gerhard Peters and John T. Woolley, The American Presidency Project, available at www.presidency.ucsb.edu/node/208062.

Saco, Alfredo. "Aprista Bibliography." *The Hispanic American Historical Review*, 23: 3 (1943): 555–585.

Programa agrario del aprismo. Lima: Ediciones populares, 1946.

Sánchez, Luis Alberto. *Waldo Frank in America Hispana*. New York: Instituto de las Españas en los Estados Unidos, 1930.

"On the Problem of the Indian in South America." *The Journal of Negro Education*, 10: 3 (1941): 493–503.

"A New Interpretation of the History of America." *The Hispanic American Historical Review*, 23: 3 (1943): 441–456.

Víctor Raúl Haya de la Torre o el político. Crónica de una vida sin tregua. Lima: Imprenta Editora Atlántida S. A., 1979.
Haya de la Torre y el APRA. Lima: Editorial Universo, 1980 (1st ed. 1954).
Ugarte, Manuel. *El destino de un continente.* Buenos Aires: Ediciones de la Patria Grande, 1962 (1st ed. 1923).
Vázquez Díaz, Manuel. *Balance del Aprismo.* Lima: Editorial Rebelión, 1964.
Wolfe, Bertram D. *The Fabulous Life of Diego Rivera.* New York: Stein and Day, 1963.

SECONDARY SOURCES

Aguilar Derpich, Juan. *Catacumbas del APRA: Vivencia y testimonios de su clandestinidad.* Lima: Ediciones del recuerdo, 1984.
Aguirre, Carlos. "Hombres y rejas. El APRA en prisión, 1932–1945," *Bulletin de l'Institut français d'études andines*, 43: 1 (2014), http://journals.openedition.org/bifea/4234.
Aguirre Gamio, Hernando. *Liquidación histórica del APRA y del Colonialismo Neoliberal.* Lima: Ediciones Debate, 1962.
Alarcón, Daniel. "What Led Peru's Former President to Take His Own Life." *The New Yorker*, July 8 and 15, 2019.
Alba, Víctor. *Historia del movimiento obrero en América Latina.* México: Libreros Mexicanos Unidos, 1964.
Alberto, Paulina L. and Jesse Hoffnung-Garskof. "'Racial Democracy' and Racial Inclusion: Hemispheric Histories," in Alejandro de la Fuente and George Reid Andrews (eds), *Afro-Latin American Studies. An Introduction*, Cambridge, UK: Cambridge University Press, 2018, pp. 264–316.
Alcántara, Mariano. *Arte y revolución, Trujillo 1932: de pie ante la historia.* Trujillo: Secongensa, 1994.
Alexander, Robert J. *Aprismo: The Ideas and Doctrines of Víctor Raúl Haya de la Torre.* Kent: Kent State University Press, 1973.
Altamirano, Carlos (ed.). *Historia de los intelectuales en América Latina. Tomo II.* Buenos Aires: Katz editores, , 2010.
Anderson, Benedict. *Imagined Communities: Reflections on the Origin and Spread of Nationalism.* London and New York: Verso, 2006 (1st ed. 1983).
Angotti, Thomas. "The Contributions of José Carlos Mariátegui to Revolutionary Theory." *Latin American Perspectives*, 13: 2 (Spring 1986): 33–57.
Angulo Daneri, Toño. *Llámalo amor, si quieres. Nueve historias de pasión.* Lima: Santillana, 2004.
Ansaldi, Waldo. "Como carrera de antorchas. La Reforma Universitaria, de Cordoba a Nuestra América," *Revista de la Red de Intercátedras de Historia de América Latina Contemporánea*, 5: 9 (Diciembre 2018–Mayo 2019): 1–11.
Apilado, Mariano C. *Revolutionary Spirituality: A Study of the Protestant Role in the American Colonial Rule of the Philippines, 1898–1928.* Quezon City: New Day Publishers, 1999.

Appelbaum, Patricia. *Kingdom to Commune: Protestant Pacifist Culture between World War I and the Vietnam Era*. Chapel Hill, NC: The University of North Carolina Press, 2009.

Archibald, Priscilla. *Imagining Modernity in the Andes*. Lewisburgh, PA: Bucknell University Press, 2011.

Barba Caballero, José A. *Haya de la Torre y Mariátegui frente a la historia*. Lima: Amauta, 1978.

Barba Caballero, José and César Lévano. *La polémica: Haya de la Torre – Mariátegui*. s.l., n.d., 1979.

Basadre, Jorge. *Vida y la historia. Ensayos sobre personas, lugares y problemas*, 2nd ed. Lima: Lluvia Editores, 1981.

Becker, Marc. "Mariátegui, the Comintern, and the Indigenous Question in Latin America." *Science and Society*, 70: 4 (October 2006): 450–479.

Beinart, Peter. "The Rise of the New New Left." *The Daily Beat, September* 12, 2013.

Belaúnde, Víctor Andrés. *La crisis presente, 1914–1939*. Lima: Ediciones "Mercurio Peruano, 1940.

Benedetti, Mario. *El desexilio y otras conjeturas*. Buenos Aires: Nueva Imagen, 1985.

Bergel, Martín. "Manuel Seoane y Luis Heysen: el entrelugar de los exiliados apristas en la Argentina de los veinte," *Políticas de la memoria*, 6: 7 (2007): 124–142.

"La desmesura revolucionaria: Prácticas intelectuales y cultura del heroísmo en los orígenes del aprismo peruano (1921–1930)." *Nuevo Mundo/ Mundos Nuevos* (2007), doi: 10.4000/nuevomundo.5448.

"Nomadismo proselitista y revolución. Notas para una caracterización del primer exilio aprista (1923–1931)." *E.I.A.L.*, 20: 1 (2009): 41–66.

"El anti-antinortemaricanismo en América Latina (1898–1930): Apuntes para una historia ntellectual." *Nueva Sociedad*, 236 (2011).

"Populismo y cultura impresa. La clandestinidad literaria en los años de formación del Partido Aprista Peruano." *Ipotesis*, 17: 2 (2013): 135–146.

"Un partido hecho de cartas. Exilio, redes diasporicas, y el rol de la correspondencia en la formación del aprismo peruano (1921–1930)." *Políticas de la Memoria*, 15 (2014–2015): 71–85.

"De canillitas a militantes. Los niños y la circulación de materiales impresos en el proceso de popularización del Partido Aprista Peruano (1930–1945)." *Iberoamericana*, 15: 60 (2015): 101–115.

El oriente desplazado. Los intelectuales y los orígenes del tercermundismo en la Argentina. Bernal: Universidad Nacional de Quilmes Editorial, 2015.

La desmesura revolucionaria. Cultura y política en los orígenes del APRA, Lima: La Siniestra, 2019.

"Con el ojo izquierdo. Mirando a Bolivia, de Manuel Seoane. Viaje y deriva latinoamericana en la génesis del antiimperialismo aprista," in Carlos Marichal Salinas and Alexandra Pita González (eds), *Pensar el antiimperialismo. Ensayos de historia intelectual latinoamericana.*

México, DF: El Colegio de México, Colima, Universidad de Colima, 2012, pp. 283–311.

Bergel, Martín and Ricardo Martínez Mazzola. "América Latina como practica. Modos de sociabilidades intelectual de los reformistas universitarios (1918–1930)," in Carlos Altamirano (ed.) *Historia de los intelectuales en América Latina*. Buenos Aires: Tomo II, Katz editores, 2010, pp. 119–145.

Bernales, Enrique. *Movimientos sociales y movimientos universitarios en el Perú*. Lima: Pontificia Universidad Católica del Perú, 1974.

Bhabba, Homi. *Location of Culture*. New York: Routledge, 1994.

Biagini, Hugo. *La Reforma Universitaria y Nuestra América. A cien anos de la revuelta estudiantil que sacudió al continente*. Buenos Aires: Editorial Octubre, 2018.

Brenner, Anita. "Student Rebels in Latin America," The Nation, December 12, 1928, pp. 668–669.

Bruno-Jofre, Rosa del Carmen. "Social Gospel, the Committee on Cooperation in Latin America, and the APRA: The Case of the American Methodist Mission, 1920–1930." Canadian Journal of Latin American and Caribbean Studies/ Revue canadienne des études latino-américaines et caraïbes, 9: 18 (1984): 75–110.

Buchbinder, Pablo. "La Reforma y su impacto en América Latina: aportes para la actualización y revisión del problema." Revista de la Red de Intercatedras de Historia de América Latina Contemporánea, 5: 9 (Diciembre 2018–Mayo 2019). ISSN 2250-7264.

Cáceres Arce, Jorge Luis. "Haya de la Torre estudiante peregrino," in *Tercer Concurso Latinoamericano de Ensayo Vida y Obra de Víctor Raúl Haya de la Torre*, ed. Jorge Luis Cáceres, Lima: Instituto Cambio y Desarrollo, 2006, pp. 15–150.

"Haya de la Torre estudiante peregrino," in Jorge Luis Cáceres, Enrique de la Osa, Tatiana Goncharova and Carlos Lúcar (eds), *III Concurso Latinoamericano de Ensayo Vida y Obra de Víctor Raúl Haya de la Torre*, Lima: Instituto Cambio y Desarrollo, 2006.

Carr, Barry. *Marxism and Communism in Twentieth Century Mexico*. Lincoln and London: University of Nebraska Press, 1992.

"Pioneering Transnational Solidarity in the Americas: The Movement in Support of Augusto C. Sandino, 1927–1934." *Journal of Iberian and Latin American Research*, 20: 2 (2009): 141–152.

Carter, Paul A. *The Decline and Revival of the Social Gospel: Social and Political Liberalism in American Protestant Churches, 1920–1940*. Ithaca: Cornell University Press, 1954.

Casaús Arzú, Marta Elena (ed). *El Lenguaje de los ismos: Algunos conceptos de la modernidad en América Latina*. Guatemala: F&G Editores, 2010.

Casaús Arzú, Marta Elena and Teresa García Giráldez. *Las redes intelectuales centroamericanas: un–siglo de imaginarios nacionales (1820–1920)*. Guatemala: Editores F&G, 2005.

Chanamé, Raúl. *La Amistad de dos Amautas: Mariátegui y John A. Mackay*. Lima: Editora Magisterial, 1995.

Chang-Rodríguez, Eugenio, ed. *La literatura política de González Prada, Mariátegui y Haya de la Torre*. México: Ediciones de Andrea, 1957.
Manuel Seoane, páginas escogidas. Lima: Fondo Editorial del Congreso del Perú, 2002.
Antenor Orrego: Modernidad y culturas americanas, páginas escogidas. Lima: Fondo Editorial del Congreso del Perú, 2004.
Ciccarelli, Orazio A. *The Sánchez Cerro Regimes in Peru, 1930–1933*. Ph. D. diss., University of Florida, 1969.
Cornejo-Coster, Ernesto. "Creación y funcionamiento," in *Dardo Cúneo, La Reforma universitaria*. Caracas: Biblioteca Ayacucho, 1978, pp. 71–72.
Coronado, Jorge. *The Andes Imagined: Indigenismo, Society, and Modernity*. Pittsburgh: University of Pittsburgh Press, 2009.
Cúneo, Dardo. *La Reforma Universitaria*. Caracas: Biblioteca Ayacucho, 1988 (1st ed. 1978).
Davies, Thomas M. *Indian Integration in Peru: A Half Century of Experience, 1900–1948*. Lincoln, NE: University of Nebraska Press, 1974.
De la Cadena, Marisol. *Indigenous Mestizo: The Politics of Race and Culture in Cuzco, Peru, 1919–1991*. Durham, NC and London: Duke University Press, 2000.
De la Mora, Rogelio y Hugo Cancino (eds). *La Historia Intelectual y el movimiento de las ideas en América Latina, siglos XIX–XX*. México: Universidad Veracruzana, 2015.
de Vivero, Fernando León, *Avance del imperialismo fascista en el Perú*, México, DF: Editorial Trinchera Aprista, 1938.
Delmar, Serafín "Interpretación del Arte en América," *Indoamérica*, 1: 2 (August, 1928): 8.
Delpar, Helen. *The Enormous Vogue of Things Mexican: Cultural Relations between the United States and Mexico, 1920–1935*. Tuscaloosa: University of Alabama Press, 1992.
Demers, Maurice. *Connected Struggles: Catholics, Nationalists, and Transnational Relations between Mexico and Quebec, 1917–1945*. Montréal and Kingston: McGill-Queen's University Press, 2014.
Díaz, Kim. "Indigenismo in Peru and Bolivia," in Robert Eli Sánchez, Jr. (ed.), *Latin American and Latinx Philosophy: A Collaborative Introduction*. New York: Routledge, 2020, pp. 180–197.
Díaz, María Luz. *Las mujeres de Haya: Ocho historias de pasión y rebeldía*. Lima: Editorial Planeta, 2007.
Di Pasquale, Mariano and Marcelo Summo (eds). *Trayectorias singulares, voces plurales: Intelectuales en la Argentina, siglos XIX–XX*. Buenos Aires: Editorial de la Universidad Nacional de Tres de Febrero, 2015.
Di Tella, Torcuato S. "Populism and Reform in Latin America," in Claudio Veliz (ed.), *Obstacles to Change in Latin America*. London: Oxford University Press, 1965, pp. 47–74.
Dorais, Geneviève. "Indo-America and the Politics of APRA Exile, 1918–1945." Ph.D. Diss., Madison: University of Wisconsin, 2014.
"Coming of Age in Exile: Victor Raul Haya de la Torre and the Genesis of the American Popular Revolutionary Alliance, 1923–1931." *The Hispanic American Historical Review*, 97: 4 (2017): 651–679.

"Missionary Critiques of Empire, 1920–1932: Between Interventionism and Anti-Imperialism." *International History Review*, 39: 3 (2017): 377–403.

Dozer, Donald Marquand. *Are We Good Neighbor? Three Decades of Inter-American Relations 1930–1960*. Gainesville: University of Florida Press, 1961.

Drake, Paul W. *Socialism and Populism in Chile, 1932–1952*. Urbana: University of Illinois Press, 1978.

Drinot, Paulo. *The Allure of Labor: Workers, Race, and the Making of the Peruvian State*. Durham, NC and London: Duke University Press, 2011.

"Creole Anti-Communism: Labor, The Peruvian Communist Party, and APRA, 1930–1934." *Hispanic American Historical Review*, 92: 4 (2012): 703–736.

Dutrénit Bielous, Silvia (ed.). *El Uruguay del exilio: Gente, circunstancias, escenarios*. Montivedo, Uruguay: Ediciones trilce, 2006.

Enríquez, Luis Eduardo Cabrera. *Haya de la Torre, la estafa política más grande de América*, Lima: Ediciones del Pacifico, 1951.

Espasa, Andreu. "'Suppose they were to Do it in Mexico': The Spanish Embargo and Its Influence on Roosevelts' Good Neighbor Policy." *The International History Review*, 40: 4 (2018): 774–791.

Fernández Retamar, Roberto (ed.). *Cuba, Nuestra América, Los Estados Unidos, por José Martí*. México: Siglo veintiuno editores, 1973.

Fey, Ingrid E. and Karen Racine (ed.). *Strange Pilgrimages: Exile, Travel, and National Identity in Latin America, 1800–1990s*. Wilmington: Scholarly Resources, 2000.

Flores Galindo, Alberto. *La agonía de Mariátegui. La polémica con la Komintern*. Lima: Centro de Estudios y Promoción del Desarrollo, 1980.

El pensamiento comunista, 1917–1945. Lima: Mosca Azul Editores, 1982.

Obras Completas V. Lima: Casa de estudio del socialismo, 1993.

In Search of An Inca: Identity and Utopia in the Andes. Cambridge, UK: Cambridge University Press, 2010.

Flores Galindo, Alberto and Manuel Burga. *Apogeo y crisis de la republica aristocrática*. Lima: Ediciones "Rikchay Perú," 1979.

Fonseca Ariza, Juan. *Misioneros y civilizadores: Protestantismo y modernización en el Perú (1915–1930)*. Lima: Fondo Editorial de la Pontifica Universidad Católica del Perú, 2002.

"Dialogo intercultural y pensamiento religioso: John A. Mackay y la Generación del Centenario," in *Intelectuales y poder. Ensayos en torno a la republica de las letras en el Perú e Hispanoamerica (ss. XVI–XX)*, ed. Carlos Aguirre and Carmen Mc Evoy. Lima: Instituto Francés de Estudios Andinos, 2008, pp. 281–302.

Educación para un país moderno: El "Lima High School" y la red educativa protestante en el Perú (1906–1945). Lima: Pontificia Universidad Católica del Perú, n.d.

Franco, Carlos. *Del marxismo eurocéntrico al marxismo latinoamericano*. Lima: Centro de Estudios para el Desarrollo y la participación, 1981.

Franco, Jean. *The Modern Culture of Latin America: Society and the Artist*. New York, Washington, London: Frederick A. Praeger Publishers, 1967.

Franco, Marina. *Exilio. Argentinos en Francia durante la dictadura*. Buenos Aires: Siglo XXI, 2008.

Frank, Marco and Alexandra Pita González. "Irradiador y Horizonte: Revistas de un movimiento de vanguardia y una red estridentista." Catedral Tomada. Revista de Critica Literaria latinoamericana, 6: 11 (2018): 13–47.

French, John D. *The Brazilian Workers' ABC: Class Conflict and Alliances in Modern São Paulo*. Chapel Hill, NC and London: The University of North Carolina Press, 1992.

Funes, Patricia. "El pensamiento latinoamericano sobre la nación en la década de 1920." Boletín Americanista, 49 (April 1999): 103–120.

Salvar la nación: intelectuales, cultura y política en los años veinte latinoamericanos. Buenos Aires: Prometeo libros, 2006.

Gandhi, Leela. *Affective Communities: Anticolonial Thought, Fin-de-Siècle Radicalism and the Politics of Friendship*. Durham, NC and London: Duke University Press, 2006.

Gamarra, Hidalgo José Daniel. *1932: los excluidos combaten por la libertad: la Revolución de Trujillo*. Perú, 2011, https://firstsearch-oclc-org.proxy.bibliotheques.uqam.ca/WebZ/FSFETCH?fetchtype=fullrecord:sessionid=fsap02pxm1-1680-kkb5863z-7gsugs:entitypagenum=9:0:recno=2:resultset=4:format=FI:next=html/record.html:bad=error/badfetch.html:entitytoprecno=2:entitycurrecno=2:numrecs=1.

García, Alan. *Contra el temor económico: ociedad el Perú*. Lima: Planeta, 2011.

García-Bryce, Iñigo. "A Revolution Remembered, a Revolution Forgotten: The 1932 Aprista Insurrection in Trujillo, Peru." *A Contra Corriente*, 7: 3 (Spring 2010): 277–322.

"Haya de la Torre and the Pursuit of Power in Peru, 1926–1948: The Seven Paradoxes of APRA." *Jahrbuch for Geschichte Lateinamerikas/Anuario de Estudios Latinoamericanos*, 51: 1 (2014): 86–112.

"Transnational Activist: Magda Portal and the American Popular Revolutionary Alliance (APRA), 1926–1950." *The Americas*, 70: 4 (April 2014): 667–706.

Haya de la Torre and the Pursuit of Power in Twentieth-Century Peru and Latin America. Chapel Hill, NC: The University of North Carolina Press, 2018.

Pragmatic Revolutionary: Haya de la Torre and the Pursuit of Power in Peru and Latin America, 1926–1979, Chapel Hill, NC: University of North Carolina Press, 2018.

Garrard-Burnett, Virginia and David Stoll (eds). Rethinking Protestantism in Latin America. Philadelphia: Temple University Press, 1993.

Germaná, César. *El 'Socialismo Indoamericano' de José Carlos Mariátegui: Proyecto de reconstitución del sentido histórico de la ociedad peruana*. Lima: Amauta, 1995.

Giesecke, Margarita. *La insurrección de Trujillo: Jueves 7 de Julio de 1932*. Lima: Fondo Editorial del Congreso del Perú, 2010.

Giraudo, Laura and Stephen E. Lewis. "Introduction: Pan-American Indigenismo (1940–1970): New Approaches to an Ongoing Debate." *Latin American Perspectives*, 39: 5 (2012): 3–11.

Giraudo, Laura and Juan Martín-Sánchez (eds). *La ambivalente historia del indigenismo. Campo interamericano y trayectorias nacionales, 1940–1970.* Lima: Instituto de Estudios Peruanos, 2011.

Gobat, Michel. Confronting the American Dream: Nicaragua under U.S. Imperial Rule. Durham, NC: Duke University Press, 2005.

"The Invention of Latin America: A Transnational History of Anti-Imperialism, Democracy, and Race." *American Historical Review*, 118: 5 (2013): 1345–1375.

Goebel, Michael. *Anti-Imperial Metropolis: Interwar Paris and the Seeds of Third World Nationalism.* New York: Cambridge University Press, 2015.

"'The Capital of the Men without a Country': Migrants and Anticolonialism in Interwar Paris." *American Historical Review*, 121: 5 (2016): 1444–1467.

Goldstone, Jack A. "More Social Movements or Fewer ? Beyond Political Opportunity Structures to Relational Fields." *Theory and Society*, 33 (2004): 333–365.

Glusker, Susannah Joel. *Anita Brenner: A Mind of Her Own.* Austin: University of Texas Press, 1998.

Graham, Carol. *Peru's APRA: Parties, Politics, and the Elusive Quest for Democracy.* Boulder: L. Rienner Publishers, 1992.

Granados, Aimer y Carlos Marichal (eds). *Construcción de las identidades latinoamericanas. Ensayos de historial intelectual siglos XIX y XX.* México, DF: El Colegio de México, 2004.

Grandin, Greg. *The Last Colonial Massacre: Latin American in the Cold War.* Chicago and London: The University of Chicago Press, 2004.

Empire's Workshop, Latin America, the United States, and the Rise of the New Imperialism. New York: Henry Holt and Company, 2006.

"The Narcissism of Violent Differences," in *Anti-Americanism*, ed. Andrew Ross and Kristin Ross, New York: New York University Press, 2004.

Green, W. John. *Left Liberalism and Popular Mobilization in Colombia.* Gainesville: University Press of Florida, 2003.

Gronbeck-Tedesco, John A. *Cuba, the United Sates, and Cultures of the Transnational Left, 1930–1975.* New York: Cambridge University Press, 2015.

Gross, Robert N. *Keeping the Faith Outside School: Liberal Protestant Reform and the Struggle for Secular Public Education in the Upper Midwest, 1890–1926*, M.A. Thesis, University of Wisconsin-Madison, 2009.

Public vs. Private: The Early History of School Choice in America. New York: Oxford University Press, 2018.

Grossman, Richard. "The Nation Is Our Mother: Augusto Sandino and the Construction of a Peasant Nationalism in Nicaragua, 1927–1934." *The Journal of Peasant Studies*, 35: 1(2008): 80–99.

Gutiérrez, Tomás J. *Haya de la Torre y los Protestantes Liberales (Perú, 1917–1923).* Lima: Editorial "Nuevo Rumbo," 1995.

Harmer, Tanya. "The View from Havana: Chilean Exiles in Cuba and Early Resistance to Chile's Dictatorship, 1973–1977." *Hispanic American Historical Review*, 96: 1 (2016): 109–146.

Heilman, Jaymie P. "We Will No Longer Be Servile: Aprismo in 1930s Ayacucho" *Journal of Latin American Studies*, 38 (2006): 491–518.

Before the Shining Path: Politics in Rural Ayacucho, 1895–1980. Stanford: Stanford University Press, 2010.

Helms, Mary W. *Craft and the Kingly Ideal: Art, Trade, and Power*. Austin: University of Texas Press, 1993.

Ulysses' Sail: An Ethnographic Odyssey of Power, Knowledge, and Geographical Distance. Princeton : Princeton University Press, 1988.

Hilliker, Grant. *The Politics of Reform in Peru: The Aprista and Other Mass Parties of Latin America*. Baltimore: Johns Hopkins Press, 1971.

Hirsch, Steven J. "The Anarcho-Syndicalist Roots of a Multi-Class Alliance: Organized Labor and the Peruvian Aprista Party, 1900–1930." Ph. D. Diss., George Washington University, 1997.

"Peruvian Anarcho-Syndicalism: Adapting Transnational Influences and Forging Counterhegemonic Practices, 1905–1930," in *Anarchism and Syndicalism in the Colonial and Postcolonial World, 1870–1940: The Praxis of National Liberation, Internationalism, and Social Revolution*, ed. Steven Hirsch and Lucien van der Walt. Leiden and Boston: Brill, Hotei Publishing, 2012.

Horvitz, María Eugenia. *Exiliados y desterrados del cono sur de América, 1970–1990*. Chile: Erdosain Ediciones Ltda, 2017.

Ibáñez Avados, Víctor Manuel. "La influencia de la Revolución Mexicana en la formación ideológica y doctrinaria del aprismo," in *VI Concurso Latinoamericano de Ensayo Vida y Obra de Víctor Raúl Haya de la Torre*, ed. Carlos Espá *et al.* Lima: Instituto Cambio y Desarrollo, 2010, pp. 75–126.

Iglesias, Daniel. "Nacionalismo y utlización política del pasado: la historia nacional desde la perspectiva de la revista Amauta (1926–1930)." *Histtórica*, 30: 2 (2006): 91–114.

"Articulaciones relacionales y redes transnacionales: Acercamiento critico para una nueva historiografía del Aprismo continental." *Nuevo Mundo Mundos Nuevos*, 2007. DOI : https://doi.org/10.4000/nuevomundo.8602.

"Réseaux transnationaux et dynamiques contestataires en exil. Sociologie historique des pratiques politiques des dirigeants des partis politiques apristes (1920–1962)." Ph.D. Diss., Université Paris Diderot (Paris 7), 2011.

Du pain et de la liberté: Socio-histoire des partis populaires apristes (Pérou, Venezuela, 1920–1962). Villeneuve d'Ascq: Presses Universitaires du Septentrion, 2015.

"Redécouverte et idéologisation de l'Amérique latine par l'Alliance populaire révolutionnaire américaine," in Annie-Blonderl and Eliane Talbot (eds), *(Re) découvertes des Amériques. Entre conflits, rencontres et recherche d'identité*. Paris: L'Harmattan, 2013, pp. 155–166.

James, Daniel. *Resistance and Integration: Peronism and the Argentine Working Class, 1946–1976*. New York and Cambridge: Cambridge University Press, 1988.

Jansen, Robert S. *Revolutionizing Repertoires: The Rise of Populist Mobilization in Peru*. Chicago: The University of Chicago Press, 2017.

Jeifets, Victor and Lazar Jeifets. "Haya de la Torre... ¿Un comunista latinoamericano?" *Istoriia: la revista científica y educativa electrónica*, 12: 6 (2011), https://history.jes.su/s207987840000141-4-2/.

Jensen, Silvina. *La provincia flotante. El exilio argentino en Cataluña, 1976–2006*, Barcelona: Casa de América Cataluña, 2007.

Jensen, Silvina and Soledad Lastra (eds). *Exilios: Militancia y represión. Nuevas fuentes y nuevos abordajes de los destierros de la Argentina de los años setenta*. La Plata: EDULP, 2014.

Kaminsky, Amy K. *After Exile: Writing the Latin American Diaspora*, Minneapolis: University of Minnesota Press, 1999.

Kantor, Harry. *The Ideology and Program of the Peruvian Aprista Movement*. New York: Octagon Books, 1966.

Kaplan, Edward S. *U.S. Imperialism in Latin America, Bryan's Challenges and Contributions, 1900–1920*. Westport and London: Greenwood Press, 1998.

Katznelson, Ira. *Fear Itself: The New Deal and the Origins of Our Time*. New York, London: Liveright, 2014 (1st ed. 2013).

Keck, Margaret E. and Kathryn Sikkink. *Activists Beyond Borders: Advocacy Networks in International Politics*. Ithaca and London: Cornell University Press, 1998.

Kersffeld, Daniel. "La recepción del marxismo en América Latina y su influencia en las ideas de integración continental: el caso de la Liga Antiimperialista de las Américas." Ph.D. Diss., Universidad Nacional Autónoma de México, 2008.

Contra el imperio: historia de la Liga Antimperialista de las Américas. México: Siglo Veintiuno Editores, 2012.

Klaiber, Jeffrey L. "The Non-Communist Left in Latin America." *Journal of the History of Ideas*, 32: 4 (October–December 1971): 607–616.

"The Popular Universities and the Origins of Aprismo, 1921–1924." *The Hispanic American Historical Review*, 55: 4 (November 1975): 693–715.

Religion and Revolution in Peru, 1824–1976. Notre Dame and London: University of Notre Dame Press, 1977.

The Church, Dictatorships, and Democracy in Latin America. New York: Orbis Books, 1998.

Klarén, Peter F. *Modernization, Dislocation, and Aprismo: Origins of the Peruvian Aprista Party, 1870–1932*. Austin and London: The University of Texas Press, 1973.

Peru: Society and Nationhood in the Andes. New York and Oxford: Oxford University Press, 2000.

Laclau, Ernesto. "Towards a Theory of Populism," in *Political and Ideology in Marxist Theory*. Thetford, UK: Lowe and Brydone Printers Limited, 1997, pp. 143–198.

Lastra, María Soledad. *Volver del exilio: Historia comparada de las políticas de recepción en las posdictaduras de la Argentina y Uruguay (1983–1989)*, Buenos Aires: Universidad Nacional de La Plata, Universidad Nacional de Misiones and Universidad Nacional de General Sarmiento, 2016.

Liss, Sheldon B. *Marxist Thought in Latin America*. Berkeley and Los Angeles: University of California Press, 1983.

Louro, Michele L. *Comrades against Imperialism: Nehru, India, and Interwar Internationalism*. New York: Cambridge University Press, 2018.

Lowenthal, Abraham F. and Cynthia McClintock (eds). *The Peruvian Experiment Reconsidered*. Princeton: Princeton University Press, 1983.

MacPherson, John M. *At the Roots of a Nation: The Story of San Andrés School in Lima, Peru*. Edinburgh: The Knox Press, 1993.

Mannheim, Karl. *An Ideology and Utopia: An Introduction to the Sociology of Knowledge*. New York: Harcourt, Brace and Company, 1949 (1st ed. 1936).

Manrique, Nelson. *"¡Usted fue aprista!" Bases para una historia critica del APRA*. Lima: Fondo editorial PUCP, 2009.

Marchesi, Aldo. *Latin America's Radical Left: Rebellion and Cold War in the Global 1960s*. New York: Cambridge University Press, 2018.

Martínez de la Torre, Ricardo. *Apuntes para una interpretación marxista de la historia social del Perú (I-II)*. Lima: Empresa editora peruana, 1947–1949.

Martínez-Fernández, Luis. *Protestantism and Political Conflict in the Nineteenth Century Hispanic Caribbean*. New Brunswick: Rutgers University Press, 2002.

Melgar Bao, Ricardo. "Militancia Aprista en el Caribe: la sección cubana." Cuadernos Americanos, 1:37 (1993): 208–226.

Mariátegui, Indoamérica y las crisis civilizatorias de Occidente. Lima: Editora Amauta S. A., 1995.

"Redes del exilio aprista en México (1923–1924), una aproximación." In *México, país refugio*, ed. Pablo Yankelevich. México, DF: Plaza y Valdés, 2002, pp. 245–263.

Redes e imaginario del exilio en México y América Latina: 1934–1940. Argentina: LibrosenRed, 2003.

"Notas para leer un proceso a la intelectualidad oligárquica: Balance y liquidación del novecientos de Luis Alberto Sanchez." *Nostromos: Revista critica latinoamericana*, 1: 1 (2007): 18–28.

"The Anti-Imperialist League of the Americas between the East and Latin America." *Latin American Perspectives*, 35: 2 (2008): 9–24.

"Los ciclos del exilio y del retorno en América Latina: una aproximación." *Estudios Latinoamericanos*, 23 (2009): 49–71.

Metzger, John Mackay. *The Hand and the Road: the Life and Times of John A. Mackay*. Louisville: Westminster John Know Press, 2010.

Meyer, Eugenia. *Un refugio en la memoria: la experiencia de los exilios latinoamericanos en México*. México, DF: Facultad de Filosofía y Letras, Universidad Nacional Autónoma de México, 2002.

Míguez Bonino, José. "Presentación," in John H. Sinclair, *Juan A. Mackay: Un Escocés con Alma Latina*, México, DF: Ediciones Centro de Comunicación Cultural CUPSA, 1990, p. 15.

Moraga Valle, Fabio. "¿Una nación íbero o indoamericana? Joaquín Edwards Bello y el *Nacionalismo continental*," in Alexandra Pita González and Carlos Marichal Salinas (eds), *Pensar el antiimperialismo: Ensayos de historia intelectual latinoamericana, 1900–1930*. México, DF: El Colegio de México, Colima, Universidad de Colima, 2012, pp. 247–282.

Murillo Garaycochea, Percy. *Revolución de Trujillo, 1932*. Lima: Editorial Nosotros, 1982.

North, Liisa. "The Peruvian Aprista Party and Haya de la Torre: Myths and Realities." *Journal of Interamerican Studies and World Affairs*, 17: 2 (May 1975): 245–253.

Obregón, Liliana. "Regionalism Constructed: A Short History of Latin American International Law." *ESIL Conference Paper Series*, 2: 1 (2012), https://ssrn.com/abstract=2193749.

Pakkasvirta, Jussi ¿Un continente, una nación? Intelectuales latinoamericanos, comunidad política y las revistas culturales en Costa Rica y el Perú. San José: Editorial de la Universidad de Costa Rica, 1997.

Palti, Elías J. "La nueva historia intelectual y sus repercusiones en América Latina." *Histórica Unisinos*, 11: 3 (2007): 297–305.

"The 'Theoretical Revolution' in Intellectual History: From the History of Political Ideas to the History of Political Languages." *History and Theory*, 53: 3 (2014): 387–405.

Pérez Vejo, Tomás y Pablo Yankelevich (eds). *Raza y política en Hispanoamérica*. Madrid: Iberoamericana, Ciudad de México: Bonilla Artigas Editores, Colegio de México, 2018.

Petersen, Mark and Carsten-Andreas Schulz. "Setting the Regional Agenda: A Critique of Posthegemonic Regionalism." *Latin American Politics and Society*, 60: 1 (2018): 102–127.

Petersen, Mark Jeffrey. "Argentine and Chilean Approaches to Modern Pan-Americanism, 1888–1930." Ph.D. Diss., Corpus Christi College, 2014.

"The Vanguard of Pan-Americanism": Chile and Inter-American Multilateralism in the Early Twentieth Century," in *Cooperation and Hegemony in US-Latin American Relations: Revisiting the Western Hemisphere Idea*, ed. Juan Pablo Scarfi and Andrew R. Tillman. New York: Palgrave Macmillan, 2016, pp. 111–137.

Peterson, Patti McGill. "Student Organizations and the Antiwar Movement in America, 1900–1960." *American Studies (AMSJ)*, 13: 1 (Spring 1972): 131–147.

Pike, Frederick B. "The Old and the New APRA in Peru: Myth and Reality." *Inter-American Economic Affairs*, 18 (Autumn, 1964): 3–45.

The Politics of the Miraculous in Peru: Haya de la Torre and the Spiritualist Tradition. Lincoln, NE and London: University of Nebraska Press, 1986.

Pita González, Alexandra. "La discutida identidad latinoamericana: Debates en el Repertorio Americano, 1938–1945," in Aimer Granados García and Carlos Marichal (eds), *Construcción de las identidades latinoamericanas*. México, DF: El Colegio de México, 2004, pp. 241–265.

La Unión Latino Americana y el Boletín Renovación: Redes intelectuales y revistas culturales en la década de 1920. México, DF: Colegio de México; Colima: Universidad de Colima, 2009.

"Panamericanismo y nación." Anuario IEHS, 32: 1 (2017): 135–154.

Pita González, Alexandra (ed.). *Redes intelectuales transnacionales en América Latina durante la entreguerra*. México: Universidad de Colima, Miguel Ángel Porrúa, 2016.

Intelectuales y antiimperialismo: entre la teoría y la practica. Colima: Universidad de Colima, 2010.

Pita González, Alexandra and Carlos Marichal Salinas (eds). *Pensar el antiimperialismo: Ensayos de historia intelectual latinoamericana, 1900–1930*, México, DF: El Colegio de México, Colima, Universidad de Colima, 2012.

Quijano, Aníbal. *Introducción a Mariátegui*, México: Ediciones Era, S.A, 1981.

"Modernity, Identity, and Utopia in Latin America." *Boundary* 2, 20: 3 (1993): 140–155.

Racine, Nicole. "The Clarté Movement in France, 1919–1921." *Journal of Contemporary History*, 2: 2 (April, 1967): 195–208.

Radhakrishnan, Rajagopalan. *Diasporic Mediations: Between Home and Location*. Minneapolis: University of Minnesota Press, 1996.

Ramos, Julio. *Divergent Modernitie: Culture and Politics in Nineteenth-Century Latin America*. Durham, NC and London: Duke University Press, 2001.

Reedy, Daniel R. *Magda Portal: La Pasionaria Peruana. Biografía Intelectual*, Lima: Ediciones Flora Tristán, 2000.

Reveco del Villar, Juan Manuel. "Influencia del APRA en el partido socialista de Chile," in Vida y Obra de Víctor Raúl Haya de la Torre, *edited by Juan Manuel Reveco*, ed. Hugo Vallenas, Rolando Pereda and Rafael Romero, Segundo Concurso Latinoamericano, Lima: Instituto Cambio y Desarrollo, 2006, pp. 19–134.

Ricard, Serge. "The Roosevelt Corollary." *Presidential Studies Quarterly*, 36: 1 (March 2006): 17–26.

Robert, Kenneth. "Preface," in Michael L. Conniff (ed.), *Populism in Latin America*, Tuscaloosa: The University of Alabama Press, 2012 (2nd ed.), pp. IX–X.

Rodríguez, Daniel R. *La primera evangelización norteamericana en Puerto Rico, 1898–1930*. México, DF: Ediciones Borinquen, 1986.

Roniger, Luis. *The Politics of Exile in Latin America*, New York: Cambridge University Press, 2009.

Destierro y exilio en América Latina. Nuevos estudios y avances teoricos, Buenos Aires: Editorial EUDEBA, 2014.

"Displacement and Testimony: Recent History and the Study of Exile in Post-Exile." *International Journal of Politics, Culture, and Society*, 9: 2 (2016): 111–133.

"Paisajes culturales en cambio bajo el impacto del exilio, las diásporas y el retorno de le emigración." *Araucaria. Revista Iberoamericana de Filosofía, Política, Humanidades y Relaciones Internacionales*, 20: 40 (2018): 185–208.

Roniger, Luis, James N. Green and Pablo Yankelevich *Exile and the Politics of Exclusion in the Americas*, Portland, ME: Sussex Academic Press, 2012.

Roniger, Luis, Leonardo Senkman, Saúl Sosnowksi and Mario Sznajder. *Exile, Diaspora and Return: Changing Cultural Landscapes in Argentina, Chile, Paraguay, and Uruguay*. New York: Oxford University Press, 2018.

Ross, Andre and Kristin Ross (eds). *Anti-Americanism*. New York: New York University Press, 2004.

Rycroft, W. Stanley. "An Upheaval in Peru," *The Monthly Record of the Free Church of Scotland*, Edinburgh, August 1923, 133–135.

On this Foundation. The Evangelical Witness in Latin America, New York: Friendship Press, 1942.

Saco, Alfredo. "Aprista Bibliography." *The Hispanic American Historical Review*, 23: 3 (1943): 555–585.

Said, Edward W. "Intellectual Exile: Expatriates and Marginals," in *Representations of the Intellectual: The 1993 Reith Lectures*, New York: Pantheon Books, 1994, pp. 49–53,

Reflections on Exile and Other Essays. Cambridge, MA: Harvard University Press, 2000.

Réflexions sur l'exil : et autres essais. Arles: Actes Sud, 2008 [1st ed. 2000].

Salvatore, Ricardo D. "Imperial Mechanics: South America's Hemispheric Integration in the Machine Age." American Quarterly, 58: 3 (September 2006): 662–691

Disciplinary Conquest: U.S. Scholars in South America, 1900–1945. Durham, NC and London: Duke University Press, 2016.

Sánchez, Juan Martín. *La Revolución Peruana: Ideología y practica de un gobierno militar, 1968–1975*. Sevilla: Universidad de Sevilla, 2002.

Sicker, Martin. *The Geopolitics of Security in the Americas: Hemispheric Denial from Monroe to Clinton*, Westport, CT and London: Praeger, 2002.

Sinclair, John H. *Juan A. Mackay: Un Escocés con Alma Latina*. México, DF: Ediciones Centro de Comunicación Cultural CUPSA, 1990.

Scarfi, Juan Pablo. *El imperio de la ley: James Brown Scott y la construcción de un orden jurídico interamericano*. Buenos Aires: Fondo de Cultura Económica, 2014.

"In the Name of the Americas: The Pan-American Redefinition of the Monroe Doctrine and the Emerging Language of American International Law in the Western Hemisphere, 1898–1933." *Diplomatic History*, 40: 2 (2016): 189–218.

The Hidden History of International Law in the Americas: Empire and Legal Networks. New York: Oxford University Press, 2017.

Scarfi, Juan Pablo and Andrew R. Tillman (eds). *Cooperation and Hegemony in US–Latin American Relations: Revisiting the Western Hemisphere Idea*. New York: Palgrave Macmillan, 2016.

Sessa, Leandro. "'Semillas en tierras estériles': La recepción del APRA en la Argentina de mediados de la década de los treinta." *Revista Sociohistórica*, 28 (2011): 131–161.

"Aprismo y apristas en Argentina: Derivas de una experiencia antiimperialista en la 'encrucijada' ideológica y política de los años treinta." Ph.D. Diss., Universidad Nacional de La Plata, 2013.

"Los exiliados como 'traductores.' Las redes del exilio aprista en la Argentina en la década de los treinta." *Trabajos y Comunicaciones*, 40 (2014).

Sheinin, David (ed.). *Beyond the Ideal: Pan Americanism in Inter-American Affairs*. Westport, CT: Greenwood Press, 2000.

Silva-Gotay, Samuel. *Protestantismo y política en Puerto Rico 1930. Hacia una historia del protestantismo evangélico en Puerto Rico*. San Juan: Editorial de la Universidad de Puerto Rico, 1997.

Soto Rivera, Roy. *Víctor Raúl. El hombre del siglo XX*. Lima: Instituto Víctor Raúl Haya de la Torre, 2002.

Aprismo y antimperialismo. Arequipa: Editorial Mirando, 1970.

Spenser, Daniela. *The Impossible Triangle: Mexico, Soviet Russia, and the United States in the 1920s*. Durham, NC and London: Duke University Press, 1999.

Stoll, David. *Is Latin America Turning Protestant?: The Politics of Evangelical Growth*. Berkeley: University of California Press, 1990.

Stein, Steve. *Populism in Peru: The Emergence of the Masses and the Politics of Social Control*. Madison: The University of Wisconsin Press, 1980

"The Paths to Populism in Peru," in Michael L. Conniff (ed.), *Populism in Latin America: Second Edition*. Tuscaloosa: The university of Alabama Press, 2012, pp. 110–131.

Studnicki-Gizbert, Daviken. *A Nation Upon the Ocean Sea: Portugal's Atlantic Diaspora and the Crisis of the Spanish Empire, 1492–1640*. New York: Oxford University Press, 2007.

Tanaka Martín. "El giro del APRA y de Alan García." *Nueva Sociedad* 217 (2008), ISSN: 0251-3552, www.nuso.org.

Taracena Arriola, Arturo. "La Asociación General de Estudiantes Latinoamericanos de Paris (1925–1933)." *Anuario de Estudios Centroamericanos*, 15: 2 (1989): 61–80.

Tarrow, Sydney. *The New Transnational Activism*. New York: Cambridge University Press, 2005.

Tauro, Alberto. *Amauta y su influencia*. Lima: Editora Amauta, 1960.

Tejada Ripalda, Luis. "El americanismo. Consideraciones sobre el nacionalismo continental latinoamericano." *Investigaciones sociales*, 8: 12 (2004): 167–200.

Terán, Oscar. "Amauta: vanguardia y revolución," in Carlos Altamirano (ed.), *Historia de los intelectuales en América Latina, Tomo II*. Buenos Aires: Katz editores, 2010, pp. 169–191

Townsend Ezcurra, André (ed.). *Antología del pensamiento político de Haya de la Torre*. Lima: Biblioteca Nacional del Perú, 1995.

50 Años de aprismo: Memorias, Ensayos y Discursos de un Militante. Lima: Editorial DESA, 1989.

Torres Rojo, Luis Arturo. *Ucronia y alteridad: notas para la historia de los conceptos políticos de Indoamérica, indigenismo e indianismo en México y Perú 1918–1994*. La Paz, BCS: Universidad Autónoma de Baja California Sur, 2016.

"La semántica política de Indoamericana, 1918–1941," in Aimer Granados and Carlos Marichal (eds), *Construcción de las identidades latinoamericanas. Ensayos de historial intelectual siglos XIX y XX*. México, DF: El Colegio de México, 2004, pp. 207–240

Trigo, Abril. *Memorias migrantes: Testimonios y ensayos sobre la diáspora uruguaya*. Buenos Aires and Montevideo: Beatriz Viterbo Editora and Ediciones Trilce, 2003.

Tünnermann, Carlos. *Sesenta años de la reforma universitaria de Córdoba, 1918–1978*. Costa Rica: Editorial Universitaria Centroamericana (EDUCA), 1978.

Tyrrell, Ian and Jay Sexton. *Empire's Twin: U.S. Anti-Imperialism from the Founding Era to the Age of Terrorism*. Ithaca, NY and London: Cornell University Press, 2015.

Ulanovsky, Carlos. *Seamos felices mientras estamos aquí*. Buenos Aires: Editorial, Sudamericana, 2001.

Unruh, Vicky. *Latin American Vanguards: The Art of Contentious Encounters*. Berkeley: University of California Press, 1994.

Urbina, Alberto Hernández. *Los partidos y la crisis del Apra*. Lima: Ediciones Raíz, 1956.

Valderrama, Mariano, Jorge Chullen, Nicolás Lynch and Carlos Malpica. *El APRA: Un camino de esperanzas y frustraciones*. Lima: Ediciones El Gallo Rojo, 1980.

Vanden, Harry E. "The Peasants as a Revolutionary Class: An Early Latin American View." *Journal of Interamerican Studies and World Affairs*, 20: 2 (May 1978): 191–209.

"Mariátegui: Marxismo, Comunismo, and Other Bibliographical Notes." *Latin American Research Review*, 14: 3 (1979): 61–86.

Vanden, Harry E. And Marc Becker (eds). *José Carlos Mariátegui: An Anthology*. New York: Monthly Review Press, 2011.

Vasconcelos, José. *La raza cósmica*, Baltimore and London: The Johns Hopkins University Press, 1997 (1st ed. in Spanish 1925).

Vásquez-Bronfman, Ana and Ana María Araujo. *Exils latino-américains. La malédiction d'Ulysse*. Paris : L'Harmattan, 1988.

Vega-Centeno, Imelda. *Aprismo popular: Cultura, Religión y Política*. Lima: Tarea, 1991.

Villanueva, Armando and Pablo Macera. *Arrogante Montonero*. Lima: Fondo Editorial del Congreso del Perú, 2011.

Villanueva, Armando and Guillermo Thornlike. *La Gran Persecución, 1932–1956*. Lima, [s.n.], 2004.

Villanueva, Víctor. *El APRA en busca del poder, 1930–1940*. Lima: Editorial Horizonte, 1975.

Vich, Cynthia. *Indigenismo de Vanguardia en el Perú: Un estudio sobre el Boletín Titikaka*. Lima: Pontificia Universidad del Perú, Fondo Editorial, 2000.

Wallace Fuentes, Myrna Yvonne. "Becoming Magda Portal: Poetry, Gender, and Revolutionary Politics in Lima, Peru, 1920–1930." Ph.D. Diss., Duke University, 2006.

Most Scandalous Woman: Magda Portal and the Dream of Revolution in Peru, Norman: University of Oklahoma Press, 2017.

Walsh, Ellen. "Advancing the Kingdom': Missionaries and Americanization in Puerto Rico, 1898–1930s." Ph. D. Diss., University of Pittsburgh, 2008.

Weaver, Kathleen. *Peruvian Rebel: The World of Magda Portal. With a Selection of Her Poems*. Philadelphia: Pennsylvania State University Press, 2009.

White Jr., Ronald C. and C. Howard Hopkins. *The Social Gospel: Religion and Reform in Changing America*. Philadelphia: Temple University Press, 1976.

Whitney, Robert. *State and Revolution in Cuba: Mass Mobilization and Political Change, 1920–1940*. Chapel Hill, NC and London: The University of North Carolina Press, 2001.

Williams, Virginia S. *Radical Journalists, Generalist Intellectuals, and U.S.–Latin American Relations*. Lewiston, NY: The Edwin Mellen Press, 2001.

Woods, Kenneth Flint. "Samuel Guy Inman – His Role in the Evolution of Inter-American Cooperation." Ph.D. Diss., The American University, 1962.

Yankelevich, Pablo. " ¿Usted no es de aquí, verdad? Huellas de identidad entre los exiliados sudamericanos en México." *Taller: Revista de* ociedad, cultura y política, 4: 9 (1999): 107–123.

"La revolución Mexicana en el debate ociedad latinoamericano: Ingenieros, Palacios, Haya de la Torre y Mariategui." *Cuadernos Americanos*, 3: 11 (May 2005): 161–186.

Yaremko, Jason. *U.S. Protestant Missions in Cuba: From Independence to Castro*. Gainsville: University Press of Florida, 2000.

Young, Kevin E. (ed.). *Making the Revolution: Histories of the Latin American Left*. New York: Cambridge University Press, 2019.

Young, Kevin. "The Good, the Bad, and the Benevolent Interventionist: U.S. Press and Intellectual Distortions of the Latin American Left." *Latin American Perspectives*, 190: 3 (May 2013): 207–225

Index

Other Books in the Series *(continued from page ii)*

108. *The Mexican Revolution's Wake: The Making of a Political System, 1920–1929*, Sarah Osten
107. *Latin America's Radical Left: Rebellion and Cold War in the Global 1960s*, Aldo Marchesi
106. *Liberalism as Utopia: The Rise and Fall of Legal Rule in Post-Colonial Mexico, 1820–1900*, Timo H. Schaefer
105. *Before Mestizaje: The Frontiers of Race and Caste in Colonial Mexico*, Ben Vinson III
104. *The Lords of Tetzcoco: The Transformation of Indigenous Rule in Postconquest Central Mexico*, Bradley Benton
103. *Theater of a Thousand Wonders: A History of Miraculous Images and Shrines in New Spain*, William B. Taylor
102. *Indian and Slave Royalists in the Age of Revolution*, Marcela Echeverri
101. *Indigenous Elites and Creole Identity in Colonial Mexico, 1500–1800*, Peter Villella
100. *Asian Slaves in Colonial Mexico: From Chinos to Indians, Tatiana Seijas*
99. *Black Saint of the Americas: The Life and Afterlife of Martín de Porres*, Celia Cussen
98. *The Economic History of Latin America since Independence, Third Edition*, Victor Bulmer-Thomas
97. *The British Textile Trade in South American in the Nineteenth Century*, Manuel Llorca-Jaña
96. *Warfare and Shamanism in Amazonia*, Carlos Fausto
95. *Rebellion on the Amazon: The Cabanagem, Race, and Popular Culture in the North of Brazil, 1798–1840*, Mark Harris
94. *A History of the Khipu*, Galen Brokaw
93. *Politics, Markets, and Mexico's "London Debt," 1823–1887*, Richard J. Salvucci
92. *The Political Economy of Argentina in the Twentieth Century*, Roberto Cortés Conde
91. *Bankruptcy of Empire: Mexican Silver and the Wars between Spain, Britain, and France, 1760–1810*, Carlos Marichal
90. *Shadows of Empire: The Indian Nobility of Cusco, 1750–1825*, David T. Garrett
89. *Chile: The Making of a Republic, 1830–1865: Politics and Ideas*, Simon Collier
88. *Deference and Defiance in Monterrey: Workers, Paternalism, and Revolution in Mexico, 1890–1950*, Michael Snodgrass
87. *Andrés Bello: Scholarship and Nation-Building in Nineteenth-Century Latin America*, Ivan Jaksic
86. *Between Revolution and the Ballot Box: The Origins of the Argentine Radical Party in the 1890s*, Paula Alonso
85. *Slavery and the Demographic and Economic History of Minas Gerais, Brazil, 1720–1888*, Laird W. Bergad
84. *The Independence of Spanish America*, Jaime E. Rodríguez

83. *The Rise of Capitalism on the Pampas: The Estancias of Buenos Aires, 1785–1870*, Samuel Amaral
82. *A History of Chile, 1808–2002, Second Edition*, Simon Collier and William F. Sater
81. *The Revolutionary Mission: American Enterprise in Latin America, 1900–1945*, Thomas F. O'Brien
80. *The Kingdom of Quito, 1690–1830: The State and Regional Development*, Kenneth J. Andrien
79. *The Cuban Slave Market, 1790–1880*, Laird W. Bergad, Fe Iglesias García, and María del Carmen Barcia
78. *Business Interest Groups in Nineteenth-Century Brazil*, Eugene Ridings
77. *The Economic History of Latin America since Independence, Second Edition*, Victor Bulmer-Thomas
76. *Power and Violence in the Colonial City: Oruro from the Mining Renaissance to the Rebellion of Tupac Amaru (1740–1782)*, Oscar Cornblit
75. *Colombia before Independence: Economy, Society and Politics under Bourbon Rule*, Anthony McFarlane
74. *Politics and Urban Growth in Buenos Aires, 1910–1942*, Richard J. Walter
73. *The Central Republic in Mexico, 1835–1846, 'Hombres de Bien' in the Age of Santa Anna*, Michael P. Costeloe
72. *Negotiating Democracy: Politicians and Generals in Uruguay*, Charles Guy Gillespie
71. *Native Society and Disease in Colonial Ecuador*, Suzanne Austin Alchon
70. *The Politics of Memory: Native Historical Interpretation in the Colombian Andes*, Joanne Rappaport
69. *Power and the Ruling Classes in Northeast Brazil, Juazeiro and Petrolina in Transition*, Ronald H. Chilcote
68. *House and Street: The Domestic World of Servants and Masters in Nineteenth-Century Rio de Janeiro*, Sandra Lauderdale Graham
67. *The Demography of Inequality in Brazil*, Charles H. Wood and José Alberto Magno de Carvalho
66. *The Politics of Coalition Rule in Colombia*, Jonathan Hartlyn
65. *South America and the First World War: The Impact of the War on Brazil, Argentina, Peru and Chile*, Bill Albert
64. *Resistance and Integration: Peronism and the Argentine Working Class, 1946–1976*, Daniel James
63. *The Political Economy of Central America since 1920*, Victor Bulmer-Thomas
62. *A Tropical Belle Epoque: Elite Culture and Society in Turn-of-the-Century Rio de Janeiro*, Jeffrey D. Needell
61. *Ambivalent Conquests: Maya and Spaniard in Yucatan, 1517–1570, Second Edition*, Inga Clendinnen
60. *Latin America and the Comintern, 1919–1943*, Manuel Caballero
59. *Roots of Insurgency: Mexican Regions, 1750–1824*, Brian R. Hamnett
58. *The Agrarian Question and the Peasant Movement in Colombia: Struggles of the National Peasant Association, 1967–1981*, Leon Zamosc

57. *Catholic Colonialism: A Parish History of Guatemala, 1524–1821*, Adriaan C. van Oss
56. *Pre-Revolutionary Caracas: Politics, Economy, and Society 1777–1811*, P. Michael McKinley
55. *The Mexican Revolution, Volume 2: Counter-Revolution and Reconstruction*, Alan Knight
54. *The Mexican Revolution, Volume 1: Porfirians, Liberals, and Peasants*, Alan Knight
53. *The Province of Buenos Aires and Argentine Politics, 1912–1943*, Richard J. Walter
52. *Sugar Plantations in the Formation of Brazilian Society: Bahia, 1550–1835*, Stuart B. Schwartz
51. *Tobacco on the Periphery: A Case Study in Cuban Labour History, 1860–1958*, Jean Stubbs
50. *Housing, the State, and the Poor: Policy and Practice in Three Latin American Cities*, Alan Gilbert and Peter M. Ward
49. *Unions and Politics in Mexico: The Case of the Automobile Industry*, Ian Roxborough
48. *Miners, Peasants and Entrepreneurs: Regional Development in the Central Highlands of Peru*, Norman Long and Bryan Roberts
47. *Capitalist Development and the Peasant Economy in Peru*, Adolfo Figueroa
46. *Early Latin America: A History of Colonial Spanish America and Brazil*, James Lockhart and Stuart B. Schwartz
45. *Brazil's State-Owned Enterprises: A Case Study of the State as Entrepreneur*, Thomas J. Trebat
44. *Law and Politics in Aztec Texcoco*, Jerome A. Offner
43. *Juan Vicente Gómez and the Oil Companies in Venezuela, 1908–1935*, B. S. McBeth
42. *Revolution from Without: Yucatán, Mexico, and the United States, 1880–1924*, Gilbert M. Joseph
41. *Demographic Collapse: Indian Peru, 1520–1620*, Noble David Cook
40. *Oil and Politics in Latin America: Nationalist Movements and State Companies*, George Philip
39. *The Struggle for Land: A Political Economy of the Pioneer Frontier in Brazil from 1930 to the Present Day*, J. Foweraker
38. *Caudillo and Peasant in the Mexican Revolution*, D. A. Brading, ed.
37. *Odious Commerce: Britain, Spain and the Abolition of the Cuban Slave Trade*, David Murray
36. *Coffee in Colombia, 1850–1970: An Economic, Social and Political History*, Marco Palacios
35. *A Socioeconomic History of Argentina, 1776–1860*, Jonathan C. Brown
34. *From Dessalines to Duvalier: Race, Colour and National Independence in Haiti*, David Nicholls
33. *Modernization in a Mexican ejido: A Study in Economic Adaptation*, Billie R. DeWalt.

32. *Haciendas and Ranchos in the Mexican Bajío, Léon, 1700–1860*, D. A. Brading
31. *Foreign Immigrants in Early Bourbon Mexico, 1700–1760*, Charles F. Nunn
30. *The Merchants of Buenos Aires, 1778–1810: Family and Commerce*, Susan Migden Socolow
29. *Drought and Irrigation in North-east Brazil*, Anthony L. Hall
28. *Coronelismo: The Municipality and Representative Government in Brazil*, Victor Nunes Leal
27. *A History of the Bolivian Labour Movement, 1848–1971*, Guillermo Lora
26. *Land and Labour in Latin America: Essays on the Development of Agrarian Capitalism in the Nineteenth and Twentieth Centuries*, Kenneth Duncan and Ian Rutledge, eds.
25. *Allende's Chile: The Political Economy of the Rise and Fall of the Unidad Popular*, Stefan de Vylder
24. *The Cristero Rebellion: The Mexican People between Church and State, 1926–1929*, Jean A. Meyer
23. *The African Experience in Spanish America, 1502 to the Present Day*, Leslie B. Rout, Jr.
22. *Letters and People of the Spanish Indies: Sixteenth Century*, James Lockhart and Enrique Otte, eds.
21. *Chilean Rural Society from the Spanish Conquest to 1930*, Arnold J. Bauer
20. *Studies in the Colonial History of Spanish America*, Mario Góngora
19. *Politics in Argentina, 1890–1930: The Rise and Fall of Radicalism*, David Rock
18. *Politics, Economics and Society in Argentina in the Revolutionary Period*, Tulio Halperín Donghi
17. *Marriage, Class and Colour in Nineteenth-Century Cuba: A Study of Racial Attitudes and Sexual Values in a Slave Society*, Verena Stolcke
16. *Conflicts and Conspiracies: Brazil and Portugal, 1750–1808*, Kenneth Maxwell
15. *Silver Mining and Society in Colonial Mexico: Zacatecas, 1546–1700*, P. J. Bakewell
14. *A Guide to the Historical Geography of New Spain*, Peter Gerhard
13. *Bolivia: Land, Location and Politics Since 1825*, J. Valerie Fifer, Malcolm Deas, Clifford Smith, and John Street
12. *Politics and Trade in Southern Mexico, 1750–1821*, Brian R. Hamnett
11. *Alienation of Church Wealth in Mexico: Social and Economic Aspects of the Liberal Revolution, 1856–1875*, Jan Bazant
10. *Miners and Merchants in Bourbon Mexico, 1763–1810*, D. A. Brading
9. *An Economic History of Colombia, 1845–1930*, by W. P. McGreevey
8. *Economic Development of Latin America: Historical Background and Contemporary Problems*, Celso Furtado and Suzette Macedo
7. *Regional Economic Development: The River Basin Approach in Mexico*, David Barkin and Timothy King
6. *The Abolition of the Brazilian Slave Trade: Britain, Brazil and the Slave Trade Question, 1807–1869*, Leslie Bethell

5. *Parties and Political Change in Bolivia, 1880–1952*, Herbert S. Klein
4. *Britain and the Onset of Modernization in Brazil, 1850–1914*, Richard Graham
3. *The Mexican Revolution, 1910–1914: The Diplomacy of Anglo-American Conflict*, P. A. R. Calvert
2. *Church Wealth in Mexico: A Study of the 'Juzgado de Capellanias' in the Archbishopric of Mexico 1800–1856*, Michael P. Costeloe
1. *Ideas and Politics of Chilean Independence, 1808–1833*, Simon Collier

CPSIA information can be obtained
at www.ICGtesting.com
Printed in the USA
LVHW080042060422
715457LV00005B/207

9 781108 838047